The Fujian Maritime Silk Road: The Hinterland Volume

The Cultural, Historical and Educational Committee
of the Fujian Provincial Committee of the CPPCC
and Fujian Yanhuang Culture Research Association

Translated by Xiaomei Wang

CHICAGO ACADEMIC PRESS

The Fujian Maritime Silk Road： The Hinterland Volume
Author: The Cultural, Historical and Educational Committee of the Fujian Provincial Committee of the CPPCC and Fujian Yanhuang Culture Research Association
Translator: Xiaomei Wang
Language: English
Word Count (for space of all pages): 364 Thousand words
Publisher: Chicago Academic Press
Number of Pages: 462
ISBN: 979-8-901-86016-8

Publishing	Chicago Academic Press
	5923 N Artesian Ave
	Chicago IL 60659
Email	contact@chicagoacademicpress.com
Website	http://chicagoacademicpress.com/
Book Size	6X9 inches
First Edition	December, 2025

All rights reserved. No part of this publication may be reproduced, stored in a retrieval system or transmitted, in any form or by any means without prior written permission from the publisher, except for the inclusion of brief quotations in a review.

Translator Profile

Xiaomei Wang, female, a native of Longyan City, Fujian Province, China, is an associate professor at the School of Foreign Languages in Minjiang University in China. She graduated from Shanghai Jiao Tong University with a Master's degree in Foreign Linguistics and Applied Linguistics, and was a visiting scholar at Indiana University Bloomington, the United States, in 2025 for one year. Her research primarily focuses on multimodal discourse analysis, cross-cultural communication, and translation teaching. She has completed one youth research program of Humanities and Social Sciences of the Ministry of Education of the People's Republic of China, one youth research program of the Fujian Provincial Social Science Foundation, and more than ten projects funded by the Fujian Provincial Department of Education and her university. She has published one monograph, two papers in CSSCI-indexed journals, and over ten papers in other academic journals.

Contents

Introduction

Section 1 Scope of Study and Key Issues

The hinterland of the Maritime Silk Road in Fujian primarily comprises the three inland cities of Nanping, Sanming, and Longyan—collectively referred to as "Nan-San-Long." This region covers an area of approximately 68,300 square kilometers, accounting for about 55.16% of the total area of Fujian Province. Two mountain ranges, aligned roughly parallel to the coastline, divide Nan-San-Long into relatively independent geographic units. One range, extending from north to south, is composed of the Jiufeng, Daiyun, and Boping mountain chains, collectively known as the Daiyun Mountain System (also referred to as the Central Fujian Mountain Belt). Spanning about 580 kilometers in length with an average elevation of 1,000 to 1,200 meters, this range separates the hinterland from Fujian's coastal cities—Ningde, Fuzhou, Putian, Quanzhou, and Zhangzhou—thereby forming a distinctive landscape configuration of mountains in the interior and seas along the coast. The other range, comprising the Xianxia Ridge and the Wuyi Mountains, is known as the Wuyi Mountain System (also referred to as the Western or Northwestern Fujian Mountain Belt). It stretches approximately 530 kilometers, with an average elevation of 1,000 to 1,100 meters. It forms the principal watershed dividing Fujian from the provinces of Zhejiang and Jiangxi. Along this mountain system, Fujian shares borders with Zhejiang, Jiangxi, and Guangdong. This region typifies the hilly and mountainous topography of eastern China. Interspersed with valleys and crisscrossed by river systems, it serves as the headwaters and upper reaches for major rivers in Fujian Province, including the Minjiang River, Jiulong River, and Tingjiang River. In premodern times, the region established close economic and cultural ties with coastal port cities through a network of river routes and mountain pathways. These inland-waterway corridors facilitated frequent material exchanges and intensive human interactions, positioning the hinterland as a key economic and logistical support zone for the coastal ports.

The hinterland not only sustained the prosperity of these ports but was itself deeply influenced by coastal economic and cultural developments, gradually forming an integrated economic system through long-term mutual interactions.

Over the past century, scholarly research on the Maritime Silk Road has explored a broad variety of topics, including its points of origin and ports, maritime transportation, trade and economic exchange, political and diplomatic relations, and religious and cultural interactions. However, the majority of these studies have focused on ports as central nodes. Relatively few have examined the historical relationship between ports and their hinterlands—how hinterlands supported port development, how ports stimulated economic transformation in inland regions, and the broader bidirectional dynamics between the two. One of the more relevant scholarly efforts emerged from an international symposium held in 2004 by the Research Center for Historical Geography at Fudan University with the title "Port–Hinterland and China's Modernization Process". The subsequent publication of the same name compiled key findings from the event. Scholars collectively argued that, "From a historical-geographical perspective, the dramatic transformations in Chinese society after 1842 originated in the coastal port regions and subsequently diffused inland through major transportation routes. In this process, the flow of goods, people, capital, technologies, and information facilitated by import-export trade was one of the primary means through which international markets and advanced productive forces influenced the broader interior of China. In economic geography, the area that supplies exports to a port and absorbs its imports is referred to as its 'hinterland,' and the relationship between ports and hinterlands is inherently bidirectional." They further emphasized that "research on port–hinterland dynamics should not be confined to trade and transportation alone; it must extend into deeper realms including industrial, financial, informational, cultural, and political dimensions. A comprehensive understanding of this topic demands interdisciplinary collaboration across fields such as history, historical geography, economics, economic geography, and transportation." Although this research paradigm has been applied in studies of contemporary port–hinterland relationships, specific investigations into the hinterlands of the Maritime Silk Road remain notably scarce. It is undeniable that ports and their hinterlands differ significantly in economic functions, geographic structures, and cultural characteristics. However, questions remain underexplored and warrant further in-depth investigation, as to how hinterlands engaged in external exchange, how they interacted with port areas, what forms such interactions took, and how the economic and social structures of hinterlands evolved through these interactions. Conducting in-depth research on the hinterland of the Maritime Silk Road in Fujian is of significant importance for advancing the "Silk Road Spirit" summarized by General Secretary Xi Jinping, which emphasizes peace and cooperation, openness and inclusiveness, mutual learning, and mutual benefit. Such research can support joint efforts with countries along the route to build a new Silk Road characterized by peace, prosperity, openness, innovation, and cultural civility. It also aligns with efforts to promote the development of the core area of the Maritime Silk Road by leveraging the ecological and tourism resources of the hinterland, as well as cultural assets such as Zhu Xi's Confucian legacy and Hakka traditions. Furthermore, it supports expanding international cooperation and cultural exchange with primary countries and regions along the route, reviving distinctive historical routes such as the "Ten-Thousand-Mile Tea Road," integrating with the Silk Road Economic Belt, and enhancing Fujian's positioning as an internationally recognized destination for eco-cultural tourism, a model zone for green development, and a hub for Hakka culture and tea culture exchange—ultimately elevating the province's level of openness and cooperation on the global stage.[1]

1 Fujian Provincial Development and Reform Commission, Fujian Provincial Foreign Affairs Office, and Fujian Provincial Department of Commerce. *Development Plan for the Core Area of the 21st-Century Maritime Silk Road in Fujian Province*.

Section 2 The Natural Geography and Historical-Cultural Environment of Fujian's Maritime Silk Road Hinterland

Situated near the Tropic of Cancer, the hinterland of the Maritime Silk Road in Fujian lies within a subtropical climatic zone. Its saddle-shaped terrain and topography—characterized by a mountainous interior facing the ocean—expose the region to abundant precipitation brought by monsoons from the Pacific Ocean. The average annual rainfall ranges from 1,500 to 2,000 millimeters. While the region benefits from the warm, moist oceanic air currents, the surrounding mountain ranges also serve to block the cold northern air masses, resulting in a typical subtropical monsoon climate—mild winters, cool summers, and annual average temperatures ranging between 16°C and 22°C. The region receives close to 2,000 hours of sunshine per year and has an average frost-free period of nearly 300 days, conditions highly favorable for the growth and reproduction of diverse flora and fauna. With large diurnal temperature variations in the mountainous areas, the region is noted for its rich biodiversity and is celebrated as a "Green Emerald on the Tropic of Cancer," a "Treasure House of Southern Biodiversity," and a "Gene Bank for Plants and Animals."

The unique climatic and geographic features have also contributed to the formation of a dense river network in the hinterland. In Longyan, river systems primarily belong to the Tingjiang River, the Beixi Creek（(a tributary of the Jiulong River), the Shaxi Creek (a tributary of the Minjiang River), and the Meijiang River, with 110 rivers and streams each having a catchment area of 50 square kilometers or more. In Sanming, over 90 rivers are longer than 10 kilometers, most of which also belong to the Minjiang River system. In Nanping, there are 70 rivers and streams with catchment areas exceeding 100 square kilometers. Notable among them are referred to as the "One River and

Eight Streams," namely: Minjiang River, Jianxi Creek, Futun Creek, Chongyang Creek, Nanpu Creek, Songxi Creek, Maxi Creek, Shaxi Creek, and Jinxi Creek. The river and streams have high discharge volumes, wide drainage areas, and deep channels with relatively low sediment content. Although subject to seasonal floods, many of these were navigable in ancient times and thus held considerable value for transportation. The three major rivers—Minjiang River, Jiulong River, and Tingjiang River—have historically served as vital conduits linking the mountainous hinterland with the coastal regions. Before the advent of modern railways and road systems, the movement of people and goods between inland and coastal areas relied heavily on these waterways. Moreover, the network of tributaries feeding into these rivers facilitated a web of interregional cooperation and division of labor between remote mountain villages, urban centers, and coastal hubs, enabling synchronized development across otherwise isolated regions of western and northern Fujian.

The intricate river network, combined with the mountainous region's suitability for commercial agriculture, laid a solid foundation for the hinterland's participation in regional economic and cultural exchange with the coastal zones.

Northern Fujian experienced relatively early economic development. Before the Southern and Northern dynasties period, northern Fujian had already emerged as a political, economic, and cultural center of the province. During the early Eastern Han Dynasty, four of the five earliest counties established within the territory of present-day Fujian were located in northern Fujian: Jian'an (now Jian'ou), Nanping (now Yanping), Hanxing (now Pucheng), and Jianping (now Jianyang).

Commemorative Stele for the Source of Three Rivers in Liancheng County

After the Han and Jin dynasties, widespread warfare in the Central Plains triggered waves of Han Chinese migration to the south. These migrants brought with them advanced agricultural and artisanal techniques, rapidly elevating local productivity and introducing the sophisticated culture of the Central Plains. The integration of Han culture with the indigenous Minyue culture formed the foundation of what later became the distinctive Min culture. During the reign of Emperor Wu of the Chen Dynasty, Fujian was first designated with a provincial-level administrative name—Minzhou, with its administrative seat established in Jin'an (now Fuzhou), marking the shift of Fujian's political center to the coastal area. Later, in the Kaiyuan period of the Tang Dynasty, Tingzhou was established in Longyan, western Fujian.

Under Wang Shenzhi's rule in the early tenth century, policies such as "encouraging agriculture and sericulture" and "light taxation with lenient punishments" attracted displaced populations and refugees, fostering population growth, land reclamation, and the development of agriculture, industry, and commerce. New counties were established in both northern and western Fujian—including Jianpu and Jianning in the north, and Guihua in the west. Wang Shenzhi also promoted Confucianism and established schools throughout the regions, thereby fostering "the spread of scholarly culture throughout the local communities." Despite its status as a regional warlord regime during the Five Dynasties period, the Min Kingdom made significant contributions to the development of Fujian, particularly its mountainous hinterland, laying a solid foundation for the region's prosperity in the Song Dynasty.

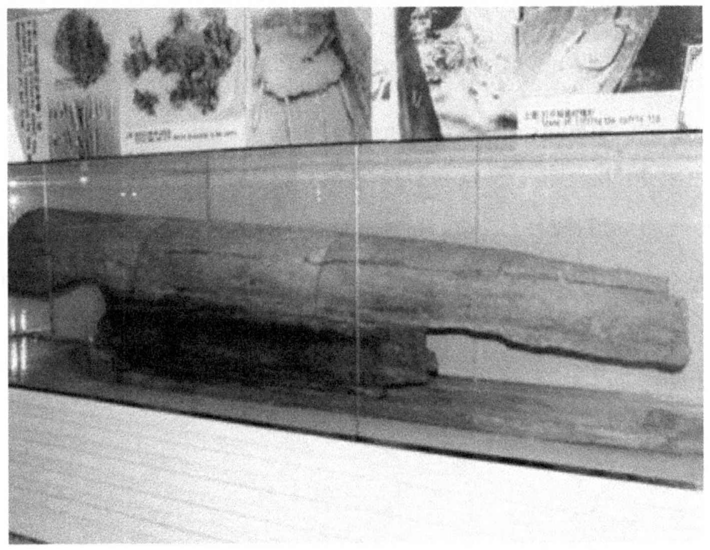

The Boat Coffin of Wuyi Mountain

During the Song Dynasty, China's economic and population centers shifted southward, and Fujian entered a historical peak of development. The hinterland experienced its golden age, marked by social stability, demographic expansion, agricultural and industrial prosperity, and flourishing education and culture. In terms of population, by the end of the Southern Song Dynasty, Longyan alone (including the areas under Tingzhou

Prefecture and the Longyan region under Zhangzhou's jurisdiction) housed over 400,000 households and more than one million people. This population boom outpaced the local land's carrying capacity, driving the rapid development of handicrafts such as tea processing, ceramics, and woodblock printing. Commercial agriculture expanded, with increased production of timber, indigo, and tea. Mineral resources, particularly in western Fujian, were intensively exploited. According to the *Gazetteer of Linting*, during the Southern Song Dynasty, two prefectures were unable to remit taxes and levies to the central government, and Tingzhou paid them on their behalf— an indication of the region's economic prosperity. Culturally, the region saw a renaissance, with Jianyang emerging as a major center for printing and publishing, while academies flourished throughout the region. Numerous candidates succeeded in the imperial examinations, achieving the rank of *Jinshi* (the highest degree in the imperial examination system), and Wuyi Mountain earned the title "Cradle of Neo-Confucianism in the South," where Zhu Xi and his disciples studied and developed Neo-Confucian doctrines.

The Ancient City of Jian'ou

The Ming and Qing dynasties witnessed the rapid development of commercial agriculture and industry in western and northern Fujian. This period also marked the region's critical contribution to the Silk Road economy and growing cultural exchange with overseas communities. Products such as tea, books, Jianyang black-glazed teacup (*Jian Zhan*), tobacco, and traditional handmade paper were transported via the Jiulong, Tingjiang, and Minjiang rivers to coastal ports and beyond. Waves of residents migrated for trade or livelihood, carrying with them Zhu Xi culture and Hakka culture to foreign lands. Coming upstream along the rivers to inland towns were sea products such as salt, foreign missionaries, letters from abroad (including remittances) —known as *Qiaopi*—that conveyed news from abroad.

In the late Qing and Republican periods, commercial activities in the hinterland were significantly disrupted by the encroachment of Western capitalism and domestic turmoil, entering a period of decline. As recorded in the *Gazetteer of Longyan County*,

> After the Xianfeng and Tongzhi reigns, goods lost their value, and the wealth of the region dried up. Rebellions brought devastation, and villages fell into desolation. Over the past decades, capital dwindled, many businesses failed, essentials became scarce, and financial circulation stagnated—the suffering of the commercial sector was immense.

Nevertheless, the commercial sector in northwestern Fujian saw two brief revivals during the Republican era. The first occurred during the period of the Central Soviet Area, when the Soviet government promoted commerce to support the development of the revolutionary base and supply the Red Army, transforming Changting into the so-called "Red little Shanghai" and Ninghua into "the Ukraine of the Central Soviet Region." The second occurred during the War of Resistance against Japanese Aggression, the large-scale inland migration of merchants from Fuzhou, Xiamen, Chaoshan and other areas brought about wartime prosperity. At its peak, Fengshi in

Yongding hosted seven shipping docks, six provincial guild halls, five banks, and over 300 commercial firms. This tiny town had a permanent population of over 20,000 and a floating population of 30,000 to 40,000, marking the most economically prosperous period in Fengshi's history. Meanwhile, Fujian's provincial capital relocated to Yong'an for seven and a half years, attracting many leading intellectuals and cultural figures and turning the city into a prominent cultural hub of southeastern China. Dozens of factories and enterprises from Fuzhou were relocated to Nanping, where a government-run institution called the "Fujian Provincial Enterprise Company" was established to manage industrial operations. Some armament factories originally from Zhejiang were also moved to Nanping. Wooden sailboats carrying local specialties from various regions converged there. At the time, 21 of the province's 82 factories were located in Nanping, making northern Fujian the industrial center of the entire province. Meanwhile, modern banking also began to develop. In addition to the wartime context, two factors greatly influenced the commercial resurgence of western and northern Fujian during this era. First, during the 1920s and 1930s, the construction of highways and the rise of automobile transport, combined with the advent of modern telecommunications such as the telegraph and telephone, brought about a qualitative change in the way commercial information was transmitted. Traditional waterways and trade routes were supplemented and integrated with a growing network of roads and communication lines, forming a comprehensive commercial system for the region. Second, the late 19th and early 20th centuries brought profound changes to Chinese society with the rise of capitalism. China's traditional economic and political foundations began to shift, and the emerging industrial and commercial bourgeoisie came to realize that the old-style guilds were no longer sufficient to protect their interests—especially in the face of growing competition from foreign capitalist forces. At the same time, industrial and commercial entrepreneurs developed a strong sense of economic nationalism. Aspiring individuals devoted themselves wholeheartedly to commerce and industry, and the idea of revitalizing the nation through industry deeply resonated with the public. New-style chambers of commerce centered on emerging capitalist enterprises were established, forming a network with chambers at the core and various trade associations, business academies, and related organizations as supporting bodies. With their extensive social connections and growing economic and political influence, chambers of commerce gained high prestige and authority in local affairs, becoming one of the de facto leading civil organizations of the time.

Section 3 Economic Characteristics and Commercial-Cultural Traits of the Hinterland

I. Economic Characteristics

First, the hinterland largely consisted of mountainous regions, and its natural resource endowments had determined the commercial nature of its agricultural and industrial production. Due to the limited availability of arable land, essential commodities such as grain, cotton, and salt were heavily reliant on external sources. To obtain these external resources, the region must possess goods suitable for exchange, which in turn fostered a strong commercial orientation in its agricultural and industrial sectors. The inhabitants either exported primary products such as timber, rosin, shiitake mushrooms, and black fungus, or processed these raw materials into paper, ironware, books, ceramics, and tea for external trade in exchange for wealth and necessities.

Second, the hinterland fell within the economic radiation zone of port cities, and maritime trade had influenced the direction of its product development. During the Ming and Qing dynasties, maritime trade in Fujian and Guangdong flourished, and the hinterland served as a major source of export goods. The types of goods demanded overseas inevitably shaped local production structures. For example, there was strong demand for paper products in Southeast Asia and Japan. Handmade paper from the mountainous areas was exported via Fuzhou, Xiamen, Shantou, and Guangzhou to Vietnam, Thailand, Myanmar, Singapore, the Philippines, Indonesia, Malaysia, Japan, and other countries. The *Gazetteer of Linting*, compiled in the seventeenth year of the Jiaqing reign in Qing Dynasty (1812), records, "Of all goods from Tingzhou, only paper is traded far and wide." As early as the twenty-eighth year of the Qianlong reign (1763), Tingzhou paper merchants had established the Tinglong Guild Hall in Chaozhou, which was subdivided into 13 units called *gang*, such as Louzhi Gang, Lyutai Gang, Fuzhi Gang, Longyan Gang, and Lianfeng Gang. This, in effect, promoted the prosperity of the paper industry in the hinterland. According to the *Fujian Provincial Gazetteer: Light Industry Volume*, "After the founding of the People's Republic of China, there were over 400 paper-making troughs in Gutian, Liancheng County, producing more than 400 tons of handmade paper annually for export." Simultaneously, overseas trade also gave rise to the prosperity of the shipbuilding industry. Ship construction required large quantities of timber, leading to the extensive planting of Chinese fir in the mountains during the Ming and Qing periods. The fir logs were transported along the Tingjiang, Jiulong, and Minjiang rivers to coastal regions. Maritime trade also introduced new species, transforming the agricultural and husbandry structures of the mountainous areas. For instance, tobacco introduced in the late Ming period was widely adopted in Yongding County, western Fujian, forming a complete industry chain encompassing tobacco cultivation, tobacco knife manufacturing, tobacco processing, and sales. Every stage in the process from tobacco shred production to sales—including the preparation of tobacco beds, tools, cutting knives, and packaging paper, as well as the transportation of tobacco—was characterized by specialized division of labor and dedicated production. This specialization stimulated the development of other industries in Yongding. For example, the production of fine tobacco shavings required special tobacco planers. The most renowned tobacco knives were the *Risheng* brand produced by the Lin family in Hongkeng Village, Hukeng Town, Yongding. These knives were sold across vast regions of China, including Shanghai and the Yangtze River region, where specialized shops were dedicated to selling them. Similarly, Yongding's fine-cut tobacco gained the prestigious title of "Tobacco King" during the Qing Dynasty, with stores, merchants, firms, and trading houses established not only in major cities throughout China but also in countries across Southeast Asia.

Third, the hinterland served as a critical hub for both land and water transportation. This locational advantage fostered the prosperity of local trade. Located in the transitional zone between the coastal and inland regions, the hinterland served as a key hub for the transfer and distribution of a large volume of goods. This led to a concentration of merchants in the area and drove urbanization at major transportation nodes. For example, the role of supplying goods to Fuzhou Port and transshipping products overseas contributed to the growth of Nanping, shifting the central city of Northern Fujian from Jian'ou to Nanping. As a crucial junction for the northward transport of southern salt and the southward movement of grain from Jiangxi, the cities of Tingzhou and Shanghang experienced substantial development. Tingzhou long held the status of a major commercial center at the junction of Fujian, Guangdong, and Jiangxi. The development of Yuegang Port in Zhangzhou spurred the growth of Longyan city, leading to its elevation to a directly governed prefecture during the Qing Dynasty. As a result, Longyan emerged as a new economic center in western Fujian, ultimately surpassing Tingzhou in regional significance. During the War of Resistance against Japanese Aggression, Fengshi in Yongding earned the moniker "Little Hong Kong" for its role as a key node linking coastal and mountainous regions.

Fourth, the region's proximity to the coast, mountainous geography, and tradition of migration from the Central Plains collectively contributed to a prevailing custom of seeking livelihoods overseas, driven by both internal and external forces. By the Song Dynasty, and especially during the Ming and Qing periods, population pressure in the mountainous regions had already exceeded their carrying capacities, triggering waves of outmigration. A typical case was the western Fujian highland, which had a population of around two million by the late Southern Song Dynasty. The imbalance between people and land prompted Hakka people migration to Guangdong and Jiangxi provinces. In the Ming and Qing dynasties, particularly after Zheng He's voyages broadened people's horizons, the vast profits of maritime trade attracted many Hakka people to make a living overseas. They brought Hakka culture to Southeast Asia, China's Taiwan Province, and other regions. These expatriates never forgot their homelands; upon achieving success, they either remitted funds or returned to invest in local development, which objectively strengthened the region's external connections and promoted its economic growth. They actively participated in public affairs and played important roles in local society. Such cases are well documented in local gazetteers and genealogies. Take Lai Kuiwang of Yongding County as an example,

> From the profits he earned through trade, he made annual donations for public affairs, ultimately fulfilling his aspirations. In the fifth year of the Jiaqing reign, he independently built the Qiaxi Tea Pavilion in Fuxi Township and endowed it with 42 *tong* of land tax. In the eleventh year, he independently built the stone arch bridge with a tea pavilion at Yuanba in Jinsha Township, at a cost of over 1,800 *taels* of silver, and further contributed over 200 *taels* to endow an additional 42 *tong* of land tax. In the thirteenth year, he alone constructed the Chongsheng Hall outside the East Gate, renovated the worship pavilion of the Mazu Temple, and purchased 40 *tong* of land tax for incense and lamps. He also funded the paving and repair of dozens of *zhang* (a customary Chinese unit of length, 1 *zhang is* about 3.3 meters),) of official roads outside the city and the reconstruction of over 20 *li* (a customary Chinese unit of length, 1 *li* is 500 meters) of the rugged trail at Sanceng Ridge, at a total cost of more than 800 *taels* of silver. At first, the Lai clan ancestor Bai Erlang had pooled a mere 60,000 cash for public use, which was entrusted to Changzhao for management. From the Xinyou to the Jisi years, over an eight-year period, the fund had grown to over 1,000 *taels*, with which sacrificial land was purchased. Additionally, 150 *taels* were donated for the renovation of the Guandi Temple at Donghua Mountain. Other charitable acts, such as the construction of stone bridge at the Mingqi Ridge and donations for coffins and emergency relief, are too numerous to detail.[1]

1(Qing) Fang Lyujian, ed., and Wu Yifu, comp. *Gazetteer of Yongding County,* Daoguang

II. Characteristics of Commercial Culture

The history of commercial activities of merchants in western and northern Fujian can be examined from the perspective of commercial culture. This region has long served as a crucial transportation hub connecting the four provinces of Fujian, Guangdong, Jiangxi, and Zhejiang. It is an important intersection of China's maritime and inland civilizations and has historically functioned as a key hinterland for coastal trade. Throughout history, merchants and commercial activities had facilitated the exchange of goods, people, and information between mountainous regions, inland areas, and coastal zones, thereby promoting economic development and the division of labor in these mountainous areas. The merchant class was the representative of the economy of the era, an important embodiment and participant of regional culture, and the most distinctive symbol of the economic development level and characteristics of the time. The entrepreneurial spirit cultivated through sustained commercial activity and deep-rooted local culture became a driving force in regional development. These hinterland merchants, though based in the mountains, were outward-looking and oriented toward the sea. Their business practices were profoundly influenced by a hybrid inland-coastal culture marked by diversity and compatibility.

First, integrity, benevolence, and a commitment to moral conduct were fundamental to the merchants' code of conduct. Merchants from the hinterland valued honesty, kindness, and personal cultivation. As recorded in the *Gazetteer of Longyan County* (Republican Period),

> In the past, merchants were skilled and resourceful, often amassing wealth and excelling in trade. They traveled

edition, vol. 16. Edited by the Fujian Provincial Local Gazetteer Compilation Committee, Xiamen University Press, 2012, p.301.

> far and wide, commanding influence in the marketplace; at home, they were generous and charitable, earning reputations throughout society. With bundles of tea and tobacco, they journeyed across many rivers and ridges and brought back great profits. Gold and silver flowed in by the millions, and wealthy households lined the villages and alleys.

Such values were passed down through generations of merchants.

Second, a reverence for education and adaptability to change contributed to these merchants' ability to seize business opportunities. Many of their ancestors had migrated from the Central Plains. In ancient times, it was mainly large clans that could withstand the risks of a journey that could last years or even generations. These clans were not only financially strong but also placed a high value on cultural and educational inheritance. Hence, this region became renowned for its scholarly traditions. The widespread presence of academies, private schools, and bookshops in both urban and rural areas was clear evidence of this emphasis on learning. Given the mountainous terrain's inability to produce sufficient staple goods such as grain and cotton, commerce became a necessary means of livelihood, allowing communities to exchange goods and supplement their subsistence. However, business activities were usually not undertaken by entire clans. Even the widely known clans engaged in book carving and printing did not involve all family members. Instead, roles were divided. Typically, members who failed to succeed in scholarly pursuits (those who studied but had no hope of attaining official titles) turned to commerce, using their earnings to support the family's livelihood and the education of other members. As a result, Confucian values were deeply embedded in the identity of hinterland merchants, who can aptly be described as Confucian merchants.

Third, solidarity, mutual aid, and cooperative spirit formed the social credit networks essential to merchant success. The region's mountainous terrain and treacherous roads, coupled with the fact that many clans were migrants, meant that only through diligence, endurance, and unity could they overcome the difficulties of life in unfamiliar lands. This resilience allowed merchants to thrive in foreign environments and support each other in business endeavors, fostering mutual prosperity. For instance, clan-based commerce in western Fujian exhibited dual characteristics of kinship and business relations. Clan power and industrial-commercial forces mutually supported, interconnected, and reinforced one another. With the backing of clan networks, family-based merchants in the book-printing and tobacco-knife industries were able to reduce internal transaction costs, organizational costs, frictional costs, and production costs. This enabled the clan economy to achieve expanded reproduction and fostered collaboration in industry and commerce, ultimately forming influential commercial groups.

Fourth, creativity, adaptability, and mutual empowerment revealed the enterprising spirit of these merchants. Merchants from mountainous areas demonstrated strong independence. Their businesses largely looked outward, and due to geographic and historical factors, they were less reliant on official structures and more market-oriented. For example, merchants in western Fujian were the first to capitalize on the introduction of tobacco, making the region the biggest domestic tobacco supplier. They harnessed local bamboo and timber to develop a national center for carved-book printing. They ventured to Southeast Asia and earned titles such as "Tin King," "Badminton King," and "Newspaper King." In the modern era, they have played leading roles in the rise of China's internet economy, forming what is known as the Longyan Internet Corps. Their capacity for innovation is reflected in their transformation of remote mountain villages into thriving communities, the emergence and prominence of merchant groups across historical periods, and their integration into new environments, where migration routes often became trade routes, and distant lands became new homes. Their commitment to "helping others to succeed and cultivating oneself" is reflected in their mutual support and in commerce's role in improving the quality of life.

Interior View of the Shanghang Hakka Genealogy Hall

Fifth, patriotism, love for one's hometown, and inclusive compassion embodied the merchants' broader moral vision. Those who have experienced the hardship of leaving their native land often feel a deeper attachment to their homelands and motherland. Many overseas Hakka people, though living abroad, have always remembered that they are descendants of China, and constantly longed for their homelands. They have passed on this awareness to their children—encouraging them to trace their roots, honor their ancestors, and always remember their motherland and ancestral home. A couplet found in the Xiangong Park in Dongxiao, Longyan expresses the sentiments of overseas Chinese, "Though the world may serve as a home, the mountains and rivers of the motherland are ever in our hearts.// Though we reside across the five continents, the customs and scenery of our homelands remain dear to us." This profound emotional attachment reduced their risks when doing business abroad while earning them support and care from their homelands. Once successful, these merchants rarely forgot their roots. They often gave back to the hometowns that had nurtured them or their ancestors. Their philanthropic acts provided significant support for China's economic development and social progress and earned them admiration and respect from the Chinese people at home and abroad. For instance, the *Genealogy of the Wu Clan of Peitian: Draft of the Memorial Arch for Yiting Gong* records,

> Donating rice for military use, caring for orphans, building bridges, funding the repair of academies, storing grain to guard against famine, and offering tea to aid travelers—these were all beneficial to the local community, not just to the clan itself.

The *Gazetteer of Changting County* records,

> Liu Wenduan, a native of Cikeng in Pingyuan, frequently engaged in trade in Chuzhou, Zhejiang, during the eleventh year of the Qianlong reign. When a great fire broke out, destroying hundreds of homes and shops, he spent his entire capital hiring workers to fetch water and extinguish the fires. The local magistrate, Zheng Gong, awarded him a plaque inscribed "Light on Wealth, Heavy on Righteousness."*Inclusiveness* is also reflected in the merchants' ability to coexist harmoniously with local communities and other traders. For example, during the War of Resistance against Japanese Aggression, when commerce from cities like Fuzhou, Xiamen, and Shantou was relocated inland, merchants from various regions collaborated to create a period of commercial prosperity in western Fujian in the 1940s.

Chapter 1

The Port–Hinterland Relationship and the Development of the Maritime Silk Road in Fujian

Section 1 Theoretical Framework of the Port–Hinterland Relationship

I. Basic Concepts of Port and Hinterland

In economic geography, port is a key term typically referring to coastal or inland locations—along seas, rivers, or lakes—that provide services such as ship berthing, cargo handling, goods distribution, and passenger and freight transit. Ports serve as crucial nodes for land–water transfers and intermodal transportation. They are usually the starting points or transit hubs in the flow of goods and passengers, playing a pivotal role in moving cargo to destination ports, where it is transferred to other modes of transport for final delivery. Depending on the geographical environment in which they are situated, ports are commonly classified as seaports, river ports, or lake ports. Historically, inland areas along rivers or waterways prioritized waterborne transportation, and regions equipped with ports often opened to foreign trade earlier than others.

The term hinterland originally emerged about a port hinterland. In 1885, George Chisholm first introduced the German term *Hinterland* (the land behind) in his *Handbook of Commercial Geography*, defining it as the area from which a port gathers and distributes goods. According to the *Concise Encyclopedia Britannica*, a hinterland is the city or regional area lying geographically behind a port, which engages in foreign trade, imports and exports, and product sales via the port. Modern scholars commonly define a port's hinterland as the geographic area involved in the intake and distribution of cargo and passengers through that port. If an area sends or receives import/export goods via land transportation to and from a particular port for onward water transport, that area is considered part of the port's hinterland.

The classification of hinterlands varies depending on the criteria applied. According to existing literature, one prevalent method categorizes hinterlands based on the intensity of port–hinterland connections. This system includes four types: core hinterlands, direct hinterlands, indirect hinterlands, and mixed hinterlands—the latter also referred to as competitive hinterlands. The core hinterland is geographically very close to the port and maintains strong economic ties with it, often comprising the port city itself or adjacent industrial zones. The direct hinterland lies relatively near the port and is linked through one or more modes of transport. It relies on the port for the shipment of goods by water and typically encompasses the economic region or urban belt in which the port city is located. The indirect hinterland is located farther from the port, requiring transfer via additional transportation methods. Its volume of goods transported via the port is usually smaller. The mixed/competitive hinterland is typically situated between two similarly ranked ports and constitutes a shared or contested region between the two.[1]

Professor Wu Songdi of Fudan University has pointed out that the structure of commodity distribution via ports in modern China was quite complex, and the concept of a hinterland cannot be simply equated with the source area of a port's exports or the destination of its imports. For imported goods, some were transported inland directly via transport routes behind the port, while others were re-exported to other ports (a process known as *transshipment*). For exported goods, some came directly from the inland areas connected to the port, while others, due to factors like transportation, taxation, or political considerations, were routed through more distant ports instead of geographically closer ones. In the aforementioned content, only regions that are geographically contiguous with a port's landward

1 Sha Yumeng. *Research on the Methods of Defining Port Hinterlands*. MA thesis, Dalian Maritime University, 2015, p.9.

connections and that directly consume imported goods or directly supply export goods should be considered as that port's hinterlands. Areas that deal in a port's transshipped goods or transport goods over longer distances for export through the port do not qualify as part of its hinterlands. According to the general principles of human geography, the peripheral areas of a port's hinterlands often maintain logistics links not only with the associated port but also with neighboring ports—though the latter usually account for a smaller share of overall cargo volume. These overlapping zones are referred to as shared or overlapping hinterlands. This phenomenon is quite common along the peripheries of port–hinterland systems. If we define hinterlands without such overlap as core or exclusive hinterlands, then any given port's hinterlands are composed of both core and overlapping zones.[1]

II. The Relationship Between Ports and Their Hinterlands

The relationship between ports and their hinterlands is fundamentally characterized by mutual dependence and reciprocal support. Together, they constitute a relatively complete regional economic system. From the perspective of regional economic geography, existing research on the port–hinterland relationship has primarily given rise to several significant theoretical frameworks, including seaport location theory, theory of regional division of labor, and synergy theory.

1.Seaport Location Theory

The location of a port refers to the site where the port engages in economic activities and its position within the broader economic-geographical space. The locational conditions of a port encompass a range of geographical and economic factors that influence its survival and

1Wu Songdi. "Port–Hinterland Relations and the Spatial Process of Modernization in China." *Hebei Academic Journal*, no.3, 2004, p.161.

development, including the economic development level of the port city and its surrounding areas, the state of the integrated transportation system, the port's capacity to attract and sustain cargo flows, and its natural hydrological conditions.[1] Seaport location theory examines the relationship between ports and their economic hinterlands mainly from the perspectives of port location, harbor conditions, hinterland positioning, and regional economic development. Ports and hinterlands form an economic system characterized by mutual influence and interaction. On the one hand, the larger the hinterland and the more developed its economy, the stronger its capacity to support the port with cargo, thereby driving the growth of port throughput and contributing to the economic development of the host city. On the other hand, relative to other regions, hinterlands enjoy comparative advantages in terms of resource distribution and cargo transshipment. The more developed the port's role as a transportation hub, the more capable it is of attracting cargo from the hinterland, thus promoting industrial agglomeration and large-scale economic development within the hinterland.

2. Theory of Regional Division of Labor

The theory of regional division of labor refers to the development of advantageous industries in different geographical regions based on their inherent resource endowments. These regions produce goods in which they have a comparative advantage and subsequently engage in interregional exchange. To illustrate simply, suppose there are two regions, A and B. Region A possesses favorable natural conditions such as climate and soil, as well as abundant labor resources, making it well-suited for large-scale cotton cultivation. Region B, by contrast, is more suitable for the large-scale aquaculture of aquatic products. In cotton production, Region A has a

1Xiao Zhongxi. "The Role of Location and Opportunity in Port Development." *Water Transport Management*, no.12, 2005, p.12.

comparative advantage over Region B; in aquaculture, Region B holds an advantage over Region A. Both regions can thus specialize in producing goods aligned with their respective advantages. After satisfying internal demand, surplus products can be exchanged to maximize overall benefits. According to this theory, a well-structured division of labor exists between ports and their hinterlands. Ports, with their unique advantages in cargo handling, distribution, and transportation, are capable of conducting specialized, large-scale, and intensive cargo throughput operations. Hinterlands, by virtue of their broader territorial expanse and more diverse production conditions, are better positioned to engage in the large-scale production of goods such as agricultural products and manufactured goods. The orderly division of labor between ports and hinterlands fosters a specialized production structure that enhances productivity on both ends and creates greater economic returns.

3.Synergy Theory

Synergy refers to the interaction and coordination among various elements or subsystems within a broader system, resulting in an organic whole. To achieve effective synergy among different geographical regions, at least three fundamental conditions must be met. First, the regions must be geographically proximate or adjacent, sharing similar or compatible cultural attributes such as social customs and lifestyles. Second, the regions must exhibit similarity or complementarity in terms of natural resources, industrial distribution, and market demand, thereby enabling cross-sectoral production cooperation and coordination facilitated by favorable spatial connectivity. Third, the regions' key actors—governments, enterprises, and other stakeholders—must be committed to collaborative development, thus creating favorable conditions for interregional industrial coordination and advancement.[1] According to regional synergy theory, the port and its hinterlands constitute a relatively integrated system. Within this system, the port and the hinterlands engage in cooperative, supportive, and coordinated development. The port provides essential transportation services for the import and export of goods from the hinterlands, while the hinterlands supply the port with necessary cargo resources. Together, they coordinate the flows of goods, information, and capital, forming an organically interconnected whole.

In summary, ports provide essential transportation services that enable hinterlands to engage in trade with external markets, expanding their avenues for international and interregional exchange and thereby promoting the development and growth of hinterland economies. At the same time, the hinterland's active participation in external exchanges and trade activities leads to sustained growth in demand for transportation services, which in turn drives improvements in port operations and enhances the port's cargo distribution and collection functions. As such, the relationship between ports and their hinterlands is one system of mutual interdependence, orderly division of labor, and coordinated development.

1Liu Bo, and Cheng Changchun. "Theoretical Foundation of Port–Hinterland Economic Relationships." *Resources Development and Market*, no.11, 2013, p.1162.

Section 2 The Relationship Between Fujian Ports and Their Hinterlands

I. Historical Evolution of Fujian Ports

The formation and development of ports is a gradual and evolutionary process. Historically, most ports had undergone a progression from a "completely natural state" to a "semi-natural, semi-socio-cultural state" and eventually to a "socio-cultural state".[1] In the "socio-cultural state", economic exchanges between ports and their hinterlands became more frequent compared to those in the "semi-natural, semi-socio-cultural" stage. Located in southeastern China, Fujian Province is characterized by mountainous and hilly terrain, which accounts for approximately 89.3% of its total area. The province is traversed by four major river systems: Minjiang River, Jinjiang River, Jiulong River, and Tingjiang River, earning it the description "eight parts mountain, one part water, one part farmland".[2] Most of Fujian ports boast a long history and have played vital roles in the development of foreign trade in commodities such as porcelain, silk, tea, and spices. Numerous archaeological discoveries and cultural relics indicate that Fujian ports held a significant place in the history of the Maritime Silk Road.

1.Fuzhou Port

Situated at the mouth of the Minjiang River, Fuzhou Port originated from Dongye Port, according to historical records, and has a history spanning over 2,000 years. Wu Zhu, the King of Minyue State, established the Minyue

1 Gong Gaojian, and Zhang Yanqing. "An Exploration of the Development of Port Economy in Ancient Fujian." *Fujian Tribune (Social Science and Education Edition), Special Issue*, 2007, p.241.

2Song Jiapeng, and Chen Songlin. "Coupling and Coordination Analysis of Implicit Land Use Forms and Land Ecological Security in Fujian Province." *Research of Soil and Water Conservation*, no.4, 2020, p.302.

Kingdom with its capital in Dongye (now Fuzhou). During the Eastern Han and the Three Kingdoms periods, Dongye Port, located in the Fuzhou Bay at the mouth of the Minjiang River, gradually rose to prominence. According to the *Book of the Later Han: Biography of Zheng Hong*, in the eighth year of the Jianchu reign in Eastern Han Dynasty (83 CE), "Tributes and transported goods from the seven commanderies of Jiaozhi were all shipped via Dongye." Additionally, the *Records of the Grand Historian: Biography of the Eastern Yue* notes that the capital of the Minyue Kingdom was located in Dongye, "In the fifth year of Emperor Gao of the Han Dynasty, Wu Zhu was re-established as King of Minyue, ruling over the former Minzhong territory with Dongye as the capital."[1] This confirms that Dongye was the administrative center of the Minyue Kingdom at the time. During the Han Dynasty, the mountainous terrain hindered northward land transportation, making Dongye Port the primary hub for the transfer of tributes from the seven southern commanderies, including those in Guangdong, Guangxi, and Vietnam.[2] As a natural deep-water harbor on the southeast coast, Dongye was renamed Fuzhou during the Tang Dynasty, when Fuzhou Port became one of the three major ports for foreign trade. During the late Tang and Five Dynasties periods, Wuzhu Port and Gantang Port were established as the inner and outer harbors of Fuzhou respectively. In the early Northern Song Dynasty, Fuzhou emerged as the maritime transport and trade center of Fujian. In the second year of Yuanyou reign of the Song Dynasty (1087), the imperial court established the Maritime Trade Supervisorate in Quanzhou, which gradually led to Quanzhou Port surpassing Fuzhou Port in importance. During the Ming Dynasty, before each of his seven expeditions to the Western Seas, Zheng He anchored at Taiping Port in Changle, Fuzhou. In the tenth year of the

1Xie Zaihua. "On the Important Position of Fuzhou in the Ancient Maritime Silk Road." *Fujian Historical Records*, no.2, 2015, p.17.

2Ou Tanhua. "The Earliest Starting Point of the Maritime Silk Road —Dongye Port of Minyue State in Fuzhou." *Fuzhou Evening News*, 24 Dec. 2016.

Chenghua reign in the Ming Dynasty(1474), the Maritime Trade Supervisorate was relocated from Quanzhou to Fuzhou, which became a key port for trade with the Ryukyu Kingdom.[1] From the opening of the five treaty ports to the late Qing Dynasty, Fuzhou Port remained a major hub for tea exports.

2.Quanzhou Port

Located at the estuary of the Jinjiang River, Quanzhou Port, known historically as Citong Port, rose to prominence during the Tang Dynasty. It is a natural deep-water port and one of the starting points of the Maritime Silk Road. During the Tang Dynasty, a military commissioner was stationed in Quanzhou to oversee foreign trade and transportation. In the Five Dynasties period, Quanzhou Port expanded its maritime routes, broadening its trade networks. During the Song and Yuan dynasties, it developed into a major international trading port, facilitating navigation and trade across the Eastern and Western seas, with routes extending eastward to Japan, southward to Southeast Asia, and westward to Persia, Arabia, and East Africa. In the Ming Dynasty, thesignificance of the foreign trade in Quzhou Port began to wane, and it gradually declined during the Qing Dynasty.[2]

3.Sandu'ao Port

Located in northeastern Fujian, Sandu'ao Port serves as a gateway for access to and from the eastern Fujian coast and is a natural deep-water harbor. The port was partially developed even before the Tang Dynasty. During the reign of Wang Shenzhi in the Five Dynasties period, the development of the port was intensified, enhancing maritime connectivity between Fujian and

---

1Xie Zaihua. "On the Important Position of Fuzhou in the Ancient Maritime Silk Road." *Fujian Historical Records*, no.2, 2015, p.18.

2Zheng Naihui, Gao Xiangfeng, and Jiang Ling. "Historical Tea Trade Routes of Fujian Ports." *Fujian Tea Industry*, no.6 2015, pp.48–49.

northern China. In the Ming Dynasty, a dedicated grain-shipping route was established at Sandu'ao. In the Guangxu era of the Qing Dynasty, Fuhai Customs (Fu Hai Guan) was set up at the port, officially opening it to foreign trade. Sandu'ao Port thus became an important coastal port for international commerce, with much of the tea produced in eastern Fujian exported via this gateway. However, during the Republic of China period, the port declined due to the impact of warfare.

4. Yuegang Port in Zhangzhou

As Quanzhou Port fell into decline in the late Yuan Dynasty, Yuegang Port, located in the relatively remote Haicheng area of Zhangzhou, rose to prominence due to its long-standing smuggling activities. The development of Yuegang Port can be divided into two phases: the first phase, from the 15th century to the mid-16th century, during which it mainly facilitated illegal overseas smuggling; the second phase, from the mid-16th century to the early 17th century, during which partial lifting of the maritime trade ban by the Ming government led to the establishment of a "foreign market" in Yuegang Port, allowing for regulated private maritime trade under government supervision.[1] With the rise of Zheng Chenggong's anti-Qing campaigns in the late Ming and early Qing periods, Yuegang Port entered a period of decline.[2]

5. Xiamen Port

Located at the junction of Jimen Bay and the Jiulong River estuary, Xiamen Port served as a subsidiary port to Quanzhou Port during the Song Dynasty. In the Yuan Dynasty, it functioned as a military harbor, where "Jiahe

---

1Zhong Jianhua. "From Yuegang Port to Xiamen Port: A Historical Study of Putou Port in Zhangzhou During the Ming and Qing Dynasties." *Journal of Minnan Normal University (Philosophy and Social Sciences Edition)*, no.3, 2015, p.9.

2Chen Ziqiang. *An Introduction to the Maritime Culture of Southern Fujian During the Ming and Qing Dynasties*. Lujiang Publishing House, 2012, pp. 8–9.

Thousand-Household Office" was established. In the Ming Dynasty, it became a major hub for private smuggling activities. During the Shunzhi reign of the Qing Dynasty, Xiamen Port served as the maritime base for Zheng Chenggong's "Five Merchants" (with *Ren*, *Yi*, *Li*, *Zhi*, and *Xin*—benevolence, righteousness, propriety, wisdom, and trust—as the code names of five trading firms) which facilitated trade with Taiwan Province, Japan, Luzon, and other parts of the South Seas. After the reunification of Taiwan during the Kangxi reign, Fukien Maritime Customs was established, with Xiamen Port designated as the principal port. In the Yongzheng era, Xiamen Port became the primary port for overseas trade from Fujian. In the 22nd year of the Daoguang reign (1842), Xiamen was designated one of the five treaty ports. By the Guangxu era, it had developed into a relatively advanced modern comprehensive port.[1]

II. Historical Definition of the Hinterlands of Fujian Ports

Based on the definition of the hinterlands of ports by Professor Wu Songdi from the Historical Geography Research Center of Fudan University, and referring to Shui Haigang's delineation of the hinterland of modern Fuzhou Port, we may consider the Minjiang River Basin as the hinterland of both Fuzhou Port and Sandu'ao Port, the Jiulong River Basin and Tingjiang River Basin as the hinterlands of Zhangzhou Port and Xiamen Port, and the Jinjiang River Basin as the hinterland of Quanzhou Port. The Minjiang River is the largest river within Fujian Province, originating from the Xianxia Ridge, Wuyi Mountain, and the Shanling Ridge at the junction of Fujian, Zhejiang, and Jiangxi provinces. The upper reaches of the Minjiang River comprise three main tributaries: the Jianxi, Futun, and Shaxi creeks; its lower reaches

1Zheng Naihui, Gao Xiangfeng, and Jiang Ling. "The Tea Trade Routes of Fujian Ports in History." *Fujian Tea Industry*, no.6, 2015, p.51.

include the Gutian Creek, Youxi Creek, Meixi Creek, and Dazhang Creek.[1] The Minjiang River Basin, defined by the reach of its various tributaries, primarily encompassed areas that, during the Tang Dynasty, included parts of Fuzhou, Jianzhou, and Tingzhou, as well as regions in northern Fujian bordering Zhejiang and Jiangxi provinces. These areas constituted the key hinterland for Fuzhou Port and Sandu'ao Port. According to the *Old History of Tang Dynasty: Geographical Treatise* and the *New History of Tang Dynasty: Geographical Treatise*, the name of Fuzhou changed multiple times in the early Tang Dynasty, successively known as Fengzhou, Quanzhou, Jian'an Commandery, Minzhou, and eventually Fuzhou. The *New History of Tang Dynasty* records that Fuzhou then administered ten counties: Minxian, Houguan, Changle, Lianjiang, Futang, Yongtai, Changxi, Gutian, Meixi, and Youxi. Jianzhou governed five counties: Jian'an (now Jian'ou), Jianyang, Pucheng, Jiangle, and Shaowu.[2] According to the *Fujian Provincial Gazetteer: Transportation Volume*, the transport of goods by wooden sailing vessels was already flourishing on the upper reaches of the Minjiang River—namely the Jianxi Creek, Futun Creek, and Shaxi Creek—during the Tang Dynasty. After the Southern Song period, native Fujian specialties and daily goods from Zhejiang were frequently collected in Pucheng and transported via the Nanpu Creek to Nanping and Fuzhou. After the opening of the five treaty ports, Wuyi tea was largely shipped along the Jianxi Creek to Fuzhou Port for overseas export. Bulk commodities transported from Fuzhou Port to Shaowu and Guangze included salt, sugar, seafood, and daily necessities.[3] During the Qing Dynasty, Sandu'ao was under the jurisdiction of Funing

---

1Shui Haigang. *Port Trade and Hinterland Society: A Study on the Development of the Minjiang River Basin in Modern Times from a Regional Perspective*. Xiamen University Press, 2019, p.19.

2(Song) Ouyang Xiu and Song Qi. *New History of Tang Dynasty,* vol. 41, *Geographical Records*. Zhonghua Book Company, 1975, p.1064.

3Fujian Provincial Local Gazetteer Compilation Committee. *Fujian Provincial Gazetteer: Gazetteer of Transportation*. Fangzhi Publishing House, 1998, pp.170–177.

Prefecture and located between the counties of Fu'an and Ningde. It was officially opened to foreign trade in the 25th year of the Guangxu reign (1899), when the Qing government established Fuhai Customs at Sandu'ao. Funing Prefecture comprised five counties: Fu'an, Ningde, Xiapu, Fuding, and Shouning. After Sandu'ao Port was opened, part of the commercial trade and transportation within Funing Prefecture shifted from Fuzhou Port to Sandu'ao Port. Thus, in the late Qing period, Funing Prefecture became a shared hinterland for both Fuzhou Port and Sandu'ao Port.

The Jiulong River, the second largest river in Fujian, is mainly composed of the Beixi, Xixi, and Nanxi tributaries. During the Tang Dynasty, the river basin formed by these tributaries primarily encompassed the region of Zhangzhou. According to the *New History of Tang Dynasty*, Zhangzhou then governed three counties: Longxi, Zhangpu, and Longyan. The Tingjiang River, referred to in the Song, Ming, and Qing dynasties as the Yinjiang River, originates from Laijia Mountain on the southern slopes of the Wuyi Mountains. Its main tributaries include the Jiuxian River, Huangtan River, Zhuotian Creek, and Taolan Creek. At that time, Tingzhou administered three counties: Changting, Shaxian, and Ninghua.[1] According to the *Fujian Provincial Gazetteer: Transportation Volume*, as early as the Tang Dynasty, wooden sailing ships were the primary mode of transport in the Jiulong River Basin, facilitating frequent exchange of local specialties and coastal goods such as salt and seafood among the counties in the basin. Goods such as bamboo, timber, and paper, which were abundant in the Tingjiang River Basin, were mostly transported downstream to Guangdong, with some rerouted via Longyan County to the Jiulong River Basin for export to the

---

1Yang Jingjing. *A Study of Fujian During the Tang Dynasty — Focusing on the Economy and Imperial Examinations after the An Lushan Rebellion*. MA thesis, Yangzhou University, 2015, p.12.

coast. Consequently, the Jiulong River Basin and Tingjiang River Basin became important economic hinterlands for Zhangzhou Port and Xiamen Port.

The Jinjiang River originates in Yongchun County, located in central Fujian Province, and comprises Xixi Creek as the main trunk and Dongxi Creek as a tributary. In the Tang Dynasty, the areas reached by these streams formed the core of Quanzhou's jurisdiction. According to the *New History of Tang Dynasty*, Quanzhou then governed four counties: Jinjiang, Nan'an, Putian, and Xianyou. The *Fujian Provincial Gazetteer: Transportation Volume* states that as early as the Southern and Northern dynasties period, wooden sailing vessels were already used to transport goods along the Jinjiang River. With the development of Quanzhou Port's foreign trade, wooden sailing shipping on the river intensified during the Song and Yuan dynasties and reached its peak, followed by gradual decline during the Ming Dynasty. Local products such as tea, porcelain, sugar, and dried longan were primarily transported via the Dongxi Creek and Xixi Creek to Quanzhou, and from there, redistributed domestically or exported overseas. Imported goods at Quanzhou Port, including kerosene, textiles, and general merchandise, were likewise distributed inland through the Dongxi Creek and Xixi Creek. Thus, the Jinjiang River Basin served as a critical economic hinterland for Quanzhou Port within Fujian.

Section 3 The Impact of Fujian Port Trade on the Hinterland Economy and Social Development

Ports serve as vital hubs for the distribution of imported and exported goods and as key nodes for multimodal transport, providing essential channels for the outward flow of inland goods and the inward movement of overseas commodities. Since the Han and Tang dynasties, coastal ports such as Fuzhou and Quanzhou in Fujian have engaged in overseas trade. The expansion of coastal port trade not only stimulated the development of the commodity economy in the inland mountainous regions of Fujian but also exerted a profound influence on their social development.

I. The Economic Impetus of Fujian Port Trade on Its Hinterland

1. The Impact of Commodity Exports on the Economic Development of Mountainous Areas

Northern and western Fujian are located in the inland regions of the province, characterized by mountainous terrain and abundant in timber, traditional handmade paper, tea, and other local products. During the Song Dynasty, with the southward shift of China's economic and cultural centers, these regions experienced accelerated development in agriculture and handicrafts, alongside a gradual rise in commercial activities. The growth of foreign trade via coastal ports facilitated the gradual entry of many inland products into overseas markets. The export of these native products significantly influenced the development of agriculture and handicrafts in northern and western Fujian, contributing to the prosperity of local marketplaces.

(1) Promotion of Handicraft Industry Development

The export of handicraft products from these regions first contributed to the expansion of production scales. During the Song and Yuan dynasties, the ceramic industry in northern Fujian flourished, with large volumes produced not only for imperial tribute but also for export. As ceramics from northern Fujian—particularly Jianyang black-glazed teacup—gained popularity in Japan, Korea, and Southeast Asia, the variety of ceramic products increased, and the scale of production expanded. For instance, in the Northern Song period, the Jiulong kilns in Songxi operated thirteen kilns, producing tribute "hare's fur tea bowls" for domestic and overseas markets. Pucheng's Dakou kilns were said to have had as many as thirty-six kilns during their peak. The Qingyun kilns in Shaowu were even larger, comprising three sites—the upper kiln, the lower kiln, and the Shuiwei kiln. Among these, the "lower kiln" covered the largest area and was primarily composed of dragon kilns. In the Yuan Dynasty, ceramic products from the Qingyun kiln were extensively exported; the site reportedly had over 130 kilns at its height. In the Song Dynasty, the dragon kilns of Yulin Pavilion in Wuyi Mountain primarily produced commercial and export ceramics, firing tens of thousands of pieces in a single session—testimony to the vast scale of production. Such large-scale kilns necessitated the employment of numerous handicraft workers. In the Qing Dynasty, western Fujian became a major producer of various types of traditional handmade paper, which was exported in large quantities to Japan and Southeast Asia due to its superior quality. Papermaking in Wuping County was the most prominent local industry. By the Daoguang era, annual output in Changting County exceeded 100,000 *dan* (a traditional Chinese unit of weight,one *dan* = 50 kg). Lianshi paper from Liancheng was prized for its bright color, smooth texture, and translucency, and was highly popular in the regions of Southeast Asia. In the late Qing and early Republican periods, Liancheng's paper industry expanded significantly, reaching over 130,000 *dan* in annual sales. Besides, the export of handmade products promoted advances in craftsmanship. The textile industry in northern Fujian also experienced notable growth during the Song and Yuan dynasties. The region had a long history of sericulture. By the Song Dynasty, foot-powered spinning wheels were in common use, and brocades produced in Jianyang were exported abroad. The external demand for silk products spurred the growth of economies of scale in local textile production and drove improvements in production techniques. To expand their export markets, local silk and cotton weavers continually refined their skills. Jianyang brocade, known for its exquisite craftsmanship, earned imperial praise from Emperor Huizong of the Song Dynasty. Furthermore, the robust export trade in handicrafts facilitated the movement of labor from agriculture to industry and commerce. During the Song Dynasty, Jianyang in northern Fujian emerged as one of the three major printing centers in China. In the Qing Dynasty, Sibao in Liancheng County in western Fujian was one of the four major publishing hubs. Books printed in these two areas were not only distributed across the provinces but also exported to Japan and Southeast Asia. The growth of the printing industry attracted many rural laborers to enter engraving and printing work. At its peak, 60% of Sibao's population was employed in the printing industry. Additionally, due to high levels of tea and tobacco exports in the Qing period, related processing industries thrived in northern and western Fujian, drawing many peasants into handicrafts.

(2) Transformation of Agricultural Structures

The export of tea from northern and western Fujian also reshaped local agricultural cropping patterns. Tea cultivation in northern Fujian has a long history. During the Song Dynasty, tribute tea from the Beiyuan tea gardens in Jianzhou was widely renowned. In the early Qing Dynasty, the successful development of Wuyi black tea shifted the center of tea production and trade to Chong'an. As black tea catered to European tastes, its exports to Europe surged. The original production area—ranging from Xingcun Town in Chong'an to Tongmuguan—became known for "Zhengshan Xiaozhong Black Tea " (Lapsang Sauchong Black Tea). In the mid-Qing period, the sharp rise in exports of Wuyi black tea led to a situation where "local production could no longer meet global demand." Driven by this surging demand, local farmers began converting rice paddies into tea plantations. As tea cultivation expanded, many counties in northern Fujian shifted from primarily growing food crops to focusing on tea as a cash crop, transforming grain-producing areas into tea-producing regions. By the Qing Dynasty, tea cultivation in various counties of western Fujian had taken shape. During the Tongzhi and Guangxu reigns, Longyan County experienced a boom in tea production and exports. Given the significantly higher profit margin of tea compared to rice, tea plantations spread widely across the region, resulting in the notable phenomenon of "tea-covered hills."

2.The Impact of Commodity Imports on the Economic Development of Mountainous Areas

From the mid to late Ming Dynasty, a variety of foreign crops were introduced to the inland mountainous regions of Fujian through coastal ports. Among them, sweet potatoes, tobacco, corn, and peanuts had significant effects on local agriculture in norther and western Fujian. Sweet potatoes were first introduced to coastal Fujian from Luzon in the 21st year of the Wanli reign (1593), and were subsequently promoted in the inland areas. As a drought-resistant and easy-to-grow crop, sweet potatoes served as a vital grain substitute, helping people survive during times of famine and food shortage. Tobacco was introduced from Luzon to Quanzhou and Zhangzhou in the late Ming Dynasty and was subsequently planted in Yongding during the early Qing period. The favorable climate and soil in Yongding facilitated the expansion of tobacco cultivation. Between the Qianlong and Guangxu reigns, Yongding's tobacco was sold nationwide and exported to Southeast

Asia. As a mountainous county with limited arable land, Yongding derived substantial profits from tobacco, often earning several times more than rice farming. Many peasants consequently converted fertile farmland into tobacco fields.

3. Prosperity of Commercial Centers and Marketplaces Driven by Foreign Trade

The expansion of import-export trade invigorated commercial hubs along transportation routes, giving rise to influential merchants and trade groups. Key transit points on the water and land routes between inland areas in northern and western Fujian and coastal ports often became major commercial centers. This was primarily because such nodes served as transshipment stations and distribution centers for both land and water transport. Imported and exported goods were frequently reloaded there, transport personnel and pack animals rested and reorganized there, and merchants conducted trade there. As a result, commercial establishments, inns, and marketplaces gradually emerged. In early Qing times, Xingcun and Xiamei in Chong'an, northern Fujian, became thriving tea trading centers with numerous tea houses, earning the nicknames "Little Suzhou" and "Little Shanghai" respectively. From the Song Dynasty to the Republic of China, Fengshi in Yongding County was a vital transit hub between Fujian and Guangdong. Local specialties from Tingzhou Prefecture were shipped via the Tingjiang River to Fengshi, then unloaded and carried over the mountains on shoulder poles to Shishang Port in Dabu, Guangdong, and finally shipped to Chaozhou for maritime export. Imported goods from the coast also traveled upstream via Fengshi to Changting, making Fengshi a crucial transshipment hub linking the mountainous interior and coastal ports. By the late Qing and early Republican period, there were over 320 trade agencies (known as "*Hangdian*") engaged in transshipment trade (known as "*Guozai Hang*") along the streets of Fengshi. Its seven wooden docks accommodated nearly

200 boats daily, with more than 400 porters handling the loading and unloading of goods.[12] Jian'ou, located at the confluence of the Chongyang Creek, Nanpu Creek, and Songxi Creek, was another vital inland port and transshipment center on the upper Minjiang River. Goods from Chong'an, Pucheng, and Jianyang were often assembled here. Nanping Port, situated at the junction of the Shaxi Creek, Jianxi Creek, and Futun Creek, was a key waterway hub connecting counties in the northern Fujian to Fuzhou Port. During the Ming and Qing dynasties, it witnessed remarkable commercial prosperity, with a bustling scene described as "a convergence of boats and carts, abundant goods and lively crowds, unmatched north of the provincial capital."[3] Furthermore, counties such as Guangze and Shaowu along the ancient Fujian-Jiangxi route, and Pucheng and Chong'an along the Fujian-Zhejiang route, were significant inter-provincial trade centers during the Ming and Qing periods due to their proximity to provincial borders. Cross-border trade in these regions was especially vibrant.

Additionally, as trade and population exchange between the mountainous interior and the coastal regions intensified, both government authorities and local residents sought to improve transportation infrastructure to facilitate land and water transport. These efforts included clearing dangerous stretches of rivers, building roads and bridges, and adding more relay stations for horses and boats.

1Zhou Xuexiang. "Commodity Circulation and Urban–Rural Markets in Hakka Areas on the Fujian–Guangdong Border During the Ming and Qing Dynasties." *Research in Chinese Economic History*, no.2, 2007, p.100.

2 Cai Lixiong, editor-in-chief. *A Commercial History of Western Fujian*. Xiamen University Press, 2014, p.116.

3 Wu Bangcai, editor-in-chief. *A History of the Development of Fujian Merchants: Nanping Volume*. Xiamen University Press, 2016, p.108.

II. The Impact of Fujian Port Trade on Social Development in the Hinterland

1.Population Migration

The export trade of native products from mountainous regions spurred the growth of the commodity economy in these areas, which in turn led to population migration from coastal regions—where livelihoods were increasingly difficult—into the inland mountainous zones. During the Qing Dynasty, the flourishing tea export trade in the Wuyi Mountains of northern Fujian significantly promoted the development of industries associated with tea exports. The expansion of tea cultivation required a large number of tea farmers, the scaling-up of tea processing demanded many laborers, and tea packaging and transportation also necessitated a sizable workforce. Consequently, the development of tea-related industries driven by export trade created numerous employment opportunities, attracting large numbers of impoverished farmers from coastal Fujian and tea workers from Zhejiang and Jiangxi to migrate to the mountainous areas of northern Fujian, where they shifted into tea cultivation, processing, transportation, and other related trades. In the early Qing period, many residents in Jian'ou "relied on tea for their livelihoods—some cleared land for tea cultivation, some harvested tea leaves, some established tea estates and collected leaves, and others engaged in tea vending, sifting, and sorting." From the Yongzheng reign to the Qianlong reign, the tea industry supported tens of thousands of people in just one county, Ouning. By the first half of the 19th century, at least several hundred thousand people were engaged in the tea industry across the 18 tea-producing counties of northern Fujian.[1] Each year during the tea picking and

1Yan Lijin. *A Study on the Interactive Relationship Between Fujian's Tea Exports and Regional Economic Development During the Qing Dynasty*. MA thesis, Jinan University, 2004, p.20.

processing season, large numbers of tea workers migrated from Jiangxi and Zhejiang to the tea-producing regions of northern Fujian. These seasonal migrations closely coincided with periods of active tea trade. Moreover, the abundant forest resources in the western and northern mountainous areas of Fujian supported a thriving papermaking industry during the Qing Dynasty. The large-scale export of traditional handmade paper and timber attracted a considerable influx of artisans and cultivators from the coastal regions of southern Fujian and the lower Minjiang River Basin into the inland areas of northwestern Fujian. For instance, loggers from the middle and lower reaches of the Minjiang River moved into forested regions of Fujian to fell pine trees. Papermakers from Zhangzhou and Yongchun relocated to bamboo-producing areas in northwestern Fujian to establish paper workshops. And people from Xinghua moved to Jian'ou to lease mountain land for Chinese fir cultivation. The booming tea trade in northern Fujian also drew many merchants from within and beyond the province to settle in the region. During the Xianfeng and Tongzhi reigns of the Qing Dynasty, for example, the tea market in Shaxian County "flourished, with tea shops lining the streets". Most tea shop owners were merchants from southern Fujian, and there were dozens of Fuzhou merchants engaged in business in Pucheng. In the Xianfeng reign, Masha town in Jianyang, northern Fujian, had "hundreds of storefronts, all operated by merchants from Jiangxi who traded in tea." In the Guangxu era, there were "more than a dozen tea shops in Shaowu County, most of which were operated by Cantonese merchants". By the end of the Qing Dynasty, about half of the residents in the county seat of Jian'ou were migrants from Jiangxi, and the majority of key commercial establishments were run by Jiangxi natives.[1] Table 1-1 presents the population statistics for the northwestern Fujian region in the first year of the Republic of China, offering

1Dai Yifeng. "Population Migration and Urbanization in Modern Fujian." *Researches in Chinese Economic History*, no.2, 1989, p.99.

empirical support for these migration patterns.

Table 1-1. Population Classification Statistics of Northwestern Fujian in the First Year of the Republic of China ***Unit: persons***

Region	Total Population	Inter-County Migrants	Inter-Provincial Migrants	% Inter-County Migrants	% Inter-Provincial Migrants	% Non-Local Population
Yanping Prefecture	926989	136391	55095	14.7	5.9	20.6
Nanping County	203509	31115	15561	15.3	7.6	23.9
Shunchang County	48056	12482	7306	30	15.2	45.2
Jiangle County	66987	1497	2102	2.2	3.1	5.3
Shaxian County	159371	19753	9553	12.4	6	18.4
Youxi County	257404	31544	573	12.3	2.2	14.5
Yong'an County	191663	40000	20000	20.9	13.6	34.5
Jianning Prefecture	1091355	143805	311346	13.2	28.5	41.7
Jian'ou County	534847	89696	129964	16.8	24.3	41.1
Jianyang County	95122	9498	53995	10	56.8	66.8
Chong'an County	155887	8516	35470	7.3	30.6	37.9
Songxi County	75210	1405	5003	1.9	6.7	8.6
Zhenghe County	110836	2033	12936	18.3	11.7	30
Shaowu Prefecture	328286	45221	52023	13.8	15.8	29.6
Shaowu County	117496	23631	11592	20.1	9.9	30
Guangze County	40489	199	3745	0.5	9.2	9.7
Jianning County	83173	12756	19895	15.3	23.9	39.2
Taining County	87228	8635	16791	9.9	19.2	29.1
Total	2346630	325417	418464	13.9	17.8	31.7

Source: Dai Yifeng, "Population Migration and Urbanization in Modern

Fujian." *Researches in Chinese Economic History*, no.2,1989, p.100.

According to Table 1-1, it is evident that from the Qing Dynasty to the first year of the Republic of China, the flourishing tea export trade in northwestern Fujian attracted a considerable number of migrants to the region. In particular, in the various counties under Jianning Prefecture, non-native residents accounted for 41.7% of the total population—one of the highest proportions of non-local population in the entire northwestern Fujian area.

2. Influx of Missionaries

In the 1830s, the booming tea export trade in the Wuyi Mountains of northern Fujian attracted the attention of Western missionaries, who repeatedly ventured into the upper reaches of the Minjiang River to gather intelligence on tea cultivation in the Wuyi region. By the late Qing period, after the opening of treaty ports such as Xiamen and Fuzhou, various Christian missionary societies[1]—led primarily by British and American organizations—established their bases in Xiamen and Fuzhou and began to carry out evangelical activities along the coastal regions. The missionary societies based in Xiamen included the Reformed Church in America, the London Missionary Society, the English Presbyterian Mission, and the American Presbyterian Mission. Those centered in Fuzhou included the American Board of Commissioners for Foreign Missions (ABCFM), the Methodist Episcopal Mission, and the Anglican Church Missionary Society.[2] In the 1860s, these major missionary societies based in Fuzhou began extending their evangelical efforts into the mountainous regions of northern Fujian along the upper Minjiang River. According to *A Brief History of Religion in Nanping*, the Methodist Episcopal Mission established Yanping as its base and expanded into areas such as Shunchang, Youxi, Shaxian,

1 Missionary Societies: A general term for Western organizations that introduced Christianity to China, also known as Western Missionary Societies, Evangelical Associations, or Mission Alliances.

2Lu Ping. *Christianity and Hakka Society in Western Fujian*. MA thesis, Fujian Normal University, 2002, pp.7–8.

Yong'an, and Mingxi. The ABCFM focused on Shaowu, expanding into Guangze, the urban area of Shunchang, Yangkou, Jianning, Taining, and Jiangle. The Anglican Church Missionary Society used Jian'ou as a center and extended its activities to Jianyang, Chong'an, Pucheng, Songxi, Zhenghe, and other areas. [1] In the 1880s, the London Missionary Society, the Presbyterian Mission, the Baptist Mission, and others began proselytizing in the Hakka-inhabited areas of western Fujian. To expand the scale of their missions and attract more converts, these Christian societies gradually established church-run schools and hospitals throughout western and northern Fujian. These institutions provided education and medical services to the local population. The establishment of church schools objectively promoted the development of modern education in these mountainous regions and cultivated a new generation of educated youth. Likewise, the founding of missionary hospitals facilitated the dissemination of advanced western medical knowledge and helped train a local cohort of healthcare workers. Thus, the opening of coastal treaty ports facilitated the entry of missionaries into the interior of Fujian. While engaged in evangelism, these missionaries also objectively contributed to the modernization of education and healthcare in the inland areas.

3.Changes in Lifestyle

After the opening of the five treaty ports, the influx of foreign goods began to subtly reshape the lifestyles of residents in the inland regions of western and northern Fujian. For instance, the large-scale importation of American flour led to increased processing and consumption of wheat-based foods, thereby diversifying the local diet. The introduction of kerosene transformed lighting methods, matches replaced traditional fire-starting techniques, imported fabrics altered local modes of dress, and western items such as clocks, watches, and sewing needles began to influence everyday life.

1Wu Weiwei. *Christianity and Modern Society in Northern Fujian: A Case Study of the American Board of Commissioners for Foreign Missions.* MA thesis, Fujian Normal University, 2006, p.10.

Section 4 The Supportive Role of Hinterland Economic Development in Port Growth

The hinterland not only provides the geographical space for port development but also supplies the essential flow of goods necessary for its growth. It serves as the fundamental prerequisite and necessary foundation for a port's survival and development. The hinterland supports port development in two main ways. First, the industrial structure and developmental trends of the hinterland exert a guiding influence on port development. The hinterland offers material support to the port's growth, and its comprehensive economic strength, industrial layout, export market orientation, and export development trends all significantly impact the transportation of goods through the port. The direction of export development in the hinterland shapes the port's trajectory, and the volume of goods exported through the port largely depends on the status of the export industries in the hinterland. Second, the economic scale of the hinterland affects the port's cargo throughput. A hinterland with strong prospects for sustainable development can promote the sustainable growth of the port and enhance its competitiveness. The broader the geographical scope of the hinterland, the richer its natural resources, and the more developed its economy, the greater the support it can provide for port development. In addition, economic development in the hinterland facilitates improvements in transportation infrastructure, providing critical facilities for the inward transfer, transit, and distribution of port cargo. A well-developed transportation network between the hinterland and the port fosters the circulation of people, goods, and capital. Overall, if the hinterland has a high degree of economic openness, frequent trade interactions, and a robust export economy, ports within that region typically possess large cargo throughput capacities and, in comparison to other ports, exhibit stronger capabilities and competitiveness.

I. The Guiding Role of Hinterland Industrial Structure in Port Development

Northern Fujian, as the source of the Minjiang River, is rich in forest resources. The ancient Minyue people were skilled in crafting dugout canoes from timber. Due to the mountainous terrain and inconvenient overland transportation in the region, and because the Jianxi Creek, Shaxi Creek, and Futun Creek all flow into the Minjiang River, the people of northern Fujian placed great importance on using the region's developed river system for boat transportation from as early as the pre-Qin period. During the Three Kingdoms period, when the Eastern Wu regime governed Fujian, Jian'an Commandery in northern Fujian became an important shipbuilding base. Once constructed, vessels were launched into the Jianxi Creek, floated downstream to Fuzhou via the Minjiang River, and then dispatched from the river's mouth to locations along the Yangtze River. The shipbuilding industry in ancient northern Fujian enabled vessels to travel from the source of the Minjiang River all the way to the vast expanses of the East China Sea. This brought the region closer to the ocean and facilitated the exchange of goods and the movement of merchants between northern Fujian, the coastal areas, and overseas. Moreover, the materials and techniques for shipbuilding developed at the river's source were later adopted across Fujian during the Song and Yuan dynasties, laying a solid foundation for the creation of the renowned "*Fuchuan*" (Fujian ships), which became famous in global maritime history. This, in turn, laid the groundwork for the flourishing of Fujian's maritime trade in subsequent eras.[1] Northern Fujian also has a long history of ceramic production. As early as the late Neolithic period, pottery

1 Wu Bangcai, editor-in-chief. *A History of the Development of Fujian Merchants: Nanping Volume*. Xiamen University Press, 2016, p.18.

was already being fired in the upper Minjiang River region. A stamped hard pottery jar from the Western Zhou period unearthed in Pucheng is considered a representative product of "Northern Fujian manufacture," and the dragon kilns in Pucheng are hailed as the progenitors of dragon kilns in Shang Dynasty in China. During the Spring and Autumn period, the area around Jianyang in northern Fujian began producing proto-porcelain. By the Han, Wei, and Six Dynasties periods, regions such as Jian'ou, Nanping, Shaowu, Guangze, and Jianyang in northern Fujian successively began firing celadon wares—part of the historical phase of ceramics known as "southern celadon and northern whiteware". The celadon products from kilns along the tributaries of the Futun Creek were easily exported via convenient water routes.[1] During the Tang Dynasty, dragon kilns or large kiln complexes were built in Jianyang, Pucheng, Songxi, and other parts of northern Fujian, primarily producing celadon wares. By the late Tang and Five Dynasties period, black-glazed ceramics, known in the Song Dynasty as "Jianyang black-glazed teacup" (Jian Zhan), were being fired around Xiaosong and Shuiji in Jian'ou. In the Song Dynasty, the Fujian Circuit was established, comprising six prefectures—Fu, Quan, Zhang, Jian (renamed Jianning Prefecture in the Southern Song Dynasty), Nanjian, and Ting—and two military jurisdictions: Shaowu and Xinghua.[2] Among these, Jianzhou, Nanjian, Tingzhou, and Shaowu approximately correspond to modern-day Nanping, Sanming, and Longyan. This mountainous area, though limited in arable land, was rich in timber, minerals, bamboo, tea, and other resources, and developed a flourishing commodity economy during the Song Dynasty. The ceramic industry in northern Fujian reached its peak during the Song and

1 Wu Bangcai, editor-in-chief. *A History of the Development of Fujian Merchants: Nanping Volume.* Xiamen University Press, 2016, p.20.

2 Wu Songdi, "The Significant Development of the Commodity Economy in Fujian During the Song Dynasty and Its Relationship with Geographical Conditions." *Research on Chinese Socio-Economic History*, no.3,1988, p.82.

Yuan periods. Numerous and large-scale kilns produced greenware, whiteware, and blackware for both domestic and overseas markets. Jianyang black-glazed teacup, for example, was shipped via the Minjiang River to Fuzhou and then exported through Quanzhou to Japan, Korea, and Southeast Asia. Quanzhou Port rose to prominence during the Five Dynasties period alongside the growth of overseas trade. In the early Northern Song Dynasty, Quanzhou became an official trade port, and in the second year of Yuanyou reign (1087), the imperial court established the Maritime Trade Supervisorate there to administer foreign maritime trade, further elevating the port's status. During the Song and Yuan dynasties, the main exports from northern Fujian included not only various ceramics but also local specialties such as Jian brocade and traditional handmade paper, most of which were transported via the Minjiang River to Fuzhou Port or Quanzhou Port for overseas shipment. Goods exported through Quanzhou Port included ceramics, silk, textiles, ironware, lacquerware, sugar, alcohol, tea, medicinal materials, and fruit—over sixty categories in total—with ceramics and silk being the dominant exports.[1] Most of the ceramics came from northern Fujian and Dehua. Consequently, the composition of export commodities from the hinterland largely determined the structure of outbound cargo from ports like Quanzhou and Fuzhou.

During the Song and Yuan periods, Zhangzhou Port emerged as an auxiliary port for Quanzhou in foreign trade, and overseas commerce gradually began to flourish. In the Ming and Qing dynasties, the restrictive maritime policies of the imperial court significantly affected the development of coastal ports in Fujian. In the early Ming Dynasty, the implementation of maritime prohibitions led to the gradual decline of overseas trade at Quanzhou Port, while smuggling-based foreign trade at Yuegang Port in

1Huang Tianzhu. "Quanzhou Port and the Ancient Maritime Silk and Porcelain Route." *Theoretical Reference*, no.2. 2016, p.64.

Zhangzhou began to flourish. During the Yongle and Xuande reigns, Zheng He led seven maritime expeditions and repeatedly docked at Taiping Harbor in Changle, where ship repairs, recruitment, and resupply supported the development of Fuzhou's outer port. In the Ming Dynasty, the Ryukyu Kingdom established a tributary relationship with China. In the tenth year of Chenghua reign in Ming Dynasty (1474), the imperial court designated Fuzhou Port as the official port for Sino-Ryukyu trade, relocated the Maritime Trade Supervisorate in Fujian from Quanzhou to Fuzhou, and established the Tribute Reception Bureau at the estuary south of Fuzhou to manage tribute trade.[1] In addition, the Ryukyus also served as an intermediary for private trade between Fuzhou Port and Japan, Korea, as well as Southeast Asia. Chinese envoys to the Ryukyus would transport goods from Fuzhou,[2] and products exported from Fuzhou mainly consisted of local specialties from the hinterlands of northern and eastern Fujian.

During the Chenghua and Hongzhi reigns of the Ming Dynasty, Yuegang Port in Zhangzhou even became the center of maritime smuggling in southeastern China, spurring the rise of Xiamen Port. From the Longqing reign to the Wanli reign of the Ming Dynasty, Xiamen Port and Yuegang Port opened ten sea routes, and maritime transportation began to take shape.[3] After the lifting of the maritime ban in the early Qing period, the Fukien Maritime Customs was established in the 23rd year of Kangxi's reign (1684), with Xiamen as its main port. Subsequently, Xiamen Port began exporting large quantities of Wuyi black tea and raw silk. The tea and silk trade gradually brought prosperity to the port. After the opening of the five treaty

1Gong Gaojian. "An Analysis of the Development of Port Economy in Ancient Fujian." *Fujian Tribune (Social Science and Education Edition)*, Special Issue, 2007, pp.246–247.

2Wei Xiance. "A Comparative Study of Quanzhou and Fuzhou Ports During the Ming Dynasty." *Journal of Fujian Institute of Education*, no.8, 2006, p.53.

3Zheng Naihui, Gao Xiangfeng, and Jiang Ling. "The Tea Trade Routes of Fujian Ports in History." *Fujian Tea Industry*, no.6, 2015, p.51.

ports, tea remained a major export from Xiamen Port, including Wuyi black tea from Chong'an in northern Fujian, Ningyang tea from Longyan, Anxi oolong, and Taiwan oolong. In the Qing Dynasty, handcrafted paper from western Fujian was known for its quality and sold well in Japan and Southeast Asia. Some of it was transported by water from Zhangping and Punan to Zhangzhou and then exported through Xiamen; other batches were carried via land and water to Yong'an, and from there down the Shaxi Creek and Minjiang River to Fuzhou for overseas export. After the Opium War, the trade route for exporting Wuyi black tea to Guangzhou was cut off, as was the route to Shanghai. In 1853, American Augustine Heard & Co sent agents to the Wuyi tea-producing region to purchase tea, which they then shipped downstream via the Minjiang River to Fuzhou. This route required less time and was closer to the tea-producing areas, resulting in lower procurement costs, which revealed the potential of Fuzhou Port to foreign merchants.[1] The following year, multiple foreign firms entered Fuzhou to purchase Wuyi black tea. After the opening of the five treaty ports, Fuzhou's main exports included tea, timber, paper, medicinal materials, and others, with tea being the principal commodity. In sum, the export of local specialties—most notably tea—from the hinterlands of western and northern Fujian played a vital role in supporting the development of ports such as Xiamen and Fuzhou during the Ming and Qing periods.

II. The Impact of Hinterland Economic Volume on Port Throughput

Port throughput is closely tied to the availability of cargo from the hinterland and market demand; hence, the scale of economic development in

1 Liu Xitao, and Huang Ting. "A Preliminary Exploration of the Impact of Modern Minjiang River Tea Trade on the Rise and Fall of Fuzhou Port." *Tea Science and Technology*, no.2, 2009, p.46.

the hinterland significantly influences the scale of port development. When industrial development in the hinterland reaches a certain level, overall economic growth accelerates, thereby exerting a stronger impetus on exports. As export-oriented industries in the hinterland expand in scale, the volume of exports through the port also grows in a corresponding and increasingly large-scale manner. During the Song and Yuan dynasties, Jianning Prefecture in northern Fujian was a major center for raw silk production. The textile industry had already achieved economies of scale during this period, and the silk fabrics woven from raw silk were not only supplied to the domestic markets but were also exported in large quantities. In the Song Dynasty, numerous dragon kilns were established in northern Fujian, including in Shaowu, Pucheng, Chong'an, and Songxi. These large-scale kilns could load tens of thousands of porcelain blanks at a time and required the employment of a substantial workforce for specialized production. Aside from tribute wares, the majority of the products they fired were "foreign trade porcelain," which was exported in large volumes to Japan, Korea, Southeast Asia, Europe, and other regions. The massive export of silk and porcelain made Quanzhou Port one of the world's most significant trading ports during the Yuan Dynasty. After the implementation of maritime prohibitions in the early Ming Dynasty, Yuegang Port in Zhangzhou and Xiamen Port rose to prominence through maritime smuggling, driven by exports of hinterland goods such as porcelain, tea, and silk. These ports opened multiple overseas shipping routes. After the maritime ban was lifted in the early Qing Dynasty, Xiamen Port began to flourish due to the large-scale export of tea, gradually becoming the primary seaport for overseas trade in Fujian Province. In July 1697, the 400-ton *Nassan* sailed from London to Xiamen, carrying 600 barrels of tea and 30 tons of raw silk. Three months later, the 250-ton clipper *Trumball* also arrived in Xiamen with a cargo of 500 barrels of tea among other goods. In 1698, a 280-ton fast sailing ship, the *Fleet*, departed from London for Xiamen and returned with 300 barrels of tea.[1] After Xiamen was designated as one of the five treaty ports, its tea exports increased rapidly. As Xiamen lacked indigenous export commodities, the port was highly dependent on the supply of goods from the hinterland. Its development was closely tied to the export of products such as tea and traditional handmade paper from the interior. In 1853, the tea route transporting Wuyi black tea from northern Fujian to Fuzhou via the Minjiang River was reopened. This attracted major foreign trading firms to Fuzhou to purchase tea, significantly boosting the volume of tea exported through the Fuzhou port, as detailed in Table 1-2.

Table 1-2 Tea Exports from Fuzhou Port During 1856–1866

Unit: Pounds

Year	Total Export Volume	Year	Total Export Volume	Year	Total Export Volume
1856–1857	35,280,000	1860–1861	61,666,500	1863–1864	63,468,298
1857–1858	32,050,300	1861–1862	55,713,433	1864–1865	65,951,916
1858–1859	29,305,600	1862–1863	52,316,780	1865–1866	65,545,036
1859–1860	41,348,600				

*Source: Liu Xitao, and Huang Ting. "A Preliminary Study on the Impact of Modern Minjiang River Tea Trade on the Rise and Fall of Fuzhou Port." *Tea Science and Technology*, no.2, 2009, p47. Cited from Banister, *Recent Century of China's Foreign Trade History (1831–1881):Ten-Year Reports of Chinese Maritime Customs.*

As shown in Table 1-2, between 1856 and 1866, the volume of tea exported from Fuzhou Port increased significantly. At the time, Fuzhou,

1Zheng Naihui, Gao Xiangfeng, and Jiang Ling. "The Tea Trade Routes of Fujian Ports in History." *Fujian Tea Industry*, no.6, 2015, p.51.

together with Wuhan and Shanghai, was recognized as one of the three major tea markets in China. According to customs statistics, in most years during the 1870s, tea exports from Fuzhou Port remained above 600,000 *dan*. From 1874 to 1876, the value of tea exports accounted for 95.5% of Fuzhou Port's total export value; between 1867 and 1894, the proportion consistently exceeded 80%.[1] In 1878 alone, over 800,000 *dan* of tea were exported from Fuzhou Port, accounting for approximately one-third of the nation's total tea exports. During the mid-Guangxu reign of the Qing Dynasty, Wuyi Mountain annually exported about 600,000 *jin* (1 jin=0.5kg) of oolong tea, with an average value of 500,000 *taels* of silver, and 200,000 *jin* of black tea, valued at 200,000 *taels*—making tea the most significant export commodity from northern Fujian.[2] These facts demonstrate that the scale of tea exports from the northern Fujian hinterland had a substantial impact on the development of Fuzhou Port's export trade. The port's prosperity after the opening of the five treaty ports was largely attributable to the large-scale tea trade. However, by the late 19th century, the successful cultivation of black tea in India and Ceylon led to a sharp decline in Fujian's tea exports, and Fuzhou Port's prominence in foreign trade diminished rapidly.

---

1 Liu Xitao, and Huang Ting. "A Preliminary Exploration of the Impact of Modern Minjiang River Tea Trade on the Rise and Fall of Fuzhou Port." *Tea Science and Technology*, no.2, 2009, p.46.

2Zheng Naihui, Gao Xiangfeng, and Jiang, Ling. "The Tea Trade Routes of Fujian Ports in History." *Fujian Tea Industry*, no.6, 2015, p.50.

Section 5 Integrated Development of Hinterland–Port Region Supporting the Prosperity of the Maritime Silk Road

The "hinterland–port" region constitutes a distinctive economic system characterized by internal linkages. In practical terms, the development of this system objectively demands a high degree of synergy, integration, and coordination between ports and their hinterlands. [1] The continuous development of hinterland economies promotes the improvement of regional infrastructure, thereby laying the material foundation for port cargo transshipment. Conversely, the ongoing expansion of port economies facilitates the enlargement of their hinterland reach. The more developed the hinterland economy and the more frequent its foreign trade activities, the greater the potential for coastal ports to increase their cargo throughput. Moreover, hinterland economic development helps improve transportation conditions between the hinterlands and ports. A well-developed transportation system, in turn, strengthens the interconnection between hinterland and port economies, thereby influencing the growth of port-based commerce. The development of Fujian's coastal ports cannot be separated from the support of their hinterlands, just as maritime routes opened by coastal ports provide essential transport channels for the export of hinterland products. Therefore, the integrated development of hinterlands and coastal ports can serve as a powerful driver of the development and prosperity of the Maritime Silk Road.

---

1 Lang Yu, and Li Peng. "On Several Theoretical Issues Concerning the Economic Integration of Ports and Hinterlands." *Economic Geography*, no,6, 2005, p.767.

I. Driving Mechanisms of Economic Integration Between Hinterlands and Ports

The "hinterland–port" region, as a unified economic territorial system, is the outcome of regional productive forces. Only when the development of productive forces in the hinterland reaches a level sufficient to manufacture waterborne transport vessels such as boats and ships, and when there is a sufficient labor force capable of operating them, do transshipment points for switching between water and land transport gradually give rise to docks. With increasing cargo throughput and the expansion of dock scale, ports begin to emerge. As economic and trade exchanges between the hinterland and external regions grow, ports start to provide outbound services for the hinterland, thereby forming an interactive relationship. This lays a necessary foundation for the formation and development of an integrated hinterland–port regional economy. The growth of regional productive forces serves as the fundamental driving force behind the continued advancement of the hinterland–port economic region. The development of regional productivity promotes economic growth within the region by expanding the use of various production factors—such as raw materials, products, labor, capital, information, and technology—thereby facilitating economic interactions and trades both within and beyond the region. Meanwhile, ports enhance their capacity to facilitate the inflow and outflow of goods and people, especially in terms of improved loading and unloading services brought about by increased cargo volumes. Furthermore, regional economic prosperity fosters tighter connections between hinterlands and ports, and improves the transportation infrastructure within the regional system, thereby accelerating the process of hinterland–port integration. The overall open development of the hinterland–port economic region, alongside the strengthening of an export-oriented economy, increases the connectivity among regions and between production factors within the economic system, further accelerating the process of economic integration within the hinterland–port region.[1]

II. Integrated Economic Development of Hinterland–Port Region Jointly Supporting the Prosperity of the Maritime Silk Road

Fujian lies within the sea. Northern Fujian is the source of the Minjiang River and also the cradle of the Minyue civilization. The Minyue people were skilled artisans and adept at building and navigating boats. The discovery of a Shang Dynasty dragon kiln in Xianyang Town, Pucheng County, northern Fujian, indicates that the ancient Min people had already begun specialized ceramic production during that time, exchanging pottery for grain and other daily necessities. The discovery of shell currency from the Shang Dynasty in Jian'ou suggests that commercial exchange activities may have existed between the inland region of northern Fujian and the coastal areas as early as the Shang and Zhou periods. Cowrie shells from the Shang period unearthed in Jian'ou suggest that commercial exchange between northern Fujian and the coastal regions may have existed during the Shang and Zhou periods. Although northern Fujian had no jade mines, jade artifacts found at the site of Mazai Mountain from the Shang and Zhou periods in the Wuyi Mountains suggest that commodities were likely exchanged with the Central Plains during that time.[2] During the Spring and Autumn and Warring States periods, the "Chu–Yue wars" led to the annexation of the ancient Yue territory, north of the ancient Min kingdom, by the State of Chu. Lacking weapons, the ancient Min kingdom was then occupied by the ancient Yue people, and the Minyue state replaced it. Large quantities of iron weapons and agricultural

1 Lang Yu, and Li Peng. "On Several Theoretical Issues Concerning the Economic Integration of Ports and Hinterlands." *Economic Geography*, no.6, 2005, p.769.

2 Wu Bangcai, editor-in-chief. *A History of the Development of Fujian Merchants: Nanping Volume*. Xiamen University Press, 2016, p.2.

tools unearthed in the upper reaches of the Minjiang River—specifically in the Jianxi Creek Basin and Futun Creek Basin—indicate that much of the commodity production of the Minyue state was related to military equipment.

In the Han Dynasty, northern Fujian became the first stop for migrants from the Central Plains entering Fujian. Jian'ou, located at the confluence of the Songxi Creek, Chongyang Creek, and Nanpu Creek, was selected as an administrative center. From the Three Kingdoms period to the late Tang and Five Dynasties period, northern Fujian enjoyed relative social stability, allowing for rapid development of commodity production, particularly in shipbuilding and ceramics. During the Three Kingdoms period, Fujian became an important shipbuilding base for Eastern Wu. The development of shipbuilding in northern Fujian laid a crucial transportation foundation for the flourishing of maritime trade during the Song and Yuan dynasties.

From "the southward migration of Central Plains gentry" in the late Western Jin to the Tang Dynasty, the Minjiang River became a "golden waterway" linking northern Fujian to the coast, and a vital channel for northern Fujian merchants to expand outward. In the eighth year of the Taihe reign of Emperor Wenzong of the Tang Dynasty (834 CE), an imperial edict was issued to encourage maritime trade, "Apart from ship levies, market fees, and tribute, all other exchanges shall be freely conducted, and no additional taxes shall be imposed." This policy not only encouraged coastal merchants but also promoted trade between inland and overseas regions. As a result, numerous wharves emerged in Jian'ou, located at the transportation chokepoint of the Minjiang River. Controlling the inland areas upstream and directly connected to the Minjiang River estuary downstream, Jian'ou served as a major hub through which grain, tea, ceramics, timber, and minerals from northern Fujian were transported to Fuzhou, and from there shipped overseas.[1]

During the late Tang and Five Dynasties period, Wang Shenzhi governed Fujian for 27 years. His effective administration vigorously promoted the economy, attracted merchants to engage in trade, and placed great emphasis on education and culture. His development of the mountainous regions of western Fujian focused on the cultivation of grain, tea, and timber as well as mining. During his tenure, grain production in western Fujian steadily increased, the cultivation of bamboo and timber expanded, and the smelting industry achieved modest growth. The tea mountain around the Fenghuang Mountain in Jian'ou became an imperial tea garden under Wang Yanzheng's administration, forming the precursor to the Northern Garden Tribute Tea of the Song Dynasty. In addition, archaeological evidence suggests that during the Tang Dynasty, silk weaving and papermaking technology at the source of the Minjiang River also experienced significant advancement. "*Jinhualian*" fabrics produced in Jian'ou were offered as tribute during the Kaiyuan reign of the Tang Dynasty, and the "*Kouzhi*" paper produced along the Futun Creek likewise became one of the tribute items. Among them, *Kouzhi* paper from Shunchang was granted the honorary name "*Jinxi* Paper" by Emperor Xuanzong of the Tang Dynasty. Therefore, the development of ceramic, textile, papermaking, and tea industries in northern Fujian, as well as improvements to Minjiang River navigation during the Tang and Five Dynasties periods, laid a solid foundation for the growth of maritime trade in the Song and Yuan dynasties.

Wang Shenzhi actively developed foreign trade and improved the navigability of Fuzhou Port so that large vessels could dock directly at its wharves. He also opened a secondary port—Gantang Port—in northern

---

1Wu Bangcai, editor-in-chief. *A History of Fujian Merchants: Nanping Volume*. Xiamen University Press, 2016, p.11.

Fuzhou. At that time, two primary maritime trade routes were established from Fuzhou. The first was the northbound route: departing from Fuzhou Port, passing through the East China Sea, and reaching countries such as Japan, Silla, and Goryeo. The second was the southbound route: departing from Fuzhou Port, passing through the South China Sea, and reaching Champa, Srivijaya, India, and Dashi (the Arab Caliphate and related regions), making Fuzhou an important commercial port connecting Northeast Asia.[1]

Since the late Tang Dynasty, large numbers of Han Chinese from the Central Plains migrated south into Fujian, with northwestern Fujian serving as the first stop of their journey. The migration of Han Chinese not only increased the labor force in the region but also introduced advanced northern production techniques and experience, significantly promoting local agricultural and handicraft development. In the Song Dynasty, as the national economic center shifted southward, agriculture and handicrafts in northern and western Fujian developed rapidly, laying the groundwork for commodity circulation and trade. Northern Han migrants introduced crops such as millet and beans to Tingzhou, and Champa rice, initially introduced to coastal Fujian from overseas, gradually spread inland to Tingzhou as well. In addition, the six counties of Tingzhou cultivated tea, sugarcane, indigo, tung trees, and other cash crops during the Song Dynasty. Agricultural development not only improved local livelihoods but also spurred the growth of handicrafts in western Fujian. During the Northern Song period, Tingzhou had substantial output of gold, silver, copper, iron, and lead, making it an important mining center of the time. Meanwhile, the textile, papermaking, ceramics, and printing industries in western Fujian also flourished in the Song Dynasty. More than 50 kiln sites from the Song Dynasty have been discovered in the Hakka regions of western Fujian. The ceramics produced

1Zhang Zhenyu. “Wang Shenzhi and the Maritime Silk Road in Fuzhou.” *Fujian Cultural Relics and Museology*, no.4, 2013, p.44.

at these sites include a wide variety of items such as bowls, plates, dishes, cups, teapots, jars, vats, basins, urns, tea bowls, and saucers. The abundance and diversity of these products indicate that, in addition to meeting local demand, a significant portion of the ceramics was manufactured for export. However, during the Yuan Dynasty, the six counties of Tingzhou Circuit were designated as belonging to the lowest social class of "southern people", resulting in harsh governance, heavy taxation, and a sharp decline in living standards, which severely disrupted the commodity economy.

During the Song and Yuan dynasties, northern Fujian saw the flourishing development of industries such as ceramics, tea, papermaking, textiles, metallurgy, and coin casting. Celadon, white porcelain, bluish-white porcelain, and black-glazed porcelain not only became tribute items to the imperial court but were also exported to Japan, Korea, and Southeast Asia. Teas such as Beiyuan compressed tea from Jian'ou and Shiru tea from Yanping became imperial tribute teas due to their unique production techniques and superior quality. As early as the Tang Dynasty, the region had already mastered the techniques of making hemp paper from bast fibers and letter paper from the bark of the paper mulberry tree. By the Song Dynasty, bamboo paper began to be produced on a large scale. In the Jianyang area, bamboo papermaking was done manually using tender bamboo and involved complex procedures, resulting in high-quality paper marketed under the well-known export brand "*Jianyang Kou.*" The development of papermaking also stimulated the flourishing of woodblock printing. During the Song and Yuan dynasties, Jianyang became one of the three major printing centers in the country. The "Jian brocade" produced in various counties of Jianning Prefecture was sold across the country and to Southeast Asia. During the Tianxi reign of the Northern Song Dynasty, the "*Fengguo* Mint" was established in Jianzhou, making it one of the four major coin-casting centers in the country, operating for more than 150 years. The development of the coin-casting industry in northern Fujian reflects the vitality of the commodity economy during the Song and Yuan periods. The growing volume of commercial trade increased the demand for coinage, while the enhanced supply of coinage in turn further stimulated commerce in the region. During the Song and Yuan periods, transportation in northern Fujian significantly improved, resulting in more frequent commercial interactions with the outside world. Several hazardous shoals along the Jianxi Creek, an upper tributary of the Minjiang River, were effectively managed during the reign of Emperor Renzong of the Northern Song Dynasty. Besides the water routes from Jianzhou to Yanping and from Yanping to Fuzhou, overland travel was also possible. Ancient roads were widened during the Song Dynasty, and numerous postal stations were established, improving traffic flow. In the second year of the Chongning reign in the Song Dynasty (1103), the overland distance between Fuzhou and Jianzhou was reduced to only 400 *li* , 182 *li* shorter than during the Tang Dynasty, with postal stations established every 30 *li*.[1] The improvement of transportation infrastructure facilitated closer connections between northern Fujian and the coastal ports of Fuzhou and Quanzhou, further stimulating the export of local products such as ceramics, tea, and raw silk.

Meanwhile, the Song Dynasty adopted an open-door policy. To facilitate trade with incoming foreign merchants at Quanzhou, the imperial court emphasized port construction, building the "Three Bays and Twelve Ports" of Quanzhou—namely, Chongwu, Xiutu, Houzhu, and Hanjiang ports in Quanzhou Bay; Shihu, Xiangzhi, Yongning, and Shenhu ports in Shihu Bay; and Fuquan, Shijing, Dongshi, and Anhai ports in Weitou Bay. It also constructed numerous bridges—Quanzhou was renowned for its bridges, earning the reputation "the best bridges in central Fujian"—including the

1Wu Bangcai, editor-in-chief. *A History of Fujian Merchants: Nanping Volume*. Xiamen University Press, 2016, p57.

Luoyang, Anping, Shisun, Shunji, and Xianian bridges, as well as navigation markers and lighthouses such as the Shihu Tower and Gusao Tower. Quanzhou Port became bustling with masts and sails, and foreign and Chinese merchants gathered in large numbers, creating a thriving scene of "ten thousand merchants trading under the sound of rising tides."[1] During the Yuan Dynasty, the Maritime Trade Supervisorate continued to operate in Quanzhou. The imperial court encouraged local officials to actively engage in overseas commerce, further promoting Quanzhou Port's foreign trade. The regions engaged in foreign trade gradually expanded from the islands of the Malay Archipelago, the Indochinese Peninsula, and the Indian Peninsula to the Arabian Peninsula, East Africa, and North Africa. Although Zhangzhou Port was not as prosperous as Quanzhou Port during this period, it still experienced notable growth in maritime trade. The development of the ceramics, tea, silk weaving, and shipbuilding industries in northern Fujian, Fuzhou, and Quanzhou during the Song and Yuan dynasties laid the material foundation for the expansion of Quanzhou Port's export trade and the prosperity of the Maritime Silk Road. Moreover, the dredging of the Minjiang River waterway, the opening of sea routes to and from Quanzhou Port, and the improvement of port docking services further strengthened ties between the hinterland and the port, increasing the frequency of personnel, cargo, and capital flows. Thus, the economic integration of the hinterland and Quanzhou Port during the Song and Yuan periods powerfully propelled the development and prosperity of Fujian's Maritime Silk Road. The frequency and scale of foreign trade at coastal ports in Fujian during this time were unprecedented in previous dynasties.

The Ming and Qing dynasties marked a period of decline in Fujian's overseas trade and external exchanges. During the Ming Dynasty, Tingzhou

---

1 Shi Xuanyuan. "Why Quanzhou Port Prospered for Centuries in History." *Proceedings of the China Institute of Navigation Conference*, P167.

Prefecture replaced Tingzhou Circuit, and society in western Fujian remained relatively stable, with notable improvements in transportation. Connections between Tingzhou, Zhangzhou, and Chaozhou became more frequent. Western Fujian gradually introduced crops such as corn, potatoes, sweet potatoes, and tobacco, promoting agricultural development in this period. The rise of commercial agriculture in turn stimulated the growth of handicrafts, and industries such as textiles, papermaking, printing, metallurgy, and the processing of daily necessities and food products flourished during the Ming Dynasty. However, due to the strict maritime prohibition policies implemented in early Ming Dynasty, very few goods from western Fujian were exported overseas. In the mid-Ming period, with the rise of private maritime trade in Zhangzhou, Yuegang Port gradually prospered, and interactions and exchanges between Tingzhou and Zhangzhou became more active, gradually leading to regional economic integration. In the fourteenth year of the Chenghua reign in Ming Dynasty (1478), Yongding County was established. With the opening of the Yongding Road, transportation between Tingzhou and Zhangzhou improved significantly, and the Hanjiang River opened up a direct transport route between Zhangzhou and Chaozhou. From then on, economic and trade exchanges among Tingzhou, Zhangzhou, and Chaozhou became increasingly frequent. Local products from Tingzhou—such as handmade paper, timber, and tobacco—were transported via the Jiulong River and Hanjiang River to Zhangzhou and Chaozhou, and then exported overseas through Yuegang Port and Chaozhou Port. After the maritime prohibition was lifted in the sixth year of the Longqing reign (1567), the Ming government officially permitted limited private overseas trade at Yuegang Port in Zhangzhou. This trade was unidirectional, regionally restricted, and quantitatively controlled (e.g., trade with Japan was prohibited; foreign merchant ships were barred from Yuegang Port; the annual number of ship permits was initially limited to 88, and later increased to 110). This partial lifting of a nearly 200-year ban on maritime trade allowed for the revival of overseas commerce and established a connection between the eastern and western Pacific trade routes, thereby enabling the trans-Pacific

"Great Galleon Trade" that brought large quantities of silver and American species from Mexico.[1] In the Ming Dynasty, the ceramics industry of northern Fujian declined relative to its Song and Yuan peaks, with white porcelain being the predominant product and exports decreasing significantly. The cotton textile industry gradually rose, and fabrics from Youxi, Shunchang, and Pucheng were widely distributed. The tea industry shifted from state-controlled to predominantly privately run operations, and loose-leaf tea replaced the compressed tea of the Song Dynasty. The regional commodity economy in northern Fujian further developed, with increased commercialization of agricultural products and bustling rural markets in Ming Dynasty. Wooden boats frequently traveled along the upper and lower reaches of the Minjiang River. Besides, during the maritime prohibition in the Ming Dynasty, goods from Zhejiang and Jiangxi could only be exported overseas through Yuegang Port in Zhangzhou. As a result, border areas of northern Fujian such as Pucheng, Chong'an, and Guangze, which neighbored Zhejiang and Jiangxi, became important hubs of frontier trade. The Minjiang River served as the primary waterway for transporting goods from northern Fujian to Fuzhou, Quanzhou, and Zhangzhou. After the maritime ban was lifted in the late Ming period, local products such as timber, silk, cotton, tea, and handmade paper were once again shipped via the "Three Streams and One River" (the Jianxi Creek, Futun Creek, Shaxi Creek, and the Minjiang River) to coastal ports for onward export to Japan, Europe and America, as well as Southeast Asia. Among these, Wuyi tea became the most significant export product from northern Fujian.[2]

During the Qing Dynasty, commercial agriculture and handicrafts in western Fujian further developed. Tingzhou Prefecture became an important region for the cultivation of cash crops such as tobacco, tea, indigo, and

1Zhou Bangshi. "Trade Between the Maritime Silk Road and Fujian Before the Opium War." *Theory and Contemporary Times*, no.5, 2020, p.24.

2Wu Bangcai, editor-in-chief. *A History of Fujian Merchants: Nanping Volume*. Xiamen University Press, 2016, p.115.

sugarcane. The cultivation of these crops optimized the agricultural structure of the mountainous areas and increased rural incomes, while also promoting the development of local handicraft industries. In the Qing Dynasty, the tobacco processing, papermaking, textile, and printing industries of western Fujian experienced considerable growth. Bamboo paper produced in Changting, Liancheng, and Ninghua was particularly prized for its quality and exported in large quantities to Japan, Korea, and Southeast Asia. Although the Qing court maintained the maritime ban during its early years, by the twenty-third year of the Kangxi reign (1684), customs offices were established successively in Fujian, Guangdong, Zhejiang, and Jiangsu, marking a revival of foreign trade in Fujian. In the twenty-second year of the Qianlong reign (1757), the customs offices in Fujian, Zhejiang, and Jiangsu were abolished, and only the Guangdong Customs was retained, initiating the "Canton System" of single-port trade. As a result, northern Fujian's tea had to be transported overland to Guangzhou for export. After the Opium War, the *Treaty of the Five Ports* was implemented. With the opening of Fuzhou and Xiamen, tea merchants from Xiamen, Zhangzhou, and Quanzhou once again began exporting northern Fujian tea via Fuzhou Port and Xiamen Port. Additionally, during the Xianfeng reign, the export of handmade paper, tobacco, and timber from western and northern Fujian also increased significantly. The development of coastal ports such as Fuzhou, Xiamen, and Quanzhou relied heavily on the abundant output of goods from the inland regions of western and northern Fujian. Likewise, the growth of the commodity economy in these hinterland areas required the support of coastal ports. The regional economic integration of hinterlands and ports provided mutual reinforcement for the development of Maritime Silk Road trade.

Chapter 2

Economic and Trade Exchanges Between the Maritime Silk Road Hinterland, Coastal Regions, and Overseas Areas

The history of the development of Fujian's maritime culture is also the history of its inland waterway development and the evolution of its agriculture, industry, and commerce. Although the Maritime Silk Road hinterland did not directly border the sea geographically, it was never absent from Fujian's maritime trade activities. Relying on a network of rivers—primarily the Minjiang River, Tingjiang River, Jiulong River, and their tributaries—the hinterland linked mountains and sea. The ancestors of this region took advantage of these riverine routes, using boats to navigate the waterways and explore a wider world. Among the three subregions of the Maritime Silk Road hinterland, northern Fujian was the earliest political and economic center of the province, while northwestern and western Fujian played influential roles in the inland-coastal trade during the Ming and Qing dynasties. Over the long term, the hinterland continuously supplied maritime ventures with ships, goods, and personnel. People from the hinterland were visibly present in seafaring activities. By the Ming and Qing periods, increasing numbers of people from the hinterland participated directly—either individually or collectively—in economic and trade exchanges along the coast and overseas. In this sense, the people of the hinterland were also builders of Fujian's maritime culture. Like the sea breeze, maritime culture flowed inland and profoundly shaped the social landscape of its hinterland.

Section 1 Economic Connections Between the Hinterland and the Coast Before the Five Dynasties Period

The overall development of Fujian began relatively late. Before the mid-Tang period, most of the region remained sparsely populated. During the Minyue Kingdom (ca. 202 BCE–110 BCE), the Minyue people of northern Fujian mainly settled along alluvial zones by rivers. After the Qin and Han dynasties, rudimentary mountain paths began to emerge in western and northern Fujian. During the Three Kingdoms period, the Eastern Wu regime established Jian'an Commandery in northern Fujian, with its seat at Jian'an (modern-day Jian'ou), making northern Fujian the earliest political and economic center in the province's history. During the Western Jin period, Jin'an Commandery was added (with its seat in present-day Fuzhou), expanding imperial control further into western Fujian and the coastal regions, although the Minjiang River Basin remained the core area. From the second to fifth year of the Yongjia reign (308 CE to 311 CE),in order to meet the needs of people fleeing into Fujian to escape turmoil, a number of post roads were gradually constructed in northern Fujian, with civilian ferries established at key river crossings or simple wooden bridges built. In the Southern Dynasties, Nan'an Commandery was added (with its seat in modern Nan'an County), and the Jinjiang and Jiulong river basins increasingly came under state governance. Beginning in the Tang Dynasty, due to the influx of Han Chinese from the north, the population grew rapidly. This led to the exchange of production technologies and ideological concepts among different ethnic groups, which promoted the early development of the region. However, due to the still-small population base, society remained in an early stage of labor division, and economic development lagged far behind other areas. During the Huang Chao Rebellion at the end of the Tang Dynasty, the peasant armies expanded overland transportation routes in western and northern Fujian. During the Tang and Five Dynasties periods, Fuzhou, Jianzhou, and Quanzhou were the three major cities in Fujian. Northern Fujian continued to play a significant economic role in the province, and Fuzhou Port became one of southern China's key trading ports. During the Five Dynasties period, Gantang Port and Zhangzhou Port were also developed, becoming newly emerging hubs for foreign trade and transportation.

I. The Minjiang River Basin

Before the Five Dynasties, economic development across the three regions of the Maritime Silk Road hinterland was uneven, and their connections with the coast varied. The Minjiang River Basin was the earliest to be developed. The river system is fan-shaped, with numerous tributaries, and its watershed spans more than 60,000 square kilometers—covering half of Fujian's total area. Upstream of Yanping (modern-day Nanping), the three main tributaries of the Minjiang River were the Jianxi Creek, Futun Creek, and Shaxi Creek. The Jianxi Creek and its tributaries irrigated the area of Jianning Prefecture and parts of Zhejiang Province. The Futun Creek and its tributaries served Shaowu Prefecture and the northern portion of Yanping Prefecture. The Shaxi Creek and its tributaries flowed through the Dapu area of Yanping Prefecture and the northern part of Tingzhou Prefecture. These three tributaries converged and flowed eastward, joined by the Youxi Creek and Gutian Creek and the downstream Dazhang Creek, along with many smaller tributaries, finally emptying into the East China Sea near Langqi Island in Fuzhou. The Minjiang River system was not only vast in scope but also had numerous navigable branches and channels. Through this river system, the hinterland's local products—such as tea, timber, and handmade paper—were able to reach maritime trade ports, while goods from coastal and overseas areas were imported inland. Daily necessities and trade goods circulated with few obstacles.

1.Shipbuilding and Water Transportation

During the Minyue Kingdom, the Minyue people were said to "use boats as carts and oars as horses," and watercraft were widely employed in daily life, production, and military campaigns. It is recorded that the Minyue Kingdom was capable of building various types of vessels, including riverboats, hunting boats, pontoon boats, and towered warships, which could sail north to the Shandong Peninsula, east to Taiwan, and south possibly even to parts of Southeast Asia. In the third year of Jianyuan reign of the Western Han (138 BCE), Minyue laid siege to Dong'ou, prompting Emperor Wu to dispatch troops who "sailed across the sea in aid." Later, Yu Shan—the brother of the King of Minyue and ruler of Dongyue—rebelled. In the first year of the Yuanfeng reign (110 BCE), Han forces invaded Dongyue, killed Yu Shan, and relocated the Dongyue population to the Jianghuai region. Historical records document the military strategy of Dongyue King Yu Shan in resisting Han forces, as well as the campaign led by Emperor Wu of Han. These accounts contain references to maritime routes and naval battles, indicating that the Minyue kingdom may have already possessed a large, well-equipped, and fully functional fleet at that time. During the Three Kingdoms period, the Eastern Wu regime designated the Fujian region as a key shipbuilding base. It established the "Wenma Ship Garrison" (in present-day Xiapu) and appointed a "Naval Commandant" (in present-day Fuzhou) to oversee ship construction and train naval forces. A shipbuilding center was also established in Jian'ou in northern Fujian, where shipbuilding materials could be sourced locally. Once constructed, the vessels would travel down the Jianxi Creek and the Minjiang River to Fuzhou, and from there be shipped by sea to Wu territories. The thriving upstream shipbuilding industry reinforced the strategic significance of the Minjiang River's source and, objectively, facilitated commodity exchange, merchant travel, and information flow between the mountains and the sea.

2. Overland Passes and Transportation Networks

The earliest mountain passes in northern Fujian were the Yuliang Pass (located in present-day Pucheng County), the Fenshui Pass (in present-day Wuyishan City), and the Shanguan Pass (in present-day Guangze County). Historical records note that when the Minyue went north to resist the Qin troops, and later when Emperor Wu of the Han destroyed Minyue, they passed through these three passes. This shows that the three passes must have been opened no later than the Qin period.

Yuliang Pass was located in Xianxia Ridge at the border between Fujian and Zhejiang. During the Huang Chao Rebellion in the Tang Dynasty, a mountain path stretching 700 *li* was carved through, opening up the ancient Xianxia Route. Subsequently, the pass was renamed Xianxia Pass. It was a strategic location—easy to defend, hard to attack. Fenshui Pass in Chong'an, also known as the Great Pass, was located on the watershed northwest of Chong'an, adjoining the border of Yanshan in Jiangxi. It was a vital hub for traffic between Fujian and Jiangxi, and since ancient times had been known as the "First Pass into Fujian." During the Five Dynasties period, a fort was established at this location. In the Kaiqing era of the Song Dynasty (1259), an official courier station was set up, but was later abolished during the Yuan Dynasty. In the Hongwu reign of the Ming Dynasty, the pass was reinstated and a patrol office was established for military defense. The renowned scholar-official Wang Shimao in the Ming Dynasty, who once served in Fujian, recorded,

> Every day, silk from Fuzhou, gauze and silk from Zhangzhou, indigo from Quanzhou, iron from Fuzhou and Yanping, oranges from Fuzhou and Quanzhou, lychees from Fuzhou and Xinghua, sugar from Quanzhou and

> Zhangzhou, and paper from Shunchang pass over the Fenshui Ridge and Pucheng Pass and flow into Wu and Yue like water.[1]

By the Qianlong and Jiaqing reigns of the Qing Dynasty, Fenshui Pass remained a vital stop along the Shanxi merchants' ten-thousand-*li* tea road. Shanguan Pass, located on the Fujian–Jiangxi border in Guangze County, Fujian Province, was first built during the Tang Dynasty and dubbed "the Western Gate of Oumin (Min State and Ou State)" and "the First Pass of Western Fujian." It had historically served as a military stronghold.

The overland transportation network in the Minjiang River Basin gradually formed and evolved. During the time of the Minyue Kingdom, the upper reaches of the Minjiang River had already begun to open up key routes through mountain crossings, forming a regional transportation network that combined both land and water routes. In the Han Dynasty, Shanguan Pass was first developed as an official route to the imperial capital. By the Tang Dynasty, it had become the essential passage through which all travelers from Fujian heading to the capital had to pass. Both Xianxia Pass and Fenshui Pass had become official routes as well in the Tang Dynasty. These three imperial highways were developed through the methods described as "cutting through peaks and flooding valleys, halting boats to continue by water (constructing floating bridges), and crossing wood while pulling ropes (building bridges)." The description vividly reflects the immense difficulty involved in opening transportation routes out of the province. These three main roads formed the backbone of the network, with many smaller paths added throughout northern Fujian to form channels for internal material transport. Due to the undulating terrain and rugged mountain paths of northern Fujian, it was imperative for

1(Ming) Wang Shimao. *Memorials on Fujian. First Series of Collected Works*, vol. 3161. Zhonghua Book Company, 1982, p.18.

the local ancestors to build bridges—particularly through the technique of "crossing wood while pulling ropes"—in order to traverse the numerous mountain passes. These bridges—especially ancient covered bridges—reflect the geographic and cultural distinctiveness of the upper Minjiang River region. The earliest covered bridge in northern Fujian with confirmed historical documentation was the Qingfeng Bridge in Nanshan Town, built by Wu Yi of Yanping during the Zhenguan reign of the Tang Dynasty. These covered bridges, with a history spanning over a millennium, provided shelter for merchants and travelers from wind and rain, and stretched like rainbows across the mountainous landscape. They were not only vital transportation routes, but also served as hubs of market trade and sites of local folk belief. As such, they hold special significance for understanding the economic development and socio-cultural history of northern Fujian.

3.Wharves, Ports, and Cities

During the period of the Minyue Kingdom, northern Fujian served as the economic backbone and military center of the region,[1] with cities opening to external trade relatively early. According to historical records, the Minyue Kingdom had seven cities, of which only Dongye—located in present-day Fuzhou—was outside northern Fujian. The remaining six cities—namely, the Hancheng city in Wuyishan's Chengcun, Hanyang city in Pucheng, Datang city in Jianyang, Linjiang city in Pucheng, Wuban city in

1The locations of the capital of the Minyue Kingdom and the subsequent Yexian County is a significant topic in the study of Minyue history. Scholarly debates on this issue have revolved around the "Zhejiang theory," the "Northern Fujian theory," and the "Fuzhou theory," with the latter two commanding broader academic support. Proponents of the "Northern Fujian theory," such as Jiang Bingzhao, argue that the Minyue capital of Ye was located in Pucheng, while Zhang Qihai, Lin Zhonggan, and Lin Weiwen maintain that it was situated in the Hancheng city of Chong'an, although these three scholars differ in their views regarding the precise location of Yexian County. On the other hand, scholars such as Huang Zhanyue and Wu Chunming support the "Fuzhou theory," which posits that the Minyue capital of Ye was located in Fuzhou. See Wu Chunming. "Historical and Archaeological Issues Regarding the Location of the Minyue Capital of Ye." *Archaeology*, no.11, 2000, pp.65–74.

Shaowu, and Jian'ou city—were all situated in northern Fujian. These six cities also played a crucial role in military strategy, acting as a defensive buffer zone to keep central authorities at bay. By the end of the Han Dynasty, among the four counties established in the Fujian region, three—Jian'an, Hanxing, and Nanping—were located in northern Fujian, with the exception of Houguan County. Notably, Nanping held the most significant military-geographic position, situated at the confluence of the Jianxi Creek, the Futun Creek, and the Shaxi Creek, and served as an important early commercial hub in northern Fujian.

Jian'ou was located at the confluence of the Songxi Creek, the Chongyang Creek, and the Nanpu Creek, making it one of the earliest developed cities in Fujian Province. In the eighth year of the Jian'an reign of Emperor Xian of Han Dynasty (203 CE), it was established as the prefectural seat of a Commandant's Office, and later became the seat of Jian'an Commandery at the end of the Eastern Han Dynasty. In the early Tang Dynasty, Jian'an Commandery was renamed Jianzhou, becoming the first *zhou* (prefecture-level administrative division) established in what is now Fujian. In the late Tang period, Wang Yanzheng proclaimed himself emperor of the Yin Kingdom in Jianzhou. During the Eastern Wu period of the Three Kingdoms era, a "sub-city" was built in Jian'ou, complete with city gates, giving it the rudimentary features of an urban settlement.

II. Tingjiang River Basin

The Tingjiang River originates in Changting and Ninghua counties in Tingzhou and is the only river in Fujian that flows from north to south. Within western Fujian, it passes through Changting, Wuping, Shanghang, and Yongding counties before merging with the Meijiang River and the Meitan River at Sanhe Dam in Dapu, Meizhou, Guangdong. From there, it becomes the Hanjiang River, which flows through Chaozhou and Shantou before reaching the sea. Three major county-level cities lie along the several-hundred-*li* stretch of the Tingjiang River: Changting, Shanghang, and Dapu.

Development in the Tingjiang River Basin lagged behind that of northern Fujian. During the Jin Dynasties, frequent warfare led many people from the Central Plains to migrate southward to escape the chaos, prompting rapid population growth in the northwestern Fujian region. The formal administrative division of Tingzhou occurred relatively late, not until the later part of the Kaiyuan reign in the Tang Dynasty. The establishment of counties within the area spanned a long period—for instance, Ninghua County under Tingzhou Prefecture was established during the Tang Dynasty, while Yongding County, also one of the eight counties under Tingzhou, was not established until the 14th year of the Chenghua reign of the Ming Dynasty (1478). "The emergence of counties and towns is both a manifestation and a driver of economic development. The construction of prefectural and county seats is a microcosm of development in the Tingjiang River Basin."[1] Population growth and the upgrading of administrative divisions accelerated economic development, particularly in sectors such as mining and metallurgy, agriculture, and urban construction. The mining and metallurgical industry in Tingzhou not only played a vital role in the local economic structure but also held a prominent position within the national mining and metallurgy sector. The development of water conservancy and the introduction of new crops further stimulated agricultural growth. Due to its mountainous terrain, Tingzhou suffered from poor overland transportation. According to historical records, most of its roads were built only after the Ming Dynasty. As a result, Tingzhou remained isolated in terms of transportation for an extended period, which hindered economic development and left trade activities relatively underdeveloped.[2]

1Xie Chongguang. *A General Discussion of Hakka Culture.* China Social Sciences Press, 2008, pp.96–100.

2Lin Tingshui. "Some Observations on the Evolution of Ancient Transportation Routes in Fujian." *Studies in Chinese Social and Economic History*, no. 1, 1994.

III. Jiulong River Basin

The Jiulong River is the second largest river in Fujian Province, after the Minjiang River. Compared with downstream Zhangzhou, the upstream Longyan area was developed later, approximately at the same time as the Tingjiang River Basin. In the third year of the Taikang reign of the Jin Dynasty (282 CE), Xinluo County was established under Jin'an Commandery. In the 24th year of the Kaiyuan reign of the Tang Ddynasty (736 CE), it came under the jurisdiction of Tingzhou. In the first year of the Tianbao reign (742 CE), Xinluo County was renamed Longyan County and assigned to Linting Commandery. In the first year of the Qianyuan reign (758 CE), it was again placed under Tingzhou. By the 12th year of the Dali reign (777 CE), Longyan County was reassigned to Zhangzhou.

The geographical features of the Jiulong River Basin are similar to those of the Tingjiang River Basin, and their agricultural outputs are also broadly comparable. Although Longyan and Zhangzhou were connected via the Jiulong River's inland waterway, overland transport was relatively more convenient. During the early Tang period, Chen Zheng and Chen Yuanguang pacified the "barbarian uprisings" in Zhangzhou and, by moving upriver along the Jiulong River, also quelled the unrest in Longyan. Consequently, Longyan underwent sinicization alongside Zhangzhou in the early Tang period—earlier than Tingzhou, which was not sinicized until the Song Dynasty. Although Longyan and Tingzhou both belong to western Fujian, they differ in terms of ethnic origin, language, and customs. The residents of Longyan share similar ancestry, language, and customs with those in Zhangzhou, placing Longyan within the Minnan (the southern part of Fujian) cultural sphere. The development of Jiulong River shipping integrated Longyan's economy into the Minnan economic zone. However, with the improvement of transportation infrastructure and several waves of migration, ties between Zhangzhou and Tingzhou gradually strengthened, and Longyan emerged as a key node linking the two regions.

Section 2 The Expansion of Trade Between the Maritime Silk Road Hinterland and Coastal Regions During the Five Dynasties and the Song–Yuan Periods

In the fourth year of the Wude reign of the Tang Dynasty (621 CE), the commanderies in the Fujian region were abolished and replaced by five prefectures—Min, Quan, Jian, Zhang, and Ting—under the jurisdiction of the Jiangnan (the area south of the Yangtze River) Eastern Circuit. During the Sui, Tang, and Five Dynasties periods, the mining and metallurgical industry, tea production, and ceramic manufacturing developed in the region of northern Fujian along the upper reaches of the Minjiang River. The level of handicraft industry in this mountainous area far surpassed that of the coastal regions. This phenomenon was closely related to the diffusion route of Central Plains culture into Fujian. The cultural influence spread through northern Fujian and extended along the Minjiang River Basin, Jinjiang River Basin, Tingjiang River Basin, and Jiulong River Basin, aligning with the trajectory of economic development in Fujian.[1]

During the Song and Yuan dynasties, overseas transportation in Fujian reached its peak. Both the geographic scope of maritime connections and the scale of overseas trade far surpassed those of previous dynasties. The port of Quanzhou (Zaitun) became a major harbor in the East, bustling with exotic goods and frequented by merchants of various complexions, appearances, and ethnicities. Quanzhou came to be known as the "City of Light." The development of Quanzhou Port and coastal trade was both a reflection and a driver of Fujian's overall socioeconomic progress. This was also closely tied

1Zeng Ling. *A History of Handicraft Industry Development in Fujian.* Xiamen University Press, 1995, p.8.

to remarkable advancements in shipbuilding and navigation technologies during the Song Dynasty. For the inland mountainous areas, the tempo of coastal trade significantly influenced their developmental cycles. In these regions, a monetized commodity economy became more active during the Song–Yuan period, and the handicraft industries directly supported this trend by producing goods and supplying markets. After the Song–Yuan period, China exported a substantial quantity of commodities overseas, leading to the emergence of Fujian's "export-oriented" economic structure—an economy directed toward foreign markets through production and technological exchange. At that time, surrounding Asian nations and regions were significantly less developed than China and depended heavily on Chinese products. With its strong productive capacity, advantageous geographical location, and relatively convenient land and water transportation networks, Fujian became one of the country's major manufacturing and exporting centers.

I. The Min Kingdom and the Continued Development of the Hinterland

After the development during the Sui, Tang, and Five Dynasties periods, a relative balance was established between mountainous and coastal regions, with the growth of handicraft industries in the mountainous areas surpassing those of the coastal regions. With the sustained economic development of northern Fujian, areas such as Jianzhou Prefecture, Nanjian Prefecture, and Shaowu Commandery became relatively densely populated and benefited from convenient land and water transportation, leading to the flourishing of industries such as mining and metallurgy, tea production, papermaking, and porcelain manufacturing. From the second year of Jingfu reign in the Tang Dynasty (893 CE), when the brothers Wang Chao, Wang Shengui, and Wang Shenzhi seized Fuzhou, to the second year of Kaiyun reign (945 CE), when the Southern Tang conquered the Min Kingdom, the Min polity existed for a total of 52 years. During this period, Wang Shenzhi ruled for 27 years (898–925), accounting for more than half of the Min Kingdom's existence. These 27 years represented the most prosperous phase in the Min state during the Five Dynasties period.[1]

In the third year of Qianning era in the Tang Dynasty (896 CE), Fujian was elevated to the status of the Weiwu Garrison, with Wang Chao appointed as Military Governor. The following year, upon Wang Chao's death, Wang Shenzhi succeeded him and was later granted the titles Prince of Langya and King of Min. During the governance of Wang Chao and Wang Shenzhi, they administered the region with diligence. Wang Chao implemented measures such as resettling refugees, stabilizing tax policies, inspecting prefectures and counties, and encouraging agriculture and sericulture to promote production. Wang Shenzhi further consolidated power across the Fujian region by adopting appeasement strategies to eliminate threats from local armed groups. He actively reformed the bureaucracy, revived the economy, promoted moral education, and attracted talented individuals. Notable scholars of the time, such as Yang Chengxiu, Gui Chuanyi, Han Wo, Yang Zantu, and Zheng Jian, migrated to the Min Kingdom with their families and clans. Wang Shenzhi "was frugal and courteous to scholars... He also established four academies to educate the elite of Min,"[2] actively promoting education by building schools across the realm, fostering a strong culture of study in the Eight Min regions (Fujian).

Wang Shenzhi's rule coincided with a flourishing period of maritime trade in Fujian's history. The Wang regime encouraged commerce and

---

1(America) Xue Aihua. *The Min Kingdom: A Tenth-Century Kingdom in Southern China.* Translated by Cheng Zhangcan and Hou Chengxiang, Shanghai Cultural Publishing House, 2019.

2(Song) Ouyang Xiu. *New History of the Five Dynasties*, vol. 68, *Biography of Wang Shenzhi.* Zhonghua Book Company, 1974, p.846.

industry by implementing liberal trade policies and improving river channels. “To the east, they delineated long waterways as irrigation ditches; to the west, they connected with the south, diverting tributaries into canals, all leading to the sea. The tides rose and fell daily, enriching the waters with fish and shellfish, and the shores were lined with moored boats.”[1] These efforts created favorable conditions for navigation. The Wang regime also renovated seaports, leveraging Fuzhou’s geographic advantage of being flanked by river and sea. It utilized Dongye Port, originally opened during the Han Dynasty, for foreign trade, and developed Gantang Port to expand overseas commerce, thus elevating Fuzhou Port into a vital hub along the Maritime Silk Road, becoming the “metropolitan center of Minyue and a key town in the southeast.” Jian’ou in northern Fujian, benefitting from favorable shipping conditions and strategic location, emerged as an important inland port in the upper Minjiang River and a flourishing center for the distribution of goods.

The mining and metallurgical industries also saw considerable development. By the Tang Dynasty, there were already documented records of mining and metallurgy in Fujian. During Wang Shenzhi’s administration, driven by the needs of both Buddhist and Daoist rituals and economic development, particular attention was paid to the mining and metallurgical sectors. In the Five Dynasties period, Fujian’s mining and metallurgy progressed rapidly. In the first year of Zhenming era (915 CE), Wang Shenzhi established a lead production site in Ninghua, located in northwestern Fujian.

China is the birthplace of tea, and the Minjiang River Basin has long been a key tea-producing region. The “Sage of Tea,” Lu Yyu, noted that tea “is produced in Fuzhou and Jianzhou... and is often found there with excellent

---

1 Huang Tao. *Collected Works of Censor Huang*, vol. 5, *Stele of the Northern Vaisravana King at Lingshan*, quoted in *A Historical Account of Fuzhou’s Inner Rivers*, compiled by the Fuzhou Municipal Committee of the CPPCC and the Committee for Historical and Cultural Studies, Fujian People’s Publishing House, 2018, p.13.

flavor."[1] The Banyan Tea of Mount Gushan in Fuzhou was originally created by a convict from Guangzhou Prefecture who was part of Wang Shenzhi's entourage. During the Later Liang period, tea from Jianzhou replaced Fuzhou tea as the imperial tribute tea.[2] In the fourth year of Changxing reign (933 CE) under the Later Tang Dynasty, Wang Shenzhi's son, Wang Yanjun, proclaimed himself King of Min. Zhang Tinghui, the palace gate commissioner of the Min Kingdom, presented his private tea plantation—spanning over thirty *li*—to Wang Yanjun. From that point on, the Beiyuan Imperial Tea Garden gained even greater renown. Beginning in the Southern Tang period, Beiyuan tea from Jianzhou became the tea of choice for imperial tribute.

Ruins of the Imperial Tea Roasting Site at Beiyuan

Under Wang Shenzhi's leadership, the Min Kingdom intensified its overseas connections. The kingdom's "ceramics, copperware, and iron products were traded far to foreign lands in exchange for gold and silver,

1(Tang) Lu Yyu. *The Classic of Tea.* Zhejiang Ancient Books Publishing House, 2011, p. 29.

2Xu Xiaowang. "A Study of the Tea Industry in Fujian During the Late Tang and Five Dynasties." *Fujian Tea*, no.1, 1991, pp.38–42.

much to the people's convenience."[1] Artifacts unearthed from the tombs of Liu Hua (wife of Wang Yanjun, second son of Wang Shenzhi) and Wang Shenzhi himself confirm the Min Kingdom's participation in maritime trade. Two blue-green glazed pottery vessels from the Arab region were excavated from Liu Hua's tomb.[2] Glass artifacts were unearthed from Wang Shenzhi's tomb when it was looted during the Ming Dynasty. The local authorities did not recognize the objects and summoned "*Huihui*" (Muslims) to identify them, learning they were glass bowls. In Wu Renchen's compilation *Spring and Autumn Annals of the Ten Kingdoms,* it is recorded that during the Min period, emissaries returning from the southern Foqi Kingdom (present-day Sumatra, Indonesia) presented glass bottles, further confirming the Wang regime's interactions with foreign lands. This suggests that the glass bowl was likely imported from abroad.[3]

II. Economic Development and Inland-Coastal Interactions in the Upper Reaches of Minjiang River During the Song and Yuan Dynasties

During the Song and Yuan dynasties, the upper Minjiang River region in northern Fujian was relatively populous and possessed an abundant labor force, leading to a high level of economic development. In agriculture, the widespread use of waterwheel pumps and the extensive cultivation of rice on terraced mountain fields achieved the ideal of "not a single drop of water

---

1Fujian Provincial Museum. "Excavation Report on the Tomb of Liu Hua of the Min Kingdom During the Five Dynasties," cited in *Genealogy of the Liu Family of Qingyuan: Biography of the Duke of E State*. *Cultural Relics*, no. 1, 1975, p. 78.

2 Qi Dongfang. "The Rise and Continuation of Min Kingdom Civilization." *Jilin University Journal of Social Sciences*, no. 4, 2004, pp.33–43.

3Zheng Guozhen. "A Brief Report on the Clearance of the Tomb of Wang Shenzhi, Ruler of Min, and His Wife During the Late Tang and Five Dynasties." *Cultural Relics*, no. 5, 1991, p.8.

wasted, nor a single steep slope left uncultivated."[1] Grain output was substantial, and tea cultivation was both highly developed and productive. In the mid-Northern Song period, Jianzhou alone produced over 300,000 *jin* of tea annually, a figure that rose to nearly 900,000 *jin* by the early Southern Song period. During the Yuan Dynasty, tea production in northern Fujian expanded even further, with new plantations established in Wuyi, which came to be known alongside Beiyuan. In terms of handicrafts, northern Fujian was renowned for its silver, copper, and iron smelting industries Additionally, papermaking and printing contributed to Jianyang's emergence as a prominent book publishing center that flourished for several centuries.

Illustration of Tea Drinking During the Song Dynasty (provided by Nanping Museum).

The development of Fuzhou as a trade port during the Northern and

1(Song) Fang Shao. *Essays on Retreat and Resting Places*, vol. 3. *Series of Historical Notes from the Tang and Song*. Zhonghua Book Company, 2002, p.15.

Southern Song periods led to a gradual increase in shipping volume along the Minjiang River. As a result, local governments began to pay greater attention to improving the river's navigability. Many of the dangerous shoals between Pucheng and Shuikou Town (located in present-day Gutian) were to some extent cleared or managed, and the shipping capacity of the Minjiang River section from Nanping to Fuzhou was further enhanced. Meanwhile, northern Fujian's proximity to Zhejiang facilitated overland and waterway connections with major ports such as Mingzhou, Hangzhou, and Wenzhou. A large number of northern Fujian handicraft products entered overseas markets through the ports of Fujian and Zhejiang.

In the field of publishing, the *Fangyu Shenglan*(*Comprehensive Survey of Geography*) by Zhu Mu records,"The households of the two wards, Masha and Chonghua, were known as the repository of books." The *Gazetteer of Jianyang County* from the Jiajing reign notes, "The book market is located in Chongbei Ward, where nearly every household sells books. Traders and merchants from all over the empire come in droves." Books printed in Masha Ward were known as "Masha editions," and "Masha edition books traveled across the land, reaching even the most distant places."[1] They were not only distributed domestically but also exported to Korea and Japan. The *Gazetteer of Jianyang County*: *Educational Institutions* further states, "Talented young men crossed Liangdong, and books were traded with Japan and Goryeo (Korea)."

In textiles, Marco Polo noted that Jianning Prefecture produced abundant raw silk, which was woven into various kinds of silk fabrics. Colorful cotton cloth, woven from dyed cotton yarn, was also produced and traded widely throughout regions referred to as "*Manzi* Province" (a term

1(Song) Zhu Xi. *Record of the Book Collection of Jiahe (Jianyang) County School*. In *Outline of Fujian History*, edited by Wang Zenglu, Fujian People's Publishing House, 2003, p. 61.

used by outside travelers for southern China).[1] As for ceramics, northern Fujian's industry thrived during the Song and Yuan periods. A wide variety of ceramic products were produced in large quantities and exported abroad. Among these, black ceramics were especially renowned, with significant exports to countries such as Japan and Korea.

III. Economic Development and Inland–Coastal Interactions in the Tingjiang River Basin and Upper Reaches of the Jiulong River During the Song and Yuan Dynasties

The Tingjiang River served as the most crucial external transportation channel for people living within its basin. However, due to its rugged mountainous terrain, rapid currents, and treacherous rapids, navigation was exceedingly difficult. Before the Southern Song period, water transportation in western Fujian remained underdeveloped, and overland travel was hindered by steep mountains and deep valleys, rendering external communication extremely inconvenient. Economic activity remained small in scale, and the commodity economy was underdeveloped. Taking the salt trade as an example, regulations stipulated that people in western Fujian were to consume "Fu salt", which was shipped from Fuzhou.

> The salt transported to Tingzhou, after departing from the coastal regions, was carried upstream along the Minjiang River to Nanjian Prefecture... From there, another route of the salt was carried to various counties in Tingzhou, but the process was extremely arduous. The salt had to be reloaded in Nanjian Prefecture onto boats sailing westward along the Shaxi Creek to Guihua County, and then carried by human porters overland to Tingzhou. During this lengthy

1Editorial Committee of this Book. *Past and Present Jian'ou.* Straits Literature and Art Publishing House, 2010, p.149.

> and cumbersome process, significant loss and contamination occurred—salt packages were often damaged and mixed with sand, stones, and weeds. Consequently, residents of Tingzhou counties frequently expressed strong dissatisfaction. The high cost of transportation also drove up salt prices, placing a heavy financial burden on consumers,[1] and shipments would often take years to arrive.

At the time, local mineral and agricultural products were primarily exported via the Jiulong River,[2] flowing into the Minjiang River. Due to the limited development of the commodity economy, the general standard of living among the people was relatively equal. As one source notes,

> The land boundaries are not yet established, and taxation and corvée labor are unevenly distributed. Water and land transportation is underdeveloped, which hinders commerce. Few farmers are able to support themselves through agriculture alone, leading to idle land and roaming peasants. Women do not engage in sericulture and silk

---

1Zheng Xuemeng. *The Southward Shift of China's Ancient Economic Center and the Economic Development of Jiangnan in the Tang and Song Dynasties*. Yuelu Publishing House, 2003, p.335. The *Gazetteer of Linting* offers a comparison of salt prices before and after changes in the transport of Chaozhou salt: "Previously, the quota required transporting eight *zhonggang* of Fu salt per year, with actual shipments reaching up to six *zhonggang* from an intended four. Later, due to difficulties and long delays—often taking years to arrive—there were increasing calls for reform." "Traditionally, salt in this prefecture was priced at 160 *qian* (copper coin weight) per *jin*, and sold at 180 *wen* (cash coin). Subsequently, the price was gradually reduced to six *wen* per *liang*, and 96 *wen* per *jin*."

2A Boat Ballad in Qingliu: By the clear waters of the Jiulong Shoal, boats seem to soar to the heavens above and plunge into the depths below. The boats seem made of paper, while the boatmen are of iron—a local proverb in speaks of 'paper boats and iron helmsmen'. Though at times the millet-burdened craft passes through, it often strikes against the rocks. What can one do when the boat hits the stone? Alas, how many travelers like you are drifting through these perilous waters. Quoted from (Qing) Shi Runzhang. *Collected Works of Shi Yushan*. Huangshan Publishing House, 2014, p.376.

> production for self-sufficiency but instead work only on processing hemp and ramie. As a result, there is limited accumulation of goods, and clothing and daily use items lack luxury. [1]

It further states,

> Tingzhou lies in the southern part of Fujian. The people rely on wood from the mountains and water from the valleys, eat rice, and wear cloth garments. Therefore, the gap between the wealthy and the poor is not large. Since grain is not sold beyond the borders, the price of grain remains low.[2]

In the fifth year of the Shaoding reign of the Southern Song (1232), the imperial court approved a proposal allowing "Tingzhou and its counties that found it difficult to obtain Fu salt to instead import Chaozhou salt". This policy marked the beginning of efforts to dredge and improve the Tingjiang River's lower reaches, particularly the section between Shanghang city and Fengshi in Yongding. As a result, riverine navigation between the Tinjiang River and Hanjiang River began to flourish, leading to the emergence of the popular saying in Shanghang, "Eight hundred boats upstream, three thousand downstream." The unblocking of the Tingjiang River stimulated development across the entire river basin, especially in towns and markets along the riverbanks. Some contemporary accounts even claimed, "The bustling markets and prosperous commerce are comparable to those of Jiangsu, Zhejiang, and the Central Plain." [3] which, although perhaps

1 (Song)Hu Taichu, comp., and Zhao Yumu, ed. *Gazetteer of Linting: Customs and Topography.* Fujian People's Publishing House, 1990.

2 (Song)Hu Taichu, comp., and Zhao Yumu, ed. *Gazetteer of Linting.* Fujian People's Publishing House, 1990, p.35.

3 lbid., p.13.

exaggerated, testify to the lively trade and busy harbors of the region. Southbound along the Tingjiang River, rice, bamboo, timber, and handmade paper from the Ting-Gan region were shipped to the Chaoshan area and sold throughout Guangdong. Northbound, Chaozhou salt and other marine products were transported upstream along the Hanjiang River and then landed at Tingjiang River ports for distribution throughout the region and even to southern Jiangxi. With the large-scale importation of marine products, the "ocean" became a tangible part of daily life in the Ting-Gan area. People's understanding of the sea became increasingly concrete, and the growing number of inland travelers navigating these routes further connected the mountainous interior with coastal regions.

During the Tang and Song dynasties, large waves of migrants moved into the Tingjiang River Basin, forming what would become the core of the Hakka population in later generations. Many Hakka genealogies in the region trace their founding ancestors to settlers who arrived during the Tang and Song periods. In the late Southern Song period, as the Tingjiang River's navigability improved, the economic structure of the region began to change. Population growth spurred land reclamation and commercial activity, accelerating economic development. Once primarily agrarian, the Tingjiang River Basin increasingly took on the characteristics of an outward-facing and transit-oriented commodity economy. Local goods such as handmade paper and timber were exported to overseas via the Chaoshan region, while the Tingjiang River became a major export route for goods from inland areas like southern Jiangxi. The development of the Tingjiang River also laid the groundwork for the Yuan Dynasty's postal route between Longxing and Chaozhou. With the dual support of postal routes and riverine transport, Tingzhou gradually emerged as a vital hub and key town at the junction of Fujian, Guangdong, and Jiangxi.[1] This transformation was especially evident in the development of river shipping on the Tingjiang River, mining

1 Jin Yangchun. *Regional Development of Tingzhou and the Formation of the Hakka Ethnic Group During the Song and Yuan Periods*. China Social Sciences Press, 2015.

and metallurgy industries, and agriculture. The construction of the prefectural city accelerated, reshaping the region's social landscape. As a result, an economic and cultural zone centered on Tingzhou took form, linking the border areas of Fujian, Guangdong, and Jiangxi and solidifying the foundations of Hakka culture.

The development of Jiulong Creek predated that of the Tingjiang River. In the third year of the Chuigong reign of the Tang Dynasty (687 CE), the prefect of Zhangzhou, Chen Yuanguang, dispatched the Liu brothers—Liu Zhuhua, Liu Zhucheng, and Liu Zhufu—to travel upstream along the Beixi Creek, dredge the river, and construct irrigation works, thereby enabling waterborne transportation. However, since Longyan remained under the jurisdiction of Zhangzhou for a long time and held a marginal status within it, its development lagged comparatively behind.

Section 3 The Flourishing of Inland-Coastal Interactions and the Expansion of Overseas Trade Routes During the Ming and Qing Dynasties

During the Ming Dynasty, Fujian's most significant achievements in maritime transportation included Zheng He's grand voyages to the Western Oceans launched from Fujian, maritime trade relations between China and the Ryukyu Kingdom, and private maritime trade activities conducted by Fujianese merchants based in Yuegang Port in Zhangzhou. Although maritime trade in Fujian saw new developments, it could not reverse the overall decline of overseas commerce. Maritime trade during this period often exhibited characteristics of being localized, intermittent, and short-lived. The Ming Dynasty's maritime prohibition policies significantly restricted the development of oceanic trade for a prolonged period. Even the resurgence of private overseas trade following the "Longqing Maritime Opening" ultimately declined by the mid-to-late Ming period. Meanwhile, beginning in the 16th century, western colonial powers had already extended their influence into Southeast Asia, gradually gaining actual control over shipping routes and monopolizing maritime trade. Their raids along China's coastal areas further disrupted the normal order of Fujian's maritime trade and brought suffering to coastal populations.

In the Qing Dynasty, China became increasingly integrated into the global trade network. Beneath the surface prosperity of the Kangxi and Qianlong reigns, underlying crises emerged, and the Qing court's socioeconomic power began to deteriorate. As western nations further entrenched their control over Southeast Asia and transformed it into a colonial region, Fujian's maritime power—on which it had previously relied—was significantly weakened, and its dominant position in Southeast Asian waters was lost. In early Qing period, the coastal evacuation policy, imposed to meet wartime needs, dealt a severe blow to Fujian's coastal commerce. After the borders were reopened, coastal trade activities briefly recovered and developed, but the overall trend remained in decline. By the late Qing period, Fujian's coastal trade had collapsed under the weight of internal turmoil and external threats. After the Opium War, Fujian was forced to open treaty ports, becoming a foothold for foreign capital. Its economy and external trade were passively incorporated into the global capitalist system. While this, to a certain extent, promoted the development of external trade and transportation, trade activities based on unequal treaties were fundamentally controlled by western capitalist powers. As a result, maritime economic activities became a conduit for the continuous outflow of resources to western imperialist nations.

In regard to the mountainous regions, industries such as Jianyang pottery and Jianzhou tea experienced a marked decline during the early Ming period. However, by the mid-to-late Ming and into the Qing periods, the revival of paper-making, tea processing, tobacco production, and book printing industries brought renewed vitality to these areas, enabling them to regain national prominence. Nevertheless, the fundamental trade pattern of "inland-coastal interactions" between the inland mountainous hinterlands of the Maritime Silk Road and coastal Fujian remained unchanged. The fluctuating development and overall downward trend of coastal economic and trade activities also had a significant impact on the interior mountain regions.

I. The Minjiang River Basin

By the late Ming period, the upper reaches of the Minjiang River remained a critical transportation hub for Fujian's connections with other provinces. In northern Fujian, the three prefectural cities of Yanping, Jianning, and Shaowu boasted thriving market economies and were important urban centers within the basin. Yanping Prefecture, constructed along the riverbanks, sat at the confluence of the Jianxi Creek, the Xixi Creek, the Futun Creek, and the Shaxi Creek. The city faced the river with three main water gates: Yanfu Gate (also known as the Great Water Gate), the Small Water Gate, and the Water Gate. The docks at these gates were divided to serve merchant ships arriving from the Jianxi Creek, the Shaxi Creek, the Futun Creek, and the main stream of the Minjiang River. The city itself featured a major thoroughfare and nine distinct streets, with considerable urban scale. Jianning Prefecture, during the Ming Dynasty, was regarded as one of the three major cities in Fujian alongside Fuzhou and Quanzhou. Its Linjiang Gate served as the commercial hub, with constant traffic of merchants, and the city had 23 streets in total. Shaowu Prefecture, in the late Ming period, was similarly bustling and had developed into a city of notable scale. It was divided into four quadrants, with the eastern section being the most densely populated. It had 5 main streets and 27 alleys, and each quadrant had its own market. Altogether, the city comprised 30 streets and 10 markets, making it one of the liveliest centers in northern Fujian during the late Ming period.

Old View of the Minjiang River and Nanping City

[*Photographed by John Thomson in 1870*][1]

The Minjiang River Basin formed several key transfer ports and wharves. Nanping Port served as the primary hub for the distribution of goods between the interior and the coast. During the Ming and Qing dynasties, Ergang Port in Nanping functioned more as a transshipment hub than as a commercial trading port. In the Shaxi Creek Basin, wharves such as Qiaowei and Gongchuan in Yong'an, as well as Sanyuan, Ximen, Xiaoshuimen, Shigumen, and Nanmen, were important and well-known. The Qiaowei Wharf in Yong'an gathered grain, timber, and other agricultural products from Ninghua, Qingliu, and Ningyang. In the Jianxi Creek Basin, the Linjiang Wharf in Jianning was the largest in the prefecture, collecting grain and local specialties from the Chongyang Creek and Nantong Creek. On a daily basis, some 300 to 400 ships frequented this port, most of which were Jiangxi merchant vessels. Tongji Gate Wharf received wooden sailing ships from Fuzhou, Yongtai, and Minqing. The Guanquan Wharf in Pucheng, located in the upper reaches of the Minjiang River, was an important node for inter-provincial transportation and trade. The famous Ming traveler Xu Xiake passed through Pucheng three times en route to Fuzhou via Nanping. During the Qianlong and Jiaqing reigns of the Qing Dynasty, Pucheng was known as the "grain storehouse of northern Fujian." The Guanquan Wharf had eight sections, with traffic comprising mostly local vessels, though ships from Jiangxi and Fuzhou were also common. Yangkou Port in Yangkou Town in Shunchang, situated at the confluence of two tributaries of the Futun Creek, possessed favorable port conditions and could accommodate large ships. It thus emerged as a key commercial exchange center for the Jinxi Creek Basin

1 Original Title of the Image: *View of the Min River and part of Nanping, Fujian.* Copyright: © 2018 *Historical Photographs of China.* Repository: University of Bristol Library, Special Collections. Image Caption: University of Bristol – *Historical Photographs of China* reference number: Fr01–097. Photograph by John Thomson.

and the Futun Creek Basin. Yangkou had three main docks—Xiejiadu, Zhonggeng, and Kengkou. Merchant ships from Jiangxi, Tingzhou, Fuzhou, Minqing, Nanping, and Youxi regularly trafficked this port. Due to their places of origin, ship types varied: "rooster tail boats" were typically owned by Jiangxi and Tingzhou merchants; "curved-tail boats" came from Youxi; "duck mother" boats were used by Nanping sailors; and "sparrow boats" and "rat boats" were associated with Fuzhou and Minqing. Traveling merchants and local experts could recognize a ship's place of registration at a single glance. In addition to vessels, local rafts made of wood or bamboo also formed a vital part of Yangkou's thriving river transport. Toward the end of the Qing Dynasty, a violent conflict erupted between Jiangxi and Minqing boatmen over control of upstream routes from Yangkou, ultimately ending in defeat for the Jiangxi faction. The Minjiang River Basin's role as a trade conduit was thus further solidified. During the Ming Dynasty, northern Fujian became a transit region for goods from northern provinces destined for overseas markets via the Yuegang Port. Iron, paper, and other products from northern Fujian were primarily shipped out through the Yuegang Port, and these commodities constituted the bulk of this port's maritime trade. As the Ming scholar Li Ding noted,

> Goods from Yan, Zhao, Qin, Jin, Qi, Liang, Jiang, and Huai are traded day and night to the south; goods from the Southern Seas, Fujian, Guangdong, Yuzhang, Chu, Ouyue, and Xin'an are traded day and night to the north.[1]

Most products from the Southern Seas were also imported through the Yuegang Port before being sold throughout China. The upper tributaries of the Minjiang River—the Jianxi Creek, the Futun Creek, and the Shaxi

1(Ming) Li Ding. *Collected Works of Li Changqing*, vol. 19. In *Selected Materials on Shanxi Merchants in the Ming and Qing Dynasties* edited by Zhang Zhengming et al. Shanxi People's Publishing House, 1989, p. 56.

Creek—flowed through 18 counties and cities in western and northern Fujian, forming the river's main sources. The region had a vast hinterland and was a traditional timber-producing area, supplying large quantities of Chinese fir to meet market demand in Fuzhou. Yong'an and Shaxian in the Shaxi Creek Basin supplied rice, straw mats from Gongchuan, and various local specialties to Fuzhou. As one source described Yong'an,

> The salt merchants of the county are mostly from Fuzhou; timber traders are locals and there are also many from Tingzhou. For example, the bamboo shoot traders from Fujian transport their goods to Jiangsu, Zhejiang, Hubei, and Guangdong; after selling their goods, they will purchase cloth for resale. These traders are originally all local, but in recent times also include people from Ninghua and Jiangxi. Paper traders transport their products to Jiangnan, Guangdong, and Fuzhou. Mushroom traders are from Zhejiang, who handle both production and sales. Sugar traders come from Zhangping and Ningyang (where there are brokerage firms). Cloth traders and dyers are from Jiangxi. Indigo merchants and producers are from Tingzhou.[1]

This passage clearly outlines the various industries, merchant origins, and trade flows in Yong'an. The goods included basic necessities such as salt and cloth, as well as agricultural by-products and consumer goods like sugar, demonstrating that Yong'an was a prosperous trading hub and transit center.

Timber was the primary export in the transshipment trade of the Minjiang River Basin. During the Ming and Qing dynasties, timber from the

---

1(Qing) Sun Yixiu, Chen Shulan, and Liu Chengmei, comps. *Continued Gazetteer of Yong'an,* Daoguang Edition, vol. 9, *Customs.* Chengwen Publishing House, 1974, pp.420–421.

Maritime Silk Road hinterlands was mainly exported via Fuzhou, with Chinese fir as the primary type, later expanding to pine, camphor, and other hardwoods. The timber trade flourished in the Qing Dynasty, reaching its peak by the late Qing period. Even into the Republican era, timber trading continued to occupy a significant place in the economic structure of the maritime hinterland.

An Old Photograph of Yanping Prefecture

[*Photographed by Edward Bangs Drew, 1876–1877*][1]

II. The Tingjiang River Basin

Since the mid-Ming period, transportation infrastructure in the Tingzhou

---

1**Original Title of the Image:** *City of Yen-ping Fu; River Min, above Foochow.*
Copyright: President and Fellows of Harvard College.
Repository: Harvard—Yenching Library.
Description: Historical Photographs of China album reference; Hv. 3 6 . Views in China. An album presented by Edward Bangs Drew to his wife Anna Davis Drew.

region continued to improve, stimulating regional population mobility and gradually giving the Tingjiang River Basin's economy an outward-oriented character. During this period, further dredging routes in the Tingjiang River and the Jiulong River, along with the enhancement of courier roads, significantly improved the region's historically underdeveloped transportation network. The region thus gained true access southward to Jiaozhou and Guangzhou, west (and north) to Jiangyou, bordered Jiangxi's Ganzhou and Ji'an to the west, and connected with the coastal areas of Chaozhou to the south. It emerged as a crucial town and transportation hub at the junction of the three provinces—Fujian, Guangdong, and Jiangxi—facilitating the formation of an economic zone centered on Tingzhou across the borderlands of these provinces.[1] The scope of western Fujian's economic activities thus expanded substantially.

The Tingjiang River Basin has long been described by the phrase "eight parts mountain, one part water, and one part farmland," indicating its predominantly mountainous terrain with scarce arable land and limited soil fertility. Since the Song Dynasty, waves of population migration and land reclamation led to rapid demographic growth in the basin, yet per capita farmland remained low, resulting in chronic grain shortages. The subtropical monsoon climate, with excessive rainfall, was unsuitable for mulberry cultivation and sericulture, and as a result, the textile industry was historically underdeveloped. After the Song Dynasty, the limitations of the region's agriculture-based economy became increasingly apparent due to its unfavorable natural conditions. However, the development of navigation along the Tingjiang River in the Song period created favorable conditions for the basin's shift toward an export-oriented economy, allowing Tingzhou to

1 Jin Yangchun. *Economic and Social Development and Transformation of Tingzhou During the Song and Yuan Dynasties*. PhD Dissertation, Fujian Normal University, 2011, p.96.

become a strategic center for optimal resource allocation across the Fujian-Guangdong-Jiangxi border region. During the Ming and Qing dynasties, the Tingjiang River Basin maintained particularly close economic ties with the Hanjiang River Delta.[1] In the 30th year of the Jiajing reign (1551), the prefect of Tingzhou, Chen Hongfan, organized laborers to level two dangerous rapids in the upper Tingjiang River, enabling full navigation along the river. As the Qing scholar Yang Lianbang wrote in his *Yinjiang Ci*(*Lyrics of the Yinjiang River*),

> Where two streams meet, the waters flow south,
> Until they reach the sea's end at Chaoyang.
> If you ask where the road leads beneath Jiulong Mountain,
> At Zhufeng and Yudong—that's Tingzhou's domain.
> The East Stream winds around the city, flowing south,
> Across the bank, mountains stretch, separated by a sandbar.
> Alas, once out of the mountains it seeks the sea,
> Yet how could Chaozhou surpass mighty Tingzhou?

The first feature of the outward-oriented economy in the Tingjiang River Basin was the increasing development of commercial agriculture and industry, heavily influenced by maritime trade. Western Fujian exported timber, indigo, tobacco, paper, and books to northeastern Guangdong, while importing grain and salt. This inland-coastal reciprocal economic model had originated during the Song Dynasty and remained largely unchanged through the Ming and Qing periods. After Columbus "discovered" the New World, many crops native to the Americas began spreading globally. During the Ming and Qing periods, nearly 30 types of American crops were introduced to China. Fujian served as a key gateway for these new crops, which were

---

1 Zhou Xuexiang. *Socioeconomic Changes in the Hakka Regions Along the Fujian–Guangdong Border During the Ming and Qing Dynasties*. Fujian People's Publishing House, 2007, pp.374–376.

then disseminated and cultivated throughout the country, profoundly influencing social life. These crops also represented a reverse influence of maritime culture on the inland heartland of the Maritime Silk Road. Tobacco, in particular, transformed the societal landscape of western Fujian. Tobacco cultivation began in the Hakka region of Yongding in the late Ming, and soon spread throughout the counties of western Fujian. By the Kangxi era, fertile fields in the eight counties of Tingzhou were extensively used for tobacco farming: "Three or four out of every ten households grew tobacco," with cultivation especially prevalent in Shanghang, Yongding, and Ninghua.

The second feature of the outward-oriented economy in the Tingjiang River Basin was the growing marketization of local industries and the emergence of influential merchant groups. In the Qing Dynasty, the Tingjiang River Basin witnessed increasing commercialization. Both traditional cash crops such as indigo, tea, and Chinese fir, and new industries like tobacco cultivation and marketing, as well as paper-making, printing, and metallurgy, saw widespread development. This era was marked by frequent population mobility, active goods circulation, and flourishing urban-rural markets. A merchant class began to form in the region, including notable local groups such as tobacco merchants in Yongding, indigo traders in Shanghang, merchants in Liancheng, book dealers in Sibao, and paper merchants active across all counties. With economic growth, the long-lagging cultural development of the Tingjiang River Basin also progressed. From the mid-Ming period onward, as the merchant class expanded and was influenced by the "Controversy of Great Rites" of the Jiajing reign, clan organizations played an increasingly important role in local society.

The third feature of the outward-oriented economy in the Tingjiang River Basin was the development of transshipment trade and the formation of cities and towns.[1] Due to constraints such as population size and limited local markets, internal economic prosperity within the basin was modest. However, the basin's outward-oriented economy relied heavily on transshipment trade—commonly referred to as *guozai hang* or *guobo hang*—which essentially involved the redistribution of goods. Several towns became centers for freight aggregation. The development of the region's transshipment trade underwent four stages: origin, formation, expansion, and decline. From the Southern Song to the mid-Ming period, it was in its early stage. Transfer stations for transshipment largely coincided with sites where salt transport vessels were unloaded and reloaded, forming early hubs such as Fengshi, Shanghang, Huilong, and Changting. Trade was mainly limited to commodities such as salt, iron, and marine products. In the mid-Ming period, coastal Fujian saw the rise of maritime trade groups (commonly labeled as "pirates"), which arose in response to the Ming court's maritime ban. These civilian trading groups, backed by powerful private militias, occupied coastal ports and engaged in maritime commerce. Familiar with international markets, they traded China's traditional advantage goods—silk, porcelain, indigo, tea, and tobacco—for foreign spices and handicrafts, reaping high profits to maintain their forces and operations. Many partnered with inland mountain merchants. The inland heartlands of the Maritime Silk Road supplied these maritime traders with necessary goods. For example, the smuggling syndicate at the Nanao Port in Chaozhou relied on inland support from Hakka regions along the Hanjiang River , Tingjiang River , and Meijiang River. These routes became key transshipment points connecting mountains and sea. Mountain merchants came from diverse backgrounds—some were essentially bandits, whose presence often brought social

---

1Ge Wenqing. "A Preliminary Study on the Evolution of the Export-Oriented Economy in the Tingjiang River Basin." *Selected Essays on Hakka Studies: Commemorating the 30th Anniversary of the Journal of Longyan University*, edited by the Editorial Office of Journal of Longyan University, Hebei University Press, 2013, pp.148–151.

instability. According to the *Gazetteer of Chaozhou Prefecture* from the Qianlong era, 26 bandit incidents occurred in the late Ming and early Qing periods. In his *Records of Bandit Disruptions*, Li Shixiong of Ninghua in western Fujian recorded roving bandits and refugees in the borderlands of Fujian, Guangdong, and Jiangxi. He wrote of Fengshi in Yongding, "They often collude to rebel. Shanghang and Wuping are their haunts, while Fujian and Jiangxi suffer their ravages." [1] To strengthen local governance, in the 37th year of the Jiajing reign (1558), the Tingzhou Prefecture established the *Fumin Guancheng* (Pacification and Administration Garrison) at Fengshi in Yongding, where soldiers were stationed year-round to guard the area. In the 4th year of the Wanli reign (1576), Fengshi was further elevated to the status of a sub-county under Shanghang, and Hetouping saw the construction of Hetou City. The establishment of Fengshi as a sub-county and the building of the two cities were both measures by the government to tighten control over armed smuggling in inland-coastal trade. After the lifting of the maritime ban, however, the military functions of the *Fumin Guancheng* and Hetou City weakened, and they gradually took on a commercial character.In the early Qing period, the two cities were abandoned, but Fengshi's role as a transit hub for entrepôt trade between Chaoshan and the inland remained unchanged, with merchants bustling about in an endless flow.

The fourth feature of the outward-oriented economy in the Tingjiang River Basin was the development of postal routes and communications. In the mid-Western Han period, Emperor Wu opened a route from the Central Plains to Ningdu in Jiangxi and onward to western Fujian for military

1(Ming) Yu Dayou. *Collected Works of Zhengqitang,* vol. 13. Edited by Liao Yuanquan and Zhang Jichang. Fujian People's Publishing House, 2007. Quoted in Ge Wenqing. "A Preliminary Study on the Evolution of the Export-Oriented Economy in the Tingjiang River Basin." *Selected Essays on Hakka Studies: Commemorating the 30th Anniversary of the Journal of Longyan University*, edited by the Editorial Office of Journal of Longyan University. Hebei University Press, 2013.

purposes. After the establishment of Tingzhou during the Tang Dynasty, postal routes were opened and courier stations were built. Stations were set up in Chenggong, Wenquan, Shuangxi, Shanghong, and Xiahuilei of Xinluo County, which was under the jurisdiction of Tingzhou. During the Chunxi period of the Southern Song Dynasty(1174–1189), the imperial court established the Linting courier station in the eastern part of Tingzhou city. In the 5th year of the Jiading reign (1212), a vehicle courier station was added in Longyan. The Ming Dynasty saw further development, including the addition of Guanqian Station in Tingzhou, and Dengtu (now Xinan, Xinluo) Station and Shizhong Station in Longyan. Shanghang added Pingxi Station and Lantian Station, while Liancheng, Wuping, Yongding, and Zhangping had smaller courier stops but no full stations. A total of 85 courier stops were established. In the 8th year of the Kangxi reign (1669), the system expanded again. For the delivery of urgent government and military documents, a network of mounted couriers was created, eventually forming 16 courier lines by the late Qing period. In the 31st year of the Guangxu reign (1905), the Xiamen General Post Office appointed Longyan native Lin Jing to open a postal office at Shangjing, Xinluo, marking the beginning of official postal services in western Fujian. The following year, postal offices were successively established in Changting, Shanghang, Wuping, Yongding, Zhangping, and Liancheng. This ushered in organized public communication in the region.

The fifth feature of the outward-oriented economy in the Tingjiang River Basin was the sharp increase in interregional migration and overseas labor. During the Ming and Qing dynasties, the contradiction between population growth and limited land in the Tingjiang River Basin became increasingly severe. Natural disasters and warfare exacerbated the issue. The outward-oriented economy provided a channel for population movement. Many poor Fujianese migrated—some to hilly areas in Jiangxi, Zhejiang,

Guangdong, and Sichuan to grow cash crops, produce grain, or work in handicrafts; others crossed the Taiwan Strait or ventured overseas to Taiwan and Southeast Asia for livelihoods. This large-scale population movement profoundly transformed the region's social landscape. The development of postal routes in the Ming and Qing dynasties also enabled the outward migration of Hakka people. Living in remote mountainous areas, they relied on foot transport and porters for freight and communication. By the Kangxi era, western Fujian's tobacco industry was thriving, with Yongding's fine-cut tobacco once used as the tribute to the imperial court. Tobacco shops and factories were established in major cities nationwide by merchants from Xinluo, Shanghang, and Liancheng. As demand for Fujian tobacco spread across China, outdated information systems hindered efficient logistics and communication. To address this, private mail carriers emerged in the western Fujian during the Daoguang reign, offering fee-based mail delivery. There were two types: informal couriers who were often acquaintances, boatmen, porters, or peddlers and may or may not have charged for delivery; and professional couriers who registered with the government and possessed a certain amount of capital with fixed messengers and addresses—collectively known as private mail agencies. These agencies were typically located within inns, shops, or transport companies. They handled personal letters, remittances, and small parcels, with rates determined by distance and terrain. In the Guangxu period, the Qing government formally established the Customs Postal System, with the postal bureau first set up in Shanghai and later expanded to treaty ports across the nation. However, the vast inland mountainous areas (including western Fujian) remained in the courier station era (as courier stations did not handle private correspondence), which gave rise to a situation where official postal bureaus and private mail agencies coexisted. By the Xuantong reign, as the postal offices were established nationwide, the role of private mail agencies gradually diminished. By the early years of the Republic of China, they were ordered to cease operations entirely. Government-run postal bureaus replaced private ones, and all postal services were handled by official agencies. The official and private postal routes became vital ways for the flow of capital and information among the Hakka people.

In the Qing Dynasty, the outward-oriented economy of the Tingjiang River Basin flourished. Through the artery of Tingjiang River-Hanjiang River, with Chaoshan as its central market, the basin integrated into China's coastal and Southeast Asian trade networks. Merchants from various counties also traveled frequently along this trade route. For example, Yongding's fine-cut tobacco was sold across the country and beyond, with a saying that it reached "South to Singapore, North to Zhangjiakou." The Shanghang's guild halls were found in nearly all major cities across southern China. During the Qianlong period, members of the Thirteen Hongs—who held a monopoly over foreign trade—such as Huang Yanghua and Zhu Guangju, established paper shops in places like Juxi and Gutan in Liancheng County. Along the Tingjiang River and its six main tributaries, shipping docks had organized freight guilds. More than 2,000 households along the Tingjiang River were engaged in shipping year-round. During the Yongzheng reign, Shanghang's river tax revenue reached nearly 10,000 *taels*—three times the quota.

The prefectural city of Tingzhou was a testament to the prosperity of the commodity economy in the Tingjiang River Basin. Located in present-day Changting County, it connected southward to Chaozhou in Guangdong and westward to Ruijin in Jiangxi, serving as a transshipment trade hub. During the Ming Dynasty, Tingzhou city experienced significant development. Within the city were Shizi Street and Fuqian Street; the urban area included 14 streets and five main marketplaces: Diantou Market, Hebian Market, Shuidong Street Market, Wutong Temple Market, and Hetian Market. Each marketplace had its specialty: Diantou Market focused on salt, iron, indigo, and general daily goods; Hebian Market specialized in bamboo and timber; Shuidong Street Market dealt in goods brought from the Jiangxi and Guangdong regions; Wutong Temple Market, located near Diantou Market and Hebian Market, was a particularly vibrant commercial center.

III. The Jiulong River Basin

The Jiulong River flows through the regions of Longyan, Zhangping, and Ningyang, which historically belonged to the jurisdiction of the Longyan Subprefecture. Until the Chenghua reign of the Ming Dynasty, this area remained sparsely populated and underdeveloped. In the 7th year of the Chenghua reign (1471), following the recommendations of local resident Lin Tinghu and others, the Fujian Provincial Governor, successfully petitioned the imperial court to establish Zhangping County by seperating the five administrative townships of Juren, Juxian, Ganhua, Hemu, and Yongfu from Longyan County. The newly formed Zhangping County was placed under the jurisdiction of Zhangzhou Prefecture. Later, in the 1st year of the Longqing reign (1567)—or by some accounts, the 5th or 6th year (1571 or 1572)—Ningyang County was established from the Dongyang and Xiyang Patrol Divisions of Longyan County, the 28th, 29th, and 30th districts of Yong'an County, and parts of Datian County. The name *Ningyang* reflected the desire to pacify the Dongyang and Xiyang regions: "named for the peace restored to Dongyang and Xiyang." Its county seat was located in Dongxiyang (present-day Shuangyang Town, Zhangping City, colloquially referred to as "Old Ningyang"), under the jurisdiction of Zhangzhou Prefecture. The establishment of counties in Ningyang and Zhangping during the Zhengde and Chenghua reigns was primarily driven by the need to restore social order. As recorded in the *Gazetteer of Pinghe County* during the Kangxi era in the Qing Dynasty,

> During the Zhengde period, bandits from Luxi and Jianguan were unpredictable and rampant. Tingzhou and Zhangzhou were in a state of unrest. At the time, Master Wang Yangming served as the regional inspector in the southern part of Ganzhou. He led troops from two provinces to pacify the area and establish county administrations... thus the tigers retreated and the owls fell silent (metaphors indicating peace and order were restored).[1]

After the implementation of the Ming Dynasty's maritime prohibition policies, the Yuegang Port in Zhangzhou became a major coastal trading hub. The dredging and navigability of the Jiulong River, along with improvements in overland transportation between Zhangzhou and Longyan as well as between Tingzhou and Longyan, combined with the introduction of new agricultural crops, contributed to the prosperity of agriculture in the mountainous regions. The thriving private maritime trade centered on the Yuegang Port positioned Longyan, located between Tingzhou and Zhangzhou, as a growing economic center. Its orientation toward southern Fujian and the maritime world became increasingly apparent. In the 12th year of the Yongzheng reign in Qing Dynasty (1734), Longyan County was elevated to the status of a directly-administered subprefecture, governing Zhangping and Ningyang counties.

The Jiulong River's three main tributaries—the Nanxi Creek, the Xixi Creek, and the Beixi Creek—all flowed toward the Yuegang Port and into the sea, linking the mountainous hinterlands of the Maritime Silk Road with the coast. Among them, the Xixi Creek and the Beixi Creek connected Longyan and the various counties of western Fujian and were closely involved in

---

1(Qing) Li Hong, Wang Bai, corr., Chang Tianjin et al. comp., *Preface to the Pinghe County Gazetteer* (Kangxi Edition), *Collected Series of Chinese Local Gazetteers*, no. 91. Chengwen Publishing House, 1967, p.5.

maritime trade activities. During high tide, boats could travel from the Yuegang Port through the Shima River and the Fuhe River (opposite to the Sancha River), following the tidal flow into the Xixi Creek and then reaching Zhangzhou. This section of the inland river was highly active with waterborne commerce, and many imported overseas goods were distributed along this route. Sailing upstream along the Xixi Creek, the river split near the Nanjing County (present-day Jingcheng). One branch flowed southeast to Shancheng (modern-day Nanjing County seat) and then divided into two further branches. The southern branch led to Chuanchang; from there, an overland route led east to Xiayang in Yongding and connected with the Tingjiang River, which ultimately joined the Hanjiang River en route to Guangdong. The northern branch from Shancheng flowed toward the Xiaoxi (present-day Pinghe County seat), followed by an overland route to the Pinghe County seat (now Jiufeng), through the Paicong Pass, and into Meizhou. From the area around the county seat of Nanjing, another branch flowed northwest through Longshan and north of Shuitou, then continued overland via Shizhong in Longyan to reach the city itself. This formed the overland route linking Longyan and the counties of western Fujian to Zhangzhou and the Yuegang Port.

The Beixi Creek and its many tributaries—including the Xiaochi Creek, the Xiaoxi Creek, the Yanshi Creek, the Fengcheng Creek, the Xinqiao Creek, the Ningyang River, the Xin'an Creek, the Xinan River, the Kengzikou Creek, the Zhixi Creek, the Chixi Creek, the Xijiang Creek, the Wenshui Creek, the Xianxi Creek, the Nanfang Creek, the Pingxi Creek, the Zhuxi Creek, the Lindun Creek, the Longjin Creek, the Mayang Creek, and the Xiandu Creek—connected the three counties of Longyan. These tributaries converged at Zhangping and then flowed to the sea via Zhangzhou. The water transport network was well developed, enabling the consolidation and export of local specialty products and handicrafts from each county. In the early

Qing period, the county magistrate of Longxi, Chen Tianding, recorded in his *Records of the Splendors of the Beixi Region* that the trade routes of the Yuegang Port radiated inland via the Beixi Creek,

> Roughly speaking, Longtan lies at a crossroads; the straight course is the river. Sailing northward, one can reach Ningyang... It belongs to the 25th district of Longxi County. and the 25th administrative unit of Xishu (a part of Longxi County). From there, the route continues through Yong'an, heading north toward Pucheng and exiting via the Xianxia Pass, or westward to Shaowu Prefecture and Tingzhou Prefecture. [1]

This shows that the Beixi Creek served as a vital artery linking Zhangzhou and the Yuegang Port to the wider regions of northern and northwestern Fujian. Despite its treacherous terrain and deep rapids, merchant activity along the route was ceaseless. The famous Ming-dynasty traveler Xu Xiake passed through this route during his journey in Fujian. His detailed diary records not only his travel route and the time it took, but also vivid descriptions of the terrain and hydrological conditions, giving readers a sense of the challenges faced by travelers of the time.

> On the first day of the fourth lunar month, at dawn, the boat set off. The stream flowed from the mountain gorge, cascading southward. After more than ten *li*, a peak suddenly jutted out to the west, blocking the stream across its path. The water was forced to veer westward, then turned back east, the momentum like water pouring from a tipped

1(Qing) Chen Tianding. *Records of the Splendors of the Beixi Region*. In *Historical and Cultural Materials of Xiangcheng*, vol. 16, edited by the Committee of Literature and History of Xiangcheng District, Chinese People's Political Consultative Conference, 2005,p.73.

vessel—meaning the current suddenly surged. This place was called Shizui Rapid. Jagged rocks stood in clusters, with only one opening in the middle, barely wide enough for the boat to pass. As the boat plunged through the gap, it dropped by over one *zhang*; the course continued winding, dropping several more *zhang*. Compared to the various rapids in the Andan area, although the size of the drop varied, the danger here was far greater.

All boats reached this point and descended in sequence. Before each descent, the passengers disembarked and used ropes to pull and guide the boat from the front and rear. Only after a great deal of effort could the vessel proceed. Beyond this, the gorge narrowed precipitously, sheer cliffs pierced the sky, and the river twisted sharply through cleft rock walls—it truly felt like cleaving emerald cliffs and cutting through clouds. After thirty *li*, we passed Guantou, entering the territory of Zhangping. Another peak jutted out to the east, causing the river to bend again, forming Liushui Rapid. There, mountain ridges converged, and torrents surged in a narrow stream. The boat seemed to be descending from the Milky Way, the sensation like being carried by a dragon's roar. Soon the mountain terrain opened up slightly. After more than twenty *li*, we reached Shibi Rapid, where a great rock jutted northward, constricting the current. But the water did not retreat; instead, it collided violently against the stone. The danger here was comparable to Shizui Rapid and Liushui Rapid, making these three the most treacherous. Downstream, a tributary from the northeast joined in. Further along, another stream merged from the same direction. The river grew wider, the current more gentle. Another twenty *li* east, we reached Zhangping County.

The stream from Ningyang surged and tumbled with a speed ten times that of the Jianxi Creek. From Pucheng to Min'an, where the stream enters the sea, is over 800 *li*; from Ningyang to Haicheng, it is just over 300 *li*. The shorter the journey, the steeper the descent, the swifter the flow. Consider this: from Liling to Yanping is under 500 *li*; from Yanping upstream to Maling, less than 400 *li*—yet both stretches are steep. The two mountain ridges are comparable in height, but the descent to the sea differs. The peril of this water, thundering like a subterranean explosion, is truly worthy of poetic praise.

On the second day, We descended toward Huafeng by boat. After a few *li*, the mountains closed in again, with stacked rapids and cascading torrents—more numerous than even those of Taiping or Antan on the Jianxi Creek. After sixty *li*, we reached Huafeng. At this point, the Beixi Creek plunged in steep falls over stone ridges, making navigation impossible. We abandoned the boat and climbed over the ridge. Typically, only the headwaters of rivers are too shallow for rafts or bamboo rafts. But in this case, though the upper waters were navigable, the downstream flow was obstructed. Only the confluence port at Sanmen of the Yellow River compares—where boats can neither ascend nor descend. At least in Han and Tang times, their canals still bore the marks of towropes; here at Huafeng, from ancient times until now, there has never even been a path for passage. I had hoped to follow the river and explore its dangers, but the local residents only knew how to cross the ridge—they could not guide us along the stream.

On the third day, we climbed the ridge. After ten *li*, we reached the summit. There, the stream reappeared, flowing from the west, hugging the foot of the mountain. Looking down, it looked no wider than a ribbon of silk. After another five *li*, it plunged directly downward. Two more *li* brought us to the stream's edge. We resumed by boat and sailed eighty *li*, reaching the Xixi Creek. Then we walked thirty *li* southwest by land to Zhangzhou Prefecture. Following the stream southeast for another twenty *li* brought us to Jiangdong Ferry, the eastern courier route from Xinghua and Quanzhou. Another sixty *li* downstream led us to Haicheng, where the river enters the sea.

On the fourth day, we traveled twenty *li* by sedan chair and entered Zhangzhou via the North Gate. I visited my uncle, who served as the judicial officer. His post was then in Nanjing, thirty *li* away. That evening, in the rain, we exited the South Gate and took a night boat to Nanjing.

On the fifth day, we arrived at Nanjing by dawn, having taken a winding upstream route. The stream originates from Nanping and flows to Nanjing over a distance of sixty *li*, with a mighty force comparable to that of the Xixi Creek. It passes through the South Gate in Zhangzhou Prefecture and also enters the sea at Haicheng. It remains unclear which of the two streams—the Xixi Creek or this stream—gave Zhangzhou its name.[1]

1 (Ming)Xu Hongzu, annotated and selected by Liu Huru. *The Travel Diaries of Xu Xiake*.

During the Ming and Qing dynasties, the growth of a commodity economy and the flourishing maritime trade objectively required the strengthening of inland-coastal connections. Consequently, the official roads linking Longyan with Ningyang and Zhangping were improved. In the 1st year of the Wanli reign (1573), Li Shaoxi, the magistrate of Longyan county, ordered the excavation of Guanyinzuo Rock, which had obstructed water traffic between Longyan, Yanshi, and Jintou. This allowed water transport to reach the urban center of Longyan. Longyan thus became a crucial inland transportation hub connecting Jiangxi, Tingzhou, Yanping, and Jianning with Zhangzhou. Its geographical significance became increasingly apparent, which led to its elevation from county to subprefecture in the early Qing Dynasty. The development of the upper reaches of the Jiulong River was closely tied to the growth of the lower reaches around the Yuegang Port and the Tingjiang River Basin. Together, they formed vital inland production bases for the maritime trade.

Chongwen Publishing House, 2014, pp.69–70.

Section 4 The Influence of Inland–Coastal Interactions on the Cultural and Economic Systems of the Hinterland

The hinterland of the Maritime Silk Road was connected to the maritime world via river networks. The exchange between mountains and sea not only shaped the region's economic structure, market configurations, and urban layout, but also fostered the formation of distinct cultural zones within various river basins.

I. Mountains, Rivers, and Marginality: The Economic and Cultural Zones of the Hinterland of the Maritime Silk Road

American anthropologist G. William Skinner's theory of regional systems and development cycles divides traditional China into nine macro-regions, each containing several subregions. Within each macro-region, there are both core and peripheral areas. When a macro-region experiences economic growth, it tends to attract population flows from peripheral areas. Conversely, during periods of economic decline, tensions—especially between locals and migrants—increase, often triggering reverse migration. According to this framework, the hinterland of the Maritime Silk Road discussed in this study falls within the Southeastern coastal and Lingnan macro-region. Specifically, counties in northwestern Fujian belong to the Minjiang River Basin subregion, while central and southern Fujian and northeastern Guangdong fall within the Hanjiang River Basin subregion along the southeastern coast and the broader Lingnan region. However, the mountainous zones at the Fujian–Guangdong–Jiangxi border are geographically and spatially peripheral, both to the macro-regions and their subregions.[1] Their location at a tri-provincial frontier distances them from the political and economic centers of each province, reinforcing their marginality.

Skinner's regional theory offers a contextual theoretical framework for understanding the economic and migration histories of the hinterland of the Maritime Silk Road. Situated at the margins of overlapping regional systems, this area's economic development exhibits both marginality and outward orientation. While it has a tendency to gravitate toward regional centers, its defining economic and cultural characteristic remains its marginality. Within the three areas identified in this book as comprising the Maritime Silk Road hinterland, geographical separation, differing historical development timelines, administrative divisions, and linguistic-cultural differences have all limited internal cohesion. As a result, despite sharing similar economic roles, these areas have never formed a unified or closely connected economic or cultural zone. Instead, each has followed its own developmental path, giving rise to relatively small-scale and distinct economic and cultural subregions.

Rivers played a decisive role in the formation of economic zones within the hinterland of the Maritime Silk Road. In ancient times, many county seats were established along river valleys. Rivers held a crucial position in premodern transportation—people living along navigable rivers could benefit from waterborne travel via boats and ships. Even in mountainous and hilly areas where rivers were not navigable, the valleys along riverbanks typically provided cultivable flatlands. These areas not only served as transportation corridors but also became centers of population settlement and

1 Yu Dazhong. "From the Periphery to the Center: The Construction of Hakka Identity and the Expansion of Hakka Development Space Since Modern Times." *Journal of South China University of Technology*, no. 3, 2016, pp.99–104.

economic activity. At the same time, rivers served as migration routes through mountainous regions. Migrants often moved upstream or downstream following the course of the river. As a result, an individual river basin often evolved into an economic zone, usually centered around one or two key towns.[1] Moreover, since populations within a river basin typically shared similar dialects and cultural traits, economic zones formed by river basins tended to maintain a high degree of relative independence.

The hinterland of the Maritime Silk Road, characterized as being on the "periphery of the inland",[2] had far-reaching implications for its political, economic, and cultural development. Economically, this peripheral status could foster new forces or emerging dynamics. The research of historian Fu Yiling demonstrates that, in the late feudal period, China's mountainous regions began to develop commercial characteristics. In Fujian, areas such as Jiangle, Jianning, Yongding, and Liancheng saw the rise of mountain-based merchants. After the 16th century, the economic development of the Maritime Silk Road hinterland coincided with a global trend of economic expansion. The driving forces of this economy, along with the upheaval of dynastic changes in the mid-17th century, accelerated the movement and migration of people, thereby promoting the regional economic growth of Fujian, Guangdong, and Jiangxi. From the mid-Ming Dynasty onward, economic ties between Tingzhou and Longyan, and between Tingzhou and Zhangzhou, became increasingly close. Longyan, located at the key transport junction between Tingzhou and Zhangzhou, became a transitional zone between the Hakka and Hoklo peoples. Longyan was further integrated into the economic

1 Zhou Zhenhe, and You Rujie. *Dialects and Chinese Culture*. Shanghai People's Publishing House, 1986, p.68.

2 Lu Xiqi. "The Inland Periphery: The 'Outer' Regions Within Traditional China." *Academic Monthly*, no.5, 2010, pp.121–128.

sphere in Southern Fujian. By the Qianlong and Jiaqing periods of the Qing Dynasty, Longyan had developed a distinct group of mountain merchants, highlighting the vast potential and vitality of the maritime economy in the Ming and Qing periods.

Three zones of the hinterland of the Maritime Silk Road each developed their own distinct cultural zones. "The formation of cultural zones is primarily shaped by factors such as language, religious beliefs, customs, and social mores."[1] For example, the Hakka culture of the Tingjiang River Basin is a unique cultural zone that emerged within the hinterland of the Maritime Silk Road. The scholar Sow-Theng Leong found that[2] during the 14th to 15th centuries, the three major peripheral regions of Fujian, Guangdong, and Jiangxi were all undergoing economic downturns. In this context of relative isolation from surrounding economic centers, a relatively stable cultural community with shared characteristics gradually formed — the Hakka heartland. After the 16th century, while the southeast coastal and Lingnan regions entered a period of economic growth, the Hakka heartland faced growing population pressure and land scarcity. As a result, the Hakka began migrating toward the peripheral areas of major economic centers. In the 17th century, natural disasters and the turmoil of the Ming–Qing transition pushed macro-regional economies into decline again, heightening tensions between earlier Hakka migrants and local populations. By the early 18th century, with the economic resurgence of southeastern China and the Lingnan region, Hakka populations migrated east across the Taiwan Strait, west and south into Zengcheng and Dongguan in Guangdong and Guangxi, and northwest

---

1 Tan Qixiang. "Principles and Examples of Historical Human Geography Research." *Historical Geography*, vol. 10. Shanghai People's Publishing House, 1992, p.22.

2 (Austrina) Leong Sow-Theng. *Immigration and Ethnicity in Chinese History: The Hakka, Marginal Migrants, and Their Neighbors.* Translated by Wang Dong, and Sun Yeshan. Nantian Book Company, 2014.

into Sichuan. After the mid-19th century, as Shanghai replaced Guangzhou as China's primary center for foreign trade, the Lingnan region once again entered economic decline. During this time, the outbreak of conflicts between local and Hakka populations and the Taiping Rebellion ultimately marked a turning point for Hakka culture — it evolved from an unconscious, natural state to a self-aware, deliberate identity. Through this process, Hakka ethnic identity and cultural consciousness gradually took shape and solidified.

II. Maritime Orientation and Transshipment Trade: A Common Commercial Model in the Hinterland of the Maritime Silk Road

The three zones of the hinterland of the Maritime Silk Road—stretching east to west across Zhejiang, Jiangxi, and Guangdong—represent a key junction between China's maritime and inland civilizations. Over centuries, they developed a unique commercial model shaped by this intersection.

A defining characteristic of the region's commercial model is the maritime orientation of its mountain-based commerce. As previously discussed, the Minjiang River, Tingjiang River, and Jiulong River functioned as the primary arteries through which the hinterland of the Maritime Silk Road engaged in maritime trade system. It facilitated the exchange of goods and the movement of people with China's coastal regions, Southeast Asia, and even more distant parts of the world, thereby becoming an important hinterland of the maritime economy. The region's mountainous commerce centered on commercial agriculture, handicrafts, and mineral processing, with local industries integrated into the global maritime economy. Hakka entrepreneurial activity particularly exemplified this trend. In traditional Hakka settlements across Fujian, Guangdong, and Jiangxi, due to harsh terrain and limited development, the Hakka pursued diversified livelihoods from the late Southern Song onward. They emphasized mountain and dryland cash crops to supplement limited rice yields and established local markets in emerging basins for small-scale trade. Population growth led to diminishing marginal returns on land, making industrial expansion a crucial outlet for the growing population. Industries such as mining, gold panning, iron smelting, coal extraction, indigo cultivation, papermaking, and related sectors like dyeing and weaving, as well as woodblock printing, developed in various regions—often characterized by a distinctive specialization in one particular trade per locality. Notable examples include the remarkable achievements of the Ma and Zou families of Sibao in the woodblock printing industry, and the family-run tobacco industry in Yongding, which supported the construction of earthen buildings, forming a culturally distinctive regional landscape.

The prominence of transshipment trade—another key feature—was not only a result of the economic development in the Maritime Silk Road hinterland, but also a reflection of its marginal position within the broader economic landscape. Skinner's theory of the market hierarchy classifies economic centers based on scale and functional level into three categories: standard market, intermediate market, and central market. Although these three types are hierarchical in nature, their development is interrelated and integrated. Among them, the standard market (or grassroots market) serves as "the entry point for agricultural and handicraft goods into higher-level market networks and is the endpoint for consumer goods flowing down to rural households".[1] The intermediate market occupies a middle position in the vertical flow of goods and services both upward and downward. The central market is of a higher level and holds an important strategic position in the market circulation network. The central market has the function of transmitting information and goods up and down within the entire market system — as a goods transfer center, it disperses received goods to lower-

1 (America) Skinner G. William. *Marketing and Social Structure in Rural China.* Translated by Shi Jianyun and Xu Xiuli. China Social Sciences Press, 1998,pp.5-7.

level markets while also receiving goods from those lower-level markets and sending them to higher-level markets.

It is worth noting that the three main areas of the hinterland of the Maritime Silk Road produced highly similar goods. For instance, Chinese fir was widely cultivated. Ming scholar He Qiaoyuan observed, "Fir trees flourish in Jianyang, Yanping, Tingzhou, Shaowu, and Funing— They are propagated through cuttings."[1] The fir-producing centers were primarily in the mountainous regions of Fujian, including the hinterland of the Maritime Silk Road. Before the mid-Ming period, most buildings in Shaowu used pine wood, but by the Wanli reign, fir had become more prevalent—resulting in market competition with Yanping and Jianyang. Similar dynamics applied to other goods such as handmade paper and forest products. Therefore, the three regions within the hinterland were unable to form economically complementary relationships with one another. They lacked internal mechanisms to drive trade and exchange, and in fact, the high degree of similarity in their products may have even led to potential competition. Historically, the three regions never formed a unified market system. Instead, each participated in broader market activities through their own outward-oriented market systems. As with fir, regions like Yanping, Tingzhou, Shaowu, and Jianyang all developed export channels during the Ming Dynasty. Timber merchants transported fir logs along river routes to Fuzhou for overseas shipment, making use of Xinghua sea vessels that traveled to and from the southeastern coast, ultimately delivering the timber to fir-scarce regions in the Jiangnan area. Within this context, the markets of the Maritime Silk Road hinterland were undoubtedly situated at a relatively low level in the market hierarchy. In fact, the hinterland never developed an economic center that exceeded the level of a central market. The number of central

1 (Ming) He Qiaoyuan. *Gazetteer of Fujian*, vol. 150, *Records of Southern Products*. Fujian People's Publishing House, 1995, p.4452.

markets within the region remained limited, and it notably lacked cities with influence that extended beyond provincial boundaries. Instead, the region was predominantly characterized by standard markets that met the basic transactional needs of rural households and intermediate markets that served a wholesale function. Markets at various levels within the hinterland rarely participated directly in maritime trade activities. Instead, they functioned as intermediary hubs within a multi-tiered trading network, operating in a sequential and interconnected manner. Much like a waterway system, these markets linked inland regions even farther removed from the sea, as well as mountainous markets within the hinterland itself, to the maritime world, thereby establishing a tightly integrated connection with the oceanic trade system. Nonetheless, the prosperity of transshipment trade and the proliferation of local markets demonstrate expanded trade coverage and growing volume, indirectly reflecting the region's increasing level of rural development. The emergence of township markets provided goods and services to neighboring economic zones and functioned as essential links in the supply chain connecting rural areas to economic centers. Riverine towns throughout the region developed into key nodes of transshipment commerce, embodying one of the hinterland's most distinctive commercial patterns.

Chapter 3
Goods from the Hinterland and Guilds Along the Maritime Silk Road

During the Ming and Qing dynasties, commercial activities in the hinterland of the Maritime Silk Road were not as widespread as along the coast. However, certain regions nonetheless developed notable commercial operations, with merchant groups often specializing in a single trade and sharing strong geographical ties. In the late Ming period, whether due to unfavorable natural conditions that restricted agricultural output or due to relative abundance of local resources, commerce and industry emerged as vital means of subsistence for the inland population, leading to regionally specialized trades. The commercial activities of hinterland merchants were closely tied to the rise and fall of maritime trade. When overseas trade flourished, the hinterland served as a crucial supplier of materials; when maritime activity was disrupted, commerce in the mountainous regions inevitably suffered. During the Ming–Qing dynastic transition, Fujian's coastal regions were in turmoil, and banditry was rampant in the inland mountains, seriously disrupting trade. For instance, in Liancheng County of Tingzhou Prefecture, records note,

> The flight of the coastal Fujian population did not begin with Liancheng County, nor did it end there; yet it was most severe in Liancheng County. Moreover, the migration of the people of Liancheng did not start in the present day, but it has now reached its peak. This is due to the region's lack of commercial connectivity and the absence of a trading economy. Although the area possesses modest resources, their exploitation has increasingly been hindered in recent times. For instance, in the case of paper production: when maritime trade with foreign markets is disrupted, paper that once yielded high profits overseas fetches only minimal returns when sold in Jiangxi. The same applies to brick and ceramic production—due to their coarse quality,

> these goods can only be sold locally, bringing little profit. As for timber, rampant theft in Guangdong renders transport difficult. In such circumstances, subsistence farming on barren land becomes an arduous struggle for survival.[1]

Such conditions in Liancheng were not unique among hinterland counties. Hinterland merchants and coastal traders often operated in tandem, sometimes even switching roles—occasionally blurring into mountain or maritime banditry. This phenomenon was closely tied to the temporary power vacuum in the hinterland during the dynastic transition, when normal commercial activities could not be conducted in an orderly fashion. It also indirectly reveals the degree to which inland merchants relied on maritime trade. During the Qing Dynasty, changes in national maritime policy directly affected the pace of inland commodity trade. Inland and coastal merchants maintained a closely coordinated relationship—sharing in prosperity and decline alike.

When engaging in trade along the Maritime Silk Road, hinterland merchants typically relied on locally produced agricultural or specialty products, or provided logistical services for trade between mountain and coastal regions. This naturally gave rise to trade groups with distinct specializations and geographical characters, which in turn led to the emergence of representative regional commodities and merchant communities with unique local identities.

---

1 (Ming) Zhang Laifeng. *Preface to the Record of Flight from Liancheng County*. In *Gazetteer of Liancheng County*, (Kangxi Reign, collated version), compiled and edited by (Qing) Du Shijun, vol. 8, *Bibliography of Literature and Arts*. Fangzhi Publishing House, 1997, p.195.

Section 1 Main Categories of Foreign Trade Goods from the Hinterland of the Maritime Silk Road

I. Porcelain

1.The Minjiang River Basin

The Minjiang River Basin was a major center for export ceramics. The history of pottery-making in northern Fujian dates back over 4,000 years. Kiln sites from the Late Neolithic and Xia–Shang periods discovered in the Hulu Mountain in Xingdian Town, Wuyishan City, reveal the origins and early development of prehistoric kiln technologies in Fujian. At Mao'er Mountain in Pucheng, the kiln known as the "progenitor of the Chinese dragon kiln" marked the first emergence of a long, elongated kiln form. The large-scale production of black-coated pottery from this site, noted for its exceptional durability and aesthetic appearance, was widely utilized in the daily life and production activities of early inhabitants. By the Tang Dynasty, northern Fujian had already produced celadon wares, with notable kiln sites including Anwei Mountain and Jiangkou. Celadon pieces from the Jiangkou kiln were often inscribed with the names of workshop owners or kiln artisans, reflecting an early form of brand consciousness. In the late Tang and Five Dynasties periods, the famed "Jianyang black-glazed teacup" (Jian Zhan) emerged in northern Fujian and was exported overseas. The custom of "tea contests" also arose alongside this development. During the Northern and Southern Song dynasties, tea contests became popular throughout East Asia, and large quantities of black-glazed teacups were exported to countries such as Japan and Korea. The Jian kiln products from Shuiji, Jianyang, were renowned for the saying "uniform in color when entering the kiln, but displaying myriad hues upon emergence". As one of the principal production centers of black-glazed ceramics during the Song Dynasty, the Jian kilns primarily produced bowls, commonly referred to as Jianyang black-glazed teacup. Among them, the hare-fur black-glazed teacup (*Tu Hao Zhan*) stood out for its unique aesthetics and gained widespread recognition both domestically and internationally. During the Song and Yuan periods, porcelain production and export in the Minjiang River Basin reached their peak. Prominent kiln sites in northern Fujian that exported via the maritime port of Fuzhou included the Jian kilns in the Jianxi Creek Basin and the Songxi kilns in the Songxi Creek Basin. The Minjiang River also functioned as a critical transit route for the porcelain trade.

Chayang Kiln Site in Nanping

Porcelain was long one of China's most competitive goods in the international market. Before the 15th century, Arab traders transported Chinese porcelain to Europe via the overland Silk Road, where it fetched extremely high prices. In order to meet the growing demand of the European market, direct trade routes between Europe and the East were established in the 16th century, leading to the large-scale procurement of porcelain. Jingdezhen porcelain was especially popular, leading to the production of imitation wares in coastal Fujian. Moreover, the Minjiang River waterway served as a vital maritime route for the export of Jingdezhen porcelain, thereby making northern Fujian an important transshipment hub for its overseas trade. There were two primary export routes for Jingdezhen porcelain through Fujian. The first route involved overland transport to Hekou Town in Qianshan County, Jiangxi, from where the goods crossed the Wuyi Mountain into Chong'an, then followed the upper reaches of the Minjiang River, the Jianxi Creek, downstream into the Minjiang River. The second route also began overland, entering Fujian via Guangze and Shaowu, then proceeding downstream along the Futun Creek, another upper tributary of the Minjiang River, ultimately reaching the main Minjiang River channel. In 2005, a Qing Dynasty shipwreck from the Kangxi period carrying large quantities of Jingdezhen porcelain was discovered near a reef called "Wanjiao" just south of the Minjiang River estuary. Named "Wanjiao No. 1," the ship's location suggests it likely traveled from southeastern Jiangxi into the Minjiang River system before heading out to sea via the estuary.

2.The Tingjiang River Basin and Jiulong River Basin

In the southern part of the hinterland of the Maritime Silk Road, particularly the Tingzhou region, ceramics were not a major local product, yet there is historical evidence of ceramic exports. The Qihe Cave in Zhangping is one of the earliest Neolithic sites in Fujian. Pottery unearthed there—dating from 10,000 to 7,000 years ago—included jars, cauldrons, basins, and bowls. Early pottery was primarily sand-tempered and mostly gray in color. In later periods, decorative patterns became more diverse, with cord-marked designs and incised checkerboard or mesh patterns becoming predominant. Roughly 150 kilometers away, the Nanshan site in Chengguan

Township, Mingxi County, dating from 6,000 to 4,300 years ago, contained abundant cultural remains from five cultural phases. From the second phase onward, decorated pottery appeared with zigzag and vortex patterns. By the third and fourth phases, decorations diversified further to include spiral-dot patterns, lattice patterns, grid patterns, leaf-vein patterns, and mat impressions. Kiln sites from the Song to Qing periods have been discovered in Changting, Longyan, and Zhangping. The bluish-white glazed wares produced by the Yongfu Kiln in Zhangping were highly esteemed in their region. These ceramics were characterized by a relatively thin glaze layer, which made them prone to yellowing due to seepage. The vessels often featured incised decorative patterns, and their bodies were noted for being delicately thin and elegant. These wares were supplied not only to local and regional markets but also exported via the Jiulong River to Japan and Southeast Asia. In 1987, archaeologists excavated two Song Dynasty kiln sites in Tangkengpai, Nanshan Town, Changting. The kiln remains exhibited thick stratified deposits and covered a broad area, indicating several centuries of continuous ceramic production. The ceramics unearthed from the Nanshan kilns in Changting primarily included everyday wares such as teacups, rice bowls, jars, plates, cups and saucers, along with a small number of ornamental craft items. The kilns demonstrated advanced ceramic-firing techniques, with fine porcelain bodies and decorative motifs mainly consisting of stamped and incised patterns. Rich deposits of porcelain clay and dense forests in the surrounding area provided ample fuel and raw materials. The kilns were located near the Nanshan River, a major tributary of the Tingjiang River. Goods were transported via the Nanshan River for about 10 kilometers to the main Tingjiang River, and from there to Chaozhou and beyond for overseas trade. The celadon produced at the Wanquan kilns in Jiangle, also a Hakka area like Sanming, was once exported to Japan. During the Song Dynasty, the ceramic industry in Chaozhou—linked to the Tingjiang River—flourished, likely influenced by developments in Jiangxi and Tingzhou. However, the relationship between the production and distribution of Chaozhou ceramics during the Song Dynasty and Tingzhou still requires further support from historical documents and archaeological evidence.

II. Timber

The hinterland, being predominantly mountainous, was rich in forest resources, particularly Chinese fir. Fir trees were a high-quality construction material mainly produced in Yanping, Jianyang, Tingzhou, Shaowu, and Funing Prefectures. As historical records describe,

> Fir trees that are propagated through branch cuttings can grow to substantial girths and are commonly used for constructing houses and making coffins, with timber primarily sourced from them. Even when used to make utensils, their wood is tough and durable, superior to that of trees grown from seed. When first planted by cuttings, they span across mountains and valleys in dense, continuous rows, often extending for dozens of *li*. After ten years, their value is no longer measured merely by the volume of the valleys they cover.[1]

This shows that fir trees were well suited to the natural geography of the hinterland. Their rapid growth could meet the continuous demand for logging and transport. In Jian'an, for instance, fir production reportedly reached "hundreds of millions annually."[2]

1(Qing) Yang Lan. *Collected Studies on Linting,* vol. 4, *On Local Products.* Woodblock edition, 4th year of the Guangxu reign.

2(Ming) Li Mo. *Collected Writings from the Jade Tower,* vol. 7, *A Record of the Deeds of My Late Father, the Minister of Personnel.* In *Cumulative Bibliography Series of the Four Treasuries*, vol. 77. Qilu Publishing House, 1997, p.776.

The Minjiang River Basin possessed abundant and high-quality forest resources, including premium timber suitable for shipbuilding, which provided essential raw materials for the construction of ocean-going vessels to support maritime trade. In addition to meeting local demands, timber from the Minjiang River Basin was also extensively exported. The significant advancement of shipbuilding techniques in Fuzhou during the Tang Dynasty was closely linked to the supply of superior timber from the upper reaches of the Minjiang River. Beginning in the Song Dynasty, shipyards in coastal prefectures like Fuzhou, Xinghua, Quanzhou, and Zhangzhou relied on superior raw materials—iron, fir, pine, camphorwood, rattan, and lacquer—from the upper reaches of the Minjiang River to build *Fuchuan* (Fuzhou ships), a major class of Chinese ocean-going vessel in maritime history. Many of the ships used in Zheng He's voyages to the Western Seas were constructed in Fujian, with much of the timber for shipbuilding felled from the Nanping region in the upper reaches of the Minjiang River. The discovery of the "Zheng He Bell" in Nanping City illustrates the close connection between Zheng He's maritime expedition fleet and the inland region of Nanping.

Jianning and Tingzhou were both renowned for their timber output. Merchants from these two prefectures were collectively known as the "Jian-Ting Guild". By the late Ming Dynasty, fir from Fujian's four major inland prefectures had earned widespread acclaim. One account notes,

> The four prefectures—Yanping, Tingzhou, Shaowu, and Jianning—produce fir in abundance. Local timber merchants transport the wood by rafting it down streams to markets such as Hongtang, Nantai, and Ningbo for sale. Outward shipments consist of fir timber, while the inward cargo often includes silk and cotton. Each large sea-going vessel chartered in Xinghua costs over eighty taels, yielding

substantial profits.[1]

The Zheng He Bell (The Zheng He Bell was cast in Nanping Town before Zheng He's 7th voyage to pray for safety. It measures 83 cm in height, 49 cm in diameter, 2 cm in thickness, and weighs 77 kg. The bell features a double-dragon handle with a double kettle and a sunflower-shaped mouth. Inscribed on the bell are auspicious phrases such as "Favorable winds and timely rain, national peace and people's safety." The lower part of the bell bears an inscription stating, "On an auspicious day in midsummer of the sixth year of the Xuande reign in the Ming Dynasty, Eunuchs Zheng He, Wang Jinghong, and accompanying officers and soldiers devotedly cast this bronze bell, to be eternally offered for longevity and to pray for a safe and auspicious return from the Western Seas." Originally a first-class cultural relic housed in the Nanping City Museum, it is now preserved in the National Museum. This bell is a rare physical artifact commemorating Zheng He's voyages to the Western Seas.)

1(Qing) Ji Liuqi. *Records of Northern Region of the Late Ming Dynasty* (Ming Ji Bei Lue), vol. 5, "Zhang Yandeng's Petition on Maritime Prohibition." In *Taiwan Historical Documents Series*. Datong Publishing House, 1987, p.239.

During the Qing Dynasty, timber trade in the mountainous regions of Fujian was highly prosperous. Especially in the late Qing period, as domestic economic development accelerated, the demand for timber rose sharply, leading to increased activities among timber merchants in the hinterland. These merchants used Fuzhou as the primary central and resale market, where a clearly defined division of labor within the industry emerged. At forest production sites, timber merchants were typically divided into three types: mountain brokers, procurement agents, and timber company operators. Mountain brokers acted as intermediaries between forest landowners and procurement agents, knowledgeable about local timber markets and earning commissions from brokering deals. Some mountain brokers also acted as buyers, reselling timber procured from forest landowners to agents for profit. Procurement agents, also known as "timber agents" , traveled deep into the inland forested areas to purchase timber, which they then transported to Fuzhou for resale. By the late Qing period, there were over a hundred such agents in counties like Shanghang and Jian'ou, more than sixty in Shaowu, and no fewer than twenty to thirty in other timber-producing counties of the hinterland.[1] In addition, some merchants operated timber businesses that combined local retail with procurement and transport, primarily supplying the Fuzhou market. In Fuzhou, timber merchants were categorized based on their business operations into timber brokers and operators of timber firms. Timber brokers, also known as "fire brokers", specialized in the procurement of wood. Some merchants established timber firms that not only acted as procurement agents but also served as intermediaries between inland timber firms, timber brokers, and merchant clients from Jiangsu and Zhejiang. Based

1Lin Feng, and Song Danling. "Interactions Between Inland and Coastal Regions: The Business Orientation of Fujian Merchants During the Ming and Qing Dynasties." In *Marine Culture and the Development of Fujian: Proceedings of the Second Cross-Strait Symposium on Marine Culture*, edited by Fujian Provincial Department of Ocean and Fisheries, Fujian Yanhuang Culture Research Association, Fujian Federation of Social Sciences Circles, and Fujian Academy of Social Sciences, 2011, pp.131–136.

on their places of sale, timber brokers were organized into different guilds, such as Tian (Tianjin), Nan (southern Fujian, including Zhangzhou and Quanzhou), Fu (local sales of tree roots to woodworking businesses), Tai (Taiwan), and Chang (various ports along the Yangtze River), among others.[1]

The mountainous region of Tingzhou was densely forested and rich in timber resources, particularly Chinese fir, pine, camphor, and other miscellaneous woods. The Chinese fir produced in this area, known as "Ting Fir", was highly regarded for its superior quality. In particular, coffins made from Ting Fir were renowned across a wide region. Tingzhou was also a major producer of camphor wood, which was used to craft high-end furniture, architectural components such as beams and window frames, as well as religious statues. According to late Qing Dynasty statistics,

> In Changting County alone, the annual production of fir timber reached as much as 2,000 to 3,000 *ju* (a unit of timber), while the annual output value of timber from Liancheng and Wuping each exceeded one million yuan. Yongding, Shanghang, and Pinghe counties also reported significant timber exports. Furthermore, the number of forest-dwelling households and timber merchants engaged in the industry was considerable.[2]

This situation continued into the Republican period. Archival data indicates

---

1Weng Lixin, ed. *Fujian's Timber*. Fujian Provincial Government Secretariat Statistics Office, 1940. Cited in: Lin Feng. "Interactions Between Inland and Coastal Regions: The Business Orientation of Fujian Merchants During the Ming and Qing Dynasties." In *Marine Culture and the Development of Fujian: Proceedings of the Second Cross-Strait Symposium on Marine Culture*, edited by Fujian Provincial Department of Ocean and Fisheries, Fujian Yanhuang Culture Research Association, Fujian Federation of Social Sciences Circles, and Fujian Academy of Social Sciences, 2011, pp.131-136.

2"Timber Industry in the Tingjiang River Basin of Fujian." *Fujian Statistical Monthly*, no.4, 1936.

that among the five counties of Changting, Shanghang, Liancheng, Wuping, and Yongding, Wuping had the highest timber production, with an annual output value reaching 400,000 yuan. Before the outbreak of the War of Resistance against Japanese Aggression, the five counties produced more than 900,000 trees annually, valued at over one million yuan. Though output declined slightly during the war, in 1939 the region still produced approximately 534,000 trees, with a total value of around 530,000 yuan. Hakka timber merchants from Tingzhou took advantage of the spring floods on the Tingjiang River to float rafts of timber and bamboo downstream. Workers would construct small rafts at logging sites in mountain streams and then direct them to collection hubs along the Tingjiang River. Important distribution points included Nanzhai, Sanzhou, Shuikou, and Yanggu. From there, merchants would bundle smaller rafts into large ones and float them downstream to Chaozhou and Shantou. Timber acquired by merchants in the Chaozhou and Shantou regions was then shipped via maritime routes to Guangzhou and Foshan for resale. The export of bamboo and timber provided essential raw materials for the shipbuilding and construction industries in Chaozhou, Guangzhou, Macao, Hong Kong, and the Philippines.[1]

The timber hauling chants, sung in Liling Village, Buyun Township, Shanghang County, were a form of labor chant created by local logging workers during their labor. Located in the heart of the Meihuashan Nature Reserve, Buyun Town is the headwater region of the Jiulong River , Minjiang River, and Tingjiang River and has long been a major forest zone in western Fujian. Local genealogies note that as early as the Qianlong period (18th century), merchants in this area engaged in timber trading. After felling, logs

1Ge Wenqing. "An Initial Exploration of the Evolution of the Hakka Economy in the Tingjiang River Basin." *Journal of Longyan Teachers College (Social Science Edition)*, no.2,1996.

were carried downhill to the headwaters of the Jiulong River and floated downstream through Wan'an (Xinluo District of Longyan), Zhangping, and Hua'an, ultimately reaching Zhangzhou. The descent of logs down the mountain was both difficult and dangerous, prompting laborers to sing simple, rhythmic chants such as: "Hey... hey... hey... hey-yeh hmm hey... hey ai-yo..." These chants helped to coordinate the work and boost morale. In December 2021, the Timber Hauling Chant of Liling was officially inscribed on the Representative List of Intangible Cultural Heritage of Fujian Province.

The Timber Hauling Chant of Meihuashan

(Photographed by Lan Shanxiang)

III. Tea

After the mid-Ming period, with the development of the commodity economy, a trend of "luxury" became prevalent among the people, and the demand for tea increased significantly in both quantity and quality across the nation. The upper reaches of the Minjiang River had long been an important tea-producing area. By the late Ming period, the tea industry had become one of Fujian's pillar industries.

Wuyi Mountain is an important tea-producing area in Fujian. After the abolition of the tribute tea system in Wuyi Mountain, more and more local planters and traders emerged. In the late Ming, Xu Bo stated,

> Within the area surrounding the Nine-Bend Stream, there are no fewer than several hundred households, all engaged in tea cultivation. Their annual output amounts to several hundred thousand *jin*, which is transported by both water and land and sold throughout the country, making the name of Wuyi renowned across the empire.[1]

This document indicates that by the late Ming period, Wuyi Mountain's tea industry had already grown to a considerable scale. The phrase "water floating and land circulation" suggests that Wuyi tea was not only sold inland but also exported via water transport (the Minjiang River). By the early Qing period, Wuyi tea entered the international markets. Initially, tea from Wuyi Mountain was primarily purchased by Shanxi merchants who came to the county for procurement. From the town of Xiamei in Chong'an County, Fujian, it was transported via Hekou in Jiangxi, northward to Hankou, and then further distributed to Henan and Shanxi, eventually extending to Mongolia and the Siberian plain—forming the so-called "Ten-Thousand-Mile Tea Road." In addition, tea from Anhui and Fujian was shipped via the Fenshui Pass through the Qianshan River into the Ganjiang River, then over Dayu Ridge to Guangzhou, from where it was exported to Europe by sea. After the Qing court opened the five treaty ports, procurement shifted to merchants from Xiafu, Chaozhou, and Guangzhou, who came to the county to purchase tea. The tea was then concentrated in Fuzhou for export, with only a small portion routed through Xiamen. Before the Opium War, due to

1(Ming)Xu Bo. "A Study on Tea." In *Gazetteer of Mount Wuyi*, compiled by Dong Tiangong, vol. 21, *Bibliography of Literature and Arts*. Fangzhi Publishing House, 2007, p.699.

Qing government regulations, Wuyi tea was primarily exported through Guangzhou. With the opening of the port, Guangzhou merchants monopolized the tea trade. "In the past, Fujian tea was transported to Guangdong, where the Thirteen Hongs of Canton would store the tea and then gradually ship it overseas. Due to this, foreign markets were always short of supply, and tea prices were often high." A small amount of tea was exported from Xiamen, and the tea arriving in Xiamen included four types: Gongfu, Huaxiang Baihao, Zhulan tea, and Oolong tea, with oolong tea being the most common. The tea-producing regions closest to Xiamen included Anxi (4 days), Ningyang (7 days), the Jianning area along the Beixi Creek (6 days), and Longyan (7 days). After the Taiping Rebellion broke out, land routes from Fujian to Guangzhou were interrupted, and Wuyi tea shifted to be exported via the Minjiang River. Since 1854, tea exports from Fuzhou began.

The Tea Garden in Pucheng County

In the late Qing period, Wuyi tea trade attracted tea ships from around the world to Fuzhou's Mawei Port. According to statistics from Fukien Maritime Customs, in 1866, a total of 364 British ships entered the Mawei Port of Fuzhou, with a combined tonnage of 175,192 tons; 366 British vessels departed from the port, totaling 175,422 tons. Merchant ships from other countries also called at Mawei, including 15 from the United States, 3 from

France, 17 from Prussia, 8 from Hamburg, 13 from Bremen, and 11 from Denmark. Additionally, individual ships from Norway, Sweden, the Netherlands, Hanover, and Hawaii also visited the port. In total, 451 merchant ships from 15 different countries and ports entered Mawei in 1866, with a total registered tonnage of 197,834 tons, the majority of which were British. In the ninth year of the Xianfeng reign (1859), Fuzhou Port briefly became the largest tea export port in China.

The High-grade Tea Porter[1]

The Low-grade Tea Porter[2]

In the 17th century, tea drinking began to spread from European courts to the nobility and commoners, significantly increasing the demand for tea in European markets. By the early 18th century, tea had replaced silk as China's largest export commodity, a significant shift in China's foreign trade history known as the "Silk-Tea Exchange." The growing international influence of the tea trade was largely due to the widespread popularity of tea drinking in Europe. By the 19th century, tea had become an indispensable part of daily

1Fortune Robert. *Two Visits to the Tea Regions of China.* Translated by Ao Xuegang. Jiangsu People's Publishing House, 2016. Illustration from *A Third Visit to China: 1853–1856*, originally published in the United Kingdom in 1857, cited on p. 322.

2 Ibid., p321.

life among the British aristocracy, and this lifestyle gradually spread from the upper class to the general public, increasing Britain's demand for tea. China monopolized the production of high-quality tea, and although Britain exported industrial products such as wool and worsted to China, they were not well-received. To correct the trade imbalance with China, Britain began to smuggle opium into China in exchange for silver to purchase tea. After Lin Zexu's destruction of opium at Humen in the mid-19th century, the Opium War broke out, and the *Treaty of Nanjing* was signed between China and Britain, marking the beginning of the unequal treaties. Despite this, the British were still concerned that tea trade would be affected, and thus they decided to steal tea plants and production techniques from China.

Robert Fortune was assigned this mission. Between 1839 and 1860, he visited China four times, wearing traditional Chinese robes and keeping a braid hairstyle, employing Chinese servants, and traveling deep into major tea-producing regions such as Hangzhou, Anhui, and Fujian in search of the finest tea varieties and the most advanced cultivation and processing techniques. He subsequently transported tea seedlings and seeds via Shanghai to India for cultivation.[1] Fortune documented his search for tea in China,[2] which also indirectly recorded the state of the tea industry in the Maritime Silk Road region at the time. He also corrected some misconceptions about tea held by Westerners. In 1845, during his first trip to China, he discovered that the British belief that black tea and green tea came from different varieties of tea trees was incorrect. Fortune sent green tea seedlings and seeds collected in Songluo, Anhui, to India, but they were unsuccessful in cultivation. In order to further investigate high-quality black

---

1(America) Rose Sarah. *For All the Tea in China: How England Stole the World's Favorite Drink and Changed History*. Translated by Meng Chi. Social Sciences Academic Press, 2015.

2(Britain) Fortune Robert. *Two Visits to the Tea Regions of China*. Translated by Ao Xuegang. Jiangsu People's Publishing House, 2020.

tea production regions, in May 1849 he departed from Ningbo and traveled by water through present-day Lanxi and Changshan in Zhejiang, Yushan, Hekou, and Qianshan in Jiangxi, and Chong'an in Fujian, eventually arriving at Wuyi Mountain. He ventured deep into Wuyi Mountain's core black tea area, even reaching the mother tree of *Da Hong Pao*, and collected over 10,000 seeds. Fortune secretly stole tea tree seeds and smuggled them out of China, along with Chinese technicians. The seeds were successfully cultivated in the Darjeeling region of India, which gradually came to dominate the global tea trade. As a result of this tea trade war, China, the original birthplace of tea, ultimately lost its leading position.

Mr. Xu Xiaowang has highly praised the status of northern Fujian's tea exports, noting that the traditional Maritime Silk Road of China has over 2,000 years of history. On this trade route, China exported goods such as silk, porcelain, sugar, and tea. Among them, the export of Wuyi tea through the Fuzhou Port during the late Qing period can be considered the peak of China's Maritime Silk Road trade. It had a profoundimpact on both China and the global economy and also served as a crucial foundation for the development of the Self-Strengthening Movement in modern China. Due to the prosperity of the tea industry in Fuzhou, the silver flowing into Fuzhou for tea purchases ranged from several million to tens of millions annually. For instance, in 1865, the silver flowing into Fuzhou from Hong Kong and other places reached 6,987,837 yuan, and in 1866, it was 10,606,943 yuan. From 1855 to 1885, the annual surplus of several million silver dollars made Fujian one of the regions with surplus funds in the country. The Qing government established the Mawei Naval Yard in Fuzhou at great expense, with the majority of its funding borne by Fujian Province itself. Similarly, much of the late Qing government's investment in the development of Taiwan was also financed by Fujian. The province's fiscal revenue relied heavily on the taxation of tea.

IV. Tobacco

Tobacco, also transliterated phonetically as "*Dan Ba Gu*," originated in the Americas. After the Spanish conquest of Luzon, tobacco was introduced to Zhangzhou, Fujian during the Wanli reign of the Ming Dynasty. Nearby Yongding rapidly began cultivating tobacco, earning it the reputation that "Yongding's sun-cured tobacco stands alone in the world—though other regions in the province and elsewhere produce it, none match its quality in color, texture, or flavor."[1] Tobacco cultivation soon spread across the entire province, with the mountainous hinterland areas becoming the main centers of both production and trade. By the Kangxi period, places like Longyan saw the phenomenon of "prosperity in tobacco, decline in grain." Merchants from Shizhong, a town in Longyan, gained fame for their tobacco trade, amassing significant wealth from it, which they used to build the iconic square-shaped earthen buildings of Shizhong.

In the 30th year of the Jiajing reign (1551), the Tingjiang River was once again dredged, allowing navigation as far upstream as Shuikou in Changting County. This opened the full length of the river from Shuikou to Fengshi in Yongding, making Fengshi a key hub and distribution center for goods transported between western Fujian and eastern Guangdong. During the Qianlong reign (1736–1795), "many planted tobacco on fertile lands in Yongding."[2] "Merchants from the region traveled as far as Wu, Chu, Yunnan, and Sichuan, often settling temporarily in these distant places; residents of Jinfeng, Fengtian, and Taiping even crossed the seas to various foreign lands as if visiting familiar homes."[3] Before 1926, Yongding exported 50,000 to

1 (Qing) Fang Lyujian, ed., and Wu, Yifu, comp. *Gazetteer of Yongding County,* Daoguang edition, vol. 16, *Customs*. Xiamen University Press, 2012, p.279.

2 (Qing) Wu Wei comp., and Wang Jianchuan, ed. *Gazetteer of Yongding County* (Qianlong Reign), vol. 3, *Local Products*. Xiamen University Press, 2012, p.83.

3 (Qing) Fang Lyujian, ed., and Wu, Yifu, comp. *Gazetteer of Yongding County,*

60,000 boxes of fine-cut tobacco annually, with destinations including Zhangzhou, Xiamen, Taiwan, Guangzhou, Hong Kong, Macao, Nanjing, Shanghai, Wuhan, most major cities in China, and countries across Southeast Asia.

Earthen Buildings

Yongding's tobacco was transported via three main routes:

1. From Gaotou in Yongding to Qujiang in Nanjing County, then to the county seat and onward to Zhangzhou and Xiamen ports for maritime export to Hong Kong, Macao, Taiwan, and Southeast Asia.

2. From Gaopei, Kanshi, Fushi, and Hulei in Yongding, downstream along the Yongding River to Luxi Dam in Xianshi Township, then overland

---

Daoguang edition, vol. 16, *Customs*. Xiamen University Press, 2012, p.279.

to Shishi on the Fujian–Guangdong border (in Dapu County, Guangdong). From there, it followed the Tingjiang River and Hanjiang River to Chaozhou and Shantou, then shipped from Shantou Port to Guangzhou, Liuzhou, Kunming, Chongqing, or via sea to Hong Kong, Macao, Taiwan, and Southeast Asia.

3.Following the Yongding River upstream through Fengshi Town and continuing along the Tingjiang River to Shanghang and Changting, then overland or by riverboat to Jiujiang, Nanchang, Wuhan, Changsha, Chongqing, Chengdu, Shanghai, Nanjing, and other major domestic commercial cities.

Since the Qing Dynasty, the fine-cut tobacco shops and firms established by residents of Yongding gradually expanded into major cities across southern China, as well as into Hong Kong, Macao, Taiwan, and various countries in Southeast Asia. According to incomplete statistics, during the Qing period, there were 121 tobacco shops and firms within Yongding County itself. Yongding natives went on to establish hundreds of tobacco enterprises in 39 cities across 14 provinces in southern China. Additionally, a significant number of tobacco shops and firms were opened in Hong Kong, Macao, Taiwan, and throughout Southeast Asia.

Yongding's fine-cut tobacco reportedly once awarded the honorary title of "King of Tobacco"

Table 3-1 Distribution of Yongding's Fine-cut Tobacco (Tobacco Knife) Firms and Trade Names

No.	Location	Tobacco Firms or Trade Names
1	Shanghai	Yihecheng, Tianshengde, Yonglongchang, Sudekang, Songwanmao, Wanyouqian, Wanchang
2	Guangzhou	Huangfulong, Luwanan, Quedelong
3	Nanjing	Wanqingquan, Daidechang, Longxinggui
4	Wuhan	Sudemao, Sudexing, Luhengmao, Sanyizhuang
5	Changsha	Yishuilong, Yimaoyuan
6	Hangzhou	Dayouding
7	Suzhou	Wanshuren
8	Yangzhou	Taifeng, Taichangyi
9	Xiamen	Dechanglong, Taiyixiang

The operational model of tobacco processing workshops and trading firms in Yongding was governed by merchant guilds or tobacco associations, with a tightly coordinated structure linking production and sales. The merchant guild functioned as a county-wide social organization of merchants, whose president was elected by general consensus. The tobacco association, as a trade organization encompassing both production enterprises and sales operations, primarily consisted of members who were relatives of the business owners.

The operation of the Yongding's fine-cut tobacco industry generated substantial economic benefits and significantly influenced local social landscape. In particular, it contributed to the large-scale construction of the region's distinctive earthen buildings. Notable examples such as *Yonglongchang* Building in Fushi Town, *Yijing* Building in Gaobei Town, *Dihui* Building in Guzhu Town, and the *Dafu* Residence in Hongshan Town were all closely tied to the economic prosperity brought about by the fine-cut tobacco trade.

V.Paper Products

The mountainous regions of the Maritime Silk Road hinterland have long been rich in bamboo and timber, making them ideal areas for high-quality paper production.

1. The Minjiang River Basin

The Minjiang River Basin was one of the principal paper-producing areas in Fujian. As early as the Tang Dynasty, paper manufactured in northern Fujian was known for its fine craftsmanship. In the Ming Dynasty, it was recorded that,

> In the Yanping district of central Fujian, newly sprouted bamboo shoots exceeding one *chi* (about 33 cm) in length are routinely harvested and sun-cured into bamboo shoot slices. The annual production reaches tens of millions of *jin*, and these products are sold across the country, generating incalculable profits. Additionally, bamboo is

> processed into paper, yielding economic benefits measured in the tens of thousands.[1]

During the Ming period, handmade paper from northern Fujian was even exported to Vietnam. After the establishment of a tributary relationship between Vietnam and the Ming court, Vietnam sought to emulate Chinese culture, greatly increasing its demand for books and paper. However, due to its local limitations, Vietnam lacked the capacity to produce paper independently. As a result, merchants from the Minjiang River Basin dominated the paper trade market along the Beibu Gulf, exporting Fujian-made bamboo paper in bulk and thereby promoting education and cultural development in the region.

By the modern era, traditional handmade paper remained the backbone of handicraft industries in northern Fujian. Over 20 counties in the upper and middle reaches of Minjiang River produced paper, with Shaowu, Shunchang, Nanping, and Jianyang being the most prolific, forming a well-structured sales network. During this period, paper-industry stakeholders in northern Fujian were known by various titles, such as *caohu* (paper pulp producers), *zhifan* (paper traders), *zhizhan* (paper depots), *zhuangke* (itinerant agents), *guotanghang* (intermediate brokers), *zhihang* (paper firms), *xingke* (traveling merchants), and *chengyou* (partners).[2] The handmade paper was transported downstream along the Minjiang River to Fuzhou, which thereby became the province's largest central market for paper products. Beyond local and provincial consumption, this handmade paper was further redistributed from Fuzhou to external markets—northward to coastal ports in North and Northeast China, and eastward and southward to Japan, Annam (present-day

1(Qing) Zhu Wenyu, comp., and Li Shixiong, ed. *Gazetteer of Ninghua County (Kangxi Reign)*, vol. 2, *Local Products.* Fujian People's Publishing House, 1989, p.75.

2Wu Bangcai, editor-in- chief. *History of the Development of Fujian Merchants: Nanping Volume*. Xiamen University Press, 2016, p.137.

Vietnam), and the various islands of Southeast Asia—to meet the demands of overseas Chinese communities and enthusiasts of Chinese culture. Mingxi County, located in the upper reaches of the Minjiang River, was a principal producer of five-colored paper. According to the *Gazetteer of Mingxi County* from the Republican period,

> Five-colored paper is a major product of Mingxi (formerly Guihua), widely sold in Hunan, Hubei, Guangdong, Jiangxi, and Fuzhou. Products bound for Hunan and Hubei are handled by the Hankou Guild, while those for Fuzhou are managed by the Rongcheng Guild. Both guilds reported profits tripling their investment. Many wealthy merchants of the past made their fortunes in this trade. Prior to the Daoguang reign, more than 200 paper workshops operated in the region, producing substantial quantities. After the Xianfeng and Tongzhi reigns, production sharply declined, and by the Republic era, only a few businesses remained. Tin-foil paper is another major product of Mingxi, primarily produced by female laborers. Thousands of women depend on this industry for their livelihoods. The paper was sold in Jiangxi, Shaowu, Taining, and Fuzhou, with Jiangxi being the largest market. Each year, dozens of Jiangxi merchants station representatives in the county to procure the product for export.[1]

Paper from Qingliu County—including *Changxing*, *Yukou*, D*aguang*, and *Gaolian* varieties—was sold not only in nearby counties like Ninghua, Changting, and Liancheng, but also in Yong'an, Fuzhou, Jiangxi, Hankou,

1Wang Weiliang, and Liu Zizhi, comps. *Gazetteer of Mingxi County (the Republican Period)*, vol. 15, *Miscellaneous Records*. Xiamen University Press, 2008, p.498.

Chaozhou, Hong Kong, and Vietnam.[1]

2. The Tingjiang River Basin and Jiulong River Basin

Paper was also a key export product in the Tingjiang River Basin. Liancheng specialized in high-quality bleached paper. Changting produced *Yukou* paper and *Maobian* paper. Shanghang and Wuping were known for *Haizhi* paper, used in folk rituals. Zhangping produced *Liansi* paper and *Dabian* paper. The Ming and Qing dynasties marked the golden era of Tingzhou's paper industry, where paper was a major export commodity for each county. Historical sources state, "The bamboo forests in Tingzhou are dense and lofty, blocking out the sun. Paper is produced and sold afar, yielding great profits."[2] Since the Song Dynasty, Tingzhou had been a key center of handmade papermaking. By the Ming and Qing periods, Tingzhou's traditional paper not only met local demand but nearly monopolized the Guangdong market and was exported to Southeast Asia. Historically, people in Guangdong and Chinese communities in Southeast Asia relied on Tingzhou's *Yukou* paper, easily identified by its distinctive red-stamped label. According to the statistics in 1939, Changting had 620 papermaking workshops spreading across more than 100 villages, with an annual output of 3,190 tons of handmade paper—a figure that remained consistent through 1946.[3] In addition to selling locally produced paper, paper merchants along the Tingjiang River also purchased and resold handmade paper from neighboring areas such as Ninghua, Qingliu, Shanghang, Liancheng, and Jiangle. These paper goods were transported via the Tingjiang River to the

---

1 Lin Shanqing, comp., and Wang Qiong, ed. *Gazetteer of Qingliu County (the Republican Period)*, vol. 13, *Industrial Affairs*. Shanghai Bookstore Publishing House, 2000, p.350.

2 (Qing) Zhao Cheng, comp., and Zhao Ningjing, ed. *Gazetteer of Shanghang County* (Qianlong Reign), vol. 1, *Customs*. Woodblock edition, the 18th year of the Qianlong reign (1753).

3 Local Gazetteer Compilation Committee of Changting County, ed. *Gazetteer of Changting County: Handmade Paper*. Sanlian Bookstore, 1993, p.255.

Chaoshan region, then shipped by sea to Guangzhou, and from there exported overseas by maritime routes to Hong Kong, Macao, and various Southeast Asian countries.

To better manage the paper trade, Hakka merchants from Tingzhou established paper firms in cities like Chaozhou and Guangzhou, forming a Tingzhou paper merchant guild. In the 11th year of the Yongzheng reign (1733), paper merchants from Changting and Liancheng counties established the Lianfeng Guild Hall in Foshan, Guangdong, which "served as a hub for distributing paper products to surrounding rural areas and distant regions, including Guangzhou and Zhaoqing jurisdictions".[1] Later, in the 28th year of the Qianlong reign (1763), merchants from Tingzhou and Longyan jointly established the "Tinglong Guild Hall"in Chaozhou, which primarily focused on paper trade. Paper products produced in Liancheng, such as mid-to-high level *Lian* paper, *Yukou* paper, *Yuban* paper, and *Piaogong* paper, were exported to Annam (present-day Vietnam), Siam (present-day Thailand), Burma (Myanmar), the Philippines, and other countries. The total volume of paper exported domestically and internationally reached 78,000 *dan*, each valued at 60 silver dollars, with a total value exceeding 4.68 million silver dollars.[2] According to statistics, in 1939, the five counties along the Tingjiang River produced over 316,000 *dan* of paper, with a production value of 4.506 million yuan, accounting for more than one-third of the province's total output and value.[3] As recorded in the *Gazetteer of Changting County* , during the late Qing and Republican periods, Tingzhou merchants established

1Xian Baogan, ed., and Foshan Library, comp. *Gazetteer of Zhongyi Township, Foshan (Republican Period*, annotated edition). Yuelu Publishing House, 2017, p.224.

2Zhou Xuexiang. *Socioeconomic Changes in the Hakka Regions Along the Fujian–Guangdong Border During the Ming and Qing Dynasties*. Fujian People's Publishing House, 2007, p.246.

3Fujian Provincial Department of Construction, ed. *An Overview of Fujian's Economy*. 1947, pp.116–123.

dozens of paper firms outside the region. Major ones included:

Chaozhou: Over ten trading firms such as Changan Co. (Xu Weiying), Rongfeng Co. (Tong Ziyi), and Changfeng Co. (Li Hongkai).
Shantou: More than ten firms such as Jian'an Co., Lianxing Co., and Gongxing Co..

Guangzhou: Several firms including Changxing Co. (Li Tisheng), Gong'an Co. (Luo Zuoheng), Dehe Co. (Chen Xuhe), Yongfeng Co. (Chen Bochun), Anlezhuang (Chen Bochun and Lan Qiwei), Jianchanglong (Tong Shaoqing), etc.

Foshan: A number of firms including Changlian Co., Changxing Co., Jianxing Co.

Hong Kong: A number of firms including Tingzhou Co. (Zheng Yunsong), Nanlianchang, among others.[1]

Beyond these major trade firms, Tingzhou merchants also established paper businesses in Shaoguan, Huizhou, Laolong, and Meixian in Guangdong, and in Ganzhou, Ji'an, and Nanchang in Jiangxi. In 1935, Changting town had 101 paper firms, rising to 125 by 1945.

In addition to local paper merchants engaging in external commercial operations, merchants from other regions also came to western Fujian to establish paper firms. For instance, in the 45th year of the Qianlong reign (1780), Guangdong merchants Huang Yanghua and Zhu Guangju arrived in the handmade paper-producing area of Liancheng and successively established paper firms such as Tai'an, Hong'an, Yisheng, and Yongchang in Gutan and Juxi. These firms purchased handmade paper and transported it back to Guangdong, where it was sold in markets such as Foshan, Hong Kong,

1 Local Gazetteer Compilation Committee of Changting County, ed. *Gazetteer of Changting County: Handmade Paper*. Sanlian Bookstore, 1993, p.255.

and Macao.[1]

Different grades of Tingzhou handmade paper were sold through distinct commercial channels. For printing books, ledgers, and account books, high-grade Tingzhou-produced *Yukou* paper of Grades 1, 2, and 3 was preferred. This kind of paper was characterized by its fine texture, white color, and strong durability. It did not allow ink to bleed during writing. Cigarette paper for hand-rolled tobacco typically used Grades 4 and 5 of *Yukou* paper, valued for its toughness and resistance to disintegration when held in the mouth. Colored paper, literacy primers, and calligraphy practice books mainly used Grade 6 of *Yukou* paper, a mid-grade product. This type of paper was widely used in weddings and funerals as well as for mass-printed educational materials, making it highly demanded annually. Packaging paper generally utilized Grades 7 and 8 of *Yukou* paper—classified as low-grade—characterized by a coarse texture and yellowish tint. Despite its rough appearance, it was tough and non-toxic, making it suitable for packaging in pharmacies, general stores, and fabric shops. Another popular variety was *Maobian* paper, which, while less durable than *Yukou* paper for long-term preservation, was cheaper, lightweight, and portable. It was commonly used for practicing brush calligraphy or dyed into various colors, and also represented a significant segment of the market.[2] The Hakka merchants of Tingzhou virtually monopolized the handmade paper market in Guangdong. As Luo Xianglin noted in his *Introduction to Hakka Studies*, paper produced in the Hakka regions of Fujian was widely sold throughout South China. From the Song Dynasty through the Republican era, Tingzhou's Hakka paper

---

1Zhou Xuexiang. "A Comparative Study of the Regional Economies of the Two River Basins in Tingzhou During the Qing Dynasty." *Journal of Gannan Normal University,* no.1, 2012.

2Mao Xing. "Fragments of Commercial Trade in Changting Before the Founding of the PRC." *Historical Materials of Changting*, vol. 12, edited by the Literature and History Editorial Office of the CPPCC Changting County Committee, 1987, pp. 34–39.

merchants developed a tightly organized distribution network for handmade paper and successfully integrated this network into maritime trade routes.

In the Jiulong River's upper reaches, Longyan was the most important center of paper production. According to the county gazetteer,

> The natural resources of Longyan are abundant, and it possesses a wide variety of raw materials suitable for manufacturing. Presently, industrial goods are sold in the region of the Beixi Creek. Products from communities such as Hubang, Longmen, Dachi, Xiaochi, and Shizhong are transported and sold in the region of the Xixi Creek. The Xixi Creek primarily deals in coarse materials, while the Beixi Creek also transports fine white material. The white paper produced here is of excellent quality and is sold as far as the Southeast Asia. Although annual sales do not reach a million units, they provide a livelihood for the poor. In the paper-producing villages, even women and children can find employment. Thus, it is evident how crucial industry is, and how necessary it is to promote its development. [1]

VI. Books

1.Jianyang Imprints

During the Southern Song period, Jianyang rose to become one of the three major book engraving centers in China, earning the title of "the Forest of Books". Jianyang's engraved books not only fostered the prosperity of Fujian's cultural and educational endeavors but also exerted influence across

1Ma Heming, ed., and Du Hansheng et al. comp. *Gazetteer of Longyan County*, vol. 17, *Treatise on Industry*. In *Series of Chinese Local Gazetteers*. Reprint of the lithographic edition from the 9th year of the Republic of China. Chengwen Publishing House, 1967, p.186.

the entire province and even the nation. Moreover, they became integrated into the trade routes of the Maritime Silk Road. According to Volume 4, *Local Products*, of the *Gazetteer of Jianyang County* compiled during the Jiajing reign of the Ming Dynasty, "Categories of goods include: books, embroidered blankets, cloth, paper, ... products from bowl kilns and black kilns." Books were listed first, indicating their prominent role in Jianyang's commercial activities.

In the Ming Dynasty, the book market at Chonghua Ward in Jianyang was the largest in the region. A major fire in the 12th year of the Hongzhi reign (1499) destroyed a vast number of woodblocks, dealing a heavy blow to the local book trade. However, in the late Ming period, in response to the growing market demand, many woodblocks were re-engraved and reissued, significantly increasing in quantity compared to the Hongzhi era. By the end of the Ming Dynasty, the commercial nature of the book trade intensified. Among the main centers of book engraving at the time, Jianyang stood out in terms of sheer quantity—"The books from the book markets of Jianyang flourish across the realm,"[1] and merchants from all over China gathered there in droves. Nonetheless, Xie Zhaozhe criticized the quality of Jianyang publications, stating," Jianyang has the most prolific book market, but its printing paper and woodblocks are of the poorest quality, for publishers are driven solely by profit rather than the desire to produce lasting works."[2] His critique suggests that the books produced in Jianyang were often of low quality due to publishers' eagerness for quick returns, which led them to use inferior materials. Nonetheless, this account also reflects the keen market sensitivity of Jianyang's book merchants and the intense commercial

1(Ming) He Qiaoyuan. *Book of Fujian*, vol. 38, *Treatise on Customs.* Fujian People's Publishing House, 1995, p.943.

2(Ming) Xie Zhaozhe. *Five Miscellanies*, vol. 13, *Section One on Affairs.* Shanghai Bookstore Publishing House, 2001, p.266.

competition that characterized the publishing industry.

During the Song, Yuan, and Ming dynasties, Jianyang imprints were exported overseas. Xiong He, a scholar from Jianyang during the late Song and early Yuan periods, stated that "Books reach Goryeo and Japan, bridging the ten-thousand-li distance between our realm and theirs," [1] highlighting the dissemination of Jianyang imprints to neighboring countries such as Japan and Goryeo (Korea).

Based on the era in which Xiong He lived, it is evident that Jianyang imprints were transmitted to Japan no later than the late Southern Song period, likely beginning in the mid-Southern Song. The Qing scholar Yang Shoujing composed a verse stating, "After reading the Seven Classics, I opened the Kaibao treasury, handed down by Ashikaga to promote Confucian teachings,"[2] succinctly describing that Chinese books transmitted eastward to Japan were primarily Buddhist and Confucian classics. Existing evidence shows that a significant number of these Chinese books printed in Jianyang made their way to Japan. Examples include the 120-volume *Book of Han* printed by Huang Shanfu in Jian'an during the Song Dynasty, the *Guangyun* published by Huang Sanbalang's bookshop in Jianning Prefecture in the Song Dynasty, and the *Revised Jade Chapters* from Cuiyan workshop in Yuan Dynasty. Japan also reprinted many Jianyang imprints. For instance, in the seventh year of Genna (1621), Emperor Go-Mizunoo used copper movable type to print the *Huang Song Shishi Leiyuan (Categorized Compendium of Historical Accounts in the Song Dynasty)*, originally a Jianyang edition from the 23rd year of Shaoxing reign (1153), and presented it to the court nobles

---

1 (Yuan) Xiong He. *Collected Works from the Wuxuan Studio*, vol. 4. Photographic Reprint of the Complete Library of the Four Treasuries (Wenyuan Pavilion Edition), vol. 1188. Taiwan Commercial Press, 1986, pp.804–805.

2 (Qing) Yang Shoujing. *Rhymed Verses on Book Collecting*. Classical Literature Publishing House, 1957, p.15.

and shogunate, calling it the "Genna Imperial Edition." During the Kansei era, a Japanese court physician reprinted the Yuan Dynasty's *Xinkan Xutian Shizhai Baiyi Xuanfang*, originally published by Liu Chengwen in Jianyang, Fujian. In his *Bibliography of Chinese Popular Fiction*, Sun Kaidi recorded five types of vernacular novels published by the book workshop of the Yu Family in Jian'an (modern-day Jianyang, Fujian) during the Zhizhi era (1321–1323) of the Yuan Dynasty, which he saw in Japan. The saying "Fujian editions circulate throughout the world" is the highest praise for books printed in Masha (a major printing center in Jianyang). From the mid-Ming to the early Qing periods, Fujian merchants played a key role in Sino-Japanese trade, and Jianyang books reached a new peak in exports to Japan. Aside from traditional products such as silk and medicine, books were a major trade item in Sino-Japanese trade. From the late Ming through the Qing Dynasty, many of the Jianyang editions circulating in the domestic markets were popular and practical works intended for the general public. These included fictions, dramas, encyclopedic compendia, and medical texts. As a result, a significant portion of the Jianyang editions transmitted to Japan also consisted of such popular literature—novels, plays, reference works, and medical manuals. The dissemination of stories like *Water Margin, Romance of the Three Kingdoms, Journey to the West* and *Romance of the Western Chamber* further strengthened cultural ties between China and Japan. Narratives from *Romance of the Three Kingdoms* and *Journey to the West* remain widely appreciated in Japanese society to this day. Although the book printing industry in Jianyang declined during the Qing Dynasty, Jianyang books continued to be shipped to Nagasaki, and Japan. These included not only works on the philosophies of Zhu Xi and Wang Yangming, but also technical treatises such as *The Exploitation of the Works of Nature*, which introduced Chinese technological achievements. Such works had a significant impact on Japan's educational and intellectual spheres, as well as on aspects of everyday life during the Tokugawa period.

In Korea, An Hyang and his disciple Kwon Bu promoted the spread of Chinese culture and Zhu Xi's philosophy. In the 26th year of the Zhiyuan reign of the Yuan Dynasty (1289), An Hyang, serving as an envoy to the Yuan court, brought back to Goryeo a number of important Zhu Xi works, including *Collected Commentaries on the Four Books, Collected Works of Master Zhu Xi* and *Classified Conversations of Master Zhu Xi*. Later, *Collected Commentaries on the Four Books* was printed in Korea by Gwon Bu. During the Ming Dynasty, frequent tributary missions between the Joseon (Korean) court and Ming China facilitated the continuous influx of Chinese texts into Korea. For instance, the Yongle Emperor bestowed upon the Korean delegation a number of Chinese works in Jianyang editions, such as *Collected Memorials of Officials*, *Extended Meaning of the Great Learning*, *Comprehensive Interpretation of the Spring and Autumn Annals*, *Zhen Xishan's Reading Notes*, and *Complete Works of Master Zhu Xi*. In addition to canonical texts, fiction was also a major category among the books that entered Korea. During the Ming Dynasty, Jianyang was a major publishing hub for classical Chinese novels, and many of these Jianyang editions were transmitted to Korea. Notable examples include *Popular Romance of the Three Kingdoms with Phonetic Annotations Based on an Ancient Corrected Edition*, *Legend of the Loyal General Yue Fei*, *Illustrated New Edition of the Five Manifested Spirits: Biography of the Deity Huaguang*, and *Judge Bao's Judgments on a Hundred Cases*. These novels, which narrated well-known Chinese historical and legendary tales, not only enriched the cultural and entertainment life of the Korean people, but also played a significant role in disseminating Chinese civilization.

After the Jiajing and Wanli reigns of the Ming Dynasty, western missionaries who came to China served as intermediaries in the exchange of books between China and the West. By carrying and sending books abroad, they introduced Chinese works to the Western world, including editions printed in Jianyang. Although the number was limited, what is particularly valuable is that some of these were unique copies already lost on the Chinese mainland. According to the research of Fang Yanshou, these rare editions are now preserved in national libraries in France, Germany, Belgium, Austria, Spain, and the United States, as well as in institutions such as Harvard University. The preserved works include: the *New Edition of the Ten Deeds of Han Peng*, printed by Yu Shaoya's Zixin Studio during the Ming Dynasty; the *Illustrated Romance of the Three Kingdoms*, printed by Liu Rongwu's Liguan Workshop in Fusha during the Ming Dynasty; the *Records of the Daonan Academy*, a Jiajing-period Jianyang edition; a reprinted edition of the *Newly Compiled Biographies of Ancient Exemplary Women* by the Ruan family in Yangzhou in the Qing Dynasty, based on the Song-era Jian'an edition by the Yu family's Qinyoutang; *The Lychee Chronicle*, printed by Ye Wenqiao's Nanyang Workshop during the Ming Dynasty; the *Romance of the Three Kingdoms*, printed by Ye Fengchun during the Jiajing reign of the Ming Dynasty; *Classified Treatises on Cold Damage with Illustrative Diagrams*, printed by Xiong Zongli during the Zhengde reign of the Ming Dynasty; *Supplemented and Annotated Comprehensive Reference of the Complete Works*, printed by Zheng Shangxuan in the Ming Dynasty; *Four Competing Curious Works*, printed by the Yu family's Cuiqing Workshop in Jianyang during the Tianqi reign of the Ming Dynasty; *Commentaries on the Doctrine of the Mean* and *Questions on the Doctrine of the Mean*, printed by Zhongde Workshop in Jianyang during the Hongzhi reign of the Ming Dynasty; and *Principles Reflected in the Jade Hall*, printed by Zhiyun Workshop in Masha during the Ming Dynasty.[1]

From the Song to the Ming dynasties, Mashan Town in Jianyang was an

1Fang Yanshou. "Development and Influence of Jianyang's Role as a Book-Engraving Center in External Dissemination." *Research on the History of Chinese Publishing*, no. 3, 2019, pp.7–21.

important center for woodblock printing and book publishing. Some scholars argue that by the late Ming period, a unified book market had emerged across central and southern China, with Jianyang, Suzhou, Hangzhou, and Nanjing serving as its major hubs. Jianyang's rise as a printing center since the Song Dynasty can be attributed to two primary factors: the local abundance of natural resources necessary for book production, and a plentiful supply of labor. As a result, the cost of producing Jianyang editions was significantly lower than that in other regions. However, this does not imply, as some critics have claimed, that Jianyang editions were cheap and of inferior quality. A wealth of historical evidence indicates that Jianyang imprints encompassed a wide variety of genres, including Confucian classics, historical works, medical texts, encyclopedic compilations for daily use, elementary primers, operatic and lyrical collections, and historical novels. These publications not only had a profound influence on the general readership across China, but also traveled overseas, impacting countries such as Japan and Korea.[1]

2.Woodblock Printing in Sibao

Sibao, located in present-day Sibao Town, Liancheng County, lies at the junction of four counties in western Fujian—Liancheng, Changting, Ninghua, and Qingliu. It represents a pan-regional village cluster that transcends administrative boundaries. The mountainous area around Sibao was rich in timber and had a well-established paper-making industry, which provided the essential resources for the rise of its printing sector. By the Wanli reign of the Ming Dynasty, Sibao had already begun engaging in woodblock printing and publishing. After more than a century of growth, the industry reached its peak during the Qianlong, Jiaqing, and Daoguang reigns of the Qing Dynasty. In the early 19th century, the number of local printing workshops expanded

1(America) Chia Lucille. *Printing for Profit: The Commercial Publishers of Jianyang, Fujian (11th -17th Centuries).* Translated by Qiu Kui, et al. Fujian People's Publishing House, 2019, pp.187-188.

from the original 13 to an additional 46.[1] During the Qing period, Sibao in Liancheng, along with Xuwan (Jiangxi), Hankou, and Beijing, was regarded as one of the four major printing centers in China.[2] Book merchants in Sibao dominated southern China's publishing and book distribution network, giving rise to the saying, "Monopolizing the South, selling books across the entire nation."[3]

The Papermaking Workshop in Liancheng

Sibao's book trade was typically managed through family-operated businesses. The local clans, especially the Zou and Ma families, built extensive family-based commercial networks. The trade routes and primary markets developed by Sibao merchants covered major parts of Fujian, Jiangsu, Zhejiang, Hubei, Hunan, Jiangxi, Guangdong, and Guangxi. These areas included prefectural capitals, county seats, market towns, and rural areas. Starting in the early Qing period, Sibao held a book market every year after the Lantern Festival, attracting book dealers from Guangdong, Jiangxi,

1(America) Brooks Joanna. *Cultural Trade: Book Commerce in Sibao from the Qing to the Republican Era*. Translated by Liu Yonghua et al., Peking University Press, 2015, p.86.

2 Zou Risheng. "Sibao: One of China's Four Major Woodblock Printing Centers." *Historical Materials of Liancheng*, vol. 4, 1985, p.102.

3 Ibid.

Zhejiang, Guangxi, Hunan, and other parts of Fujian. These provinces were also the main destinations where Zou and Ma family merchants sent their clansmen to sell books. The dealers would either set up permanent bookstalls, carry books on shoulder poles from town to town, engage in wholesale trade, or sign futures contracts with buyers. Through these diverse and cross-regional business strategies, Sibao book merchants established a vast and intricate book distribution network across southern China. Sibao books and booksellers also entered maritime trade networks, exporting to Vietnam, Java, Siam (Thailand), and other parts of Southeast Asia.

The Woodblock Printing Exhibition Hall in Sibao

The publications produced in Sibao encompassed a wide variety of genres. According to Cynthia J. Brokaw's statistical analysis of genealogies, account books, and surviving woodblocks, woodblock printing in Sibao could be broadly categorized into three main types: educational texts, instructional manuals, and literary works. Educational texts primarily included elementary primers, character compilations, basic learning materials, anthologies of poetry, and Confucian classics such as the *Collected*

Annotations of the Four Books and early childhood moral texts like the *Standards for Being a Good Student and Child.* Instructional manuals comprised medical books, pharmacological texts, almanacs, practical reference works, moral books and family ritual texts—materials essential for daily life among the common people, such as *Essential Formulas Worth a Thousand in Gold* and *Everyday Use for the Household.* Literary works included opera librettos, novels, poetry collections, anthologies of painting and calligraphy, and lyric songbooks. Notable examples were *The Literary Mind and the Carving of Dragons* and the *Songs of Chu*. Interestingly, even proscribed works from the Ming and Qing dynasties, such as *The Plum in the Golden Vase*, were among the titles printed in Sibao. In addition, the commercial distribution networks of Sibao publishers exhibited a notable correlation with the migration routes of Hakka communities during the Ming and Qing dynasties. Their primary markets were typically located in inland regions near urban centers, which also coincided with major areas of Hakka settlement. In addition to the popular titles mentioned above, Sibao booksellers also printed specialized books for Hakka readers, such as *Everyday Characters for Use* by Ma Linlan Workshop and *A Year's Worth of Everyday Characters* compiled by Lin Baoshu of Wuping. These books were written in the Hakka dialect using simple and accessible language, which contributed to their widespread circulation in Hakka regions.

The Zou family of Sibao primarily specialized in woodblock printing.[1] From the mid-Ming to the early Qing periods, due to the imperial maritime ban , Sibao book merchants operated exclusively within domestic markets. However, from the late 17th to early 18th centuries, Southeast Asia rapidly flourished as a hub of Sino-Western commerce. In the competition between

1Chen Zhiping, and Zheng Zhenman. "A Study of Clan Merchants in Sibao, Western Fujian, During the Qing Dynasty." *Researches in Chinese Economic History*, no. 2, 1988, pp.93–109.

the British and the Dutch over the Wuyi tea trade, the Dutch ultimately prevailed, and Batavia (present-day Jakarta) emerged as a key maritime trade center. On the first day of the ninth lunar month in 1684, the Qing government issued an edict to "open maritime trade". By 1689, indirect trade between China and Batavia had commenced. The Dutch East India Company relied on Chinese junks to carry out import and export trade between Fujian, Guangdong, and Batavia. These favorable conditions created new opportunities for Fujian merchants to enter overseas markets. Against this broader historical trend, Sibao clan-based merchants began expanding their markets overseas in the late 17th to early 18th centuries. In the 33rd year of the Kangxi reign (1694), the 17th-generation descendants of the Zou family—Zou Xinguo (courtesy name Juchen) and Zou Jingguo (courtesy name Weichen)—were the first to explore the market in Siam.[1] In addition, Zou Shizhong traveled to Ba Kingdom[2] (referring to Batavia and its surrounding areas, approximately modern-day Jakarta), accompanied by his uncles and younger clansmen. In the 39th year of the Kangxi reign (1700), Zou Zhangguo (courtesy name Feichen), Xinguo, Shizhong (courtesy name Guanhui), and Zongfa (courtesy names Shibai and Xingzu) ventured abroad with books to sell in Ba Kingdom. Zou Zhangguo even married a local woman and had two sons, both of whom remained in the region. Many from the Zou clan followed suit and settled in Southeast Asia. His experience demonstrates how the Zou clan merchants had begun integrating into local societies. By the generation of the18th-descendant Zou Shizhong, this integration had deepened. According to the records of the family genealogy, Shizhong traveled extensively among the "islands of Siam and Ba Kingdom."

1Editorial Committee of the Sixth Revision of the Zou Family Genealogy, Wuge, Sibao, Liancheng, Tingzhou, Fujian Province. *Genealogy of the Zou Family of Fanyang (Dunben Version)*, vol. 3, *Selected Historical Records and Annual Highlights*. 1996.

2 Longzu Branch of the Zou Clan in Sibao, Changting. *Genealogy of the Zou Family of Fanyang,* fifth Revision, vol. 33, *The Life of Zou Shizhong*. 1947.

Though local "languages, clothing, and diets differed markedly from those of the Central Plains," Shizhong, through his talent and character, earned their respect over long-term interaction. "The locals became close to him and admired his loyalty to the country, so that they were in complete harmony with him and regarded him as a bosom friend."[1]

The Process of Woodblock Printing

1Longzu Branch of the Zou Clan in Sibao, Changting. *Genealogy of the Zou Family of Fanyang,* fifth Revision, vol. 33, *The Life of Zou Shizhong*. 1947.

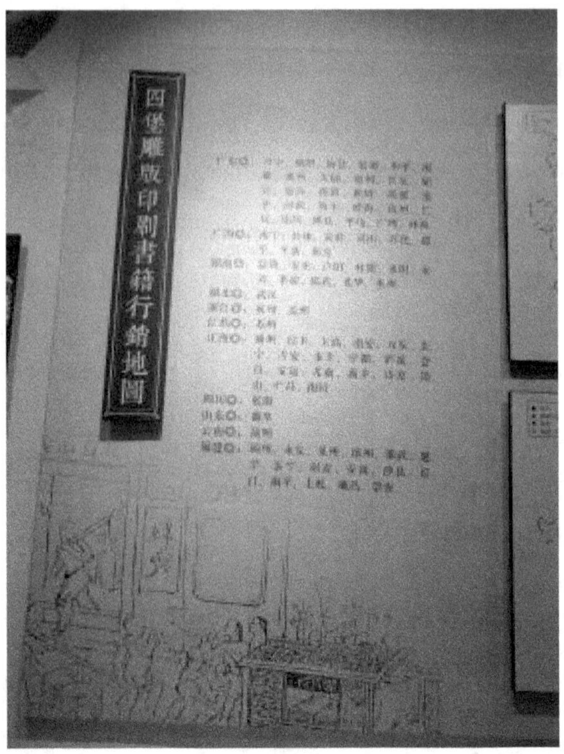

The Domestic Distribution Map of the Printed Books by Sibao

Ancient Woodblocks from the Exhibition Hall of the Collection of Sibao Woodblock Printing in China

In the late Qing period, Sibao's decline was hastened by multiple factors:

the disruption caused by the Taiping Rebellion, the successive emergence of lithographic and lead-type printing technologies, and Sibao's failure to keep pace with technological advancements or acquire the technical knowledge and machinery necessary for mechanized printing. During the era of the imperial civil service examinations, Sibao's primary printing output consisted of examination preparation texts. However, with the abolition of the imperial examination system in 1905 and the emergence of modern educational institutions, Sibao quickly lost its competitive edge in the publishing market for modern textbooks and reading materials. As a result, during the late Qing and early Republican periods, Sibao—positioned on both the geographic and cultural periphery—inevitably entered a period of decline. Branch outlets outside the region began to break free from the control of the family-run publishing houses, transforming into independent bookstores or retail distributors of modern publishing institutions. The last few printing shops struggled to survive until just before 1942, when Sibao's centuries-old woodblock printing industry came to a quiet end.

Section 2 Hinterland Guilds Spreading Across the Coastal Regions

In transshipment trade activities, guilds and merchant associations played crucial roles as important commercial organizations. Guilds were geographically-based entities that arose to meet the practical commercial or social needs of certain stages in the traditional society, and they served vital social and economic functions.[1] Merchant associations, on the other hand, were groups of merchants formed around economic activities, typically consisting of people from the same region or involved in similar trades. The physical buildings of these guilds were often funded and constructed by merchants of the same locality, who also used these guild halls as a base for their commercial activities, leading to the formation of merchant associations. During the Ming and Qing dynasties, merchant associations from various regions established guild halls in key port cities along the Maritime Silk Road and inland cities. As paper merchants from Tingzhou and Longyan regions in Chaozhou stated during the Tongzhi reign, "The establishment of a guild hall serves four main purposes: to foster local fellowship and kinship, to honor gods with reverence, to maintain order and propriety in relations, and to ensure trust through scheduled meetings."[2] Guilds not only facilitated trade activities for merchants in foreign lands but also played an important role in strengthening bonds among merchants, reinforcing their identity, promoting education, and encouraging healthy competition. Merchants from the hinterland of the Maritime Silk Road also expanded their networks, leaving traces in various regions across the country. Additionally, as trade hubs, guild

---

1(America) He Bingdi. *A Study on the History of Chinese Guild Halls*. Zhonghua Book Company, 2017, p. 1.

2(Qing) Tang Shibiao. *Gazetteer of the Tinglong Guild Hall in Chaozhou*, vol. 2, book 3 of the *Series on the Compilation and Research of Mazu Documents*. Strait Literature and Art Publishing House, 2017, pp.115–242.

halls were established by merchants from other provinces and regions in the hinterland of the Maritime Silk Road.

In the Jiangnan region, from the late Ming period onward, the development of the regional commodity economy transformed it into a competitive field for merchant associations from various parts of the country. Merchants from the hinterland of the Maritime Silk Road also thrived in this environment. During the Jiajing and Wanli periods of the Ming Dynasty, the Jiangnan region served as the main transit point for goods being transferred from Fujian to northern China. After the Qing Dynasty was established, Fujian merchants, including those from the Maritime Silk Road hinterland, became highly active in business activities in Jiangnan. In Suzhou, the most prosperous and wealthy city in Jiangnan during the Ming and Qing dynasties, merchants from the hinterland of the the Maritime Silk Road formed the Shaowu, Yanjian, and Tingzhou merchant associations. Both the Shaowu and Tingzhou merchant associations established guild halls during the Kangxi period, while the Yanjian merchants pooled resources to purchase land and build a guild hall during the Qianlong period. After the opening of the seas in the Kangxi period, Shanghai quickly rose as a central hub for trade connecting the north and the south. Merchants from Jianning, situated in the upper reaches of the Minjiang River, and Tingzhou, formed the Jian-Ting merchant association, mainly engaging in the trade of paper, palm, and indigo. In modern times, timber became the main industry for the Jian-Ting merchant association, which also expanded into tobacco and medicinal materials. During the Jiaqing and Daoguang periods of the Qing Dynasty, the Jian-Ting guild hall was established. Merchants from the hinterland of the Maritime Silk Road were also present in Hangzhou, Nanjing, and other cities, engaging in industries such as timber and paper, although their numbers were relatively smaller compared to other Fujian merchants.

In addition to the Jiangnan region, guilds were also gradually established during the Ming and Qing dynasties in key trading centers long operated by merchants from the Maritime Silk Road hinterland, such as

Chaozhou and Fuzhou. Among them, Tingzhou merchants stood out, and they established guilds in many cities across the country. Merchants from Tingzhou and Longyan established warehouses and trading firms in Chaozhou to serve as hubs for the export of native products from Tingzhou and Longyan and the import of salt and sugar. To maintain the ritual practices of the merchant association, Tingzhou paper merchants opened the Lianfeng Guild during the Yongzheng period, focusing on paper products "made from bamboo shoots from the various mountains of Tingzhou. In years of abundance, the paper is plentiful, but in years of scarcity, it declines. The guild sell various paper products such as *Yukou*, *Shanbei*, *Guanbian*, *Gongxin*, *Shouben* and *Gaolian* across rural areas, other regions, and even in the Guangdong and Zhaoqing areas."[1] During the Qianlong period, merchants from Tingzhou and Longyan jointly built the Tinglong Guild. Internally, the guild was divided into sub-groups based on locality, each of which contributed financially to the guild and participated in ritual offerings and ancestral sacrifices with their own designated resources.[2] This system balanced the overall interests and individual competition, helping the Tinglong merchants solidify their position in Chaozhou's commercial activities.

1 *Gazetteer of Zhongyi Township, Foshan*, vol. 6, *Industry* (Republican period). Quoted in *Economic Materials from Inscriptions in Foshan During the Ming and Qing Dynasties*. Guangdong People's Publishing House, 1987, p.350.

2 (Qing) Tang Shibiao. *Gazetteer of the Tinglong Guild Hall in Chaozhou*, vol. 2, book 3 of the *Series on the Compilation and Research of Mazu Documents*. Strait Literature and Art Publishing House, 2017, pp.115–242.

Table 3-2 Overview of Tingzhou Guild Halls

Name of Guild Hall	Location	Establishment Year	Target Audience
Tinglong Guild Hall	Chaozhou	28th year of the Qianlong reign (1763)	Merchants from Tingzhou and Longyan
Jianting Guild Hall	Shanghai	29th year of the Daoguang reign (1849)	Paper merchants from Jianning and Tingzhou
Tingzhou Guild Hall	Zhapu, Jiaxing	4th year of the Yongzheng reign (1726)	Indigo merchants from Tingzhou
Tingzhou Guild Hall in Tamsui (Yinshan Temple)	Tamsui, Taiwan	2nd year of the Daoguang reign (1822)	Fellow villagers from Tingzhou
Tingzhou Guild Hall	Wenzhou	Late Qing period	Merchants from Tingzhou
Tingzhou Guild Hall	Taijiang, Fuzhou	-	Paper and indigo merchants from Tingzhou
Tingzhou Guild Hall	South Gate, Gulou, Fuzhou	Qianlong period	Scholars and merchants from Tingzhou
Tingzhou Guild Hall	Taxiang alley, Gulou, Fuzhou,	Early Qing period	Scholars and merchants from Tingzhou

In the 28th year of the Qianlong reign(1763), merchants from Tingzhou and Longyan established the Tinglong Guild Hall, located west of the Kaiyuan Street in Chaozhou. According to the *Gazetteer of the Tinglong Guild Hall in Chaozhou*, "Tingzhou and Longyan are closely connected, situated in the upper reaches of Fujian, neighboring the Chaozhou region to the south. The Tingjiang River flows southward to Chaozhou, making waterborne travel highly convenient."[1] In the early years of the Republic of China, the Tinglong Guild Hall established the Tinglong School for migrant

1(Qing) Tang Shibiao. *Gazetteer of the Tinglong Guild Hall in Chaozhou*, vol. 2, book 3 of the *Series on the Compilation and Research of Mazu Documents*. Strait Literature and Art Publishing House, 2017, pp.115–242.

children in Chaozhou, which specifically enrolled the children of merchants from Tingzhou and Longyan. By the 24th year of the Republic of China (1935), the school had grown to eight classes with more than 300 students, indicating the vibrant commercial ties between Tinglong merchants and Chaozhou.

The Jianting Guild in Shanghai was founded by merchants from Jianning and Tingzhou in Fujian. During the Ming and Qing dynasties, Shanghai emerged as the national distribution center for handmade paper products. Paper from Jianning in northern Fujian and Tingzhou in western Fujian—such as *Maobian*, *Yukou*, and *Haizhi*—was widely traded in Shanghai.

Zhapu in Jiaxing, located on the northern shore of Hangzhou Bay, served as the maritime outlet of the Hangjia Plain and enjoyed strategic advantages of "linking to both Shanghai and Hangzhou, and providing access to the Taihu Lake area." During the Song and Yuan periods, Zhapu Port thrived, and traders from Guangdong, Fujian, Taiwan, Japan, Ryukyu, Annam, Siam, Java, Luzon, and other countries and regions conducted business there. During the Ming and Qing periods, merchants from Tingzhou established commercial activities in Zhapu. The Tingzhou Guild Hall in Zhapu was located in the Zongguan Alley just outside the South Gate of Zhapu in Jiaxing, and was also known as the Yinjiang Guild Hall. The hall worshipped the deity Mazu. In the 14th year of the Qianlong reign (1749), Tingzhou merchant He Yuanrui and others rebuilt the guild hall. Since most Tingzhou merchants in Jiaxing specialized in the indigo trade, the hall was also known colloquially as the "Zhapu Indigo Guild Hall," making it the only Fujianese regional association in the Hangjia Plain. It was later maintained by fellow Tingzhou natives from Wenzhou.

The Tingzhou Guild Hall in Tamsui, Taiwan, is the only surviving Hakka temple from western Fujian in the region. The main deity enshrined is

Dingguang Buddha, a protective figure for the Hakka people. In the second year of the Daoguang reign (1822), Tingzhou native Zhang Minggang funded and oversaw the construction of a temple to honor Dingguang Buddha, naming it after Yingshan Temple in Yongding County, Fujian. Upon completion, the temple also served as a residence for newly arrived Tingzhou migrants engaged in farming and commerce in Tamsui, and thus became known as the Tingzhou Guild Hall.

Fuzhou, the political center of Fujian and an important trade port along the southeastern coast of China, served as a gateway for the Maritime Silk Road. During the Ming and Qing dynasties, Tingzhou merchants sold goods such as handmade paper, indigo, and grain in Fuzhou, which were then exported through the port to other cities within China and overseas markets. A significant number of Tingzhou merchants settled in Fuzhou and established three Tingzhou guild halls. Among them, the earliest, the Tingzhou Guild Hall in Taijiang, was initially organized by merchants from Changting and Shanghang, who were involved in the paper and indigo industries. Later, the "paper and indigo guild hall" expanded into the "four-county guild hall," and eventually evolved into a formal Tingzhou Guild Hall. The guild hall near the South Gate of Gulou served as a residence for Tingzhou scholars taking the imperial exam and merchants conducting business in Fuzhou. Another hall in Taxiang Alley was originally built in the early Qing Dynasty and underwent renovations during the Qianlong and Jiaqing periods, and again in the early Republic of China.

These guild halls facilitated mutual support and economic cooperation among merchants of the same regional origin, playing a crucial role in the formation and cohesion of merchant associations. Overall, merchants from the hinterland of the Maritime Silk Road typically established guild halls composed of people from the same county or region. Some halls were organized by merchants from adjacent regions or within the same trade, leading to associations such as Yanjian, Jianting, and Tinglong. Guild halls also encouraged solidarity among neighboring regional merchant groups. The Tingzhou Guild Hall in Suzhou, built in the 47th year of the Kangxi reign (1708), was originally founded by Shanghang paper merchants. In the mid-19th century, the hall was destroyed during the Taiping Rebellion and its assets were lost. Later, Luo Shaogeng, a local official from Shanghang, led efforts to recover the property and rebuild the hall. However, by this time, Shanghang's paper industry was in decline, and the reconstruction of the hall could no longer rely solely on paper merchants. Luo Shaogeng therefore expanded the guild's membership beyond Shanghang to include merchants from all counties within Tingzhou Prefecture. As the tobacco industry in Yongding County was thriving and many Yongding merchants were active in Suzhou, merchants from both counties agreed to jointly rebuild the hall after consultations. The new Tingzhou Guild Hall, completed in the 13th year of the Guangxu reign (1887), retained its original name. The history of the Tingzhou Guild Hall in Suzhou from the early Qing through the late Qing illustrates that due to fluctuations in commercial development, the dominant merchant group within a guild was not fixed to a particular locale or trade. However, the guild itself remained a central and enduring institution in the organization of merchant associations.

Chapter 4
The Impact of Maritime Silk Road Development on Economies in Mountainous Regions

Since the establishment of the Maritime Silk Road, ports in coastal Fujian have played a vital role in foreign trade and exchange. On the one hand, the abundant resources of inland regions such as western and northern Fujian were exported overseas via coastal ports, thereby promoting the economic development of the hinterland. On the other hand, foreign goods imported through these ports were transported into the hinterland, influencing the industrial structure and daily lives of the local populations. Furthermore, engaging in maritime trade with overseas countries and regions required courage and acumen. This maritime spirit of seeking livelihoods from the sea had a profound influence on the cultural development of inland regions.

Section 1 Port Development Driving Hinterland Economic Prosperity

I. The Influence of Coastal Port Development on Hinterland Economies During the Tang, Song, and Yuan Dynasties

During the Tianbao era of the Tang Dynasty, the disruption of the overland Silk Road to the Western Regions necessitated reliance on the Maritime Silk Road for foreign trade. Situated along the southeastern coast, Fuzhou emerged as a pivotal port for overseas commerce. Under the governance of Wang Shenzhi during the late Tang and Five Dynasties period, Wuzhu Port and Gantang Port were developed as Fuzhou's inner and outer harbors. He actively attracted "foreign merchants from overseas" to promote maritime trade, thereby laying the foundation for Fuzhou Port's role as a pivotal hub in north–south maritime trade.[1] Thereafter, the scope of Fuzhou's overseas trade gradually expanded. Building upon existing maritime routes to the Indo-China Peninsula and the Malay Archipelago, three new trade routes were established. The first route extended northward from Fuzhou Port through the East China Sea and the Yellow Sea to Japan and the Silla Kingdom (in present-day Korea). The second route sailed southward from Fuzhou Port through the South China Sea to India and the Dashi Kingdom (in present-day Arab regions). The third was a tributary route connecting Fuzhou to Dengzhou and Laizhou via Wenzhou, Taizhou, and Mingzhou. During the reign of Wang Yanxi, a specialized agency for overseeing overseas trade, the Maritime Trade Supervisorate, was established in Fuzhou. In the second year of Yuanyou under Emperor Zhezong of the Song Dynasty (1087), another Maritime Trade Supervisorate was also

1Xie Zaihua. "On the Importance of Fuzhou in the 'Ancient Maritime Silk Road'." *Fujian Historical Records*, no.2, 2015, p.18.

established in Quanzhou, propelling Quanzhou Port to rapid development and eventually surpassing Fuzhou Port as the region's major maritime hub. During the Song Dynasty, Quanzhou maintained six major maritime trade routes:

(1) Quanzhou — Wanlishi Reef (Xisha Islands) — Champa;

(2) Quanzhou — Champa — Sanfoqi (comprising Sumatra, Java, and Javanese territories) — Boni (Kalimantan);

(3) Quanzhou — the South China Sea — Sanfoqi — Malacca — India — the Persian Gulf;

(4) Quanzhou — India — the Persian Gulf — the Gulf of Aden — Bipaluo (Somalia) — Cengba (Zanzibar);

(5) Quanzhou — Mayi (Mindoro) — Sanyu (Calamian Islands, Palawan, and Busanga);

(6) Quanzhou — Mingzhou — Goryeo — Japan.[1]

The rulers of Yuan Dynasty placed great importance on overseas trade, which led to the further development of Quanzhou Port, establishing it as one of the world's leading maritime trading hubs of the time.

The relative stability and frequent economic and cultural exchanges during the Song and Yuan periods fostered active overseas trade in Fujian. Ports like Quanzhou and Fuzhou became crucial export hubs, facilitating the shipment of products from northern Fujian, including tea, textiles, handmade paper, and ceramics, to international markets. The proliferation of overseas trade spurred the development of local markets and economic prosperity in the hinterland. During the Song and Yuan dynasties, tea drinking became a prevailing cultural trend. Northern Fujian emerged as a major tea-producing region, with Longfeng Compressed Tea Cakes from Beiyuan in Jianzhou

1 Huang Tianzhu. "Quanzhou Port and the Ancient Silk and Porcelain Route." *Theoretical Reference*, no.2, 2016, p.64.

gaining widespread fame as a top-grade tribute tea. Due to its superior quality, tea from northern Fujian was exported in large quantities. It was transported via the Minjiang River to Fuzhou Port and then shipped through the ports of Fuzhou and Quanzhou to countries such as Japan, Goryeo and those on the Malay Peninsula. The ceramic industry, particularly the production of Jianyang black-glazed teacup, reached its zenith during this period, with significant exports to countries and regions such as Japan, Korea, and Southeast Asia via Fuzhou Port and Quanzhou Port. In addition, during the Song Dynasty, northern Fujian was renowned for its production of silk, gauze, linen, cloth, hemp, paper, and printed books, all of which were widely exported overseas through the rising maritime ports of Fuzhou and Quanzhou.

The Qianyang Ancient Commercial Street in Pucheng Emerged During the Song and Yuan Dynasties[1]

1 Image source: Wu Bangcai, editor-in-chief. *History of the Development of Fujian*

With the development of overseas trade in the Song and Yuan periods, numerous markets and commercial towns emerged along the key water and land transportation routes of northern Fujian. Some towns with thriving commerce grew into new counties due to population growth and economic prosperity. For example, Zhenghe County was established during the Northern Song Dynasty from a combination of towns, tax stations, and "a subdivided county".[1] Jian'ou, located at the confluence of the Nanpu Creek, Chongyang Creek, and Songxi Creek, became an important distribution hub and commercial center due to the export of Beiyuan tribute tea, Jian brocade, and Jianyang black-glazed teacup. During the Yuan Dynasty, overseas trade in northern Fujian remained vibrant. The Italian traveler Marco Polo, in his travel accounts, described the region: "Arriving at the grand and prosperous Jianning Prefecture, where the people are mainly engaged in commerce and handicrafts, producing large quantities of silk… passing through many towns, there are many merchants and artisans, as well as abundant goods and a great deal of silk."[2]

II. The Influence of Coastal Port Development on Hinterland Economies from the Ming Dynasty to the Republic of China

In the early Ming Dynasty, a strict maritime prohibition policy was enforced, under which Quanzhou Port was only permitted to trade with the Ryukyu Kingdom. In the 10th year of the Chenghua reign (1474), the Maritime Trade Supervisorate in Fujian was relocated from Quanzhou to Fuzhou, leading to the gradual decline of Quanzhou Port's status in overseas trade. During the Qing Dynasty, Xiamen Port gradually replaced Quanzhou

---

Merchants: Nanping Volume. Xiamen University Press, 2016, p.62.

1 Wu Bangcai, editor-in-chief. *History of the Development of Fujian Merchants: Nanping Volume*. Xiamen University Press, 2016, p.61.

2 Ibid., p.62.

Port in terms of commercial activity, further accelerating the decline of the latter. From the mid-Ming period onward, Fuzhou Port emerged as a major hub for foreign trade in Fujian, maintaining frequent trade with the Ryukyu Kingdom and engaging in active commercial exchanges with various overseas countries. During this time, products from northern Fujian—such as tea, rice, Chinese fir timber,and handmade paper—were transported down the Minjiang River to Fuzhou, and then shipped overseas to Japan, Southeast Asia, and Europe. Among these exports, tea saw the most rapid growth and became the most significant commodity exported from northern Fujian. According to *The General History of the Qing Dynasty*, "In the 13th year of the Chongzhen reign (1640) in the late Ming , red tea was introduced to Britain via the Dutch."[1] The active overseas trade through Fuzhou Port in the late Ming and early Qing periods further stimulated economic development in the northern Fujian hinterland, leading to the rise of numerous renowned merchants and commercial enterprises, such as the *Maobian* Paper of Tongshunxing in Shunchang and the Yu family's Qinyoutang publishing house in Jianyang. In the 22nd year of the Qianlong reign (1757), the abolition of Fukien Maritime Customs restricted the foreign trade of Fuzhou Port. As a result, tea from northern Fujian had to be transported overland to Guangzhou for export. After the opening of treaty ports, Fuzhou Port was reopened to international trade, and once again, local products from northern Fujian were shipped along the Minjiang River and exported overseas via Fuzhou. From the Xianfeng reign to early Guangxu reign, the export volume of tea, handmade paper, and timber from northern Fujian increased significantly. Jian'ou, a major commercial center along the Jianxi creek, witnessed commercial prosperity, with over 3,000 trading firms operating at its peak. Meanwhile, Yangkou Town, previously a relatively

1Xiao Yishan. *General History of the Qing Dynasty,* vol. 2. Commercial Press, 2019, p.847.

undeveloped area, became a major trade hub along the Futun Creek due to its role in the concentration and export of local specialties. However, after the Opium War, the massive influx of foreign goods such as western cloth, tobacco, and matches severely impacted local agriculture and handicraft industries. In particular, as tea exports declined, northern Fujian's commerce and industry entered a period of further decline.

During the Song and Yuan dynasties, handmade paper, timber, and other products from the Tingjiang River Basin in western Fujian were primarily transported downstream along the Tingjiang River to Chaozhou, and from there they were re-exported via the Chaoshan region to Southeast Asia. Imported goods from overseas were likewise carried upstream along the Tingjiang River to Tingzhou. In the early Ming Dynasty, the implementation of maritime prohibitions led to the rise of Yuegang Port in Zhangzhou, which flourished through private maritime trade and was known in the mid-Ming period as "Little Suzhou." After Yongding was established as a county in the 14th year of the Chenghua reign (1478), transportation routes between Tingzhou and Zhangzhou improved significantly, particularly with the opening of the Jiulong River waterway, which further strengthened connections between inland Tingzhou and the coastal regions in Zhangzhou. The prosperity of private maritime trade in Zhangzhou stimulated the cultivation, processing, and export of cash crops in the mountainous areas of western Fujian, promoting the development of a commercialized agricultural economy. Improvements in land and water transportation linking the Jiulong River Basin, Hanjiang River Basin, and Tingjiang River Basin facilitated increasingly frequent commercial exchanges among Tingzhou, Zhangzhou, and Chaozhou. Longyan, situated at the intersection of Tingzhou and Zhangzhou, emerged as a key distribution center for goods moving between the coastal and inland regions. In the early Qing Dynasty, Yuegang Port was gradually replaced by Xiamen Port, which had functioned during the Song and Yuan periods as a subordinate port to Quanzhou. After the Qing government's unification of Taiwan, Fukien Maritime Customs was established in the 23rd year of the Kangxi reign (1684), with Xiamen designated as "the primary customs port for all maritime vessels engaged in interprovincial and overseas trade, where duties were collected by official authorities." In the first year of the Jiaqing reign (1796), Xiamen had become a major international trade center, engaging with more than 30 countries and regions across the Eastern and Western Oceans.[1] From the Qing to the Republican period, handmade paper, tobacco, and tea from western Fujian dominated the region's exports via Xiamen Port. After the 22nd year of the Daoguang reign (1842), local paper products such as *Yukou* paper and *Maobian* paper produced in Changting were transported by land and water to Zhangzhou and then exported in large volumes via Xiamen Port, with an annual output value exceeding 2 million silver dollars. Liancheng's paper industry reached its zenith in the late Qing Dynasty, producing large quantities of high-quality, white *Dalian* paper suitable for cigarette rolling, which was exported extensively to Southeast Asia. *Xuanzhi* paper was exported to Japan, while *Yuban* paper and *Piaogong* paper were shipped to the Philippines, including Luzon Island and other regions.[2] There were two main export routes for Liancheng's paper products: One route passed through Fengshi in Yongding to Chaoshan, and from there to Vietnam, Thailand, and the Philippines; the other went through Zhangping and Punan to Zhangzhou, and then to Japan and Southeast Asia via Xiamen. After the opening of the treaty ports, Longtian's *Yukou* paper was exported in large quantities to Singapore, Malaysia, Indonesia, Siam (Thailand), the Philippines, and other

1Zheng Naihui, Gao Xiangfeng, and Jiang Ling. "The Historical Tea Trade Routes of Fujian Ports." *Fujian Tea Industry*, no.6, 2015, p.51.

2 Cai Lixiong, editor-in-chief. A *History of Commerce in Western Fujian.* Xiamen University Press, 2014, p.103.

countries.[12] The expansion and opening of coastal ports spurred the overseas export of western Fujian's paper, which in turn promoted the growth of the region's papermaking industry. Numerous commercial firms emerged, such as Yitai, Guilan, and Xiangxing in Liancheng. From the Qianlong reign to Guangxu reign in the Qing Dynasty, large quantities of Yongding's fine-cut tobacco were sold nationwide and to Southeast Asia. The tobacco exported to Southeast Asia was mainly transported by land to Zhangzhou and then shipped via Xiamen to Taiwan and other Southeast Asian destinations. Before the 15th year of the Republic of China (1926), Yongding exported 50,000 to 60,000 crates (1,562.5–1,875 tons) of fine-cut tobacco annually, with a total value exceeding 2 million silver dollars.[3] In addition, from the Kangxi reign to Daoguang reign of the Qing Dynasty, tea produced in Ningyang County was exported overseas via Chaozhou and Xiamen for a period of time. During the Tongzhi and Guangxu reigns, the oolong tea produced in Longyan County was likewise exported in large quantities via Chaozhou and Xiamen to Southeast Asia. The growth of overseas trade also drove economic development at key transportation nodes and market towns along the Tingjiang River and Jiulong River. For instance, during the Jiajing reign of the Ming Dynasty, the city of Changting had three main streets and four marketplaces within its walls, and 11 streets beyond the city walls. In the Qing Dynasty, Shanghang County was home to numerous forwarding firms dealing in paper, timber, Beijing dry fruits, and more. In the early Republican era, there were over 700 shops along the Tingjiang River banks in the urban area of Shanghang. Although only 220 meters long, Zhetan Street in

1Zhou Xuexiang. "The Circulation of Commodities and Urban–Rural Markets in Hakka Regions Along the Fujian–Guangdong Border During the Ming and Qing Dynasties." *Research in Chinese Economic History*, no.2, 2007, p. 95.

2Huang Majin, editor-in-chief. *A History of Papermaking in Changting*. China Light Industry Press, 1992, p.35.

3 Cai Lixiong, editor-in-chief. A *History of Commerce in Western Fujian*. Xiamen University Press, 2014, p.108.

Yongding hosted over 80 stores dealing in paper, tobacco, cloth, and general goods. After Xiamen was opened to trade in the early Qing Dynasty, Fengshi in Yongding rapidly developed into a center of entrepot trade. By the late Qing and early Republican periods, streets in Fengshi housed over 320 transshipment firms (known as *guozai hang*), and its seven wooden-dock wharves accommodated nearly 200 vessels daily. The commercial tax bureau in Fengshi generated an annual revenue of 15,457 silver dollars, equivalent to 68.7% of the total collected in Shanghang County.[1][2] These figures reflect the vibrant commercial scene in Fengshi at the time.

1Zhou Xuexiang. "The Circulation of Commodities and Urban–Rural Markets in Hakka Regions Along the Fujian–Guangdong Border During the Ming and Qing Dynasties." *Research in Chinese Economic History*, no.2, 2007, p. 100.

2Cai Lixiong, editor-in-chief. A *History of Commerce in Western Fujian.* Xiamen University Press, 2014, p.116.

Section 2 The Transformation of the Economic Structure of the Hinterland by Foreign Commodities

Since the opening of the overland and maritime Silk Roads during the Han Dynasty, commercial exchanges between China and regions such as the Western Regions, the states in the South China Sea, and the Indian subcontinent steadily increased. During the Sui and Tang dynasties, these foreign interactions became more frequent, resulting in the introduction of numerous foreign crops into China via these routes. For example, peppers and Persian dates from Persia, *Niuma* hemp, and ginseng from Korea, lettuce from the Mediterranean, sword beans from India, and spinach from Nepal were successively introduced. From the Song, Yuan, Ming, and Qing dynasties onward, further introductions included Champa rice, sweet potatoes, corns, peanuts, potatoes, citrus fruits, and tobacco. After the Opium War, the influx of foreign goods caused considerable disruption to domestic agriculture and industry. During the Republican period, new breeds of pigs, cattle, and sheep were also introduced and crossbred with local breeds. The introduction of overseas commodities not only enriched the variety of domestic products, but also had a significant impact on the structure of local industries.

I. The Importation and Impact of Foreign Commodities Prior to the Qing Dynasty

Since the late Tang and Five Dynasties periods, two main categories of foreign products were imported into Fujian: first, luxury goods such as spices, pearls, and medicinal herbs that were tributes from countries of the South Seas; second, goods imported by private merchants from Southeast and East Asia. Tribute goods were primarily reserved for imperial use and had minimal impact on the general populace. From the Song and Yuan dynasties, as the economic center of China shifted southward, overseas trade in Fujian became increasingly vibrant, with Quanzhou Port emerging as a significant hub for foreign commerce. Fujian merchants shipped ceramics and other goods to Southeast Asia and the Arab world and returned with local products such as spices, medicinal herbs, and amber. According to historical records, over 300 types of foreign goods passed through Quanzhou Port during the Song Dynasty, including agarwood, sandalwood, ambergris, storax, cloves, pepper, mother-of-pearl, tortoiseshell, rhinoceros horn, ivory, agate, coral, refined iron, and gold and silver artifacts.[1] Most of these goods were consumed by the wealthy elite, though a portion entered the domestic markets. During the Southern Song period, Quanzhou merchants sold foreign commodities such as agarwood, borneol, imported fabrics, and sappanwood in the capital Hangzhou.[2] The influx of "foreign goods" promoted the development of processing industries for imported products.

> Within and around the capital, there were no fewer than several hundred establishments specializing in the production of gold foil and decorating with inlaid jade and gold. In the markets, where they were sold, the number of itinerant merchants and traders involved in their circulation often reached several thousand.[3]

In the early Ming Dynasty, tribute trade was dominant, and private foreign trade was strictly limited, leading to a flourishing of smuggling along the Fujian coast. Tribute items brought in by foreign countries mainly consisted

1Huang Tianzhu. "Quanzhou Port and the Ancient Maritime Silk and Porcelain Route." *Theoretical Reference*, no.2, 2016, p.64.

2(Song) Hong Mai. comp., and He Zhuo. ed. *Records of Foreign Lands*, vol. 1, *Records of Foreign Lands: Ding Volume*, scroll. 6. Zhonghua Book Company, 1982, p.588.

3(Qing) Xu Song, comp. *Collected Manuscripts of the Song Huiyao*, vol. 166, *Criminal Law II*. Zhonghua Book Company, 1957, p. 6565.

of spices, medicinal products, handicrafts, and exotic items. During the Longqing reign in Ming Dynasty (1567–1572), foreign trade policies were gradually liberalized, facilitating the integration of eastern Pacific maritime routes (e.g., Yuegang Port in Zhangzhou to the Philippines and Japan) with western Pacific maritime routes (e.g., the Philippines to Mexico), thereby forming the trans-Pacific "Galleon Trade." [1] The emergence of this transoceanic trade encouraged many merchants in coastal Fujian to resume overseas commercial activities. While exporting Chinese goods, they also introduced a wide variety of plant species from the Americas. From the Song and Yuan dynasties through the mid-Ming period, numerous foreign crops were brought back by Fujian merchants and subsequently promoted for cultivation in the inland regions of Fujian, thereby transforming the agricultural production structure of the mountainous areas.

1. Champa Rice

Rice has long been the staple grain in Fujian, and references to various rice varieties appear in numerous local gazetteers. Historical evidence indicates that, as early as the Tang Dynasty, merchants from Quanzhou conducted trade with Champa and Annam. It is likely that Champa rice was introduced into coastal Fujian via these merchants and then diffused into the inland. Champa rice, also referred to in historical texts as "Champa grain," "dryland rice," "hundred-day rice," and most commonly "Champa rice", was named after its place of origin —the ancient kingdom of Champa,[2] located in what is now south-central Vietnam. This variety was known for its early maturity, drought resistance, slender grains, and short growing cycle. According to the *History of Song Dynasty: Treatise on Food and Goods*,

1Zhou Bangshi. "Fujian's Trade and the Maritime Silk Road Before the Opium War." *Theory and Contemporary Times*, no.5, 2020, p.24.

2Zhu Xingyu. "An Analysis of the Champa Rice Issue in the Northern Song Dynasty." *Journal of Liaoning Administration Institute*, no.1, 2008, p. 83.

Emperor Zhenzong of Song dispatched officials to Fujian to procure 30,000 *hu* (a traditional unit of volume) of Champa rice because the Jiangnan, Huai, and Zhejiang regions experienced frequent droughts, which rendered water-based paddy farming unproductive. This record indicates that Champa rice was already cultivated on a considerable scale in Fujian during the early Northern Song period. Because of its drought-resistant property and short growth cycle, Champa rice was initially adopted in the coastal areas of Fujian, including Quanzhou, Zhangzhou, Xinghua (present-day Putian), and Fuzhou, and then gradually spread to the inland mountainous regions of western and northern Fujian. The hilly terrain and limited arable land in these interior regions made Champa rice especially suitable for dry upland cultivation. Since rice generally yielded higher outputs than other grains such as millet, wheat, and legumes, local populations in western Fujian began reclaiming lower hill areas to expand paddy cultivation. After the introduction of Champa rice, the sown area for rice in western and northern Fujian increased significantly, leading to higher grain production and supporting substantial population growth. During the Song Dynasty, the population in western Fujian grew rapidly. Compared with the Yuanhe era of the Tang Dynasty, the number of households in the Yuanfeng era of the Northern Song increased more than 200-fold. In the Ming Dynasty, indica rice, including both early and late-maturing varieties, was also introduced, well-suited to the region's climate and soil. By the Ming and Qing periods, northern Fujian had become a major grain-producing area in the province. Surplus grain was used in rice wine production, which in turn stimulated the growth of the local brewing industry.

2. Sweet Potatoes

Sweet potatoes, also known as red yams, yams, or *fan shu* (foreign tubers), are native to regions in South America, including present-day Mexico and Colombia. After Columbus's arrival in the Americas in the 15th century, sweet potatoes were brought back to Spain and subsequently spread to Luzon Island, the Malay Peninsula, and beyond. In the 22nd year of the Wanli reign of the Ming Dynasty (1594), Chen Zhenlong, an overseas Chinese merchant from Changle County, Fujian, and his son Chen Jinglun brought sweet potatoes from Luzon to Fujian via Quanzhou and presented them to the then Governor-General of Fujian, Jin Xuezeng. Lingshui Village in Anhai Town, Jinjiang County, was the earliest area in southern Fujian to begin cultivating sweet potatoes.[1] According to *Miscellaneous Notes on Fujian*,

> During the Wanli reign, the people of Fujian obtained sweet potatoes from foreign lands. Even barren and gravelly land was suitable for the cultivation of sweet potatoes. They were initially planted in Zhangzhou Prefecture, then gradually spread to Quanzhou, then to Putian, and more recently to Changle and Fuqing. South of the Fujian Sea lies the country of Luzon. West across the ocean lies the Western Sea, rich in gold and silver, where silver circulates like currency in China. These western countries ship gold and silver through Luzon for trade, and so many Fujian merchants trade there. The country produce red tubers that spread over mountains and fields, growing wild without cultivation. Indigenous people often gather them for food. The vines and leaves resemble those of gourds, Polygonatum, and yams, and are moist and edible—either cooked or ground into flour. The roots are like yams, squat and bird-shaped, with thin red skin that can be peeled. They

1 Huang Shuikan. "A Brief Study of Agricultural Crops Imported and Exported via Quanzhou Throughout the Dynasties." *Fujian Agricultural Science and Technology*, no.3, 1980, p.31.

> are edible raw or cooked and can also be used to brew alcohol. When eaten raw, they taste like kudzu root; when cooked, their color resembles honey, and they taste like ripe water chestnuts. When stored, they emit a sweet fragrance that fills the room.[1]

From this account, it is evident that when sweet potatoes were introduced to Fujian during the Ming Dynasty, people mistakenly believed they were native to Luzon, though they held the crop in very high regard. Sweet potatoes are drought-resistant, high-yielding, and can serve as a staple food. They can be sun-cured for storage, consumed raw or cooked, and their leaves serve as pig fodder, while the tubers can be fermented into alcohol. Once widely planted in coastal southern Fujian, the crop was then promoted in western and northern Fujian. During years of severe drought and crop failure in these mountainous regions, sweet potatoes often became a primary food source. Yields could reach 3,000–4,000 *jin* per *mu* (approximately 1,800–2,400 kg/hectare), and planting just two to three *mu* of sweet potatoes could meet the basic food needs of nearly one hundred people. If the sweet potatoes harvested in a given year were not fully consumed, they could be sliced and sun-cured during the Winter Solstice for storage, to be consumed during the following year's lean season. From the Ming and Qing periods, the cultivation of sweet potatoes in western Fujian became widespread. In Longyan Prefecture, for example, red and white varieties of sweet potatoes, with a sweet taste, were commonly grown as grain substitutes.[2] In Ningyang County and Zhangping County, sweet potatoes were also widely planted:

1(Ming) Zhou Lianggong. *Miscellaneous Notes on Fujian*, vol. 3. In *Collected Local Gazetteers of China*, photocopied edition of the Qianlong edition in Qing Dynasty. Chengwen Publishing House, 1967, p.12.

2(Qing) Peng Yantang, ed., and Chen Wenheng, comp. *Gazetteer of Longyan Prefecture* (Daoguang Edition), vol. 8, *Local Products*. Compiled in the 15th year of Daoguang reign and reprinted in the 16th year of Guangxu reign.

"Now sweet potatoes can replace grain, and people rely on them to avoid hunger." [1] Thus, for mountainous areas with limited arable land and insufficient rice production, the cultivation of sweet potatoes played a vital role in ensuring the survival of the local population.

3. Peanuts

There are two competing theories regarding the origin of peanuts: One posits that they originated in Africa, while the other attributes their origin to the West Indies of South America. During the Wanli reign of the Ming Dynasty, Fujian merchants introduced peanuts to Quanzhou from overseas, after which the crop spread across Fujian and Guangdong's coastal regions.[2] According to *Collected Writings*, authored by Wang Fengjiu in the early Qing period,

> Recently, there has appeared a crop called "*luohuasheng*" [peanut], whose stems and leaves resemble those of beans. Its flowers are also bean-like and yellow in color. It bears no fruit on its branches. Rather, when the flowers fall to the ground, they bear fruit in the soil—a curious phenomenon. The pods resemble bean shells but are slightly tougher. When roasted, they taste similar to pine nuts. This crop was introduced from central Fujian.[3]

As a drought-tolerant crop with high nutritional value, peanuts proved

---

1(Qing) Cai Shibo, ed., and Lin Dezhen et al., comps. *Gazetteer of Zhangping County* (Daoguang Edition). In *Collected Local Gazetteers of China: Compilation of Fujian Prefectural and County Gazetteers*. Shanghai Bookstore Publishing House, 2000.

2Huang Shuikan. "A Brief Study of Agricultural Crops Imported and Exported via Quanzhou Throughout the Dynasties." *Fujian Agricultural Science and Technology*, no.3, 1980, p.31.

3Wu Hai. *Inheritance and Transformation: Commercial Routes, Commodity Flows, and Regional Social Changes in the Border Areas of Jiangxi, Fujian, and Guangdong from the Ming Dynasty to the Republican Period.* MA thesis, Jiangxi Normal University, 2015, p.49.

suitable for cultivation in arid areas. However, because they could not serve as a staple food, their spread from the coastal regions of Fujian to inland areas was slower than that of sweet potatoes. After their introduction to coastal Fujian, peanuts gradually spread to inland regions such as western and northern Fujian, with Longyan County in western Fujian becoming a significant center for large-scale peanut cultivation. By the early Republican period, agricultural records noted that "grain and vegetables were the most important crops in Longyan, followed by wheat, with sweet potatoes and peanuts next in importance; cotton and sugarcane were cultivated sporadically but yielded little."[1] This indicates that peanuts had become one of the county's major crops, second only to grains and vegetables. Since the Ming Dynasty, rural townships in Longyan—such as Dachi, Yanshi, Suban, and Dongxiao—have consistently cultivated peanuts. The processing and export of peanuts developed into a key feature of the region's agricultural economy. Today, Longyan peanuts are recognized as one of the representative specialty products of western Fujian.

4. Tobacco

Tobacco originated in the Americas and Columbus observed indigenous people smoking tobacco upon his arrival. Tobacco was introduced to Spain and Portugal around 1588, and subsequently spread to France and England. In 1605, it was transmitted by the Portuguese to Turkey and India, eventually reaching Nagasaki, Japan. After its arrival in Luzon and Japan, tobacco was brought to southern Fujian during the Ming Dynasty by Fujian merchants. Upon its introduction, tobacco cultivation first took root in Zhangzhou Prefecture, where locals often planted it in rice fields. From there, it gradually

1 Ma Heming, ed., and Du Hansheng et al., comps. *Gazetteer of Longyan County* (Republican Period), vol. 17, *Industrial Gazetteer: Agriculture. In Collection of Chinese Local Gazetteers*, facsimile of the 1920 lithographic edition. Chengwen Publishing House, 1967, p.186.

spread from the coastal areas of southern Fujian to the inland regions of western and northern Fujian, as well as to eastern Guangdong, particularly the Chaoshan area. Given its high economic value, tobacco cultivation rapidly expanded across various regions in China. During the Qianlong period of the Qing Dynasty, Lu Yao authored *Treatise on Tobacco*, which states, "There is no gentleman who does not relish tobacco. Even women and children commonly carry pipes. One may go without food or drink, but never without tobacco. In social exchanges between hosts and guests, it is offered as the foremost courtesy."[1] This highlights the widespread popularity of tobacco consumption at the time.

After tobacco was introduced to western Fujian from Zhangzhou, it quickly gained prevalence across the region. According to the *Gazetteer of Ningyang County*, tobacco, "colloquially called *fen*, was first cultivated in the Chongzhen reign. Now it is widely planted."[2] This suggests that tobacco cultivation had already begun in the mountainous regions of western Fujian by the late Ming Dynasty. By the Qing Dynasty, tobacco cultivation had extended to nearly all counties in western Fujian. In Shanghang, "though arable land is scarce, people seek profit and abandon food crops to grow tobacco."[3] In Yongding, "with many mountains and little farmland, tobacco yields several times more profit than rice. It is the only local product that can

1Wu Hai. *Inheritance and Transformation: Commercial Routes, Commodity Flows, and Regional Social Changes in the Border Areas of Jiangxi, Fujian, and Guangdong from the Ming Dynasty to the Republican Period.* MA thesis, Jiangxi Normal University, 2015, p.54.

2(Qing) Dong Zhongxiu, ed., and Chen Tianshu, comp. *Gazetteer of Ningyang County* (Guangxu edition), vol. 2, *Geography: Local Products. In Collection of Chinese Local Gazetteers*, facsimile of the 1920 lithographic edition. Chengwen Publishing House, 1967.

3(Qing) Zhao Chengxiu, and Zhao Ningjing, comps. *Gazetteer of Shanghang County* (Qianlong edition), vol. 1, *Local Products.* Woodblock edition of the Qianlong reign (1753).

be sold out-of-province and sustains local finances."[1] In Changting, "the people all followed suit. In recent years, in the fertile lands of eight districts, three to four out of every ten farmers have taken up tobacco cultivation."[2] In Ninghua, "everyone grows it." In Longyan, "tobacco competes with food crops, occupying as much as half of all farmland."[3] Fujian-produced tobacco, renowned for its quality, earned the reputation of being "Fujian tobacco, preeminent under Heaven." Yongding's soil and climate were particularly suitable for tobacco cultivation, making it the center of tobacco production in western Fujian. Its fine-cut tobacco was regarded as a top-grade product with a broad export market. "Not a single household in the entire county does not grow tobacco," because "the profit from growing tobacco surpasses all other crops."[4] Local residents derived substantial profits from tobacco cultivation. The *Gazetteer of Yongding County* from the Daoguang reign notes, "The profit from tobacco planted in fertile lands is double that of grain. Four out of every ten plots are used for tobacco. After the court received its taxes, the land demonstrated its productivity, and the quality of the tobacco was outstanding. Many local residents relied on this to amass considerable wealth."[5] In the late Qing and Republican periods, however, the influx of foreign cigarettes into China led to the rise of paper-wrapped

---

1(Qing) Fang Lyujian, ed., and Wu Yifu, comp. *Gazetteer of Yongding County,* Daoguang edition, vol. 10, *Local Products*. Xiamen University Press, 2012, p.204.

2(Qing) Wang Tinglun. *Investigative Essays on the Affairs of Linting*, vol. 6, *Eight Proposals on Consulting the Benefits and Drawbacks.* In *Photographic Reprint of the Complete Library of the Four Treasuries (Wenyuan Pavilion Edition)*. Beijing Publishing House, 2000.

3 Cai Lixiong, editor-in-chief. *A Commercial History of Western Fujian.* Xiamen University Press, 2014, p.101.

4You Haihua. "Agricultural Change and Transformation in the Border Regions of Jiangxi, Fujian, and Guangdong from the Late Qing to the Republican Period." *Historical Monthly*, no.6, 2005, p.103.

5(Qing) Fang Lyujian, ed., and Wu Yifu, comp. *Gazetteer of Yongding County,*Daoguang edition, vol. 16, *Customs.* Xiamen University Press, 2012,p.279.

cigarettes. This trend significantly impacted the local tobacco industry in western Fujian, causing a decline in leaf tobacco sales and a reduction in cultivation.

During the Wanli reign of the Ming Dynasty, tobacco seeds were introduced from southern to northern Fujian's Pucheng area. Subsequently, Yanping, Shaowu, and Jianning also began cultivating the crop. Pucheng's tobacco was prized for its golden hue and mellow flavor and was known as "*sheyan*" or "yellow tobacco." The finest product was called "*jinsi*" (golden threads). By the Qianlong reign, *jinsi* tobacco from Pucheng was designated as tribute to the court. During the Jiaqing reign, Pucheng's tobacco cultivation expanded significantly. Owing to its substantial profitability—a single *mu* of tobacco yielding the equivalent income of ten *mu* of grain—and increasing competition in the tea market during the Daoguang and Xianfeng periods, many tea farmers in northern Fujian shifted to tobacco cultivation.[1]

In addition to the aforementioned crops, numerous other agricultural species were introduced via the coastal regions of Fujian, including cotton, pumpkin, eggplant, pineapple, papaya, lemon, cabbage, taro, mango, guava, and tomato. In the Song Dynasty, Fujian merchants also brought back muscovy ducks and turkeys from Southeast Asia. The introduction of these foreign agricultural products had a profound impact on agricultural production and daily life in Fujian's inland mountainous regions. High-yield, drought-resistant staple crops helped alleviate food shortages caused by population growth in these areas. Cash crops such as peanuts and tobacco enabled rural populations to achieve higher incomes, thereby stimulating the development of a commodity-based economy. Meanwhile, the arrival of various fruits and vegetables enriched local diets.

---

1 Wu Bangcai, editor-in-chief. *A History of the Development of Fujian Merchants: Nanping Volume*. Xiamen University Press, 2016, p.81.

II. The Importation and Impact of Foreign Commodities from the Qing Dynasty to the Republican Era

1. Cotton Cloth and Yarn

On November 2, 1843, Xiamen was officially opened as a treaty port, after which large quantities of foreign goods from Britain and the United States began flooding into the port. Between 1846 and 1847, imports at Xiamen Port were primarily composed of textiles from Britain and the United States, as well as cotton yarn from India, a British colony. According to a report by T.H. Layton, the British Consul at Xiamen, in 1846 the city imported 1,772 bales of cotton yarn, 272 bolts of woolen fabric, 25,537 bolts of bleached cotton cloth, 21,870 bolts of unbleached cloth, 5,280 bolts of twill, and 2,529 bolts of printed and dyed cloth. By 1847, these numbers had increased to 2,073 bales of cotton yarn, 4,809 bolts of woolen fabric, 32,618 bolts of bleached cotton, 35,509 bolts of unbleached cloth, 10,848 bolts of twill, and 3,987 bolts of printed and dyed fabric.[1] Despite the growing volume of imported British cotton cloth and yarn in the early years of the treaty port era, sales in Xiamen were sluggish, and unsold stock accumulated. Fuzhou was officially opened as a treaty port on July 3, 1844. In September of that year, an American merchant vessel carrying foreign cloth and other merchandise arrived in Fuzhou Port, but lingered for over a month without a single sale, ultimately having to offload its goods at reduced prices. By 1850, although British merchant ships occasionally docked at Fuzhou Port, demand for imported cloth remained extremely low. The British government repeatedly petitioned the Qing court to swap other treaty ports for Fuzhou, to no avail.[2] Thus, in the initial years after the opening of Xiamen and Fuzhou,

1Dai Yifeng. "Foreign Trade in Fujian During the Treaty Port Period." *Fujian Tribune (Humanities and Social Sciences Edition)*, no.1, 1988, p. 54.

2Ibid.,p.55

foreign goods saw limited market penetration. It was not until the early 1860s, following a boom in tea exports from both ports, that imports of foreign goods saw notable growth. Cotton cloth and yarn occupied a significant proportion of imported goods along the Minjiang River Basin. According to the *Annual Trade Report of Fukien Maritime Customs (1865)*, the value of imported cotton cloth at the Fuzhou Port between 1861 and 1865 is recorded in Table 4-1.

Table 4-1 Value of Imported Cotton Cloth at Fuzhou Port, 1861–1865 (Unit: *Yuan*)

Year	Unbleached Cotton	Bleached Cotton	Unbleached Marked Cloth	American Twill	Striped Velvet	Sheared Velvet	Camel Hair Fabric	Total
1861	58,720	13,127	127,335	78,030	22,978	12,771	24,462	337,423
1862	120,233	23,401	277,009	23,944	80,484	26,020	44,787	595,878
1863	299,222	48,941	114,919	121	111,581	66,500	60,849	702,133
1864	207,430	76,745	217,459	112	97,900	51,058	56,034	706,738
1865	178,448	38,358	60,081	960	66,452	18,456	62,611	425,366

Source: "Annual Trade Report of Fukien Maritime Customs (1865)." In *An Overview of the Socio-Economic Conditions in Modern Fuzhou and Eastern Fujian*, edited by Chi Xianren. Huayi Press, 1992, pp.2–3.

The data above show a rapid increase in cotton cloth imports through Fuzhou between 1861 and 1865. Thereafter, the growth rate of imported cotton yarn outpaced that of cloth, becoming the fastest-growing category of imported goods. This was primarily because imported yarn was cheaper, and weaving cloth from foreign yarn was more cost-effective than spinning yarn from domestically grown cotton.[1] To reduce dependence on imported cloth and produce affordable fabric for the working class, the Fuzhou Weaving Bureau was established in 1888. It employed simple wooden looms to produce two grades of cloth: "one finer grade, 15 *cun* (1 *cun* =3.33 centimeters) wide and 22.6 *chi* (1 *chi* =33.3 centimeters)long, is sold for 40 *fen* per piece, and one coarser grade, 20.6 *chi* long, is sold for 35 *fen* per piece. Both grades closely resemble imported unbleached cloth in color and texture."[2] Thus, cotton cloth woven from imported yarn on wooden looms gained market share in Fujian, leading to a steady decline in imports of foreign cotton cloth. According to the *Decennial Report of Fukien Maritime Customs (1892–1901)*, from 1892, imports of foreign yarn—especially from India and Japan—increased rapidly, while demand for foreign-woven cloth declined significantly. With the influx of foreign cloth and yarn, cultivation of ramie and cotton in inland western and northern Fujian dwindled. During the Republican period, cotton cultivation in western Fujian was rare: "Cotton is scarcely grown; ramie is planted occassionally, but not in large quantities."[3] Moreover, imported indigo was ten times more efficient than local indigo, with one *jin* of foreign indigo equivalent to ten *jin* of native product. As imported indigo flooded the market during the late Qing and Republican eras, locally produced indigo from western and northern Fujian became unsellable, leading to the decline of its cultivation. Thus, the large-scale importation of cotton cloth and yarn significantly impacted the cultivation of cotton, ramie, and indigo in Fujian's inland regions, while also transforming the province's

---

1Lin Renchuan. *A History of Fujian's Foreign Trade and Customs*. Lujiang Publishing House, 1991, p.206.

2"Decennial Report of Fukien Maritime Customs (1892–1901)." In *An Overview of the Socio-Economic Conditions in Modern Fuzhou and Eastern Fujian*, edited by Chi Xianren. Huayi Publishing House, 1992, p.375.

3You Haihua. "Agricultural Change and Transformation in the Border Regions of Jiangxi, Fujian, and Guangdong from the Late Qing to the Republican Period." *Historical Monthly*, no.6, 2005, p.104.

methods of textile production and manufacturing.

2. Kerosene

After the opening of the five treaty ports, kerosene was imported into Fujian primarily through the ports of Fuzhou and Xiamen, with sources including Russia, the United States, and Sumatra. Prior to its importation, local residents relied mainly on tung oil, pine oil, and rapeseed oil for lighting. Due to kerosene's affordability and higher luminosity, it quickly gained widespread use among both coastal and inland populations, pushing traditional oils out of the market. In the early treaty port era, such as in Jian'ou County of northern Fujian, the decline in traditional oil production was already noticeable:

> Tung oil is extracted from tung seeds. Those harvested from rocky hills are especially rich in oil. Twenty years ago, exports were counted in the tens of thousands of *dan*, but today they amount to only a tenth or less. Ever since kerosene was introduced, fewer people have cultivated tung trees.[1]

Similarly, in Yongtai County, "Local oils include three types: tung, tea, and sesame. With the prevalence of foreign oil, only one or two out of ten tung trees are still used for oil pressing."[2] Although a series of fires occurred in the mid-1880s due to improper kerosene usage, prompting the Qing government to issue edicts banning its use, kerosene remained popular due to its cost-effectiveness. With subsequent improvements in refinement techniques, its safety increased, leading the public to resume the use of

---

1 Zhan Xuanyou, ed., and Ca Zhenjian et al., comps. *Gazetteer of Jian'ou County* (Republican Period), vol. 25, *Treatise on Industry*. Lithographic edition from the 18th year of the Republic of China , p.8.

2 Don Bingqing et al., eds., and Wan Shaoyi, comp. *Gazetteer of Yongtai County* (Republican Period), vol. 7, *Treatise on Industry*. Lithographic edition from the 11th year of the Republic of China, p.7.

kerosene for lighting. The rising demand for kerosene significantly increased import volumes. In 1892, 43,730 gallons of American kerosene were imported. By 1893, this had risen to 514,300 gallons. During the same period, imports of Russian kerosene increased from 213,050 gallons to 1,147,500 gallons.[1] During the Republican era, as machinery use became more widespread in factories, kerosene's function expanded beyond lighting to serve as fuel for industrial equipment. In the inland regions of western and northern Fujian, kerosene-powered engines were adopted in rice mills and lumber-processing factories. For example, Jian'ou's Dafeng Rice Mill, established in the 14th year of the Republic of China (1925), utilized kerosene as its primary power source.[2] Additionally, with the growing use of kerosene lamps, glass manufacturing factories began to appear in the Minjiang River Basin to produce kerosene lamp chimneys.[3] Thus, the importation and proliferation of kerosene played a role in advancing industrial development in the inland regions of Fujian.

3. Sugar

Despite being a sugar-producing region, coastal and northern Fujian experienced a surge in imported sugar beginning in the late Qing period. Most of this imported sugar came from Java (white sugar) and Hong Kong (refined sugar). The superior quality and lower price of foreign sugar made it difficult for locally produced, traditionally processed cane sugar to compete. For instance, Zhenghe County in northern Fujian, once a significant sugar-

1Shu Haigang. *Port Trade and Hinterland Society: A Study of the Development of the Modern Minjiang River Basin from a Regional Perspective.* Xiamen University Press, 2019, p.118.

2Zha Xuanyou, ed., and Cai Zhenjian et al., comps. *Gazetteer of Jian'ou County* (Republican Period), vol. 25, *Treatise on Industry*. Lithographic edition from the 18th year of the Republic of China , p.13.

3"Decennial Report of Fukien Maritime Customs (1892–1901)." In *An Overview of the Socio-Economic Conditions in Modern Fuzhou and Eastern Fujian*, edited by Chi Xianren. Huayi Publishing House, 1992, p.413.

producing area, lacked the modern chemical knowledge necessary to refine white sugar, limiting producers to crude brown sugar. As a result, high-quality, sweet, and clean white sugar relied heavily on imports. During the Republican era, the backwardness of sugar-processing techniques made it impossible for local sugar producers in coastal and northern Fujian to match the competitiveness of imported products. Consequently, many producers were forced to shut down, and sugarcane cultivation declined. In western Fujian, where sugarcane was not widely grown, sugar had long been sourced from coastal areas such as Zhangzhou, Chaozhou, and Shantou. As imported sugar became increasingly available, the sugar consumed in western Fujian also came primarily from abroad. Thus, the influx of foreign sugar significantly accelerated the decline of the sugar industry in Fujian's traditional sugar-producing areas.

4. Matches

After the opening of the treaty ports, the importation of matches into Fuzhou and Xiamen increased rapidly. The main reason was the lack of domestic production capacity, while matches were a daily necessity. Initially, most imported matches came from Europe. By the reign of Emperor Guangxu, however, imports from Japan began to dominate. According to the *Decennial Report of Fukien Maritime Customs*, from 1892 to 1901, matches imported from Japan accounted for approximately 75% of the total, while those from Europe made up only about 15%. During the Republican period, Lin Mijyu, a native of Changle, established a small match factory named Kangji in Fuzhou. His matches were cheaper and of better quality, which gradually reduced the demand for imports. Around 1933, the Japanese-run match factory in Fuzhou ceased operations. Lin Mijyu purchased its equipment and facilities, expanded production, and renamed the company Jianhua Match Factory. In 1938, the factory had been relocated to Nanping, and branch factories were subsequently established in Shaxian, Longyan, Guangze, and

Ganzhou in Jiangxi. From the late Qing to the Republican era, the match industry in Fujian underwent a transition from heavy dependence on imports to local production. This shift illustrates the importation of matches also contributed to the development of indigenous industries in the Fujian region.

5. Opium

Before the opening of the five treaty ports, foreign opium was mainly imported into Fujian via Quanzhou. After the ports of Fuzhou and Xiamen were opened,, ships laden with opium sailed directly to these ports. Among all imported goods, opium held the highest value. Although the Qing government officially banned the opium trade during the early years of the treaty port era, many officials were themselves addicted and profited from the trade. As a result, opium imports remained high. According to foreign accounts, by the end of 1863, the total value of imported goods at the Fuzhou Port exceeded 10.5 million yuan, with opium alone accounting for 5 million yuan.[1] After the signing of the *Supplementary Article to the Chefoo Convention* in 1885, the opium trade was legalized. Upon importation, each chest of opium was levied a regular duty of 30 taels and a *likin* (a form of transit taxation in China) tax of 80 taels, after which Chinese merchants, holding the receipt, could freely distribute it inland without paying any further taxes. Thereafter, large quantities of opium flowed into the Minjiang River Basin.[2] Once it was legalized, the number of users in inland regions such as northern and western Fujian located in the upper reaches of the Minjiang River began to increase steadily. Opium consumption inflicted serious harm on both the physical and mental health of the

1Lin Xing. *A Study on Urban Development in Modern Fujian (1843–1949): Focusing on Fuzhou and Xiamen.* PhD dissertation, Xiamen University, 2004, p.40.

2Shui Haigang. *Port Trade and Hinterland Society: A Study of the Development of the Modern Minjiang River Basin from a Regional Perspective.* Xiamen University Press, 2019, p.127.

population, and also depleted household finances. In response, various anti-opium campaigns emerged, including the establishment of a dedicated anti-opium association in Fuzhou. These movements achieved a certain degree of success, and from 1910 onward, the volume of opium imports began to decline gradually.

From the late Qing through the Republican era, in addition to the aforementioned imports, Fujian also received foreign wheat, flour, clothing, and other goods. These imported commodities significantly influenced both the production and daily life of people in coastal and inland areas of the province.

Section 3 Inland–Coastal Trade Propelling the Modernization and Development of the Hinterland Society in the Early Modern and Modern Periods

With the opening of the ports of Xiamen and Fuzhou, the influx of foreign goods into Fujian was accompanied by the introduction of capitalist modes of production, ideological and cultural influences, and new educational models, all of which had a profound impact on social transformations in both the coastal and inland regions of the province.

I. Development of Modern Industry

From the Tongzhi reign to early Guangxu period of the Qing Dynasty, the export of high-quality tea and timber from northern Fujian attracted a considerable influx of western capital, which was invested in establishing factories that employed modern machinery for tea and timber processing. This marked the onset of modern industry in the region. The earliest mechanized tea processing was introduced by Russian merchants. In 1872, the first brick tea factory was established by Russian traders in Fuzhou, where tea from northern Fujian was processed into brick tea for easier transport and longer preservation. Between the 12th year of Tongzhi reign (1873) and the second year of Guangxu reign (1876), Russian merchants built seven mechanized brick tea factories in Nanping and Jian'ou's Nanya, Taiping, and Sanmen. "In the 11th year of Guangxu reign (1885) alone, brick tea output reached 3,595.6 tons."[1] In 1875, in response to competition from Russian traders, some Fujian industrial capitalists attempted to emulate their practices

1 Wu Bangcai, editor-in-chief. *A History of the Development of Fujian Merchants: Nanping Volume*. Xiamen University Press, 2016, p.140.

by founding mechanized brick tea factories —one in Xiqin, Yanping Prefecture, and another in the city of Jian'ou. However, due to the overwhelming capital strength of the Russian merchants, who dominated the brick tea export market, "the brick tea factory in Xiqin ceased operations the following year. Shortly thereafter, the factory in Jianning Prefecture was also relocated to Sanmen for undisclosed reasons."[1] Despite these setbacks, the initial attempts of domestic capital to engage in modern industry in northern Fujian reflected an innovative spirit and laid valuable groundwork for future endeavors. By the 17th year of Guangxu reign (1891), tea merchants in Jian'ou had imported modern tea-processing machinery from abroad and intended to establish a machine-operated tea roasting plant for local tea production.[2] As most local tea farmers could not afford such expensive equipment yet desired to roast their tea more effectively, they were inclined to use machines whenever machine roasting became cheaper than manual roasting. This demonstrates that after the opening of treaty ports and the influx of foreign capital, traditional tea production methods in northern Fujian were gradually supplanted by modern industrial techniques. However, with the decline of tea exports in the early Republican period, mechanized tea processing in the region progressed slowly.

Northern Fujian also possessed abundant timber resources, which were in high demand in Japan and Southeast Asia. In the 25th year of Guangxu reign (1899), British merchants established Xiangtai Timber Company in Jian'ou and operated large-scale logging of pinewood along the local riverbanks. They also opened a mechanized sawmill in Fuzhou. [3]

1Su Yutang. *Materials on the History of Modern Chinese Industry,* vol. 1 (1840–1895), part I. Science Press, 1957, p. 59.

2 Ibid.,p. 1016.

3 Wu Bangcai, editor-in-chief. *A History of the Development of Fujian Merchants: Nanping Volume*. Xiamen University Press, 2016, p.140.

Subsequently, as timber processing proved highly profitable, several other foreign firms—such as the British firm Tianxiang Trading Co., the German firm Chancheng Trading Co., and the Japanese firm Jianxing Trading Co.—successively established mechanized sawmills in Fuzhou. Timber from northern Fujian was shipped to Fuzhou Port, where it was cut into boards for the manufacture of kerosene crates and tea chests. During the Republican era, foreign merchants opened local processing factories in northern Fujian for pine and Chinese fir, enabling on-site processing prior to export.

Handmade paper products from northern Fujian were also widely exported. With the rise of modern industry, the Minjiang River Basin gradually saw the emergence of mechanized papermaking factories. During the Republican period, the northeastern part of Fujian saw the establishment of paper manufacturing plants that adopted modern machinery throughout the entire production process, such as the Huantai Paper Mill in Yong'an, the Maotai Paper Mill in Shaxian, and the Futai Paper Mill in Shuikou.[1]

The opening of treaty ports and the expansion of inland and coastal trade also facilitated the arrival of foreign missionaries in inland Fujian. In the fifth year of the Republic of China (1916), a Christian pastor in Yangkou Town, Shunchang, purchased a 25-kilowatt kerosene generator through an intermediary, which powered lighting for the church, the Sino-American School, and the Gongpu Hospital—marking the first instance of thermal electricity being used for lighting in northern Fujian.[2] Inspired by the missionary's use of kerosene-powered generator, local entrepreneurs began establishing their own thermal power plants. In the ninth year of the Republic of China (1920), Zheng Bochun and others raised funds to build a thermal

1(Japan) East Asia Research Association, ed. *A Survey of Industries in South China*. Sanseidō, 1939, p.140.

2Wu Bangcai, editor-in-chief. *History of the Development of Fujian Merchants: Nanping Volume*. Xiamen University Press, 2016, p.142.

power plant in Jian'ou, which officially began supplying electricity in the 11th year of the Republic of China (1922). Following the success of Jian'ou's plant, similar ventures soon appeared in Nanping, Jianyang, Shunchang, Chong'an, Guangze, and Shaowu. In the 16th year of the Republic of China (1927), Ji Tinghong, a native of Nanping, raised funds to purchase hydroelectric equipment from abroad. He leased the Liu family's water-powered mill in Xiadao Town, Nanping, and established the first hydroelectric power station in northern Fujian. The construction of these thermal and hydroelectric power plants significantly promoted the development of the electrical industry in the region. In addition, northern Fujian during this period saw the emergence of machine-based industries such as sugar refineries, match factories, rice mills, and shipyards. Although these modern industries were primarily concentrated in the primary processing of local agricultural and specialty products, they nonetheless played a fundamental role in advancing the region's industrial modernization.

During the Republican period, the development of modern industry in western Fujian remained relatively underdeveloped. Factories that adopted modern machinery were primarily limited to rice mills, electric lighting companies, hydroelectric power plants, chemical plants, and cigarette factories. Notable examples include the rice mill established in Zhangping in 1916, the Guanghua Electric Lighting Company in Longyan in 1924, the Fuyao Electric Lighting Company in Shanghang in 1925, the Jyulun Hydroelectric Power Plant in Longyan in 1943, and the Sanyou Cigarette Factory in Longyan in 1947. Most of these mechanized industrial enterprises were small to medium-sized, with few large-scale operations. This was primarily due to the limited accumulation of capital among local merchants, which hindered their ability to purchase expensive large-scale machinery and expand production capacity.

II. The Rise of Modern Education

After China's defeat in the Opium War, the country gradually descended into a semi-colonial, and semi-feudal state. In response, the establishment of modern education emerged as a crucial pathway to national rejuvenation. Since the Self-Strengthening Movement, the Qing government established numerous modern industrial and technical schools aimed at cultivating skilled labor for the machinery and manufacturing sectors. These institutions marked the beginning of modern vocational education in China. During the late Qing reforms, several industrial schools were established in Fuzhou, which further evolved into vocational schools during the Republican period and gradually expanded into the inland regions of northern Fujian. Simultaneously, with the opening of treaty ports such as Xiamen and Fuzhou, western missionaries began to enter coastal Fujian in significant numbers, establishing a wide array of missionary schools as a means of promoting Christianity. From their bases in Fuzhou and Xiamen, these missionaries rapidly extended their educational activities into the inland areas of northern and western Fujian.

1. Government-Run Vocational Schools

In the fifth year of the Tongzhi reign (1866), the Qing court established the Fujian Naval Academy in Mawei, Fuzhou. Also known as the *Qiushitang Yiju* (Academy for the Pursuit of Practical Knowledge), this institution was founded by the Self-Strengthening Movement reformers in the aftermath of the First Opium War and is recognized as China's first modern technical school, marking the beginning of modern vocational education in the country.[1] Between the 26th and 34th years of the Guangxu reign (1900–

1Shui Haigang. *Port Trade and Hinterland Society: A Study of the Development of the Modern Minjiang River Basin from a Regional Perspective.* Xiamen University Press, 2019, p.227.

1908), the Qing government successively founded various vocational schools in Fuzhou, including a sericulture school, a nursing school, Yinghua Academy, girls' vocational school, an intermediate commercial school, and an intermediate industrial school. During the Republican era, these late-Qing vocational schools were retained and further expanded with the establishment of new vocational institutions. The Ministry of Education at the time defined the purpose of vocational education as "to impart knowledge and skills essential to agriculture, industry, and commerce." In Fuzhou, several new institutions such as nursing schools, commercial schools, and girls' vocational schools were established. In Northern Fujian, vocational education also developed progressively during the Republican period. For instance, in 1914, the first and second craft training institutes were founded in Nanping County, where professional technicians were hired to teach skills in rattan and bamboo furniture making, wood furniture production, lacquering and spray painting, and soap manufacturing. Many of the products created by graduates were even exported abroad. In 1916, to facilitate local access to training, the first craft institute was relocated to Jian'ou, making it more convenient for local students to attend. In 1919, it was renamed the Public Craft Training Institute of Jian'ou County. Due to the large influx of imported textiles, the local traditional weaving industry was on the verge of collapse. To revitalize the domestic cotton and silk textile industries, a Weaving Bureau was established in 1914 at the Tianguan Ridge, Nanping, with funding raised to support training and innovation. As there was a shortage of forestry professionals in northern Fujian, the Daoli Forestry School (first-Class) was founded in the city of Jian'an. The school recruited overseas-trained forestry graduates as leading instructors to cultivate professional forestry talents. In addition, a sericulture internship school was established in 1916 as part of the first high elementary school in Shaxi County, followed by the public Sericulture Internship Institute in Jian'ou County in 1921, which focused on teaching silkworm cultivation techniques. In 1920, two additional institutions were founded: the Second-Class Agricultural School of Chong'an County and the Second-Class Commercial School of Jian'ou County, both aiming to develop technical and commercial professionals. In western Fujian, Liancheng County was renowned for its skilled handmade paper production, including *Xuanzhi* paper and *Yukou* paper, which were sold widely both domestically and internationally. The paper industry was one of Liancheng's pillar sectors. In 1942, leveraging this advantage, the Fujian Provincial Department of Education established the Provincial Advanced Industrial Vocational School in Gutian, Liancheng, aimed at training technical talents in the paper industry.[1] In the Republican era, the curriculum design of modern vocational schools was typically aligned with local industrial development. Programs were designed based on the principle of "meeting local needs," and were characterized by a high degree of practicality and applicability.

2.Missionary-Run Schools

In the 22nd year of the Daoguang reign in the Qing Dynasty (1842), American missionaries introduced Christianity into Fujian Province. From the mid-19th century to the early 20th century, the influence of Christianity expanded rapidly across both coastal and inland regions of Fujian. To advance their evangelical mission, major Christian denominations established a significant number of missionary schools throughout the province. Taking the Hakka regions of western Fujian as a representative example, missionaries initially employed itinerant preaching as a primary method of evangelism. However, these efforts achieved limited success. One of the main reasons was the lack of a stable audience. Furthermore, due to the underdeveloped economy in western Fujian, school enrollment rates were low, leading to widespread illiteracy, which in turn hindered the public's

1Deng Jinkun. *The Xuanzhi Paper in Liancheng*. Economic Science Press, 2008, p.8.

ability to read the *Bible*. To increase the number of believers, cultivate Chinese evangelists, and expand the scope of Christian influence, various major Christian missionary societies [1] established missionary schools, offering tuition-free education for impoverished children. In western Fujian's Hakka regions, the primary missionary societies involved in the founding of such schools included the London Missionary Society, the Presbyterian Mission, and the Baptist Mission. Tables 4-2 to 4-4 present the schools founded by these three major societies, respectively.

1 Missionary Societies : A general term for Western organizations that introduced Christianity to China, also known as Western Missionary Societies, Evangelical Associations, or Mission Alliances.

Table 4-2 Schools Established by the London Missionary Society in Western Fujian

School Name	Founded Year	Notes
Ducun Primary School	1892	Founded within the Hetian Chapel; moved to Changting in 1901
Huaying Girls' School	1909	Later merged with Chongzheng Primary School to form Leyu Primary School
Yashengdun Medical School	1909	—
Zhongxi School	1909	—
Chongzheng Primary School	1913	Founded at the Hetian Chapel; schoolhouse adjacent to the right of the church
Longtoufang Primary School	1917	Established by the Longtoufang Chapel
Shufeng Primary School	1917	Founded in Qingliu by Wu Cunzong
Jiesan Primary School	1919	Established by the Sibao Chapel in Liancheng; renamed Desan Primary School in 1927, and closed in 1930
Peide Primary School	1920	Founded in the ancient city of Changting; closed in 1929
Mingde Primary School	1923	Founded in Huling, Longyan; boys only, later merged with Dingxin Girls' School
Baohe School	1925	Founded by the Longtoufang Chapel
Seminary	1934	Founded by Dr. Lai Chali
Tongfang Central Primary School	1939	Rebuilt by the Tongfang Chapel of the London Missionary Society
Peide Girls' Middle School	1947	Founded on Zongjie Street in Longyan; specially junior high classes to train girls for church service

Source: Lu Ping. *Christianity and Hakka Society in Western Fujian*. MA thesis, Fujian Normal University, 2002, pp. 28–29.

Table 4-3 Schools Established by the Presbyterian Mission in Western Fujian

School Name	Founded Year	Notes
Yude Primary School	1899	Founded in the church at Yongding; closed in 1941, later repurposed as a women's literacy school
Fuying Primary School	1906	Established within Shanghang church; four-year elementary program, closed in 1929
Peihua Middle School	1921	Founded in the Chen family's Ancestral Hall in Ganquan Lane, Shanghang; later moved to Kongxiangkou in the West Gate area, with three junior high classes
Mingde Girls' School	1921	Founded in the Zhou Family's Ancestral Hall, Shanghang; closed in 1928
School for Blind Children	1921	Founded in the Huang Family's Ancestral Hall, Shanghang; offered courses in braille and weaving

Source: Lu Ping. *Christianity and Hakka Society in Western Fujian*. MA thesis, Fujian Normal University, 2002, p.30.

Table 4-4 Schools Established by the Baptist Mission in Western Fujian

School Name	Founded Year	Notes
Meihua Primary School	1912	Founded in Hengsi and Hengwu Streets, Shanghang; closed in 1929
Meihua Girls' School	1916	Founded in "Meihua Garden" near East Gate, Shanghang; closed in 1929
Meihua Middle School	1919	Founded in Hengsi and Hengwu Streets, Shanghang; destroyed in 1929
Zhendong Girls' School	1920	Founded in Hexi, Yongding; closed in 1929
Zhendong Middle School	1920	Founded in Hexi, Yongding; closed in 1929
Chongwen Primary School	1922	Founded within the Hugang Sub-Chapel in Yongding; closed in 1929
Bible School	1917	Founded in "Meihua Garden," Shanghang. In 1919, a sericulture school and a craft learning institute were added but later destroyed in 1929

Source: Lu Ping. *Christianity and Hakka Society in Western Fujian*. MA thesis, Fujian Normal University, 2002, p.31.

As evidenced by Tables 4-2 through 4-4, the Christian missionary societies established three main types of schools in western Fujian: primary schools, secondary schools (including vocational institutions), and theological or specialized schools, with a focus on the first two categories. Although the primary intention behind these schools was to accelerate the spread of Christianity in Fujian, they objectively played a positive role in improving the cultural literacy of the local population and in promoting modern education content. In addition to basic courses in Chinese and Western cultural subjects, many missionary schools offered instructions in English, mathematics, medicine, and natural sciences (referred to at the time as *Gezhi*), thus nurturing a generation of educated youth in the region. One notable example is Dr. Fu Lianzhen, a founding figure in the modern Chinese healthcare system, who graduated from the Yashengdun Medical School in his youth and later became a physician at the Gospel Hospital in Tingzhou. The curricula and educational models introduced by these schools played a significant role in the emergence and spread of modern education in western Fujian.

3. The Establishment of Modern Hospitals

In addition to founding schools, Christian missionary organizations began to increasingly recognize, starting in the 1880s, the auxiliary role that medical work could play in advancing their evangelical efforts. Consequently, more missionary doctors were dispatched to Fujian, and the establishment of Christian hospitals followed. These hospitals were typically founded in a pattern that expanded from the coastal areas to the interior and from major urban centers to smaller towns. After the opening of the five treaty ports, missionaries initially concentrated their medical institutions in coastal cities such as Fuzhou, Xiamen, and Quanzhou. By the late 19th and early 20th centuries, the reach of these hospitals had gradually extended to the inland regions of northern and western Fujian. In 1866, Dr. Nathan Sites, a missionary from the Methodist Episcopal Mission, arrived in Nanping and introduced Christianity there. The Chinese Anglican Church was the first denomination to combine medical services with religious missions in northern Fujian. In 1888, Dr. J. Rigg, a physician affiliated with the Chinese Anglican Church, founded the Rigg Memorial Hospital in Jianning. In 1890, British missionary Lu Zhengrong arrived in Jianyang, where he purchased land outside the northern gate of the city and established a church called *Tianfutang*, which included a medical clinic. In 1921, the American Board of Commissioners for Foreign Missions opened the Sacred Teachings Hospital on Gongde Street in the northern gate area of Shaowu.[1] In 1904, the Alden Speare Memorial Hospital was built opposite Putong Temple on Ziyungang Hill in Nanping by the American Methodist Episcopal Mission. The hospital was directed by the American Dr. James E. Skinner, and staffed by American physicians, missionary doctors, and nurses. It was equipped with western medical technology, including X-ray machines, microscopes, and facilities for physical therapy and laboratory testing, all donated by a church in New York. In 1935, the hospital established medical training and nursing programs, cultivating a number of local medical professionals. In 1941, due to a restructuring of the church, the hospital was renamed the Nanping Methodist Hospital of the Chinese Christian Church. It was taken over by the People's Government in 1949. In September 1951, it was renamed the Nanping Prefectural Hospital.

In 1902, the Presbyterian Mission sent Pastor James Wasson and Dr. Charles Blair to Changting to begin evangelistic work.[2] At the initial stage of Christianity's introduction into Changting, some missionaries abused their powers and privileges to oppress the common people, resulting in widespread local resentment toward the religion. Later, as missionaries altered their preaching strategies and began offering free medical consultations and distributing medicine, public attitudes began to shift. In 1904, the London Missionary Society began constructing a church hospital in Changting. Completed in 1908, the Yashengdun Medical Clinic not only treated patients but also recruited students and taught western medical knowledge. In 1926, it was renamed the Gospel Hospital and, in 1931, it served as a Red Army hospital in the Central Soviet Area. The hospital's equipment and medications were largely imported from Britain, and the facility was modeled

---

1Zhou Dian'en. "A Preliminary Study on the Historical Evolution of Protestant Mission Hospitals in Fujian." *Journal of Maritime History Studies,* no.1, 2005, p.97.

2Ibid.

after Western-style hospitals, featuring independent operating rooms, laboratories, gender-segregated wards, and sterilization boilers. It also included residences for doctors, nurses, medical students, a chapel, missionary quarters, and dining facilities. Departments included internal medicine, surgery, gynecology, and emergency care. Additionally, in 1917, the British Dr. John McPhun and Ding Zengbi established a Gospel Hospital in Shanghang County.[1]

Although the initial goal of building these hospitals in inland Fujian was to facilitate the acceptance of Christian doctrine and increase the number of converts, these hospitals laid an essential foundation for the emergence of modern medicine in western and northern Fujian. Before the founding of the People's Republic of China, the inland regions of Fujian had extremely limited healthcare resources, with rudimentary equipment and poor living conditions. The establishment of missionary hospitals not only contributed to safeguarding the physical and mental health of local residents, but also introduced advanced western medical knowledge, public health practices, and modern hospital management systems. These efforts significantly promoted the development of modern healthcare in western and northern Fujian.

1Editorial Committee for Historical and Cultural Materials, Chinese People's Political Consultative Conference, Shanghang County Committee, Fujian Province. *Historical and Cultural Materials of Shanghang*, vol. 5, 1986, p.73.

Section 4 Inland-Coastal Interactions Shaping the Maritime Character of the Hinterland Culture

I. The Emergence and Characteristics of Fujian's Maritime Culture

Located on the southeastern coast of China, Fujian Province is characterized by mountainous terrain and scarce arable land, yet it boasts an expansive maritime territory, abundant aquatic resources, and an extensive, rugged coastline. These natural conditions fostered the development of numerous natural harbors. The Minyue people—early inhabitants of the region—fully utilized marine resources to develop their means of production and meet material needs for survival. As a result, they established close and enduring ties with the ocean in both productive and daily activities, gradually giving rise to a distinctive maritime culture. A large quantity of accumulated shells and mollusk carapaces unearthed from the Keqiutou cultural site, dating to the early Neolithic period, indicates that the early Minyue people had already acquired the ability to gather and harvest shellfish from shallow seas and tidal flats for subsistence. These early practices exhibit the initial signs of maritime cultural traits and are widely considered the earliest manifestations of maritime culture in Fujian. The Qin, Han, and Three Kingdoms periods mark the formative stage of Fujian's maritime culture. During this era, the Minyue people had mastered the construction and operation of watercraft, and began building sea-going vessels and marine navigation on a considerable scale. This period laid the necessary foundation for the full-scale development of maritime culture in later dynasties. Notably, northern Fujian became a key shipbuilding base for the state of Wu during the Three Kingdoms period, supplying a large number of experienced seafarers. During the Tang Dynasty, the imperial court actively promoted foreign trade, and Fuzhou Port saw rapid development in maritime transportation and commerce. In the Five Dynasties period, under the rule of Wang Shenzhi in Fujian, particular emphasis was placed on maritime trade. He developed Gantang Port in northern Fuzhou, establishing trade routes to Japan, India, the Abbasid Caliphate, and Srivijaya. In the Song and Yuan dynasties, Fujian not only emerged as a major center of shipbuilding, but also adopted the magnetic compass and celestial navigation techniques such as "star following", enabling long-distance oceanic voyages. Ports in Quanzhou, Fuzhou, and Zhangzhou flourished, with Quanzhou Port becoming one of the world's largest trade hubs due to the massive scale of overseas commerce. It attracted merchants from across the world, resulting in a convergence of diverse cultures that further enriched Fujian's maritime culture through intercultural exchanges. Fujian merchants rose swiftly in prominence during the Song and Yuan dynasties, undertaking large-scale overseas ventures throughout Asia and engaging in a wide range of frequent commercial transactions. However, during the Ming and Qing dynasties, strict maritime prohibition policies significantly curtailed interactions between coastal regions and foreign countries. Despite these constraints, Zhangzhou merchants in the Ming era defied the bans and engaged in maritime smuggling, contributing to the prosperity of Yuegang Port. Nonetheless, maritime cultural development during the Ming and Qing dynasties was considerably constrained by state-imposed maritime prohibition policies.

In contrast to inland cultures, maritime culture values strength, and is marked by greater adventurousness, pioneering spirit, creativity, openness, and outward orientation. Fujian's maritime culture is both long-standing and multifaceted, exhibiting four defining characteristics across different dimensions: creativity in material culture, adventurousness in behavior, practicality in institutional practices, and spirituality in religious belief.[1][2] Creativity is particularly reflected in the innovation and refinement of shipbuilding techniques. In order to facilitate long-distance navigation and improve cargo capacity, Fujian craftsmen continuously improved ship designs and cabin structures, employing techniques such as mortise-and-tenon joints and seam caulking to enhance hull durability. Compared to the relative stability of the land, the ocean is characterized by greater uncertainty and unpredictability. The mountainous terrain and limited arable land in Fujian compelled local merchants to seek their livelihoods from the sea. Confronted with the vast and perilous ocean, survival depended on having the courage to explore and take risks, thereby fostering a maritime ethos defined by boldness and resilience. Practicality at the institutional level manifested in the collective adherence of Fujian merchants to commercial regulations. In engaging in overseas trade, they emphasized tangible profits and practical effectiveness, which enabled them to expand their trading networks and sustain long-term operations. On the level of spiritual belief, this maritime character was also marked by a strong devotional tradition centered on the worship of Mazu—the deity of the sea—who was venerated as a divine protector of seafarers.

II. The Maritime Character of Fujian's Inland Hinterland Culture

Although western and northern Fujian are situated in the inland hinterland of the province, they have long maintained close connections with the coastal areas. This geographic and cultural proximity places these regions

1Ye Zhijian. "A Tentative Discussion on the Emergence, Evolution, and Characteristics of Fujian's Maritime Culture." In *Proceedings of the First Academic Symposium on Maritime Culture in Fujian Province*, October 12, 2007, p.23–24.

2 Fujian Yanhuang Culture Research Association & CPPCC Fuzhou Municipal Committee, eds. *Research on Fujian's Maritime Culture*. The Straits Literature and Art Press, 2009, p.39.

at the intersection of inland and maritime cultures. The unique topography of being "backed by mountains and facing the sea" gave rise to a maritime character within the hinterland's inland culture. In this context, merchants from western and northern Fujian served as key agents in the cultural fusion between land and sea during the long history of inland-coastal exchange.

1. Commercial Consciousness

Commercial consciousness refers primarily to an awareness of commodity exchange, including both the exchange of goods and the exchange between goods and money. In Fujian's coastal regions, limited farmland and low grain yields compelled fishing communities to rely on marine production—offshore fishing and sea salt processing—as the basis of their livelihoods. These products were then traded for grain, textiles, and other daily necessities from inland and other areas. Consequently, coastal fishermen developed a strong sense of commercial exchange early on. The development of this commercial mindset greatly contributed to the growth of handicrafts, commerce, and monetary use in northern Fujian. As the headwaters of the Minjiang River, the region had boat-building capabilities even in ancient times. By the Three Kingdoms period, northern Fujian had become a major shipbuilding base for the state of Wu. In the Tang Dynasty, the Yongfeng Mint was established in Jianzhou, marking the beginning of local coin minting. The circulation of currency further accelerated commodity exchange. Since the late Tang and the Five Dynasties, the handicraft industries such as ceramics, tea processing, silk weaving, papermaking, and metallurgy flourished in northern Fujian. During the Song and Yuan dynasties, the region exported large quantities of ceramics, Jian brocade, tea, and handmade paper. In the Ming and Qing periods, the development of the regional commodity economy further deepened, with tea—especially Wuyi tea—playing a central role in trade. The growth of the commodity economy also led to the rise of private financial services such as pawnshops, silver shops, and native banks. Western Fujian, located at the headwaters of the Tingjiang River and Jiulong River, occupied a critical juncture among Fujian, Guangdong, and Jiangxi provinces. These waterways linked the inland with the coast and enabled access to overseas markets. Merchants from western Fujian were likewise profoundly influenced by both hinterland and maritime cultures during their engagement in the inland-coastal interactions. In the Song Dynasty, trade already flourished between Tingzhou and the regions of Chaozhou and Ganzhou. Salt produced in Chaozhou was transported via the Tingjiang River to Tingzhou, where it not only met local needs but was also redistributed to Ganzhou. Conversely, rice from Ganzhou was shipped to coastal regions like Chaozhou. As a result, Tingzhou became a key transshipment center for salt and grain. In the Ming and Qing periods, the region's abundant timber, handmade paper, and tobacco were exported overseas, contributing significantly to the local economy.

2.Spirit of Adventure and Perseverance

Spirit of adventure and perseverance refers to the capacity to confront and endure harsh natural conditions, the willingness to take risks, and the determination to improve one's own destiny through hard work and struggle. The Hakka ancestors, for instance, migrated south from the Central Plains to Ganzhou, then into western Fujian and eastern Guangdong, eventually spreading to the southeastern coast, Taiwan and even to Southeast Asia. This north-to-south migration route also illustrates the gradual extension of inland culture into maritime culture. The pathways from the inland to the southeastern coast were forged by the Hakka people. With their fearlessness in the face of hardship, pioneering spirit, and perseverance, they opened up crucial routes for inland-coastal interactions. One major route extended from Shicheng in southern Jiangxi into Ninghua and Changting, then followed the Tingjiang River downstream into the Hanjiang River, providing access to eastern and northern Guangdong and ultimately reaching coastal areas such as Chaozhou and Zhangzhou. Another route crossed the Nanling Mountain from southern Jiangxi via Wuping and Shanghang, passed through Jiaoling, and led to the Chaozhou and Shantou regions. These routes were critical for the southern migration of Han Chinese from the Central Plains to the coastal regions. From the Ming and Qing periods onward, waves of Hakka people moved from the hinterland to coastal Fujian and Southeast Asia, opening up difficult migration, trade, and communication routes that helped integrate the inland with the maritime world.[1] In this process, Hakka people actively absorbed elements of maritime culture, blending it with traditional inland and Central Plains traditions. Over time, the Hakka came to embody distinctive cultural traits shaped by both the mountains and the sea. Since the first half of the 19th century, large-scale tin mining began in the central and northern regions of the Malay Peninsula in Southeast Asia, attracting waves of Hakka migrants. The journey "to *Nanyang*" (literally "going south to the seas") became one of the longest-lasting population migrations in Chinese history, known colloquially in Hakka regions of Fujian and Guangdong as "*guo fan*"

1Yu Ruxian. "The Historical Transformation and Reasons for the Hakka People's Shift from 'Heart Toward the Central Plains' to 'Facing the Ocean'." *Research on Fujian Commercial Culture*, no.2, 2018, p.57.

(crossing the seas).[1] Many "crossing songs" passed down in Hakka mountain ballads recount this experience. The Hakka migrants who settled in Southeast Asia were bold and enterprising, making significant contributions to the region's mining industry and becoming a driving force in its economic and social development. They played important roles both in their host countries and in their ancestral homelands. Moreover, the mountainous terrain and treacherous paths of western and northern Fujian—with their swift rivers and steep ridges—led to the saying, "The roads in Fujian are harder than those in Sichuan." As such, people from these regions had to possess the courage and determination to "cut paths through mountains and build bridges over waters." It was through this spirit of perseverance—undaunted by the hardships of traversing rugged terrain and enduring the arduous journeys of trade—that they were able to create a thriving commercial and trading network. Merchants from these inland regions were risk-takers and strivers. They transported valuable mountain products to coastal ports for export and, in turn, brought back advanced technologies and cultural influences from overseas. Through this historical process of mountain-sea exchange, the hinterland culture of these regions naturally took on a maritime character.

3.Openness and Inclusivity

Openness and inclusivity refer to the positive and receptive

1Leng Jianbo. " 'Crossing the Seas' as a 'Lifestyle': A Study on the Migration of Hakka People from Eastern Guangdong to Malaya in Modern Times." *Local Cultural Studies*, no.4, 2019, p. 84.

attitude that people in inland regions such as western and northern Fujian adopted toward maritime culture. Since the mid-Ming Dynasty, with the opening of trans-Pacific trade routes to the Americas, Fujian's coastal trade gradually expanded beyond Southeast Asia to reach the American continent. Coastal regions such as Quanzhou and Zhangzhou began introducing crops like corn, potatoes, sweet potatoes, tobacco, and tomatoes from the New World. Over time, these exotic crops spread inland to the western and northern regions of Fujian, where some even became important export commodities. After the opening of five treaty ports, Christian missionaries extended their evangelical activities from Fujian's coastal areas into the inland regions of western and northern Fujian. Rather than outright rejecting this foreign religion and culture, the people of these inland areas adopted a relatively open and tolerant attitude. As missionaries established hospitals and schools while preaching the gospel, many local residents converted to Christianity. In this process of cultural interaction, the indigenous culture of the inland regions engaged with the incoming Christian culture in a spirit of mutual respect, tolerance, and harmony. Moreover, certain elements of inland food culture also reflect maritime influences. For example, many Hakka dishes incorporate a variety of seafood ingredients, such as squid and dried shrimp in the renowned dish: *Kourou* (braised pork belly) of Longtan Town in Yongding. Since the Song Dynasty, merchants from western and northern Fujian, with an open-minded spirit and pioneering drive, forged commercial routes between the inland and coastal regions.

They exported the inland's abundant products—such as ceramics, tea, handmade paper, tobacco, and silk textiles—through coastal ports to overseas markets, boosting maritime trade. Through these long-standing mountain-sea trade exchanges, merchants from these regions organically blended Central Plains civilization and inland culture with maritime culture, ultimately shaping a hinterland cultural identity rich with maritime characteristics.

Chapter 5
Transportation and Commerce in the Hinterland of the Maritime Silk Road

Due to a lack of pack animals such as donkeys, mules, and horses, and the region's mountainous terrain, Fujian had virtually no constructed roads before the Republic of China. Land transportation primarily relied on manual labor—goods were carried on shoulder poles by humans. From the Republican period up until the eve of the founding of the People's Republic of China, 18 counties in Fujian still had no roads at all, and although 28 counties had built roads, they were essentially impassable for vehicles. The total length of roads open to vehicles across the entire province amounted to only 945 kilometers. [1] Fujian was traversed by several river systems, including the Minjiang River, Jiulong River, Tingjiang River, and Jinjiang River. In the river basins, transportation mainly depended on a combination of land and water routes. In northern Fujian, before the Opium War, land transport largely depended on the postal relay system, with human portage as the dominant mode of transport and very little use of pack animals. Waterborne transport was primarily conducted via the Minjiang River and its tributaries, with wooden sailboats serving as the principal means of shipping. During the Republican era, advancements in shipbuilding technology led to a transition from traditional wooden sailboats to steamships and steamboats in northern Fujian. Road construction began on a large scale in 1934, gradually expanding the regional road transportation network. In western Fujian, where mountainous terrain and limited arable land prevailed, land transport similarly relied on human labor with minimal animal power. Water transport depended on the Tingjiang River, but the river's lower reaches, especially below the section of Shanghang, were treacherous and featured numerous rapids, making navigation difficult. As a result, the export of local specialties and the import of goods had to be routed through northern Fujian and eastern Guangdong. Due to these transportation constraints, large-scale exploitation of forest and mineral resources in the region remained largely unfeasible prior to 1949.

1Fujian Provincial Map Compilation Committee. *Atlas of Fujian* (General Maps). 1963, pp. 23–24.

Section 1 Inland Waterway Navigation and Trade Routes

I. The Minjiang River Navigation and Trade Routes

The Minjiang River system originates in Junkou Town, Jianning County, located on the border between Fujian and Jiangxi provinces. It flows from west to east into the East China Sea. Its primary upper tributary is the Shaxi Creek, which passes through Yong'an and Shaxian. After merging with the Futun Creek—which flows through Shaowu and Shunchang—it forms the main stream, commonly known as the Xixi Creek. It later joins the Jianxi Creek (also called the Dongxi Creek), which flows through Jianyang and Jian'ou, at the Shuangjiantan confluence in Nanping. From this point downstream, the river is known as the Minjiang River. The section from the source to Shuangjiantan in Nanping is generally referred to as the upper reaches. Below Nanping, the Minjiang River primarily flows through Gutian, Minqing, Minhou, Fuzhou, and Lianjiang, eventually emptying into the East China Sea at Changmenkou.

The Minjiang River plays a vital role in facilitating economic trade and population movement between upstream and downstream regions. For inland areas, the Minjiang River serves as one of the primary channels for engaging in external economic and trade relations. For coastal regions, it is an essential pathway through which port functions are extended into the inland hinterland. Historical records indicate that prior to the construction of roads in northern Fujian, over 70% of goods exported from or imported into the upper Minjiang River Basin relied on the Minjiang River and its tributaries for transshipment or transportation.[1] Spanning nearly 600 kilometers, the Minjiang River has more than 120 tributaries in its upper reaches and drains a basin that covers

1"Highway Construction in Fujian Province." *Minzheng Series*, 1939, p. 11.

nearly half of Fujian Province, granting it the geographical advantage of being "short but powerful" and directly opening into the sea.

1. Overview of Waterways of the Minjiang River

The Shaxi Creek, Futun Creek, and Jianxi Creek are the three major tributaries in the upper reaches of the Minjiang River and form critical waterways for transporting goods out of northwestern Fujian. The Shaxi Creek originated in Yanfeng Mountain in Jianning County, flowed eastward through Ninghua, Qingliu, Guihua (now known as Mingxi), and Yong'an and then turned northeastward, passing through Sanming and Shaxian. Located 20 kilometers upstream of Nanping, the mouth of the Shaxi Creek was where it converged with the Futun Creek. This point was approximately 120 kilometers from Yong'an and was navigable by medium-sized civilian vessels. Upstream from Yong'an, the stream branched into two tributaries: the Jiulong Creek, which reached Ninghua with a navigable length of 130 kilometers suitable for small boats; and the Nanxi Creek, which flowed toward Xiaotao with a 60-kilometer stretch navigable by small boats.[1] The Shaxi Creek was an essential water route connecting the counties of Ninghua, Qingliu, and Guihua in Tingzhou Prefecture with Fuzhou. It also served as an important link connecting southeastern Jiangxi with the lower reaches of Minjiang River. Historical accounts suggest that prior to the Tang and Song dynasties, the eighteen rapids in Jiulong, located at the boundary between Ninghua and Qingliu, were too shallow and rocky for boats to pass through. During the late Yuan Dynasty, Chen Youding, then the Deputy Administrator of Fujian, organized laborers to remove rocky obstructions by chiseling through them, thereby rendering the waterway navigable.[2] Subsequently, grain from the three upstream counties of the Minjiang River under Tingzhou

---

1 Shui Haigang. *Port Trade and Hinterland Society: A Regional Perspective on the Development of the Modern Minjiang River Basin*. Xiamen University Press, 2019, p. 63.

2 (Ming) Chen Guifang, comp. *Gazetteer of Qingliu County*, Jiajing Edition, vol. 2, *Mountains and Rivers*. Edited by the Gazetteer Compilation Committee of Qingliu County, Fujian People's Publishing House, 1992, pp. 22–23.

Prefecture, along with agricultural produce from southeastern Jiangxi, could be shipped downstream via the Shaxi Creek to the lower reaches of the Minjiang River and on to Fuzhou. According to the *Gazetteer of Tingzhou Prefecture* compiled during the Jiajing era of the Ming Dynasty,

The confluence of the Xixi Creek and Jianxi Creek in the urban area of Nanping (Shuangjiantan): the origin of the Minjiang River[1]

> From the great river in front of Ninghua County, boats travel downstream to Qingliu County over a distance of sixty *li*, passing through a stretch winding through seven bends, known as the Seven Coiled Dragons, which boatmen dread... The boats used are typically three-planked small vessels, slightly larger than those used in Changting, and can reach Qingliu in half a day downstream.[2]

In Guihua County, the Mingxi Creek, a tributary of the Shaxi Creek,

> gathers various streams before the county seat of

1Photograph taken by the project team on 14 Aug, 2019 in Yanping District, Nanping City.

2(Ming) Shao Youdao, comp. and ed. *Gazetteer of Tingzhou Prefecture,* Jiajing Edition, vol. 1, *Geography.* Selected Reprints of Local Gazetteers in Ming Dynasty from the Tianyige Library: Sequel Series, Shanghai Bookstore, 2014, p. 99.

> Guihua, becoming sizable at the Shaxi Creek, where it is navigable by small boats. From the stream past Yanqian to the mouth of the Shaxi Creek spans thirty *li*, where it merges with the Jiulong River, continues downstream to Yanping, and eventually reaches Fuzhou.

This indicates that goods originating from Guihua County could also be transported via this waterway to Fuzhou.

The Futun Creek features a trellis-like drainage system. Its two primary upstream tributaries are the Beixi Creek and Xixi Creek. The Beixi Creek originates from Beidaqi Mountain in Daiping Village in the northeastern part of Guangze County, while the Xixi Creek, the main source of the Futun Creek, rises from Chahua Pass to the south of Wushan Mountain in Guilin, Shaowu. These two tributaries converged below the county seat of Guangze, from which point the lower reaches of the stream were navigable by small civilian boats. The Futun Creek flowed mainly through Shunchang, Shaowu, and Guangze before joining the Shaxi Creek at its mouth. The 160-kilometer waterway from Guangze to Yangkou Town in Shunchang typically took 3 to 4 days downstream and 7 to 10 days upstream. Yangkou was 270 kilometers by water from Fuzhou, a route that required 3 to 4 days downstream and 8 to 9 days upstream.[1] Historical records show that during the Ming Dynasty, the waterway of the Futun Creek was heavily trafficked. Many local products from Shaowu Prefecture were shipped via this waterway to Yanping and Fuzhou. In the fifteenth year of the Hongzhi reign (1502), there were 498 registered civilian vessels in Shaowu Prefecture.[2] Since the Ming and Qing

1(Japan) Akamatsu Sukeyuki, ed. *Economic Affairs of the Provinces of China*, vol. 16, *Fujian Province*. Japan International Association, 1936, pp. 71–72.

2(Ming) Xing Zhi, comp., and Chen, Rang, ed. *Gazetteer of Shaowu Prefecture,* Jiajing Edition, vol. 5, *Household Register*. Selected Reprints of Local Gazetteers in Ming Dynasty from the Tianyige Collection, Shanghai Ancient Books Bookstore, 1982, p. 235.

dynasties, the Futun Creek had served as a vital conduit linking various counties of Shaowu Prefecture with the middle and lower reaches of the Minjiang River. It also formed an important segment of the interprovincial transportation corridor between Fujian and Jiangxi.

The Jianxi Creek is the largest of the three major tributaries in the upper Minjiang River in terms of water volume. Its three main headwaters are the Chongyang Creek, the Nanpu Creek, and the Songxi Creek. The stream primarily flowed through the counties of Jian'an, Ouning, Pucheng, Chong'an, Jianyang, and Songxi. After the three streams converged, the Jianxi flowed southward to Yanping, where it merged with the Xixi Creek and became part of the Minjiang River. During the Southern Song Dynasty, a 10-kilometer section of the Xianxia Ridge was leveled with 3,060 stone steps, partially mitigating the steep incline.[1] Thereafter, it became possible to travel upstream from Fuzhou along the Minjiang River, transfer to the Jianxi Creek to reach Pucheng, then cross the Xianxia Ridge to Quzhou, and ultimately arrive at the capital city of Lin'an.

The main course of the Minjiang River refers to the middle and lower reaches of the river, extending from the confluence of the Jianxi Creek and the Xixi Creek to its estuary. This section passed through the counties of Nanping, Youxi, Gutian, Minqing, Minhou, Houguan, Changle, and Lianjiang. The section from Nanping to Shuikou in Gutian was classified as the middle reach, and the segment below Shuikou was the lower reach. Major tributaries in the middle reach included the Gutian Creek and the Youxi Creek, while the lower reach included the Dazhang Creek and the Meixi Creek. During the Tang Dynasty, the middle and lower reaches of the Minjaing River, from Nanping to Fuzhou, constituted not only an essential inland navigation

---

1 (Ming) Chen Guifang, comp. *Gazetteer of Qingliu County*, Jiajing Edition, vol. 2, *Mountains and Rivers*. Edited by the Gazetteer Compilation Committee of Qingliu County, Fujian People's Publishing House, 1992, p. 22.

route within Fujian Province, but also a key segment of the official courier route connecting Fuzhou with the capital city of Chang'an. During the High Tang period, official post stations were established along the route from Fuzhou to Jianzhou, with one station placed approximately every 15 kilometers. These stations were divided into land and water posts, with water posts being dominant along the route; land posts were used when dangerous rapids or treacherous stretches of river made river navigation difficult. Among these river segments, the stretch between Nanping and Shuikou along the Jianxi Creek was hazardous due to numerous shoals and rocky outcrops, making navigation challenging. However, the 100-kilometer section from Shuikou to Fuzhou had fewer such obstacles and could accommodate large civilian boats. In the period of the Republic of China, small steamships were reportedly able to navigate near Minqing. According to incomplete statistics, in the late Qing and early Republican periods, no fewer than 3,000 civilian boats navigated the Minjiang River system. Table 5-1 presents a statistical summary of these vessels.

Table 5-1 Statistics on the Number of Civilian Vessels Navigating the Minjiang River System in the Late Qing and Early Republican Periods

Location	**Moored Vessels**		**Transiting Vessels**	
	Type / Tonnage	Quantity (Vessels)	Type / Tonnage	Quantity (Vessels)
Fuzhou	Civilian boats	2,000	Ocean barges	over 100
			Small barges	70–80
			Clinker-built vessels	70–80
Nanping	20–50 *dan* load	300		
Yangkou	Civilian boats	500		
Yong'an	20–200 *dan* load	40		
Shuikou	Sparrow-shaped boats	30		
	Fuzhou boats	10		

Location	**Moored Vessels**		**Transiting Vessels**	
	Type / Tonnage	Quantity (Vessels)	Type / Tonnage	Quantity (Vessels)
	Rooster-shaped boats, knife-shaped boats	10		
Baisha	20–50 *dan* load	over 10		
Shakou	10–20 *dan* load	dozens		
Shunchang–Shaowu			20–30 *dan* load	20
Shunchang–Jiangle			20–30 *dan* load	20
Jian'ou–Songxi			20–30 *dan* load	20
Nanping–Jian'ou			20–30 *dan* load	20
Yangkou–Shaowu			Cockboats, sparrow boats	hundreds
Fuzhou–Yangkou			30–500 *dan* load	over 20
Shaxian–Zikoufang			10–20 *dan* load	16

Source: Dai Yifeng. "A Preliminary Study of Minjiang River Shipping in Modern Times." *The Journal of Chinese Social and Economic History,* no. 3, 1986, p. 108.

The sailing speed of various boats on the Minjiang River depended on multiple factors, including current speed, flow direction, vessel size, and the number and experience of crew members. In general, downstream navigation required significantly less time than upstream travel. For example, traveling downstream from Pucheng via the Jianxi Creek to Fuzhou could be completed in 4 to 5 days, whereas the upstream journey from Fuzhou to Pucheng—spanning approximately 390 kilometers—resulted in a daily travel distance of just over 20 kilometers.[1] Table 5-2 summarizes the navigability of major inland water routes in the Minjiang River Basin during the period of Republic of China.

Table 5-2 Navigability of Major Inland Waterways in the Minjiang River Basin During the Republican Era

River System	River Section	Distance (*li*)	Cargo Capacity during High Water Season	Navigation Time
Jianxi Creek	Zhenghe upstream to Songxi	20	Less than 20–30 *dan*	—
	Xijin to Jian'ou	130	—	Upstream: 5 days; Downstream: 2 days
	Jian'ou to Pucheng	320	20–50 *dan*	Upstream: 9 days; Downstream: 3 days
	Jian'ou to Jianyang	120	Large sailboats (10,000–20,000 *jin*)	Upstream: 8 days; Downstream: 3 days
	Jianyang to Chong'an	90	Small boats	—
	Jian'ou to Yanping	125	Large boats	Upstream: 2 days; Downstream: 1 day
Futun Creek	Upstream of Guangze	—	Rafts only	—
	Yangkou to Guangze	320	—	Upstream: 10 days; Downstream: 5 days
	Yangkou to Jiangle	—	—	Upstream: 3 days;

1Lai Weiyuan, comp. *Guide My Journey*. Manuscript copy held at the Shanghai Library, p. 34.

River System	River Section	Distance (*li*)	Cargo Capacity during High Water Season	Navigation Time
				Downstream: 1 day
	Yangkou to Nake	—	—	Upstream: 3 days; Downstream: 2 days
	Yangkou to Shunchang	30	—	Upstream: 6 hours; Downstream: 2 hours
	Yangkou to Shaowu	240	—	Upstream: 7 days; Downstream: 3 days
	Yangkou to Fuzhou	570	—	Upstream: 9 days; Downstream: 4 days
	Yangkou to Jianning	—	—	Upstream: 7 days; Downstream: 4 days
Shaxi Creek	Yong'an to Shaxian	340	30–50 *dan*	—
	Shaxian to Shaxi Stream Estuary	—	500 *dan* to over 10,000 *jin*	—
	Shaxian to Fuzhou	520	500 *dan* to over 10,000 *jin*	Downstream: 4 days; Upstream: 9 days
Youxi Creek	Youxi to Jiangkou	200	Sailboats	—
Mainstream of Minjiang River	Nanping to Shuikou	200	Large boats	Upstream: 3 days; large boats: 7–8 days
	Shuikou to Fuzhou	200	Small steamers also navigable	Upstream: 3 days; Downstream: 2 days

River System	River Section	Distance (*li*)	Cargo Capacity during High Water Season	Navigation Time
	Fuzhou to Minjiang River Estuary	34	Steamships can reach Luoxing Pagoda; other boats unimpeded	—

Source: Lin Yuru, Jiang Xiuxian, Zhou Zifeng, and Wang Zhan. *Modern Economic Geography of China: Fujian and Taiwan Volume*, East China Normal University Press, 2016, p.150.

As shown in Table 5-2, during the Republican period, vessels navigating the major inland waterways of the Minjiang River Basin varied widely in type. Among these, only the river segments from Jian'ou to Nanping and from Nanping to Shuikou were navigable by large vessels, while upstream sections beyond Nanping could not accommodate large ships. Overall, the Minjiang River's mainstream featured a relatively wide river surface, fewer rapids, and stronger navigability.

2. Commercial Water Routes in the Minjiang River Basin

(1) Commodity Export Routes

Prior to the Tang Dynasty, the Minjiang River had long served as a crucial channel for both the export and import of goods in the Minjiang River Basin. From Shuangjiantan in Yanping District, goods could travel upstream along the Futun Creek to Shanguan Ridge in Guangze County, where they could exit Fujian into Lichuan in Jiangxi Province. Alternatively, they could ascend the Jianxi Creek to reach Xianxia Ridge, cross into Quzhou in Zhejiang, or travel downstream along the Minjiang River to Fuzhou, and then be shipped overseas via Fuzhou Port. For this reason, the Minjiang River was often referred to as Fujian's "Golden Waterway." Beginning with the southward migration of Han elites during the Western Jin Dynasty, northern Fujian utilized this golden waterway to trade tea, salt, dried goods, and fresh fruits. Cargo transport on the river commonly employed "big-bellied boats" and "bird-shaped boats," supplemented by long-tailed wooden rafts. While the tributaries and their branches saw extensive use of smaller "rooster-shaped boats" and bamboo rafts for minor transport and trade.[1] By the early Tang Dynasty, commercial navigation on both the Minjiang River's main stream and its tributaries had achieved significant scale. Taking the Futun Creek as an example, goods from the Shaowu area could travel upstream to Guangze, exit via Shanguan Pass into eastern Jiangxi and southern Zhejiang, or descend the stream to Shunchang, then to Yanping, and finally reach Fuzhou. In the eighth year of Emperor Wenzong's Taihe reign (834 CE), an imperial edict encouraged free trade between inland regions and the coastal areas of Fujian and Lingnan, prohibiting double taxation. This policy greatly stimulated trade between the Central Plains and the coastal areas of Fujian. Situated at the confluence of the Chongyang, Nanpu, and Songxi creeks, Jian'ou controlled a strategic waterway chokepoint, making it a vital distribution center linking northern Fujian and the inland hinterland with the Minjiang River estuary. Local products such as grain, porcelain, and timber were transported downstream via the Jianxi Creek, then along the Minjiang River to Fuzhou, and from there shipped overseas via Fuzhou Port. As waterborne trade gradually flourished, the number of docks in Jian'ou steadily grew. According to historical records, it was once said that Jian'ou had "eight urban docks and eight rural docks."

The Song and Yuan dynasties marked a period of flourishing maritime trade for China. During this time, northern Fujian enjoyed relative social stability and economic prosperity. Industries such as ceramics, tea, papermaking and woodblock printing, textile production, and metallurgy all thrived. Northern Fujian's main waterborne trade routes were centered on

1 Wu Bangcai, editor-in-chief. *A History of the Development of Fujian Merchants: Nanping Volume*. Xiamen University Press, 2016, p. 10

Jianyang and consisted of two principal lines: one from Jianyang to Jian'ou via the Chongyang Creek; the other from Shuiji to Jian'ou via the Nanpu Creek, then to Nanping along the Jianxi Creek, and from there downstream along the middle and lower reaches of the Minjiang River to Fuzhou. From Fuzhou Port, goods were shipped to Quanzhou Port and then exported to Southeast Asian countries, or directly to Korea and Japan.

In 1976, a Yuan Dynasty shipwreck was discovered in the seas off Sinan, South Korea. Among the unearthed artifacts from the shipwreck were black-glazed ceramics identified as products of the Jian kiln from the Song period. According to the research of Ye Wencheng and Lin Zhonggan, Jianyang black-glazed teacup was exported to Japan during the Song and Yuan dynasties via three primary routes: (1) from Fuzhou to the Ryukyu Islands and then to Japan; (2) from Quanzhou to the Penghu Islands and then to Japan; and (3) from Ningbo directly to Japan, or via Fuzhou or Quanzhou to Ningbo and then to Japan.[1] In addition, green-glazed porcelain, white porcelain, and lead-glazed ceramics produced in Chaoyang Town were also exported in large quantities during the Song and Yuan dynasties to Korea, Japan, Indonesia, the Philippines, and the Penghu Islands. *A Brief Account of Island Barbarians* documented the overseas destinations of various ceramic exports from Fujian during the Yuan Dynasty, as detailed in Table 5-3.

Table 5-3 Export Sales of Fujian Ceramics During the Yuan Dynasty

Destination Country or Region	Types of Ceramics	Destination Country or Region	Types of Ceramics
Mishima	Green-white porcelain	Bengkulu	Porcelain
Sulu	Porcelain	Brunei	Black jars, green

1 Wu Bangcai, editor-in-chief. *A History of the Development of Fujian Merchants: Nanping Volume*. Xiamen University Press, 2016, p.62

Destination Country or Region	Types of Ceramics	Destination Country or Region	Types of Ceramics
			porcelain
The Champa Kingdom	Green porcelain flower bowls	Champa	Coarse bowls
Malacca	Green-white porcelain from Chuzhou, tile kiln	Chivanno	Large/small water jars
Japan	Green porcelain, coarse bowls	Malacca	Green porcelain, coarse bowls
Mait	Porcelain, plates, water jars, large urns	Ligor	Green-white flower bowls
Tondo, Manila	Green-white flower bowls	Sumenep	Large/small water jars
Phuket	Green-white flower bowls, jars, pots	Bangkok	Porcelain
Lovek	Green-white bowls	Pattani	Green porcelain, coarse bowls, large/small water jars
Lopburi	Green ware	Johor Lama	Chuzhou porcelain, large/small water jars, urns
Kozhikode	Green-white flower bowls, large/small water jars	Barus	Green porcelain, earthenware vessels
Surat	Green-white flower bowls, water jars	The Singapore Strait	Chuzhou porcelain
Jambi	Large/small water jars	Langkawi Island	Coarse bowls
Dai Viet	Coarse bowls, green ware	Pasai	Coarse bowls, Chuzhou greenware

Source: Wu Bangcai, editor-in-chief. *A History of the Development of Fujian Merchants : Nanping Volume*. Xiamen University Press, 2016, pp:63–64.

As Table 5-3 indicates, green porcelain dominated Fujian's ceramic exports during the Yuan Dynasty, with a wide variety of vessel types. While many of these products were manufactured in northern Fujian, some also originated from Jiangxi and Zhejiang provinces. Moreover, ceramic wares from northern Fujian during the Song-Yuan period have also been discovered in South Asia, West Asia, and Africa. These findings confirm that the Song-Yuan era represented a peak in northern Fujian's ceramic industry.

The Ming Dynasty instituted strict maritime prohibitions starting in the Hongwu reign which banned overseas trade. These restrictions were lifted only in the first year of the Longqing reign (1567), after which maritime commerce gradually resumed and river traffic along the Minjiang River from Pucheng to Fuzhou once again became busy.

After the mid-Ming Dynasty, farmers in coastal regions of Fujian—particularly the prefectures of Fuzhou, Xinghua, Quanzhou, and Zhangzhou— primarily cultivated sugarcane and other cash crops in lieu of grain, with relatively little land devoted to staple grains like rice, even as local population growth accelerated. As a result, these areas experienced grain shortages. In contrast, the regions of Shaowu, Jianning, and Yanping produced surplus rice, much of which was shipped along the Minjiang River to Fuzhou and then further distributed to coastal regions such as Xinghua, Quanzhou, and Zhangzhou. Rice from Pucheng flowed down the Nanpu Creek to the Jianxi Creek, then to Nanping, and from there along the middle and lower reaches of the Minjiang River to Fuzhou. Shaowu Prefecture's surplus grain traveled along the Futun Creek and the Jinxi Creek to the mouth of the Shaxi Creek, and then entered the Minjiang River toward Fuzhou. Nakou Town in Shaowu, Jian'ou, and Nanping became major grain trading hubs. After the Qing court unified Taiwan, the island, already short on grain, faced increased demand due to the stationing of large numbers of troops. Northern Fujian began trading grain with Taiwan, often in the form of barter—exchanging rice from northern Fujian for coal and other goods from Taiwan. This system of barter continued until the founding of the People's

Republic of China.

Northern Fujian has long had a tradition of reforestation, resulting in abundant bamboo and timber resources. "Jian fir" was one of the region's major export commodities. After the Ming Court lifted the maritime ban, timber trade in northern Fujian gradually expanded, and by the Qianlong reign in the Qing Dynasty, timber represented by Jian fir had reached markets across Southeast Asia. There were two primary transport methods for exporting northern Fujian's timber: (1) loading timber onto wooden sailing ships, which traveled down the Futun Creek, Jianxi Creek, and Minjiang River to reach Fuzhou; (2) bundling timber into rafts secured with bamboo and rattan ties, then floating them downstream via the same waterways using manpower. From Fuzhou, these logs were shipped to Jiangsu, Zhejiang, Taiwan, Guangdong, and Southeast Asian countries. Timber from Ninghua, Qingliu, and Guihua (under Tingzhou Prefecture) was mainly transported along the Shaxi Creek and then down the middle and lower reaches of the Minjiang River to Fuzhou. In the Qing period, Fuzhou was one of the three largest timber distribution centers in China. In addition to timber, northern Fujian's bamboo and bamboo shoots were also frequently exported during the Qing Dynasty, following routes similar to those used for timber trade.

Papermaking in northern Fujian originated during the Tang Dynasty, developed through the Song and Yuan periods, and gradually expanded its exports during the Ming and Qing dynasties. Although all counties in northern Fujian produced bamboo paper, it was noted that "paper from Shunchang was the finest."[1] After Zheng He's voyages to the Western Seas during the Ming Dynasty, traditional handmade paper from northern Fujian—represented by Shunchang's *Maobian* paper and Jianyang's *Yukou* paper—

1(Ming) Huang Zhongzhao, compiler. *General Gazetteer of Fujian*, vol. 25, *Food and Commodities*. Fujian People's Publishing House, 1990, p. 550.

saw a significant increase in exports. Waterways remained the primary transport routes. Paper produced in Shaowu, Shunchang, and Guangze was shipped downstream via the Futun Creek into the Minjiang River. Paper from Jianyang was transported via the Jianxi Creek into the Minjiang River. Paper from Jiangle, Mingxi, and Qingliu was carried via the Shaxi Creek into the Minjiang River, and from there to Fuzhou. From Fuzhou, the paper was distributed to Jiangsu, Zhejiang, Guangdong, Guangxi, Hunan, Hubei, and exported to Japan, Indonesia, the Philippines, and other countries. Notably, the types of paper produced in Qingliu such as *Changxing*, *Yukou*, *Daguang*, and *Gaolian* were not only shipped to Fuzhou via waterways but also exported to Chaozhou, Hong Kong, and Vietnam.[1]

In the early Qing Dynasty, black tea was first developed in the region of Wuyi Mountain in northern Fujian. With its mellow flavor aligning with European tastes, it quickly gained popularity overseas. Beginning in the early Kangxi reign, European merchants dispatched vessels to China specifically to purchase Wuyi black tea. In the early Qing period, northern Fujian tea was mainly exported via the Jianxi Creek and the Minjiang River to Fuzhou, then transported by water to Xiamen for shipment to Europe. After the Opium War and the subsequent opening of treaty ports like Fuzhou and Xiamen, tea from northern Fujian was once again shipped to these ports and exported to Southeast Asia, Europe, and the Americas. Wuyi tea shipped from Xingcun Town could reach Fuzhou via water transport in as little as four days, while the overland route through Hekou in Jiangxi to Guangzhou took up to 45 days. Thus, exporting through the Fuzhou Port significantly reduced both transportation time and cost, allowing foreign merchants to reach European markets earlier and gain competitive advantage. However, by the late 19th

1 Lin Shanqing, ed., and Wang Qiong, comp. *Gazetteer of Qingliu County*. Compiled during the Republic of China era. *Collection of Chinese Local Gazetteers: Fujian Prefectural and County Gazetteers,* vol. 38. Shanghai Bookstore Publishing House, 2000, p.350.

century, with the mass cultivation of tea in British colonies such as India and Ceylon, and the rise of tea trade, foreign merchants began sourcing tea from those regions. As a result, tea exports through Fuzhou declined, leading to a downturn in Fuzhou's tea trade and a significant reduction in tea cultivation across northern Fujian—many plantations were even abandoned.

Beyond the aforementioned commodities, other local products such as tobacco, indigo, *zexie* (Alisma orientale), and shiitake mushrooms were also widely produced and traded during the Ming and Qing periods. According to the *Gazetteer of Guangze County: Local Survey*, by the 30th year of the Guangxu reign (1904), Guangze produced over 200,000 *jin* of indigo annually, with approximately 100,000 *jin* shipped to Fuzhou by water.[1] The ceramics industry in northern Fujian experienced a relatively slower development in the Ming and Qing eras, with both the quality and quantity of exports falling short of Song and Yuan levels. Following the opening of treaty ports in the late Qing and into the early Republic of China period, many of northern Fujian's traditional exports remained active. However, between 1930 and 1949, due to wartime disruptions, agricultural and industrial production in the region declined sharply, and external trade became unstable.

(2) Commodity Import Routes

Imported goods into northern Fujian primarily included salt, seafood, textiles, Beijing dry fruits, and various daily commodities. These goods were usually shipped upstream along the Minjiang River, reaching Nanping, and then further transported via tributaries such as the Jianxi Creek, Shaxi Creek, and Futun Creek to the counties of northern Fujian. Some cargo was carried across the Xianxia Ridge by porters for sale in southern Zhejiang. Historical records show that during the Jiajing reign of the Ming Dynasty, small wooden

---

1 Wu Bangcai, editor-in-chief. *A History of the Development of Fujian Merchants: Nanping Volume*. Xiamen University Press, 2016, p.81.

boats frequently traveled along the Futun Creek, with 100–200 vessels operating daily and as many as 300–500 on market days. Large quantities of agricultural and sideline products, timber, and bamboo were shipped downstream via the Futun Creek to Fuzhou and coastal areas. On the return journey upstream, boats transported salt, seafood, fish products, textiles, and general goods to Shunchang, Shaowu, Guangze, Jiangle, Taining, Jianning, and other counties.[1] By the early Qing period, the number of vessels operating on the Futun Creek had surpassed 1,000, and commercial activity peaked during the Qianlong and Jiaqing reigns. During the Ming and Qing periods, grain from northern Fujian was shipped downstream via the Minjiang River to Fuzhou, while salt was brought upstream from Fuzhou—forming a longstanding trade network of grain and salt that lasted until the eve of the Opium War. After the opening of treaty ports, particularly Fuzhou, large quantities of Wuyi tea were exported overseas. As a result, farmers in northern Fujian began to cultivate tea on a large scale, leading to a sharp decline in rice production and turning areas such as Pucheng into grain-deficient regions. Subsequently, grain produced in Jiangsu, Zhejiang, and Southeast Asia was shipped by sea to Fuzhou and then transported upriver via the Minjiang River to supply the counties of northern Fujian.

II. Inland Waterway Navigation and Trade Routes of the Tingjiang River

1. Overview of the Tingjiang River Waterway

The Tingjiang River is the third-largest river in Fujian Province and the largest in western Fujian. It is also the province's only trans-provincial river. Originating from the northern slope of Muma Mountain in Zhiping Town, Ninghua County, located on the southeastern side of the southern Wuyi

---

1 Wu Bangcai, editor-in-chief. *A History of the Development of Fujian Merchants: Nanping Volume*. Xiamen University Press, 2016, p.107.

Mountains, the river flows from north to south through the four counties of Changting, Wuping, Shanghang, and Yongding in western Fujian. It exits the province at Fengshi Town in Yongding County and enters Dabu County in Guangdong Province, where it merges with the Meijiang River at the Sanhe Dam to form the Hanjiang River. Thus, the Tingjiang River belongs to the Hanjiang River system. Major tributaries of the Tingjiang River Basin include the Zhuotian River, Taolan Creek, Jiuxian River (its upper section is known as the Liannan River), Huangtan River, Yongding River, and Jinfeng Creek.[123] The Tingjiang River Basin is characterized by steep and rugged mountainous terrain. The section between Changting and Shanghang has relatively wide channels and is navigable, whereas the stretch below Shanghang contains many rapids and swift currents. As such, throughout history, the Tingjiang River's navigation channels have undergone multiple phases of development and improvement.

After the establishment of Tingzhou Prefecture during the Tang Dynasty, Changting's economic growth was slow, population increase was limited, and industry and commerce remained in a relatively primitive state. It can be said that before the Southern Song period, the population in western Fujian was relatively sparse and scattered, and the scale of economic development was small. Coupled with the region's rugged mountainous terrain, poor overland transportation, and inconvenient waterway transport, communication with the outside world was difficult, and the local economy primarily operated

1 He Meifeng. "Fish Diversity and Its Influencing Factors in the Upper and Middle Reaches of the Tingjiang River." *Fujian Journal of Agricultural Sciences*, vol. 31, no. 6, 2016, p. 567.

2 Zhang Jie, Zhang Zhengdong, Wan Luwen, Yang Chuanxun, and Ye Chen. "Contributions of Climate Change and Human Activities to Runoff Variation in the Tingjiang River." *Journal of South China Normal University (Natural Science Edition)*, vol. 49, no. 6, 2017, p. 85.

3 (France) Lagerwey John, editor-in-chief. *Traditional Hakka Society*. Zhonghua Book Company, 2005, p. 56.

under a self-sufficient production model. At the time, table salt was monopolized and distributed by the imperial court. Since salt was not locally produced in Tingzhou, residents in western Fujian consumed "Fu salt". Fu salt mainly came from the coastal areas of eastern Fujian. It was shipped upstream along the Minjiang River to Nanjianzhou (modern-day Yanping District, Nanping), then transferred to boats navigating the Shaxi Creek to Guihua County (modern-day Mingxi, Sanming), and finally carried overland by human porters to Tingzhou. Due to the long transportation route and multiple transfers, there was significant loss during transit, resulting in high prices and poor quality. This led to widespread complaints among the local people. During the Southern Song period, navigation along the Tingjiang River gradually developed. In the sixth year of the Jiading reign (1213), Zhao Chongmo, then prefect of Tingzhou, opened a navigation route from Shanghang to Fengshi in Yongding. In the third year of the Duanping reign (1236), county magistrate Song Ci further extended navigation from Changting to Huilong. In the thirtieth year of the Jiajing reign of the Ming Dynasty (1551), Tingzhou prefect Chen Hongfan successfully managed the rapids at Huilong, completing a navigable route from Changting through Shanghang to Fengshi in Yongding.[1] However, below Fengshi, especially around the Mianhuatan Rapids, the river was treacherous and fast-flowing. A 5.5-kilometer stretch between Fengshi and Dabu County in Guangdong was strewn with hidden reefs, making it impassable for vessels of any size. Therefore, goods shipped from Tingzhou to Chaozhou had to be unloaded at Fengshi and carried overland for five kilometers before being reloaded onto boats for continued transport along the Hanjiang River. In the early Yuan Dynasty, as Chaozhou's status as an economic hub in southeastern coastal China rose, the region sought to extend its reach into the hinterland and

1 Cai Lixiong, editor-in-chief. *A Commercial History of Western Fujian.* Xiamen University Press, 2014, p. 32.

strengthen interprovincial connections between Jiangxi, Fujian, and Guangdong. In the 21st year of the Zhiyuan reign (1284), Yuedi Mishi, the Pacification Commissioner of the Guangdong Circuit, opened a courier route from Longxing (modern-day Nanchang, Jiangxi), via Fuzhou (modern Linchuan District, Fuzhou, Jiangxi), through Shaowu (now Shaowu, Fujian), then descending through Tingzhou (modern Changting County, Fujian), and finally to Chaozhou (modern Chaozhou, Guangdong). The entire route covered approximately 800 kilometers and included 17 official courier stations.[1] During the Ming and Qing dynasties, this courier route was improved and expanded: in the sixth year of the Chenghua reign (1470), Pingxi Station (in southern Shanghang) was added; in the tenth year of Chenghua (1474), Lanwu Station (at the Huilong section of the Tingjiang River between Shanghang and Changting) was added; and during the Hongzhi reign, Sanzhou Station (in south of Changting County) was established. The Qing Dynasty added Yongding Station as well. The opening and navigation of the Tingjiang River waterway during the Southern Song Dynasty, coupled with the opening of the Longxing–Chaozhou courier route in the Yuan Dynasty, greatly enhanced economic ties between western Fujian and eastern Guangdong. The continued improvement of the Tingjiang River waterway in the Ming and Qing dynasties further promoted the flow of goods and people among Jiangxi, Fujian, and Guangdong. Shipping goods downstream from Tingzhou to Chaozhou and exiting via Shantou Port constituted the shortest and most convenient maritime route for the mountainous regions of western Fujian. As a result, Tingzhou became the economic and trade hub at the junction of Fujian, Guangdong, and Jiangxi during the Ming and Qing periods. By the Republican era, the Tingjiang River system had three major navigable waterways primarily served by

1Yan Guangwen. "The Opening of the New Postal Route from Longxing to Chaozhou in the Yuan Dynasty and Its Impact on the Border Development of Jiangxi, Fujian, and Guangdong." *China's Borderland History and Geography Studies*, no. 2, 1998, p. 11.

civilian vessels. See Table 5-4 for details.

Table 5-4 Navigable Waterways and Vessel Operations in the Tingjiang River System During the Republican Period

Waterway Name	Navigable Vessel Type	Route	Approximate Length	Notes
Tingjiang River	Civilian boats	Changting to Fengshi	260 km	Including the Shuilan Creek and Huangtan Creek
Jiuxian River	Civilian boats	Shanghang to Pengkou	60 km	Tributary of the Tingjiang River
Yongding Creek	Civilian boats	Kanshi to Shixia Dam	50 km	Tributary of the Tingjiang River

Source: Zhu Daijie, and Ji Tianyou, *Overview of Fujian's Economy.* Fujian Provincial Department of Construction, 1947, p.198.

Fengshi in Yongding served as a critical node on the Tingjiang River, becoming the largest river port on the lower reaches of the Tingjiang River and the sole transfer point along the Hanjiang River system for goods flowing among Fujian, Guangdong, and Jiangxi. During the War of Resistance against Japanese Aggression, Fengshi earned the nickname “Little Hong Kong” for its bustling commerce.

2. Waterborne Trade Routes in the Tingjiang River Basin

Western Fujian is a mountainous region, with ranges rising one after another. The Tingjiang River Basin features a relatively dense fluvial network, and throughout history, successive regimes paid insufficient attention to the development of overland transportation. As a result, the Tingjiang River and its tributaries naturally evolved into the region’s primary transportation system. Strategically located at the junction of Fujian, Guangdong, and Jiangxi provinces, the Tingjiang River Basin boasted a favorable geographic position: to the south, it connected via the Tingjiang River and Hanjiang River with the Chaoshan region, offering access to the sea through Shantou Port; to the west, overland routes led to Ruijin and then along the Ganjiang River to the Yangtze River Basin and the Central Plains; to the east, it linked to the Minjiang River via the Shaxi Creek and Jianxi Creek, reaching the sea through Fuzhou Port. Commercial activities across the counties in the Tingjiang River Basin mainly revolved around two systems: the "mountain–sea exchange" with coastal Fujian and Guangdong, and the "salt–grain trade" with southern Jiangxi. Of these, the connection with the Hanjiang River Delta was the most active.[1] According to historical records, "The county borders connect with Guangxi and Guangdong, with a constant flow of traveling merchants. As trade flourishes and people settle, the exchange of rice and salt is of utmost importance."[2]

(1) Commodity Export Routes

Western Fujian was historically one of the production centers for green-glazed ceramics exported from Fujian. During the Song Dynasty, the region boasted numerous pottery kilns, tile kilns, and jar kilns.[3] Records indicate that as early as the Song and Yuan periods, ceramics produced in western Fujian were already being exported to Southeast Asian countries through ports such as Shantou and Quanzhou. The American scholar Li Rukuan once wrote a paper mentioning a ceramic fruit plate exported from Fujian. He

---

1Zhou Xuexiang. "A Comparative Study of the Regional Economies of the Two River Basins in the Tingzhou Area During the Qing Dynasty." *Journal of Gannan Normal University*, no.1, 2012, p. 84.

2(Qing) Liu Guoguang, compiler. *Gazetteer of Changting County,* Guangxu edition. *Series of Chinese Local Gazetteers*, no. 87. Chengwen Publishing House, 1967, p. 483.

3 Cai Lixiong, editor-in-chief. *A Commercial History of Western Fujian*. Xiamen University Press, 2014, p. 79.

identified it as "Exported from Shantou, Guangdong in 1127; produced in Tingzhou, Fujian; with a diameter of 39 centimeters, a footing diameter of 16.5 centimeters, and a height of 7 centimeters." He also noted that in *The Travels of Marco Polo*, Marco Polo referred to the green-glazed ceramics of Tingzhou as high-quality and inexpensive.[1] These ceramics were transported from Tingzhou along the Tingjiang River and Hanjiang River to Shantou for overseas export. Scholars have discovered a dragon kiln from the Song-Yuan period in Nanshan Town, Changting County, measuring 80 to 90 meters in length, with ceramic layers up to 2 meters thick. Many of the collected green-glazed shards feature decorative patterns identical to those found in archaeological sites in the Philippines and Indonesia, which were rarely seen locally—suggesting that the Nanshan dragon kiln may have been a major production site dedicated to export.[2] In addition to ceramics, other goods produced in western Fujian during the Song and Yuan dynasties—such as oil tea, timber, and handmade paper—were also transported via the Tingjiang River and Hanjiang River to Chaozhou. Some were then shipped onward to Quanzhou for further maritime export to countries including Malaysia, Indonesia, the Philippines, and Japan.

From the mid-Ming Dynasty onward, as maritime bans were gradually lifted, handicrafts and commerce in the mountainous areas of western Fujian developed significantly, and regional economies became increasingly commercialized. Among the major export commodities from the mid-Ming period onward were timber, tobacco, handmade paper, indigo, and books. Each year, counties along the Tingjiang River such as Changting and Shanghang exported large volumes of China fir. According to Volume 4 *On*

1Huang Ting, and Du Jingguo. "Transportation and Economic Connections in the Fujian–Guangdong–Jiangxi Border Region from the Song to the Qing Dynasties." *Journal of Shantou University (Humanities Edition)*, no. 2, 1995, p. 81.

2Li Min. "An Analysis of the Overseas Trade of Ancient Hakka Ceramics from Western Fujian." *Sculpture*, no.5, 2016, p. 56.

Local Products of the *Collected Studies on Linting*, once the fir trees matured and were ready for harvest, merchants from Chaozhou would travel to Changting to purchase the trees based on mountain valuation. The timber would then be transported to wharves along the Tingjiang River, bundled into rafts, and floated downstream to Chaozhou. This trade brought significant wealth to riverside villages along the Tinjiangg River. The timber industry and its exports remained highly active through the Qing and Republican periods. It is recorded that in the early Republic of China, timber exports from Wuping reached an annual value of 400,000 to 500,000 silver dollars. Although this declined due to the fall of the Chaoshan region, Wuping still exported approximately 200,000 silver dollars' worth of timber annually via Chaozhou. Timber from the Tingjiang River Basin was primarily transported via the Tingjiang and Hanjiang river systems to the Chaoshan region. There were two main transportation routes. The first route relied on the main channel of the Tingjiang River, with timber shipped from four major wharves located in the county seat of Changting, Zhuotian, Xinquan, and Huilong. From there, it passed through Shanghang County or Fengren, reaching Fengshi in Yongding. The timber was then transported via Shixia Dam to Sanhe Dam in Dabu County, and finally delivered to Chaozhou, from which it was further distributed to Shantou. The second route involved timber exported from Wuping, which was shipped via the Xiaohe River, passing through Wusuo, Xiaba, and Jiaoling, and reaching Songkou Town in Meizhou. From there, it was transported to Chaozhou and further to Shantou, then distributed northward to destinations such as Taiwan, Ningbo, Shanghai, Qingdao, and Tianjin, and southward to Guangzhou, Hong Kong, the Philippines, Indonesia, and other regions. [1] Timber exported from the Tingjiang River Basin provided abundant raw materials for construction and

1 Liu Zhenggang. "Economic Development of the Tingjiang River Basin and the Hanjiang River Delta." *The Journal of Chinese Social and Economic History*, no. 2, 1995, p. 80.

shipbuilding in these importing regions. It also brought considerable wealth to the counties along the Tingjiang River, while promoting active trade and population movement between the Tingjiang River Basin, coastal areas, and Southeast Asia.

The mountainous counties of the Tingjiang River Basin were also rich in moso bamboo, an essential raw material for papermaking. During the Ming and Qing dynasties, most of the paper produced in the region was shipped via the Tingjiang River and Hanjiang River to Chaozhou, and then distributed to Guangzhou, Foshan, Hong Kong, and Southeast Asia. Chaozhou became a major distribution hub for Tingzhou's handmade paper. In addition, some merchants from Guangdong even established paper depots in Liancheng, where they directly purchased locally produced paper and transported it by water along the Tingjiang River to the Chaoshan region, eventually exporting it to Vietnam, Thailand, Myanmar, and other Southeast Asian countries and regions.

During the Ming and Qing dynasties, tobacco was also an important export commodity for counties such as Liancheng, Shanghang, and Yongding. The raw tobacco leaves used in processing the renowned *Chao Yan* (Chaozhou tobacco) in Chaozhou Prefecture were primarily sourced from Yongding and Dabu. In Yongding, tobacco leaves were carried on foot from Fengshi Town to Sanhe Dam in Dabu County, then loaded onto boats and shipped to Chaozhou. According to the *Gazetteer of Yongding County*, shredded tobacco produced in Yongding was even exported as far as to the Southeast Asia during the Republican period. The transportation route followed the same pattern: from Yongding to Chaozhou, then overseas via Chaozhou Port.

The book printing industry in western Fujian was epitomized by the woodblock printing tradition of Sibao in Liancheng. According to historical accounts, printed books from Sibao during the Qing Dynasty were distributed via three major routes, two of which utilized the Tingjiang River waterway. The first route went westward from Sibao to Changting, then down the Tingjiang River by boat through Shanghang, Chaozhou, and Shantou, before continuing by sea into the Pearl River to reach Guangzhou. From there, books were dispersed throughout western Guangdong or transported upstream along the Pearl River to Wuzhou, Guixian, Lingshan, Hengxian, Nanning, and Baise in Guangxi, eventually reaching various regions in Yunnan. The second route passed through the Pengkou Creek into the Hanjiang River, reaching eastern Guangdong's Chaoshan region, and from there books were shipped via Shantou Port to Southeast Asian countries.[1]

During the Qing Dynasty, the population of western Fujian increased rapidly. Given the mountainous terrain and limited arable land, local grain production could not meet demand, necessitating large-scale grain imports. Southern Jiangxi, the neighboring region, had abundant rice production and had been supplying grain to Tingzhou since the Southern Song Dynasty. During the Ming and Qing dynasties, grain–salt trade between Tingzhou and southern Jiangxi remained active. Merchants from Tingzhou purchased rice from Jiangxi not only for local consumption but also for resale to Meizhou and Chaozhou. The grain followed the waterway downstream along the Tingjiang River to Yongding's Fengshi, continued to Sanhe Dam in Dabu, and from there entered the Hanjiang River to reach Chaozhou. After the Opium War, Xiamen opened as a treaty port, and western Fujian became integrated into a trade network centered on Xiamen. Consequently, local products such as timber, paper, and tobacco, which were previously shipped via the Tingjiang River and Hanjiang River to Chaozhou, were now in part transported from Shantou by sea to Xiamen, then exported overseas through Xiamen Port. Goods imported through Xiamen also traveled this route in

1 Cai Lixiong, editor-in-chief. *A Commercial History of Western Fujian*. Xiamen University Press, 2014, p. 65.

reverse, moving inland.[1] During the Ming and Qing dynasties, other export products from counties along the Tingjiang River included indigo, ceramics, and more.

(2) Commodity Import Routes

Western Fujian, being mountainous and landlocked, was historically unable to produce salt locally and thus depended heavily on imports. After the opening of the courier route from Longxing to Chaozhou during the Yuan Dynasty, various local specialties produced in Chaozhou—including sea salt, fish, rice, porcelain, textiles, and rice wine—were mostly transported upstream along the Hanjiang River to Dabu County in Guangdong. From there, goods were carried overland for a short distance to Yongding's Fengshi, then shipped upstream via the Tingjiang River to Tingzhou, with some cargo continuing on to southern Jiangxi. Compared to *Fu salt*, *Chao salt* had lower transportation costs and higher quality, making it more popular among consumers. Moreover, large quantities of contraband salt were also smuggled from Chaozhou via the Hanjiang River and Tingjiang River to Tingzhou, and then transshipped to Ganzhou. In the early Ming period, salt remained a government monopoly. The residents in Chaoshan region were heavily involved in fishing and salt trading, and the salt supplies for regions such as Meizhou, Tingzhou, and Ganzhou largely originated there. According to the *Treatise on the Advantages and Disadvantages of Commanderies and States of the Empire*, one of the main trade routes for salt exports from Chaozhou was the "Chao–Ting–Gan" commercial route. Salt was purchased at markets along Dongjie, taxed at the Guangji Bridge, and then shipped via the Hanjiang River to Sanhe Dam in Dabu County, Meizhou. From there, it was carried overland and reloaded onto boats, ascending the Tingjiang River to

1Lin Yuru, Jiang Xiuxian, Zhou Zifeng, and Wang Zhan. *Modern Economic Geography of China: Modern Economic Geography of Fujian and Taiwan*. East China Normal University Press, 2016, p. 187.

Tingzhou, then transported overland across the Changting–Ruijin border to reach Ruijin, Huichang, and Shicheng in Jiangxi.[1] Since the Song and Yuan dynasties, western Fujian had also imported other goods besides salt—such as cotton, cloth, sugar, medicinal herbs, and seafood—a large volume of which was transported inland from coastal areas via the Hanjiang River and Tingjiang River. During the Ming and Qing periods, the preferred route for Fujian merchants traveling to Guangdong was likewise along this waterway. Chaozhou and Shantou became vital distribution hubs for the import and export of goods from Tingzhou and various parts of southern Jiangxi.

III. Navigation and Trade Routes of the Jiulong River

1. Overview of the Jiulong River Waterway

The Jiulong River is the second-largest river in Fujian Province. It is primarily formed by the confluence of three main tributaries—the Beixi Creek, Xixi Creek and Nanxi Creek—and flows eastward, eventually emptying into the Taiwan Strait through Xiamen. Among them, the Beixi Creek originates in Huangsheng Village, Quxi Town of Liancheng County, located in the central area of Daimo Mountain; the Xixi Creek originates from Shifang Mountain, south of Shizhong Town in Longyan City; and the Nanxi Creek rises in the Sanping watershed of Pinghe County in Zhangzhou. Within western Fujian, the Longchuan River and Huoxi Creek merge at the Hexi Creek in Suban to form the main course of the Beixi Creek, which in turn serves as the principal trunk stream of the Jiulong River. The Huoxi Creek, also known as the Wan'an Creek, flows through the northwestern part of Longyan. From the estuary of the stream onward, it becomes navigable to large wooden boats and bamboo rafts. The waterway passes through the

---

1 Huang Ting, and Du Jingguo. "Transportation and Economic Connections in the Fujian – Guangdong – Jiangxi Border Region from the Song to the Qing Dynasties." *Journal of Shantou University (Humanities Edition)*, no. 2, 1995, p. 79.

Wan'an forest zone in Longyan, and goods can be transported downstream along the Jiulong River to Zhangzhou and onward to Xiamen Port via Shima. The navigable stretch of the Xixi Creek is primarily located within Zhangzhou.

Table 5-5 Navigable Waterways and Vessels in the Jiulong River System During the Republican Era

Waterway	Navigable Vessels	Route	Approx. Length (km)	Notes
Xixi Creek	Steamships	Haicheng to Longxi	35	
	Civilian boats	Nanjing to Chuanchang	55	Including the Guanxi Creek
Beixi Creek	Civilian boats	Shima to Ningyang/Longyan	280	Including streams like Longjin, Ganhua, Jiuhe, Yanshi

Source: Zhu Daijie, and Ji Tianyou. *Overview of Fujian's Economy.* Fujian Provincial Department of Construction, 1947, p. 197.

As shown in Table 5-5, by the Republican period, the Jiulong River system had formed two major navigable routes: the Xixi Creek and Beixi Creek. The Xixi creek had better conditions for navigation and could accommodate steamships. The Beixi Creek was longer and navigable by civilian boats from Shima in Zhangzhou to Ningyang and Longyan—a distance of nearly 280 kilometers—serving as an important link between Longyan and Zhangzhou.

2. Waterborne Trade Routes of the Jiulong River

The regions through which the Huoxi Creek and the Longchuan River pass are relatively flat, with few rapids or dangerous currents, making them ideal for transportation. Consequently, a significant portion of goods from western Fujian destined for Zhangzhou was transported via the Huoxi Creek and the Longchuan River. In particular, many commodities produced in the Huoxi Creek area were shipped from its estuary, then floated downstream via the Huoxi Creek and the Jiulong River to Punan and Shima in Zhangzhou, and further to Zhangzhou and Xiamen for export. The river market at the mouth of the Wan'an Creek became a key waterborne distribution center for paper and timber from western Fujian to the coastal areas. Most exported timber was tied into rafts and floated downstream through the Huoxi Creek and the Jiulong River to Zhangzhou. After the maritime ban was lifted during the Longqing reign, the Yuegang Port emerged as an important coastal distribution hub. From the mid-Ming period onward, with the flourishing of private maritime trade in coastal Zhangzhou and Longyan's pivotal position as a transportation hub linking Tingzhou and Zhangzhou, upstream–downstream cargo movement along the Jiulong River became increasingly active. In the Qing Dynasty, there were three major export routes for handmade paper produced in Liancheng. One of these routes involved transporting the paper by human carriers to the mouth of the Huoxi Creek, then by boat down the stream to Zhangping, from there along the middle and lower reaches of the Jiulong River to Punan, and finally to Zhangzhou, where it would be distributed to Xiamen, Quanzhou, and other destinations. After the opening of the treaty ports, Xiamen became one of the most important foreign trade ports along the Fujian coast. Leveraging the advantages of the Jiulong River waterway, merchants transported goods produced in western Fujian and those brought inland to Longyan via the Huoxi Creek to Wan'an. From there, they passed through Hua'an to reach Shima and Haicheng wharves in Zhangzhou, and finally were shipped to Xiamen for export. Imported foreign goods arriving at Xiamen were also transported inland by ascending the Jiulong River to Ningyang, Longyan, and other destinations.

Section 2 Overland Transportation and Trade Routes

I. Overland Transportation and Trade Routes in Northern Fujian

1. Overland Transportation in Northern Fujian

(1) Overland Transportation in Northern Fujian from the Han to Tang Dynasties

During the Western Han period, a route from the Central Plains to Jiangxi crossed the Meiling Ridge via the Ganjia Pass and entered Jianning in western Fujian. From there, an overland path led to Huangtuzhai in the southwestern corner of Shaowu, which then was connected to Jianyang in northern Fujian. The *Essence of Historical Geography* records, "Forty *li* southwest of the prefectural seat lies Huangtuzhai, also known as Huangtu Pass, where Huangtu Ridge is located. This route leads to the counties of Guangchang and Nanfeng in Jiangxi. It is also a garrison post."[1] Yushan, the king of Minyue, took Pucheng as his stronghold and built six fortified cities to resist Emperor Wu of the Han Dynasty. In 110 BCE, Emperor Wu dispatched Commandant Wang Wenshu to lead the third army to attack Datan City in Jianyang, seeking to breach Yushan's defenses. Since the road between Ganjia Pass and Huangtuzhai already existed at that time, Wang Wenshu entered Jianning via Ganjia Pass and proceeded through Huangtuzhai to Shaowu, then into Jianyang. The fourth army, led by Generals Yuehou Gechuan and Xia Lai, advanced via Ruoye and entered Pucheng from Yueqing in Zhejiang, indicating that a route connecting Zhejiang and Fujian

1 (Qing) Gu Zuyu. *Essentials of Historical Geography*, vol.97. Shanghai Bookstore Publishing House, 1998, p. 640.

was already open by then.

According to the *New History of the Tang Dynasty: Geography*, when King Yushan of Minyue rebelled against the Han Dynasty, he killed three western Han captains at Baisha, Wulin, and Meiling Ridge. At that time, Minyue could reach Chang'an, the ancient capital of the Han Dynasty, by way of Baisha and Wulin. According to the place names of the Western Han period, Baisha and Wulin were located within the territory of Boyang County in Jiangxi. Further evidence comes from *Gazetteer of Shaowu Prefecture*, volume 13, *Mountain Passes*, which states, "The Shanguan Pass lies atop Shanling Ridge, seventy *li* northwest of (Guangze) County. It is 120 *li* west to Jianchang Prefecture in Jiangxi (present-day Nancheng County), and serves as a thoroughfare between Fujian and Henan."[1] This confirms that by the Han Dynasty, northern Fujian had established links with the Central Plains, allowing Minyue to maintain access to Chang'an.

In the first year of the Guangming reign of the Tang Dynasty (880 CE), the Tieniu Pass was established on Tieniu Ridge of Dahe Mountain in Guangze County. Exiting Fujian through this pass allowed entry to Zixi in Jiangxi. Due to its sheer cliffs and treacherous terrain, the Tieniu Pass was regarded as the " strategic stronghold of the northern Fujian–Jiangxi route." According to volume 29 *Jiangnan Circuit V* of the *Maps and Gazetteers of Prefectures and Counties in Yuanhe* compiled by Li Jipu during the Tang Dynasty, the roads of Jianzhou during the Yuanhe era formed the so-called "Eight Routes," each leading to different destinations with precise mileage. These "Eight Routes" specifically were: northwest to Chang'an (Upper Capital): 4,695 *li*; northwest to Luoyang (Eastern Capital): 3,835 *li*; due south, slightly east to Fuzhou: 600 *li*; northwest to Xinzhou (modern Shangrao,

1 Lin Tingshui. "The Development and Changes of Ancient Overland Transportation Routes in Fujian." *Historical Geography*, no. 21, 2006, p. 225.

Jiangxi): 540 *li*; southwest to Tingzhou (by water): 1,500 *li*; northeast to Chuzhou (modern Lishui, Zhejiang; by water): 900 *li*; northwest to Fuzhou (Jiangxi): 830 *li*; due northwest, slightly east to Quzhou: 700 *li*.[1] This indicates that, aside from the water routes connecting Jianzhou to Tingzhou and Chuzhou, the other six destinations were accessible via land, demonstrating that northern Fujian's outbound transportation had significantly improved.

According to the *Essence of Historical Geography*, volume 97, entry on the Fenshui Pass in Chong'an County under Jianning Prefecture, "The pass lies in the northwest of the county on Fenshui Ridge and borders Yanshan, Jiangxi, serving as the strategic gateway between Jiangxi and Fujian. From the Five Dynasties through the Song, forts were built here." The entry further cites an older gazetteer, "(Fenshui Pass) was a key artery for commercial and traveler movement."[2] During the Five Dynasties period, tributes from Fujian to the Liang Dynasty could be sent via the Minjiang River upstream to the Jianxi Creek, then along its valley route to Chong'an's Fenshui Pass by land, through which goods would exit Fujian. The route then passed through Qianshan and Shangrao in Jiangxi, and then through Quzhou in Zhejiang, and continued north to Chizhou before reaching the capital at Kaifeng. Alternatively, one could exit Fujian via the Tieniu Pass in Guangze, enter Jiangxi, cross the Yangtze River at Boyang, and proceed through Shucheng, Luzhou (modern Hefei), and Shouxian to reach the capital, Kaifeng.

(2) Overland Transportation in Northern Fujian During the Song, Yuan, Ming, and Qing Dynasties

1Wang Na. *A Study of Overland Transportation in Northern Fujian from the Han to the Yuan Dynasties*. MA thesis, Fujian Normal University, 2014, p. 23.

2Lin Tingshui. "The Development and Changes of Ancient Overland Transportation Routes in Fujian." *Historical Geography*, no. 21, 2006, p. 225.

The *Old History of the Tang Dynasty: Annals of Emperor Xizong* records,

> The forces of Huang Chao attacked Jiangxi again, capturing the prefectures of Qian, Ji, Rao, and Xin. They crossed the Yangtze River from Xuanzhou, and attempted to enter Fujian via eastern Zhejiang. Lacking ships, they instead carved out 500 *li* of mountain roads, entered Jianzhou by land, and subsequently captured the central regions of Fujian.[1]

This suggests that in the late Tang period, another route into Fujian taken by Huang Chao's uprising forces was from the southern part of Quzhou in Zhejiang, across Xianxia Ridge. Along this path, new roads were opened, establishing a passable route into Pucheng through Xianxia Ridge, and then onward to Jianzhou. There, they joined another division that had entered western Fujian via the Meiling Ridge and the Ganjia Pass, through Jianning and on to Jianyang. Because Huang Chao's forces had hastily carved the road through Xianxia Ridge without proper construction, that segment fell into disrepair for a long time. In the early Shaoxing reign of the Southern Song, the imperial court recruited laborers to rebuild the road using stone, making it gradually passable. During the Ming and Qing dynasties, as northern Fujian's economy prospered, officials and merchants increasingly traveled between Fujian and Zhejiang via this route. However, the Xianxia section remained steep and difficult. Therefore, in the Jiaqing reign of the Qing Dynasty, wealthy merchants funded improvements: "They hired labor to level the foundation, adjust elevation, and widen narrow passages."[2] From then on, the route through Xianxia Ridge became considerably more

---

1 Lin Tingshui. "The Development and Changes of Ancient Overland Transportation Routes in Fujian." *Historical Geography*, no. 21, 2006, p.227.

2 (Qing) Weng Tianyou, and Lyu Weiying, comps. *Gazetteer of Pucheng County*, Guangxu Edition, vol. 36. Shanghai Bookstore Publishing House, 2000.

accessible for inter-provincial traffic. In the Southern Song period, aside from the Xianxia route, it was also possible to exit Fujian via Chong'an's Fenshui Pass to enter Zhejiang. However, this road was more than 300 kilometers longer than the route through Xianxia Ridge to the capital Lin'an. In the Yuan Dynasty, the Fenshui route became less favorable due to banditry in the mountainous areas, and the Xianxia Ridge route became the primary link between northern Fujian and the Zhejiang–Jiangxi region. According to the *Gazetteer of Place Names of Pucheng County* in 1981, the Xianxia Ridge route had two branches: one led northeast through Wangcun Village at the provincial border, continuing north via the Anmin Pass; the other led northwest through Shangjinzhu Village, reaching Xiaojinzhu Village in Jiangshan and exiting into Zhejiang and Jiangxi. Both branches were commonly used during the Song, Yuan, Ming, and Qing dynasties by those traveling to the capital to take the imperial civil service examinations.[1]

During the Yuan Dynasty, significant emphasis was placed on the development of postal roads and courier stations. To improve connectivity between northern Fujian and Fuzhou, numerous courier stations were established along the Minjiang River Basin in regions such as Chong'an, Pucheng, Jian'ou, Nanping, Gutian, Minqing, and Minhou. The Shanguan route, which entered northern Fujian from Jiangxi, had already been opened during the Western Han period. Since the Tang Dynasty, courier stations such as Shanguan Horse Station, Hangchuan Water Station, and Qiaochuan Water and Horse Station were established, enabling access from Guangze to Chong'an and Pucheng, and onward north to Jiangsu and Zhejiang. The Yuan Dynasty further expanded the network by setting up additional stations, including the Lindun Horse Station, Nakou Water and Horse Station, and Shuikou Station. These developments greatly enhanced transportation within

1 Lin Tingshui. "The Development and Changes of Ancient Overland Transportation Routes in Fujian." *Historical Geography*, no. 21, 2006, p.227.

Shaowu Prefecture and its links to other areas of northern Fujian. By the late Qing Dynasty, numerous dual-mode courier stations (serving both water and land transport) existed along the upper and lower stretches of the Minjiang River. Examples include: Nanping to Pucheng section: Da'an Station (northwest of present-day Chong'an County), Changping Water Station (within present-day Chong'an County), Chong'an Station (in modern Wuyishan City), Xingtian Station (southeast of present-day Chong'an County), Jianxi Station (west of present-day Jianyang), Taiping Station (Taiping in southern Jian'ou), and Daheng Station (northeast of Nanping); Nanping to the Shanguan Pass in Guangze: Jianpu Station (east of Nanping), Wangtai Station (west of Nanping), Shuangfeng Station (within Shunchang), Futun Station (northwest of Shunchang), Nakou Station (southeast of Shaowu), Qiaochuan Water Station (within Shaowu), and Hangchuan Station (in present-day Hangchuan County); Nanping to Fuzhou: Chating Station (southeast of Nanping), Huangtian Station (southeast of Gutian), Shuikou Station (south of Gutian), Xiaoruo Station (west of Minqing), Baisha Station (northwest of Minhou), Yuyuan Station (within Minhou), Ximen Station (Fuzhou suburbs), and Sanshan Station (within Fuzhou).[1]

By the late Qing period, four major overland transport routes had emerged in the Minjiang River Basin of northern Fujian. All primary routes started from Fuzhou and traveled upstream along the Minjiang River through Minqing and Gutian to reach Nanping, where the route then branched into four paths leading to Zhejiang and Jiangxi. The first route went from Nanping through Shunchang, Shaowu, and Guangze to Jianchang in Jiangxi. The second route went from Nanping through the valley of the Jianxi Creek to Pucheng and onward to Jiangshan in Zhejiang. The third route went from

---

1Shui Haigang. *Port Trade and Hinterland Society: A Study of the Development of the Modern Minjiang River Basin from a Regional Perspective.* Xiamen University Press, 2019, p.73.

Nanping via Jian'ou, Jianyang, and Pucheng to Longquan in Zhejiang. The fourth route went from Nanping via the Shaxi Creek, Guihua, Qingliu, and Ninghua to Shicheng in Jiangxi.[1] Pucheng, Guangze, and Ninghua became vital transportation nodes for both goods and people moving between northern Fujian and the provinces of Zhejiang and Jiangxi. During the Ming and Qing dynasties, most cargo in the Minjiang River Basin was first shipped by water to these counties, and then transferred overland for further distribution to the provinces of Zhejiang and Jiangxi.

(3) Overland Transportation in Northern Fujian in the Republican Period

In the Republican era, road development in the upper reaches of the Minjiang River began to take shape. In 1928, in an effort to consolidate its military presence, the garrisoned troops in northern Fujian initiated the construction of multiple roads in the region. The first stretch, a 17-kilometer segment from Nanping to Ji'an, was completed and opened to traffic in April 1929. Soon thereafter, a 17-kilometer road between Jian'ou and Lukou was also constructed. In 1933, as part of a campaign to "encircle and suppress" the Red Army, the Kuomintang in the border regions of Fujian, Zhejiang, Jiangxi, and Anhui mobilized large numbers of civilian and military laborers to build a highway connecting Pucheng to Zhejiang and Jiangxi. By the end of that year, the road from Jiangshan in Zhejiang to Xiakou, and then via Fengling to Pucheng, was fully completed and opened to traffic—marking the first outbound highway from northern Fujian to another province. After the failure of the "Fujian Rebellion," the Nationalist government intensified its efforts to suppress the Red Army in the Central Soviet Area, accelerating road construction day and night throughout the region. This effort led to the

---

1Chen Wentao. *Geography Gazetteer of Fujian Modern Livelihood*. Far East Publishing House, 1929, p. 124.

completion of the second interprovincial highway connecting Pucheng—Jianyang—Jian'ou—Nanping—Yong'an—Ruijin in Jiangxi, as well as several county-level roads, including Jianyang —Shaowu—Guangze, Jianyang—Chong'an, and Nanping–Shunchang–Jiangle. By the eve of the War of Resistance against Japanese Aggression, much of the upper reaches of the Minjiang River was connected by highways, although water transport remained the primary mode between Nanping and Fuzhou. A mixed-mode transportation system (combining water and land) was thus established between the upper and lower reaches of the Minjiang River. At that time, Jianyang became the hub of road transportation in northern Fujian. In 1938, the Central-South Travel Agency, established by the Fujian Provincial Transportation Company, opened in Nanping, making the city the main hub for passenger and freight transport in northern Fujian at the time. Direct interprovincial bus services were also introduced, linking Nanping to cities such as Chongqing, Nancheng in Jiangxi, Qujiang in Guangdong, and Lanxi in Zhejiang. During the Republican period, motor vehicles gradually replaced some manual porterage, accelerating the movement of people and the turnover of goods, thereby greatly improving transportation efficiency.

2. Overland Trade Routes in Northern Fujian

After the Tang and Five Dynasties periods, the commercial economy of northern Fujian gradually became more vibrant, with the emergence of various tangible marketplaces. During the Northern and Southern Song dynasties, the region enjoyed relative social stability and rapid economic development. The scale of production in industries such as ceramics, tea, papermaking, textiles, and metallurgy continued to expand. By the Song–Yuan period, two major interprovincial overland trade routes had been established in northern Fujian, both originating from Jianyang. The first was the ancient Fujian–Jiangxi commercial route: it led from Jianyang through Chong'an, exiting via the Fenshui Pass to reach Shangrao in Jiangxi, or alternatively, from Jianyang via Shaowu, exiting through the Shanguan Pass in Guangze to reach Ganzhou in Jiangxi. The second was the ancient Fujian–Zhejiang route: it extended from Jianyang through Pucheng, exiting via the Xianxia Pass to reach Jiangshan County in Zhejiang. A wide range of products from northern Fujian—including ceramics, Jian brocade, tea, bamboo and timber, silver, copper, and iron—were transported continuously along these two trade routes to the Jiangxi–Zhejiang regions, with some eventually exported to Korea, Japan, and other countries via Ningbo and Hangzhou. At the same time, goods shipped from Wuhan, Nanchang, Shanghai, and other locations were transported into northern Fujian via the ancient Fujian–Jiangxi and Fujian–Zhejiang routes, where they were either distributed throughout Fujian or exported overseas through the province's coastal ports. Jianyang was a critical gateway through which the Central Plains accessed Fujian. There were three main overland routes for the export of local products such as handmade paper and Jianyang imprints: the first ran via the Shanguan Pass in Shaowu or through the Tieniu Pass in Guangze into Jiangxi, then onward to Anhui, Henan, and other areas in the Central Plains; the second exited Fujian through the Fenshui Pass in Chong'an and reached the Jiangsu–Zhejiang region; the third proceeded northward via the Xianxia Ridge in Pucheng to the Zhejiang–Jiangxi area. Convenient overland transportation and a thriving woodblock printing industry attracted numerous booksellers to trade in books. In addition, during the Song–Yuan period, while goods from counties across northern Fujian were transported to Fuzhou mainly via the Minjiang River, a portion also traveled overland through Jianzhou to Fuzhou, where they were then exported through coastal ports.

During the Wanli reign of the Ming Dynasty, tobacco cultivation and tobacco slicing flourished in Pucheng, Jianning, Shaowu, Shunchang, and other areas, with Yangkou Town in Shunchang becoming an important tobacco distribution center. In the Ming and Qing dynasties, numerous tobacco shops and trading firms commissioned brokers or middlemen to purchase sun-cured tobacco in northern Fujian, which was then transported through Pucheng's Xianxia Ridge and Chong'an's Fenshui Pass into Zhejiang and Jiangsu, and from there further distributed to coastal provinces. Other specialty products from northern Fujian, such as shiitake mushrooms, indigo, and *zexie* (Alisma orientale), were also transported in large quantities by land through Pucheng and Chong'an to Zhejiang and Jiangsu, with indigo serving as a crucial raw material for the dyeing industry in those regions. During the maritime prohibition period in the Ming Dynasty, goods destined for overseas markets from Jiangsu and Zhejiang could only be exported through the hands of Fujian merchants. Consequently, the ancient trade routes connecting Jiangsu–Zhejiang with northern Fujian became one of the key bridges for international trade.[1]

From the Qianlong reign to the Jiaqing reign of the Qing Dynasty, most of the yellow paper produced in Guangze was transported via the Shantou Pass to Guixi in Jiangxi, and then shipped inland through waterways such as the Ganjiang River and the Yangtze River to other inland regions. In the late Qing period, the large-scale cultivation of Wuyi tea in northern Fujian led to a substantial reduction in rice cultivation in some counties, resulting in food shortages. Rice, which was abundant in Jiangxi, was transported by land from Guangchang to Shaowu, or from Xincheng to Guangze, and finally from Shaowu and Guangze to areas facing grain shortages. After the opening of the treaty ports, the growing variety of imported goods entering Fuzhou and Ningbo led to an increasing volume of foreign cloth, kerosene, matches, paper, liquor, and other imported commodities flowing from Ningbo through Quzhou into Pucheng and Chong'an. The influx of imported goods significantly impacted the sales of local specialties in northern Fujian,

1 Wu Bangcai, editor-in-chief. *A History of the Development of Fujian Merchants: Nanping Volume*. Xiamen University Press, 2016, p.111.

leading to a gradual decline in their market share.

During the Republican period, the development of highway networks in northern Fujian led to an increase in overland commodity transport compared with earlier times. However, due to the limited number of modern transportation vehicles such as automobiles, and insufficient investment in road maintenance, the overall efficiency of goods transportation remained relatively low.

II. Overland Transportation and Trade Routes in Western Fujian

1. Overland Transportation in Western Fujian

(1) Overland Transportation in Western Fujian from the Han to Tang Dynasties

Western Fujian is characterized by rugged mountains and was historically regarded as a land inhabited by "barbarians." Overland transportation conditions in the region were poor, described in historical records as "steep cliffs and rugged gravel paths, exhausting for travelers."[1] The Wuyi Mountain Range lies at the junction of Fujian, Jiangxi, and Zhejiang provinces. Its high and precipitous terrain gives rise to many rivers that form self-contained river systems, with little hydrological interconnectivity. As a result, overland access from the Central Plains to western Fujian was significantly limited since ancient times. Historical sources indicate that before the Song Dynasty, three principal overland routes connected the Central Plains to western Fujian: The first route led from the Central Plains to the Meiling Ridge, north of Qianhua County in Jiangxi, then passed through Ganjia Pass—an important economic and military gateway—

1(Song) Hu Taichu, comp., and Zhao Yumu, ed. *Gazetteer of Linting*. Fujian People's Publishing House, 1990, p. 7.

before entering Jianning in western Fujian; the second route went from the Central Plains to Ruijin in Jiangxi, then passed through the Huangzhu Ridge, the Ailing Ridge, and the Xinlu Ridge, each of which provided access to Tingzhou in western Fujian; the third route extended from the Central Plains to Shicheng County in Jiangxi, passed through the Zhanling Pass, and then entered Shibi in Ninghua County, western Fujian.

As early as before the Qin and Han periods, the early inhabitants of Fujian and Jiangxi had already opened a route into Jianning in western Fujian through the Ganjia Pass on the Meiling Ridge (located between Qianhua and Nanfeng counties in Jiangxi Province). However, this road was rugged and narrow. In 112 BCE, during the revolt of the Nanyue Kingdom, the King of Minyue, Yu Shan, requested permission from Emperor Wu of Han to lead troops against Nanyue but secretly colluded with them. The following year, General Yang Pu, Commander of the Tower Ships, stationed his troops at the Meiling Ridge in Yuzhang Commandery (present-day Jiangxi Province) in preparation to attack Minyue. In 110 BCE, Emperor Wu dispatched four military forces deep into Minyue territory. The third army, led by Lieutenant Wang Wenshu, advanced through the Meiling Ridge[1] into western Fujian, thereby opening a military transportation route between the Central Plains and western Fujian. In the late Tang Dynasty, Huang Chao led his rebel army into Fujian by advancing along two routes simultaneously. One of these routes also entered Jianning in western Fujian through the Ganjia Pass on the Meiling Ridge, and then proceeded northeast from Jianning to Jianyang. When Huang Chao's rebel army entered Jianning, his army undertook improvements on this route during its advance. After the "Yongjia Upheaval" of the Western Jin Dynasty, large numbers of Han Chinese from the north fled the chaos of war and migrated from the Central Plains into western

1 Cha Chenglin. "A Study on Interprovincial Transportation Routes in Southwestern Fujian Before the Song Dynasty." *Shanxi Archives*, no. 5, 2014, p. 117.

Fujian—most of them also took this route. Since then, this road remained one of the major military routes connecting Fujian and Jiangxi.

Prior to the Tang Dynasty, a key route from southern Jiangxi to western Fujian passed through Ruijin in Jiangxi, across the Huangzhu Ridge and the Ailing Ridge into Tingzhou. According to the *Recompiled Gazetteer of Changting County*, Tingzhou was established in the 24th year of the Kaiyuan reign of the Tang Dynasty (736 CE), overseeing the counties of Changting, Huanglian, and Longyan. The northwestern part of Changting could access Ruijin via either the Huangzhu Ridge or the Ailing Ridge, and merchants often used these roads for trade. In the late Tang period, a new route was developed from western Changting to Ruijin, via the Xinlu Ridge at the border. According to the *Gazetteer of Linting,* the Xinlu Ridge was located 30 kilometers west of Changting and just 10 kilometers from Ruijin's county seat. The mountains of Xinlu Ridge were steep and lined with cliffs, and the road was rugged. By passing through the ancient fortress and the Luokeng Pass on the ridge, travelers could enter Changting from Ruijin. This route thus became another critical passageway for people from the Central Plains to enter western Fujian via southern Jiangxi.

After the establishment of Tingzhou during the Tang Dynasty, overland routes between Tingzhou and both Qianzhou in Jiangxi and Chaozhou in Guangdong were gradually opened, making Tingzhou a vital hub linking the three provinces of Jiangxi, Fujian, and Guangdong. Volume 271 of the *Comprehensive Mirror for Aid in Government* records,

> The Han ruler Liu Yan, advised by a soothsayer, took refuge in Meikou Town, which lies close to Fujian's western frontier. The Fujian commander Wang Yanmei led forces to attack him. Upon learning the news just tens of *li* away, Liu

Yan fled and narrowly escaped.[1]

Today, Meikou Town is known as Songkou Town in Meizhou, and this record confirms that an overland route between Tingzhou and Meizhou already existed at that time. As early as the Tang Dynasty, a road connected Tingzhou and Zhangzhou: from Changting, it passed south through Hetian to Longyan County, from Longyan to Fushan in the northwest of Nanjing, and finally reached Zhangzhou.[2] According to the *New History of the Five Dynasties*, in the late Tang period, warlord Wang Xu led tens of thousands of troops from Nankang across the Xinlu Ridge into Changting, then captured Zhangpu and operated in the Zhangpu–Chaozhou region. The *Essence of Historical Geography*, volume 98, further records that Wang Yanzheng of the Five Dynasties period constructed a fort 50 *li* southwest of Changting to defend against forces from Jiangnan. These records confirm that the road from Ruijin to Changting and then from Changting to Zhangpu had already been opened.

According to the *Gazetteer of Linting*, Ninghua was formerly known as Huanglian, named after the nearby Huanglian Cave. In the 13th year of the Kaiyuan reign (725 CE) in the Tang Dynasty, it became a county due to the settlement of over 3,000 households. In the 1st year of the Tianbao reign (742 CE), it was renamed Ninghua. Shibi Village in Ninghua was located just east of the Zhanling Pass on the border with Shicheng County in Jiangxi. Since the late Western Jin Dynasty, the route from Shicheng across the Zhanling Pass into Shibi had served as a primary corridor connecting the Central Plains with western Fujian. From the Jin Dynasty through the Tang Dynasty, Han Chinese fleeing war in the north migrated through this route into western Fujian and eastern Guangdong, where many settled and became ancestors of

---

1 (Song) Sima Guang. *Comprehensive Mirror for Aid in Government*. Zhongzhou Ancient Books Publishing House, 2003, p. 2809.

2 Lin Tingshui. "The Development and Changes of Ancient Overland Transportation Routes in Fujian." *Historical Geography*, no. 21, 2006, p. 230.

today's Hakka people. Why did Shibi in Ninghua become such an important settlement and transit point for Han migrants from the north? Historical evidence suggests three main reasons: First, the Zhanling Pass had a relatively low elevation, making travel from the Central Plains via Shicheng to Shibi more accessible; second, Shibi Village lied in a basin, favorable for agriculture and relatively undisturbed by warfare; third, the water-land transportation corridor from Ninghua through Qingliu to Yanping and on to Fuzhou had already been established, facilitating the exchange of goods with northern and eastern Fujian. Since the late Tang Dynasty, the corridor between Ninghua's Shibi and Shicheng in Jiangxi has remained one of the busiest interprovincial routes between Fujian and Jiangxi.

(2) Overland Transportation in Western Fujian During the Song, Yuan, Ming, and Qing Dynasties

During the Song Dynasty, merchants frequently traveled the routes from Ruijin in Jiangxi to Changting, and then onward to the coastal regions of southern Fujian. In particular, groups of salt traders were often seen moving between southern Jiangxi, Changting, and Zhangpu, or rerouting from Changting toward Chaozhou and Meizhou. To crack down on salt smuggling, the Song court relocated the fortified city to the western part of Changting County and established a military outpost. The former city site was converted into Liucun Town (now Hetian Town in Changting County), which later became a major transit and gathering point for merchants and travelers. In addition, during the Song period, a number of post stations were established, including Jiulong, Shiniu, Guanqian, Jiang'an, and Mingxi. From Changting, these stations enabled overland travel northeastward into Qingliu and Ninghua, and from there to Shicheng and Guangchang in Jiangxi. Alternatively, merchants could travel from Qingliu to Mingxi, then on to Jiangle and Shaxian, eventually reaching Shaowu, Shunchang, and Yanping in northern Fujian.

Although the road from Tingzhou to Zhangzhou had been opened during the Tang Dynasty, it remained largely underutilized. In the Southern Song period, Tingzhou began to rely on salt from Zhangzhou, which led to increased use of overland routes between the two regions. The counties of Changting, Liancheng, and Wuping traveled via Shanghang and Yongding, and then through Xiayang, Daxi, and Yueliu passes in southeastern Yongding County to enter Pinghe County in Zhangzhou. During the Song Dynasty, the post station Denglong was set up south of Longyan County, and another called Zhuche was established to the west, enhancing transportation between Tingzhou and Zhangzhou. This route later came to be known in the Ming Dynasty as the "Eastern Route" between Tingzhou and Zhangzhou, as it was relatively rugged and difficult. In the mid-Ming period, a new "Western Route" was developed, passing through Shanghang and Yongding to reach Zhangzhou. During the Jiajing reign, a formal postal road was constructed from Shanghang to Yongding, then via Hulei and Fuxi (now Fushi Town), through Longtan, and ultimately to Zhangzhou—this was the "Western Route." It was shorter than the "Eastern Route," "reducing the distance by one-third with fewer obstacles, being both nearer and easier, and thus preferred by travelers."[1] Consequently, after the opening of the Western Route, usage of the Eastern Route declined noticeably. From the mid-Ming period onward, a preliminary network of land and water routes connecting Tingzhou, Zhangzhou, and Chaozhou had taken shape, and Yongding emerged as a key transportation hub.

Gu Zuyu, a scholar in the Qing Dynasty, once remarked, "The southwestern border of Fujian and the Chaozhou prefecture of Guangdong are as close as lips and teeth, with both land and water routes offering swift

---

1(Qing) Zeng Riying et al., coms., and Li, Bo et al., eds. *Gazetteer of Tingzhou Prefecture*, Qianlong edition, in *Collection of Chinese Local Gazetteers*. Shanghai Bookstore Publishing House, 2000.

passage."[1] Owing to its border position with Guangdong and Jiangxi, western Fujian maintained frequent economic exchanges with these provinces. By the late Qing period, four main interprovincial overland routes connected western Fujian and southern Jiangxi: The first route was a mountain road from Anyuan Subprefecture in Ninghua County to Gaoshui Market in Shicheng County, Jiangxi; the second route was from Changting through the Huangzhu Ridge in Ruijin to Shicheng or to Xiashan Town in Ningdu, which served as a vital commercial route between western Fujian and Jiangxi in the Qing Dynasty; the third route was from Tingzhou through the Ailing Ridge and Gucheng (in present-day Changting County) to the county seat of Ruijin, which was the earliest transport route from Ganxian to western Fujian; the fourth route was from the Junmen Ridge across the Wuyi Mountains via Dongliu (in present-day Wuping County), directly to the county seat of Wuping, and then through Shifang (also in Wuping) to the county seat of Shanghang.[2] Western Fujian's overland connections with eastern and northern Guangdong followed two main routes: The first route originated from Meixian or Songkou in Guangdong, reached Jiaoling County, then from there entered Yanqian Town and Shifang Town (now under Wuping County), and proceeded to Shanghang or Liancheng; the second route started from Xingning or Meixian in Guangdong to Dapu, then from Dapu entered Yongding County, and finally reached Longyan via Yongding, the entire journey being overland. By the end of the Qing Dynasty, a relatively well-formed overland network had been established across the Fujian-Guangdong-Jiangxi border regions. Most of these ancient roads were constructed from cobblestones, tamped earth, or blue stone slabs, and ranged in width from one to several meters. Even in rainy conditions, they remained

---

1 (Qing) Gu Zuyu. *Essentials of Historical Geograph,* vol. 97. Shanghai Bookstore Publishing House, 1998, p. 643.

2Lin Yuru, Jiang Xiuxian, Zhou Zifeng, and Wang Zhan. *Modern Economic Geography of China: Fujian and Taiwan*. East China Normal University Press, 2016, p. 188.

passable for merchants and travelers.[1]

(3) Overland Transportation in Western Fujian During the Republican Period

During the Republican era, road development in western Fujian generally occurred in three main phases. From 1920 to 1930, the first stage saw various warlords constructing roads primarily to exploit local resources. Most of these roads, however, failed to serve any real transportation function. From 1931 to 1936, the second stage involved large-scale military road construction by the Nationalist government aimed at "encircling and suppressing" the Red Army in the Central Soviet Area. From 1937 to 1942, after the outbreak of the War of Resistance against Japanese Aggression, the Nationalist government built roads to facilitate the mobilization and transport of military supplies. During these three phases, five major trunk highways and six branch roads were developed.

1You Haihua. "The Continuity and Transformation of the Market Network in the Border Region of Jiangxi, Fujian, and Guangdong from the Late Qing to the Republican Era". *Researches in Chinese Economic History*, no. 4, 2006, p. 63.

Table 5-6 Roads Constructed in Western Fujian During the Republican Period

Category	Road Name	Route (Start–End)	Approx. Length (km)
Trunk Highways	Xia–Ai Line	Yongxi (Longyan) to Ailing (Changting)	254
	Yan–Peng Line	Xinting (Liancheng) to Pengkou	63
	Xin–Yan Line	Xinquan (Liancheng) to Shanzi (border, Wuping)	119
	Long–Feng Line	Longmen (Longyan) to Youxia Dam (border, Yongding)	89
	Wen–Ning Line	Wenheng (Liancheng) to Sibao (Shibi)	33
Branch Roads	Long–Zhang Line	Dongmen (Longyan) to Yanshi	23
	Yue–Bai Line	Yueshan (Longyan) to Baitu	4
Branch Roads	Shi–Wu Line	Shifang to Wuping County Seat	19
	Ting–Ning Line	Changting to Guanqian	30
	Hang–Feng Line	Shanghang via Zhongdu to Fengshi (Yongding)	68
	Long–Gao Line	Jiaopai Bridge (Gaowu) to Qianjia Village	30

Source: Cai Lixiong, editor-in-chief. *History of Commerce in Western Fujian*, Xiamen University Press, 2014, p. 178.

From Table 5-6, it is evident that during the Republican era, nearly every county in western Fujian constructed at least one road. Among them, the route from Yongxi in Longyan to Ailing in Changting spanned 254 kilometers, making it the longest road in the region at the time. However, due to a lack of maintenance and repair, compounded by destruction caused by floods and other natural disasters, the total length of operational roads at the time of the founding of the People's Republic of China was only 177 kilometers. This indicates that while road transport capacity during the Republican period remained limited, the preliminary road network laid an essential foundation for the region's transportation development in the early years of New China.

2. Overland Trade Routes in Western Fujian

From the late Tang to the Song dynasties, the population in western Fujian gradually increased due to the large-scale migration of northern Han Chinese. Since the Song and Yuan periods, external interactions also grew progressively. However, as the region was mountainous, even by the early Republican era it was still referred to as "a landlocked Tingzhou with winding mountains and obstructed transport."[1] Overland transport served as the primary connection between western Fujian and northern Fujian, as well as southeastern Jiangxi. For connections with Zhangzhou and Quanzhou, combined land-water transport was more common; and for connections with Meizhou and Chaozhou, water transport dominated.

During the Shaoxing reign of the Southern Song Dynasty, residents of Tingzhou shifted from consuming Fuzhou salt to Zhangzhou salt, prompting utilization of the land routes between Tingzhou and Zhangzhou that had been opened since the late Tang period. According to the *Gazetteer of Lin Ting*,

> In Wuping County, salt was transported from Zhangzhou... The county was more than ten-day-station away from Zhangzhou. All transport was overland, and local laborers were contracted in rotation to carry the salt. In Liancheng County, salt was likewise transported from Zhangzhou. By official custom, the government advanced funds to procure salt, hired strong local men to carry it overland, and split the salt between government and civilian

1 Party History Materials Collection Leading Group of the CPC Longyan Prefectural Committee, and Cultural Relics Administration Committee of Longyan Regional Administrative Office. *Documents on the Revolutionary History of Western Fujian*, vol. 1. December 1981, p. 79.

> use. In recent years, government officials were dispatched with silver to Zhangzhou to purchase salt, which was then loaded at Shuitou, with laborers hired to carry and unload it there.[1]

This illustrates that counties such as Wuping and Liancheng in Tingzhou Prefecture imported substantial quantities of salt from Zhangzhou.

During the Yuan Dynasty, the population of Tingzhou experienced a significant decline, leading to a contraction of market activity. It was not until the mid-Ming period that the economy of western Fujian gradually began to recover. By the late Ming period, improvements in the overland transport infrastructure connecting Zhangzhou to Longyan and Tingzhou to Longyan, coupled with the Yuegang Port in Zhangzhou becoming an important coastal port for foreign trade, enabled the export of several local commodities from Tingzhou—such as paper, indigo, tea oil, and tung oil—via the Ting–Zhang overland route to the Yuegang Port, and from there, overseas. Conversely, seafood, silk, cotton, sugar, and other goods imported from the coast also traveled via the Ting–Long overland route to reach Tingzhou. During the Ming and Qing dynasties, Chaozhou salt was transported in large quantities to Tingzhou via the "Chao–Ting–Gan" commercial route. Salt, once it arrived in Changting, was carried over the Xinlu Ridge, and through Gucheng and Ruijin reached counties like Huichang and Shicheng under Ganzhou Prefecture. This route's transported salt was known locally as Ting salt. Jiangxi's southern region was rich in grain production, and Tingzhou merchants, after selling Chaozhou salt there, would return with large quantities of grain. Hence, the salt-grain trade between Tingzhou and southern Jiangxi flourished during this period and was predominantly

1(Song) Hu Taichu, comp., and Zhao Yumu, ed. *Gazetteer of Linting*. Fujian People's Publishing House, 1990, p. 29.

conducted via overland routes. In the Qing Dynasty, an important land route emerged from Changting or Liancheng to the county seat of Shanghang, then to Shifang and Yanqian in Wuping, onward through Jiaoling to reach Songkou Town in Meixian County. This became a major passway for exporting paper and grain from western Fujian to northeastern Guangdong, and for importing salt, sundries, and textiles in the reverse direction. By the late Qing period, another busy overland trade route connected Meixian County through Dapu into Yongding, continuing on to Longyan, Nanjing or Pinghe, and eventually reaching Zhangzhou. This route played a crucial role in connecting Guangdong and Fujian, with goods transported largely by human porters. Marine products, daily necessities, kerosene, pepper, and other commodities from the Chaozhou region were transported inland to the Zhanglong area via this route.

In the Republican period, the importation of salt into western Fujian continued to rely heavily on Zhangzhou and Chaozhou sources, commonly referred to as Zhang salt and Chao salt. After the opening of the Zhang–Long highway to automobile traffic, the Zhang–Long Auto Transport Company dispatched vehicles to the salt depots in Zhangzhou to load salt for distribution in Longyan, with part of it being further transported to Zhangping, Ningyang, Yong'an, Datian, Liancheng, and other areas. Longyan served as the main distribution center for Zhang salt in western Fujian, receiving around 5,000 *dan* of salt monthly from Zhangzhou. After the Zhang–Long highway was damaged, salt transport was split into two segments: first by water from Zhangzhou to Shuichao, then by truck from Shuichao to Longyan, taking approximately 4 to 5 days. Since the Ming and Qing periods, regions such as Yongding, Shanghang, Wuping, Changting, and even parts of Jiangxi had primarily consumed Chao salt. By the Republican era, Chao salt was still being purchased in large quantities from Chaozhou, though the transportation method had changed to a combined water–land system: shipped by water to

Shuichao, then trucked via highway to Longyan and Changting. Only a small portion of the Chao salt arriving in Changting was sold locally; the majority was shipped overland through Ruijin's Huangzhu Ridge to Shicheng or Xiashan Town in Ningdu, then redistributed across Jiangxi Province. Additionally, the salt consumed in Ninghua, Qingliu, and Mingxi also partially originated from Chao and Zhang salts, which were transferred overland from Changting and Liancheng. Besides salt imports, these routes also facilitated the entry of textiles, kerosene, and sundry goods into western Fujian. These items were sold both locally and, via Changting, re-exported to Jiangxi counties such as Ruijin, Shicheng, and Huichang. Changting County housed various transshipment and brokerage firms, including paper trading firms, trading firms of Beijing goods, sundry trading firms, and pharmacies.

Section 3 Major Transportation Hubs and Commercial Centers

I. Major Transportation Hubs and Commercial Centers in Northern Fujian

Northern Fujian lies at the junction of the three provinces of Fujian, Zhejiang, and Jiangxi—bordering Jiangxi to the west and Zhejiang to the northeast. Since the Tang Dynasty, transportation routes had already been established between this region and the provinces of Jiangxi and Zhejiang. By the late Qing period, three main interprovincial routes had been established in the region: The first route passed through the Shanguan pass in Guangze County and led into Jiangxi; the second route crossed the Xianxia Ridge from Pucheng into Zhejiang; the third route departed from Chong'an (now Wuyishan City), exited Fujian via the Fenshui *Pass*, then traveled through Yushan, Shangrao, and Hengkou Town in Yanshan County, and eventually reached Kaihua, Changshan, and Jiangshan in Zhejiang. Among these three, the first route was more level but winding; the second was more direct but involved crossing higher mountains; the third combined land and river transport and had long served as a crucial commercial passageway linking northern Fujian to Jiangxi and Zhejiang. Key transportation hubs and commercial centers developed along these routes: Guangze County and Shaowu County became vital nodes along the Jiangxi-bound commercial routes; Pucheng County and Chong'an County were prominent along the routes leading to Zhejiang; Yanping served as the central node connecting northern Fujian to the middle and lower reaches of the Minjiang River and the port of Fuzhou.

1. Shaowu County

Since the Han and Tang dynasties, the ancient trade route through the

Huangtu Pass in Shaowu had been not only an important passageway for entering Fujian from the Central Plains, but also a vital commercial route linking coastal and inland regions. Travelers could pass through the pass on the Chousi Ridge in Heping Town, traverse the Huangtu Pass in Jinkeng, and reach Lichuan County in Jiangxi. The mountain path at the Chousi Ridge was rugged and steep. Since its opening in the Han and Tang periods, countless people from the Central Plains entered Fujian via this route, bringing their culture with them. In the Song Dynasty, local residents in Heping Town reinforced this path with stone paving. The route was repeatedly repaired during the Ming and Qing periods. By the Republican era, it remained an essential commercial route for northern Fujian merchants heading to Jiangxi. The two most notable markets in Shaowu were located in Heping Town and in Jinkeng Town. By the Tiancheng era of the Tang Dynasty, Heping Town had already emerged as a major trading hub. Merchants from Jiangxi, northern Fujian, and Fuzhou gathered here for trade, forming a five-day cycle market. Shaowu also had important water-based trade routes. Goods could be transported upstream via the Futun Creek to Guangze, or downstream to Shunchang, then via Yangkou and Xiayang to Yanping, and from there along the Minjiang River to Fuzhou. Seafood, sundry goods, and imported foreign items from coastal areas such as Fuzhou were redistributed through Shaowu to Jiangxi, while goods from the inland were routed through Shaowu to other parts of northern Fujian and further downstream along the Minjiang River. Thanks to its advantageous overland and water transport networks, Shaowu became a major transportation hub in northern Fujian, attracting merchants from across the country. It developed into a key distribution center for goods flowing between the coast and the inland. During the Ming and Qing periods, the commercial streets of Heping and Jinkeng were lined with diverse businesses, especially paper and tea trading firms.

2. Guangze County

Guangze County is located in the upper reaches of the Futun Creek and in the northern section of the Wuyi Mountains. It borders Zixi and Lichuan counties in Jiangxi Province to the west, and Guixi and Yanshan counties in Jiangxi to the north. According to *The General Gazetteer of Fujian,* "To enter Fujian, one must pass through the Shanguan Pass." The Shanguan Pass, located at the border between Guangze and Lichuan, was first established in the first year of Tang's Guangming reign (880 CE). Since ancient times, Guangze had maintained frequent border trade with adjacent counties in Jiangxi Province. Four of Guangze's townships—Zhima, Huaqiao, Saili, and Siqian—border Jiangxi. On market days, residents from these Jiangxi border areas often accounted for at least 40% of market participants, and Jiangxi merchants were a common presence during regular trading activities.[1] Among these counties, Guangze's trade with Lichuan was the most substantial, primarily because Lichuan possessed superior water transport infrastructure. The Lihe River merged with the Xujiang River and eventually flowed into the Fuhe River, which in turn entered the Dongting Lake, thereby linking with the Ganjiang River and the Yangtze River. From the Ming and Qing dynasties, Fujian's sea products, paper, tea, and timber were transported via the cities along the Yangtze River. Conversely, commodities from Wuhan, Nanchang, and Shanghai were transported up the river to Lichuan, and then carried into Fujian via the ancient commercial routes through Guangze and Shaowu. Goods from Jiangxi and other inland areas could be floated downstream via the Futun Creek to Yanping, and from there along the Minjiang River to Fuzhou. On the return trip, large quantities of coastal goods were transported back inland. Thus, Guangze emerged as a vital border trade

---

1 Wu Bangcai, editor-in-chief. *A History of the Development of Fujian Merchants: Nanping Volume*. Xiamen University Press, 2016, p.109.

market in northern Fujian.

3. Pucheng County

Pucheng County, located at the northernmost part of Fujian Province, borders Jiangshan County in Zhejiang to the north and Shangrao City in Jiangxi to the west. It sits on the ancient Fujian–Zhejiang trade route and has long served as an important transportation and commercial hub. Crossing the Xianxia Ridge from Pucheng leads directly into Jiangshan, Zhejiang. Owing to its location at the junction of Fujian, Zhejiang, and Jiangxi, Pucheng has long sustained vibrant border trade with adjacent areas of these provinces since ancient times. Since the Southern Song Dynasty, products from Fujian destined for the Jiangsu and Zhejiang regions would often be gathered in Pucheng, then transported by land via the Xianxia Ridge or the Fenshui Pass to Zhejiang. Meanwhile, textiles and daily necessities from Jiangsu and Zhejiang were delivered to Pucheng and then transported along the Nanpu Creek to Nanping, and finally along the Minjiang River to Fuzhou. Pucheng developed into a key hub for cargo transportation using wooden sailboats, and from the Ming and Qing periods onward, merchants from Zhejiang, Jiangxi, and even Fuzhou established guild halls in the city. Located at the confluence of the Nanpu Creek and the Malian River, Nanpu Town possessed both a water transport port and was an important collection and distribution point along the Xianxia ancient route. It became a major trading town in Pucheng. Porters carried silk textiles from Jiangsu–Zhejiang area via the Xianxia route to Pucheng, and from there the goods would travel along the Nanpu Creek through Jian'ou and Nanping, and then down the Minjiang River to Fuzhou. Likewise, Pucheng's local specialties—such as timber, tea, dried bamboo shoots, tung oil, and red mushrooms—were transported via the same route to Fuzhou. On return trips, sea products, salt, Beijing dried fruits, and daily sundries from Fuzhou and towns along the lower and middle reaches of the Minjiang River were brought upstream. After reaching

Pucheng, these goods were partially sold in northern Fujian, while the rest was carried by porters over the Xianxia route into Jiangshan in Zhejiang, and then redistributed to Shanghai, Jiangsu, and other regions.

4. Chong'an County

Chong'an County (modern-day Wuyishan City) was located in northwestern Fujian, bordered by Pucheng to the east, Jianyang to the south, Guangze to the west, and Yanshan County in Jiangxi Province to the north. Since ancient times, the Fenshui Pass in Chong'an had been one of the most important commercial gateways between Fujian and Jiangxi. According to the *Essentials of Historical Geography*, "The Fenshui Pass lies on the northwestern watershed of the county (Chong'an), bordering Jiangxi's Yanshan... it has long been a vital passageway for merchants and travelers."[1] Hekou in Yanshan County, Jiangxi, connected westward to the Poyang Lake water system and the Yangtze River via the Xinjiang River, and eastward to Jiangsu and Zhejiang, with boats able to reach Yushan directly. It served as a key distribution hub for trade among Fujian, Zhejiang, Jiangxi, and Anhui. By the Ming Dynasty, a wide array of goods from Chong'an were shipped to Jiangxi's Yanshan, and trade activity was intense. According to the *Yanshan Gazetteer*, volume 1, *Food and Commodities* (compiled during the Wanli reign), the flow of goods through Hekou was described as follows,

> Goods from all directions arrive here. From southeastern Fujian come iron from Yanping, raw cloth from Datian, bamboo shoots from Chong'an, white and brown sugar from Fuzhou, fans from Jianning, lychees and longans from the coastal region of Zhangzhou, pepper and sappanwood from overseas, tin, red copper, lacquerware

1 (Qing) Gu Zuyu. *Essentials of Historical Geography*, vol. 97. Shanghai Bookstore Publishing House, 1998, pp. 639-642.

> from Guangdong... various silk fabrics, Hangzhou silk, cotton textiles, Pengliu satin, Quzhou silk, and Fuzhou silk... These are among the most important commercial goods transported by merchant vessels.[1]

This shows that commodities shipped from Fujian to Hekou were highly diverse. From Hekou, they could be redistributed to Jiangsu, Zhejiang, and areas along the Yangtze River. Conversely, goods from these areas were transported back through Hekou, over the Fenshui Pass in Chong'an, to northern Fujian and then distributed throughout the province. Moreover, during the Ming Dynasty's maritime trade ban, many goods from Jiangsu and Zhejiang destined for overseas markets were first routed through the Fenshui Pass into Fujian, where Fujianese merchants would then ship them abroad. As a result, Chong'an became a key commodity distribution center for the tri-province region of Fujian, Zhejiang, and Jiangxi.

II. Key Transportation Hubs and Commercial Centers in Western Fujian

Located at the juncture of Fujian, Guangdong, and Jiangxi provinces, western Fujian has gradually become a central hub for trade and commercial exchange among the three provinces since the Tang and Song dynasties, owing to population growth and economic development. Three major transportation hubs and commercial centers had emerged in the region: Changting County, Longyan County, and Fengshi Town in Yongding.

1. Changting County

Situated in the upper reaches of the Tingjiang River, Changting borders Ruijin in Jiangxi to the west, Liancheng to the east, Ninghua and Qingliu to

1 Wu Bangcai, editor-in-chief. *A History of the Development of Fujian Merchants: Nanping Volume*. Xiamen University Press, 2016, p.111.

the north, and Wuping and Shanghang to the south, making it a crucial node along the ancient trade routes linking Fujian, Guangdong, and Jiangxi. After the Southern Song period, with continued population growth and economic development, along with the opening of upper-Tingjiang River navigation routes, salt and grain trade between Changting, southern Jiangxi, and northeastern Guangdong began to flourish. Salt from the Chaozhou region was transported via the Hanjiang River and the Tingjiang River to Changting. While some salt was consumed within Tingzhou Prefecture, the majority was re-exported to southern Jiangxi. Conversely, grain abundantly produced in southern Jiangxi was shipped through Changting to the regions of Chaozhou and Shantou. However, the scale of this salt-grain trade remained limited at the time. During the Ming and Qing dynasties, as the economy of the mountainous border regions between Fujian and Jiangxi further developed, and with improvements in water transport along the Tingjiang River as well as in transportation routes connecting Jiangxi, Meizhou, Tingzhou, and Zhangzhou, the scale of trade in goods such as salt, grain, handmade paper, and daily necessities across the Fujian-Guangdong-Jiangxi border regions expanded continuously. As a result, the Fujian–Guangdong–Jiangxi border area began to coalesce into a defined economic region, with Tingzhou emerging as its commercial hub. It is recorded that over 1,000 *dan* (about 50,000 kilograms) of rice from southern Jiangxi were transshipped daily via Changting to eastern Guangdong. According to the local gazetteer from the Jiajing era of the Ming Dynasty, Tingzhou Prefecture already hosted numerous large marketplaces. For instance, Diantou Market, located outside the southern gate of the prefectural city, "reaches down to the riverside, where salt, iron, indigo, and sundry goods are traded"; while Wutong Temple Market, connected to Diantou Street, was known for the "convergence of goods from all directions." In the early Qing period, merchants from regions such as Ganchuan, Chaoshan, Dapu began to open trade establishments along Diantou Street in Changting, attracting numerous merchants from both north and south to conduct business there.[1] During the early Republican era, the bulk of grain, legumes, live pigs, and cloth imported from southern Jiangxi was traded in Changting before being re-exported to Meizhou and the Chaozhou-Shantou area. At that time, over 500 shops and commercial establishments were located within the county seat of Changting. During the War of Resistance against Japanese Aggression, Changting earned the nickname "Red Little Shanghai", with stores selling dried fruits, cloth, oil, salt, and various general goods densely lining its many streets. As such, Changting became one of the most significant economic and trade centers within the Central Soviet Area.

The Restored Port Street of Changting

2. Longyan County

Longyan County (now Xinluo District of Longyan City) bordered Zhangzhou to the south and was one of the key transportation hubs linking Tingzhou and Zhangzhou. In the first year of the Wanli reign of the Ming

1Huang Ting, and Du Jingguo. "Transportation and Economic Connections Along the Fujian–Guangdong–Jiangxi Border from the Song to Qing Dynasties". *Journal of Shantou University (Humanities Edition)*, no. 2, 1995, p. 81.

Dynasty (1573), the county magistrate, Li Shaoxi, recruited local laborers to chisel through the Guanyinzuo Rock, which had obstructed the waterway between Longyan and the towns of Yanshi and Jintou. This engineering feat enabled vessels to navigate the Jiulong River upstream to the urban center of Longyan. In addition, improvements made during the Ming Dynasty to the official roads connecting Longyan with Ningyang and Zhangping further enhanced its role as a crucial transport corridor between southern Jiangxi, northern Fujian, Tingzhou, and Zhangzhou. [1] With the emergence of Longyan as a key transportation hub in southwestern Fujian, the county was elevated to the status of Longyan Prefecture in the early Qing Dynasty. In various parts of Longyan Prefecture, there were shortages of both salt and grain. Salt had to be brought in from Zhangzhou, while grain was imported from southern Jiangxi via Changting. The renowned Qing scholar Gu Yanwu noted in his *Treatise on the Salt Laws*,

> Only the counties under Zhangzhou's jurisdiction, such as Longyan, Zhangping, and Ningyang, are mountainous, remote, and impoverished, so that the local people cannot readily obtain salt. As for how salt is supplied to the people: it is transported by sea vessels to Haicheng, docked at the wharf, then transferred onto small boats that sail northwestward along two rivers to Huafeng, and from there it is distributed and sold throughout Longyan and nearby counties. Another route goes upstream from Ningyang to Majia Mountain, then across Yong'an, spreading into the jurisdictions of Yan, Jian and Shao—regions included in the official salt distribution network. The profits from this trade are many times greater, which is

---

1 Cai Lixiong, editor-in-chief. *A Commercial History of Western Fujian*. Xiamen University Press, 2014, p. 46.

> why merchants from Zhangzhou are often eager to seize the opportunity for gain.[1]

The majority of salt shipped from Zhangzhou supplied Longyan, Zhangping, and Ningyang, while a smaller share was sent to Shanghang, Wuping, and Liancheng. Goods imported from Zhangzhou into Tingzhou—such as sugar, textiles, seafood, and sundries—were also frequently rerouted through Longyan, while specialty products exported from Tingzhou to Zhangzhou, such as bamboo shoots, handmade paper, and shredded tobacco, were partially channeled through Longyan as well. Located just five kilometers from the Longyan urban center, Longmen Town functioned as the county's largest commodity distribution hub, where merchants from Fujian, Guangdong, and Jiangxi conducted substantial trade in handmade paper. After the opening of five treaty ports, some goods imported through Xiamen Port also passed through Zhangzhou and Longyan en route to Changting. Consequently, from the mid-Qing period onward, Longyan increasingly evolved into a vital transportation hub and commercial center within western Fujian.

3. Fengshi Town

Fengshi Town is located along the lower reaches of the Tingjiang River and borders Dapu County in Guangdong Province, marking the fluvial boundary between Fujian and Guangdong. Due to the obstructive terrain at Mianhua Shoal, the river segment between Fengshi and Dapu was unnavigable by boat. Consequently, goods transported from Jiangxi and Changting to the Chaoshan region had to be unloaded at Fengshi and carried overland to Dapu before continuing by water to Chaoshan. Similarly, goods

1 (Qing) Gu Yanwu. *Treatise on the Advantages and Disadvantages of Commanderies and States of the Empire*, edition of *Four Book Series*. Shanghai Bookstore Publishing House, 1985, p. 675.

shipped upstream from Chaoshan via the Hanjiang River were unloaded at Dapu, transported by land to Fengshi, and then forwarded by water to Shanghang and Changting before being rerouted to Jiangxi and northern Fujian. Fengshi thus became a critical transshipment hub for goods exchanged among the three provinces of Fujian, Guangdong, and Jiangxi. In the early Ming Dynasty, although the government implemented a maritime prohibition policy, armed private maritime trade and mountain trade remained active in the coastal regions of Fujian and Guangdong. Fengshi, located at the border of Fujian and Guangdong, gradually became a hub for smuggled goods moving between the coastal zones and inland regions of Fujian and Jiangxi. Due to frequent armed smuggling activities involving maritime and mountain trade in Fengshi at the time, the Ming court built the "Fumin Pavilion Fort" and "Hetou Fort" there during the Jiajing and Wanli periods, and stationed troops to guard the area. After the mid-Ming Dynasty, when the maritime prohibition policy was lifted, the variety and volume of goods traded in Fengshi increased significantly. By the early Republican period, merchants from Chaoshan, Changting, Liancheng, Jiangxi, and Hunan had established guild halls in Fengshi, and the town boasted over 300 commercial establishments. During the War of Resistance against Japanese Aggression, Fengshi became a crucial node in the revolutionary transport network and an important distribution center for transshipped goods among Fujian, Guangdong, and Jiangxi, making it earn the nickname "Little Hong Kong."

Chapter 6
People from the Hinterland of the Maritime Silk Road

The Push and Pull Theory in migration studies posits that population movement is influenced by push factors (unfavorable living conditions in areas of origin) and pull factors (conditions in destination areas that offer better opportunities). During the Ming and Qing dynasties, emigration from the hinterland of the Maritime Silk Road was largely driven by mountainous terrain with limited arable land and heavy subsistence pressures. Meanwhile, the rise of a market economy created more opportunities for outward population movement.

Section 1 The Seafarers from the Hinterland of the Maritime Silk Road

Historical records of population mobility from the mountainous hinterland along the Maritime Silk Road began to increase after the Song Dynasty. By that time, residents of western Fujian had already navigated the Tingjiang River and Hanjiang River to travel toward the South China Sea, Taiwan, and Hainan. The *History of Song: Biography of Java* records that Mao Xu, a merchant from Jianxi (modern-day Jian'ou), made multiple trade voyages to Java. In the third year of Chunhua reign (992 CE), Mao Xu served as an interpreter for an envoy from Java bringing tribute to China. In the fifth year of Xianping reign (1002), Zhou Shichang, a maritime merchant from Jianzhou (now Jian'ou), was blown off course to Japan, where he lived for seven years before returning to China. In the seventeenth year of Jiading reign (1224), Zhu Qian of Jianyang, a great-grandson of Zhu Xi, traveled eastward to Goryeo (modern-day Korea) with his children and disciples Ye Gongji, Zhao Yong, Chen Zushun, and four others, eventually settling in Neungseong. Zhu Qian's eldest son, Zhu Yuqing, was appointed Left Chancellor of Music and posthumously awarded the title of Director of Confidential Affairs of the Privy Council in Goryeo. His grandson Zhu Yue achieved first place in the civil service examination during the first year of Goryeo and served as magistrate of Namwon, eventually rising to the position of Inspector General. Today, Zhu Qian's descendants are numerous in South Korea.

During the Yongle reign of the Ming Dynasty, Wang Jinghong from western Fujian joined Zheng He's fleet on his expeditions to the Western Seas, helping to open up maritime routes to Southeast Asia and the Indian Ocean, thus contributing a brilliant chapter to China's maritime history. In the Zhengtong period, a Japanese man named Zhengchang, styled Lanxuan, traveled successively to Jianyang with Heqi Mingqin and others to study medicine under the renowned physician Xiong Zongli. During the Chenghua period, Xie Wenbin of Tingzhou, who had set out to sea to trade salt, arrived and settled in Siam (modern-day Thailand). He rose to the position of *Yuekun* (a scholarly rank), married a local woman, spoke the Siamese language, and wore Siamese clothing. In the thirteenth year of Chenghua (1477), he served as an envoy from Siam to pay tribute to the Ming court. This event is recorded in the books of *A Comprehensive Inquiry into Foreign Lands* and *History of Ming: Biography of Siam*, where the Siamese king dispatched two envoys, Xie Tisu Yingbi and Meiya, to present tribute. The envoy "Meiya" was in fact Xie Wenbin, who, upon his return to China, was recognized by his nephew in Nanjing, thereby confirming his identity. In the tenth year of Hongzhi (1497), a man named Tailuo (also written as Lailuo or Nailuo) returned to China as an interpreter for the Siamese court. He claimed to be from Qingliu County, Fujian, and said he had been blown off course to Siam, where he subsequently settled. Tailuo petitioned the imperial court for permission to return to his hometown to pay respects at his ancestral tombs, which was granted. Both Xie Wenbin and Tailuo initially migrated abroad as private citizens, and later took on official roles as envoys in the tributary trade system, thus playing a role in facilitating cultural exchange between China and Southeast Asia.

In the late Ming and early Qing periods, many Chinese migrated and settled in Nagasaki, Japan, among whom a significant number were overseas Chinese from Fujian. Over time, Fujianese communities began to take shape in Nagasaki and surrounding areas. Among the Fujian scholar-officials residing in Nagasaki, quite a few hailed from the mountainous regions of Fujian. In the fortieth year of the Wanli reign (1612), Lu Junyu,[1]

1Lin Guoping, and Qiu Jiduan, editors-in-chief. *A History of Fujian Migration*. Fangzhi Press, 2005, p. 188.

originally from Shaxian in Yanping County, Fujian, traveled to Nagasaki and settled in Japan after marrying a local woman. He adopted the Japanese name Shozaemon and became the founding ancestor of the Lu clan among the Japanese Chinese. In 1666, he was appointed as a Tang interpreter. The Lu family settled in Nagasaki, and Lu Junyu and his descendants played an active role in disseminating Chinese culture. Lu Junyu's grandson, Lu Caoshuo (Chinese name Xuanzhuo, Japanese name Tokubei), became a famous Chinese physician in the mid-17th century. Despite living in Japan, he remained widely known by his Chinese surname. At the age of 12, he began studying medicine under Ono Shosaku and later pursued further studies in Kyoto, gaining recognition as a scholar of pharmacognosy. He practiced medicine in Nagasaki and trained many disciples. His work, *Essential Compilation of Medicinal Properties*, earned him the title "forefather of pharmacognosy during Japan's sakoku era." Lu Caoshuo's son, Lu Caozuo —also known as Yuanmin and Baozhen, and called Usanosuke in childhood during his time in Japan—was a diligent scholar who began lecturing at the age of 17 and attracted many disciples. In his later years, he was appointed as the head scholar of the Confucius Temple and was also recommended to serve as Supervisor of Books and Records. Lu Caozhuo was proficient in Confucianism and also deeply interested in the Daoist teachings of Laozi and Zhuangzi, adopting the Daoist name Qingsuxuan. He excelled in poetry, prose, and astronomy. His son, Lu Ji, was a prominent scholar among the Chinese community in the first half of the 18th century in Nagasaki, Japan. His work *Chronicles of the Early Settlers of Nagasaki* is an important historical source on the Nagasaki Chinese diaspora.[1]

During the late Ming and early Qing periods, people from western

1Wang Xiangrong. *Japanese Instructors*. Sanlian Bookstore, 1988, p.42.

Fujian set sail via the Tingjiang River and Hanjiang River, with Taiwan and Southeast Asia being primary destinations. During the Shunzhi reign of the Qing Dynasty, Chen Qitao of Mingxi, a rice merchant operating in Guangdong, was blown off course and ended up residing in Siam. Also known as Xitao, courtesy name Yulong, Chen Qitao was born in Yangfang, Mingxi County, in the eighteenth year of Shunzhi (1661). He was intelligent from a young age and skilled in social interactions. At the age of sixteen, he began trading in eastern Guangdong. When he first arrived there, due to language barriers, he could only run a small-scale business. However, Qitao was naturally quick-witted and soon learned Cantonese, integrated into local society and gradually moved on to trade in bulk goods. He realized that Siamese rice was of high quality and low cost, so he often interacted with Siamese rice merchants. He learned the Siamese language and frequently sailed overseas to negotiate trade with the Siamese. One day, while traveling by boat, he encountered a violent storm and was blown off course to Siam. When news spread that a Chinese man had arrived in the kingdom, locals came to inquire. Qitao communicated with local merchants and civilians in Siamese and gradually built relationships with local officials and elites. When the king heard of this, he summoned Qitao for an audience. Seeing that Qitao was tall and dignified in appearance and refined in speech, the king granted him an official position and later gave his daughter in marriage to him. He served successively as Prime Minister of Siam and was known to have sent valuable items back to China during the Yongzheng and Qianlong reigns. Some rumors claimed he ascended to the Siamese throne after the king's death, though this lacks historical verification.[1] In the twelfth year of the Yongzheng reign in Qing Dynasty (1734), Hu Zhaoyou,

---

1Li Yunsheng. "A Record of Chen Qitao from Mingxi Becoming Prime Minister of Siam". *Local Historical Materials of Mingxi,* vol. 1, edited by the Editorial Office of Literature and History Materials of the CPPCC Mingxi County Committee, 1983, pp. 54–56.

a *gongsheng* (tribute student) from Zhongchuan, Yongding, traveled eastward to Taiwan. During his stay, he established the Mingzhi Academy and became the first person to promote education and culture in northern Tamsui. In 1745, Ma Fuchun, a charcoal worker from Yongding, went to sea and settled in Penang, Malaysia, where he helped develop the area. After his death, the local Chinese community venerated him as the *Tua Pek Kong*, a local guardian deity.

By the Qing Dynasty, population movements along the Maritime Silk Road had become increasingly frequent. Zhu Zizhang, a native of Tingzhou and born into a family of medical practitioners, had already gained a reputation for his medical expertise by the end of the Kangxi era. Invited by the Tokugawa Shogunate, Zhu Zizhang and his younger brother Zhu Laizhang arrived in Nagasaki, Japan, aboard a merchant ship on July 16th of the sixtieth year of Kangxi (1721), accompanied by several disciples and assistants. They brought with them more than seventy Chinese books, including a substantial number of medical texts. On December 21th of the first year of Yongzheng (1723), the Zhu brothers returned to China. Two years later, they came to Nagasaki again, this time with family members Zhu Yunguang, Zhu Yunchuan, and Zhu Shuangyu. While in Nagasaki, the Zhu brothers not only treated local patients but also responded to inquiries from Japanese physicians, making notable contributions to the advancement of Japanese medicine. Zhu Laizhang documented his medical experiences in Nagasaki in a book titled *Zhu Laizhang's Case Studies*, now housed in the Japanese Cabinet Library. In the fifth year of Yongzheng (1727), Zhu Laizhang departed Nagasaki for home. Their eldest brother, Zhu Peizhang, also traveled with them, but he was active primarily as a Confucian scholar rather than a medical practitioner. Zhu Peizhang once presented the Japanese authorities with a musical text entitled *The Subtle Principles of Musical Tuning and Temperament.*

During the transitional period between the Ming and Qing dynasties, Hakka people from Fujian and Guangdong increasingly migrated to Southeast Asia, with particularly large numbers from Dapu County in Guangdong and Yongding County in Fujian. Within Yongding, the majority of those who ventured overseas came from the towns of Jinfeng, Fengtian, and Taiping. Utilizing the water route from the Tingjiang River to the Hanjaing River, waves of emigrants continuously set sail for Southeast Asia, embarking from the Tingjiang river wharf of Chayang. In the seventeenth year of Kangxi (1678), Wu Jiqing from Yongding traveled to Malaysia; in the fifth year of Yongzheng (1727), You Qiaoqi migrated south to Java, while Hu Yingxue and Hu Yongxiang migrated south to Sarawak and other places. From Sibao in Liancheng, Zou Shizhong and Zou Xunchen journeyed to Batavia, Java (modern-day Jakarta, Indonesia) and Siam. In the tenth year of Qianlong reign (1745), a group of approximately forty Hakka migrants from Fujian and Guangdong boarded a ship at the Chayang wharf. Caught in a storm during their voyage, they were blown off course to Penang Island. The group was led by Zhang Li and Qiu Zhaojin from Dapu, Guangdong, and Ma Fuchun from Yongding, Fujian.The three men swore brotherhood, with Zhang Li as the elder brother, and together spearheaded the pioneering settlement efforts of Chinese immigrants in Penang. When British Captain Francis Light arrived at Penang in 1786, he found that significant development had already taken place: hundreds of hectares of land had been cultivated and the population approached a thousand, with Chinese making up about 40% of the total. After Zhang, Qiu, and Ma passed away, their bodies were not repatriated; instead, local Chinese buried them on the Hai Choo Island and built a temple in their honor, referring to them as the *Tua Pek Kong* of the Hai Choo Island. Zhang Li, the eldest, was revered as the "Founder and Patron of the Land." *Tua Pek Kong* became a symbol of the pioneering spirit of overseas Chinese in Southeast Asia. During their lifetimes, these individuals led immigrants in building new lives through hard work and perseverance; after their deaths, they were deified, giving rise to the *Tua Pek Kong* belief in Chinese communities across Southeast Asia, where they became revered as protective deities of the local Chinese population. From the 19th century onward, increasing numbers of people from western Fujian and eastern Guangdong migrated to Southeast Asia, and the Hakka from western Fujian emerged as a significant ethnic group within the emigrants from the Maritime Silk Road's hinterland. Some moved back and forth between their hometowns and new settlements, while others permanently settled abroad. A number of them rose to prominence as renowned merchants and tycoons—for example, Malaysia's "Pepper and Clove King" Hu Taixing, "Tin King" Hu Zichun, and "Tiger Balm King" Hu Wenhu—all typical representatives of this phenomenon.

Among these migrants, there was also a group who went to Southeast Asia either sold as "laborers" or voluntarily seeking work. For instance, in the second year of Xianfeng (1852), four impoverished men from Yong'an, including Chen Lai and Cai Liangren, were abducted and trafficked; in the twenty-seventh year of Guangxu (1901), dozens of men from Datian County, such as Tu Wulu, Tu Wenyu, Tu Sunxu, and Zhang Yuzhong, went to Malaysia under "labor contracts." Toward the end of the 19th century and beginning of the 20th, people from Chongcheng Town in Chong'an (now Wuyishan City), including Gao Jinshou, Gao Jincai, Zhang Qianzai, and Zhang Qiansun, went to Penang, Malaysia, as contract laborers in the gold mines. Their children and grandchildren later engaged in education, commerce, and medicine, obtained Malaysian citizenship, or migrated to Canada.

In the 20th century, emigration from the hinterland of the Maritime Silk Road continued in various forms. In 1906, Pei Yuqiao from Qingliu traveled to Singapore. People from places such as Jiyang, Humei, and

Pingshan in Datian County also went to Singapore, Malacca, and Kuala Lumpur in search of livelihoods. Huang Xitian from Heping in Shaowu sought work in Malaysia. In 1912, Deng Lisheng from Zhicheng Town in Jian'ou settled in Singapore after transiting through Hong Kong and founded the Huiyuan Printing House. In 1913, Lai Xiahou from Jukou in Nanping migrated to Malaysia for making a living. In 1924, Tu Nansheng from Tancheng Town in Jianyang traveled to Malaysia for commerce and later acquired Malaysian citizenship.

A notable new phenomenon during this period was the emergence of overseas study among educated youth. In 1904, Liu Chunhai from Ninghua went to study in Japan and later joined Sun Yat-sen's Revolutionary Alliance (*Tongmenghui*). In 1906, Liu Zuocheng and Li Baokun from Yong'an were sent on a government scholarship to study in Japan and later participated in China's earliest aviation research efforts. During the Republic of China period, government-sponsored students from Yong'an, such as Lai Weixun, studied in France. Other students from Ninghua, including Tong Zhiliang, Cao Zhiqian, Yi Weice, and Xu Taixian, also studied in France. Additionally, youth from Yong'an and Ninghua studied abroad in Japan, France, and Germany, while others from Jiangle, Youxi, and Datian went to North America on scholarships or at their own expense. In 1913, Zhang Guohui from Dongguan in Shaowu was admitted to Columbia University in the United States and later entered the Law School of the University of Chicago, where he earned a Doctor of Law degree. He began teaching in the U.S. in 1920 before relocating to Malaysia and Singapore. In 1947, Wei Dexin from Jian'ou was sponsored by the government to study at the University of Cambridge in the United Kingdom, where he remained to teach and was eventually promoted to professor.

Section 2 Migration and the Development of Industry and Commerce in Overseas Settlements

The overseas commercial activities and emigration of people from the Maritime Silk Road hinterland reflect the resilient and courageous pioneering spirit of the mountainous population. The economic benefits brought about by trade helped alleviate the poverty caused by the region's limited productive resources. Emigration, in turn, eased the demographic pressure of a high population on scarce arable land. Remittances and investments from overseas Chinese improved the living standards of their native communities. The new ideas introduced through maritime trade and overseas migration, like sea breezes sweeping across the hinterland, broadened the inland population's understanding of the ocean and strengthened their confidence in maritime pursuits. Overseas Chinese also brought back new products and technologies, stimulating local production. Many responded by giving back to their hometowns—constructing public facilities, establishing schools, improving transportation, and developing enterprises—thus continuously transforming the social fabric of their native places.

I. Modes of Emigration

There were two main forms of overseas emigration from the Maritime Silk Road hinterland: free migration and contract migration. During the Republican period, nearly all migrants from the hinterland to overseas destinations were free migrants. The destinations chosen and industries entered by these "new migrants" were largely influenced by kinship and geographic ties. Typically, relatives or fellow villagers had already migrated earlier, establishing a stable presence in the host country. As their businesses expanded and required additional labor, they naturally preferred to recruit those from their home village or clan. The success of these earlier migrants ("old migrants") also exerted a strong pull on the "new migrants.". Consequently, most new migrants were accompanied or sponsored by family members or fellow villagers, and a significant proportion were direct relatives. Through this mentorship and chain migration process, the hometowns of overseas Chinese continuously supplied labor to Southeast Asia. In areas with large numbers of overseas emigrants, nearly every village had "water brokers", who acted as intermediaries between "new" and "old" migrants. These brokers also facilitated the flow of funds and goods, as remittances and parcels traveled back and forth between host countries and hometowns. Escorting a single "new migrant" overseas generally cost several dozen silver dollars. If relatives or clansmen acted as sponsors, the migrant would either pay for the journey themselves or have the sponsor cover the cost, which would later be repaid after the migrant secured employment abroad. These new arrivals often worked in the same industry as their sponsors.

The second mode of emigration was contract migration, in which individuals traveled abroad as "contract laborers." In western Fujian, such activities frequently involved intermediaries known as labor brokers. These brokers would escort workers to recruitment agencies in Shantou, where they underwent questioning, medical examinations, photography, contract signing, and fingerprinting before being permitted to depart. These laborers were primarily destined for tin mines and plantations in Southeast Asia,[1] though some also journeyed across the ocean to the Americas. According to historical archives on Chinese laborers, during the Xianfeng reign of the Qing Dynasty, several individuals from Longyan, including Huang Aming, were deceived into believing that working in Macau would yield high wages. In reality, they were tricked onto a so-called "coolie ship" and sent to Cuba

1 Wu Fengbin. "A Study on the Issues of Overseas Migration from Western Fujian During the Republican Era". *Southeast Asian Affairs*, no.1, 1994, pp. 10–17.

for hard labor. En route, they endured severe storms, extreme water shortages, and the stench of disease-filled holds; those who died were thrown overboard. After more than a hundred days at sea, they arrived in Cuba and were sold to sugar refineries, where they toiled day and night, surviving on meager meals of bananas, sweet potatoes, and maize. Those who arrived even slightly late for work were immediately whipped, and many were tortured to death. In the second year of Xianfeng reign (1852), Longyan residents Liu Jinqian, Li Hai, and Chen Chahua were similarly deceived by unscrupulous labor brokers and forced to become "contracted Chinese laborers" (commonly referred to as coolies). They boarded the *Robert Bowne* bound for the United States, along with more than 400 other Chinese laborers. During the voyage, they suffered abuse and humiliation at the hands of American crew members, resulting in the deaths of over ten laborers. In response, Liu Jinqian, Li Hai, Chen Chahua, and fourteen other compatriots led a revolt on the ship, inciting all the workers onboard to rise up. They killed the captain, the first mate, and three others—five in total—before escaping to the Ryukyu Islands. This laborer uprising sent shockwaves around the world, and the heroic deeds of these seventeen Chinese men became enshrined in the history of resistance by Chinese laborers abroad.

II. Routes of Emigration

The primary route for overseas emigration from western Fujian was via Shantou, followed by Xiamen. Hakka people from Yongding, Shanghang, Wuping, Changting, and Liancheng typically chose the Tingjiang River waterway, heading south into the Hanjiang River. Those departing via Shantou usually walked to Chayang in Dapu County, Guangdong, then took a "duck mother boat" (a small passenger vessel) to Chaozhou, where they stayed at or contacted inns operated by merchants from Tingzhou and Longyan. From Chaozhou, they traveled by train to

Shantou, where inns were also available for accommodation. Emigrants from Longyan and Zhangping more often traveled downstream along the Jiulong River to southern Fujian and departed via Xiamen. Setting out from Longyan, one could walk for three days through Banliao to reach Zhangzhou, then take a boat to Xiamen; traveling entirely on foot would take four days. At that time in Xiamen, Longyan natives Rao Musun and Chen Jinshou operated the Min'guo Inn and Longhua Inn, providing affordable food, lodging, and low-cost ticket purchasing services for fellow Longyan residents who had come to Xiamen seeking opportunities overseas. Upon arrival in various ports across Southeast Asia, they were often able to receive care and assistance from fellow townsmen already settled abroad. In the 1920s, several Longyan merchants in Sumatra, including Weng Duxin (owner of Jinxiangxing in Medan), Zhang Maoxuan (owner of Xietonghe in Asahan), and Fu Zhichuan (owner of Xieyuan Company in Pangkalan Brandan), played key roles in assisting newly arrived Chinese immigrants, known as "new guests". They provided the necessary guarantees for their entry, without which newcomers could not disembark after paying the entry tax. These merchants also often provided food, lodging, and job referrals, earning them the title "Three Great Overseas Chinese of Longyan."[1]

According to statistical data in 1939, the majority of overseas Chinese from western Fujian were concentrated in Yongding (present-day Yongding District of Longyan City) and Longyan (present-day Xinluo District of Longyan City), with those from Yongding accounting for more than 60% of the region's total overseas Chinese population at the time.[2] Migrants from

1Wu Fengbin. "A Study on the Issues of Overseas Migration from Western Fujian During the Republican Era". *Southeast Asian Affairs*, no.1, 1994, pp. 10–17.

2Fujian Provincial Archives, ed. *Archival Historical Materials on Overseas Chinese in Fujian Province,* vol. 2. Archives Publishing House, 1990, pp. 1735–1736.

Yongding could generally be divided into two categories: those who emigrated to Southeast Asia and those involved in the tobacco trade. The former primarily came from the southern areas of Yongding, such as Xiayang, while the latter were mainly from villages along the Jinfeng Creek Basin, including Guzhu, Xiayang, Qiling, Daxi, and Hukeng.[1] For instance, in Zhongchuan Village, Xiayang, Yongding—the hometown of the Hu Wenhu family—over 90% of households had relatives overseas. In Longyan, large numbers of overseas Chinese originated from towns and villages such as Dongxiao (Baitu), Xipi, Longmen, and Xidou Village in Dongxiao. Besides, areas like Rentian and Jiaoyang in Shanghang County, Hetian and Tongfang in Changting County, Sibao in Liancheng, Yongfu in Zhangping, and Yanqian in Wuping were also known for having relatively high concentrations of overseas Chinese.[2] During the Republican period, overseas emigrants from western Fujian primarily settled in British Malaya, the Dutch East Indies, Burma and Thailand. Most of these migrants were originally farmers or unemployed students, many of whom had received some level of formal education. From the 11th to 16th year of the Guangxu reign (1885–1890), individuals such as Qiu Rongqing (from Xinan Lane), Chen Shuifa (from Dongxiao Community), Weng Jinshi (from Suonei Lane), and Huang Zhanfu (from Xishan Community) went abroad to make a living. Toward the end of the Qing Dynasty and the early Republican era, others including Chen Shuiwang, Chen Shoubo, Weng Zhipeng, Weng Jinquan, Liu Luosan, Qiu Duguang, Zhang Hanzong, Weng Duxin, Zhang Maoxuan, Su Caixuan, Lin Yingqing, Wang Junyuan, Wei Chengjin, Deng Yueshan, and Zhang Yuezai also made their way to Zhangzhou on foot

---

1Zhong Yifeng. *The Circulation of Tobacco: The History and Culture of Tobacco in Yongding*. PhD dissertation. Xiamen University, 2008, p.140.

2The Fujian Provincial Local Chronicles Compilation Committee, ed. *Fujian Provincial Gazetteer: Overseas Chinese Volume*. Fujian People's Publishing House, 1992.

before sailing from Xiamen to Southeast Asia. Longyan emigrants mainly headed to Siam, Burma, Malaysia, Singapore, North Borneo (present-day Sabah), and the Dutch East Indies (modern-day Indonesia), with a particularly large number settling in Sumatra. By 1920, more than 300 individuals had migrated to Southeast Asia for livelihoods, led or influenced by kinship and community networks. With the ensuing years marked by continuous military strife, social unrest, and economic hardship in Longyan, the number of people leaving for Southeast Asia grew steadily. On April 15, 1927, the right wing of the Kuomintang in Longyan launched a purge against Communists, forcing over ten progressive youths—such as Zheng Rihui, Zhang Aiting, Zhang Xugao, and Chen Qinglong—to flee overseas. By 1930, the overseas Longyan diaspora had grown to over 2,000 individuals scattered across Singapore, Malaysia, the Dutch East Indies, Burma, and Siam. According to the 1945 edition of the *Gazetteer of Longyan County*, the continual warfare and worsening living conditions after 1930 led to an ever-increasing number of people seeking livelihoods abroad. By 1940, the number of overseas Chinese from Longyan had reached 8,450.

The overseas Chinese from the maritime Silk Road hinterland were widely distributed across various regions of Southeast Asia, including Penang, a major port city located at the northern end of the Strait of Malacca in Malaysia. In 1786, British colonialists began controlling Penang and developed it into a "free port" that connected Eastern and Western trade. Prior to this, Hakka people had already begun settling and cultivating the land there. Subsequently, the Hakka population grew steadily; they initially planted pepper—earning considerable profits—and later expanded into other forms of agricultural development. During the Qianlong reign of the Qing Dynasty, Hu Taixing, a Hakka native of Zhongchuan Village in Xiayang, Yongding County, became the first Chinese industrialist on

Penang Island. The Hu family had long cultivated pepper in Penang, and by Hu Taixing's time, they owned extensive pepper plantations. With the continued development of Penang, many Hakka overseas Chinese migrated there from other parts of Malaysia to establish businesses. One of the most notable figures was Hu Zichun, the so-called "Tin King," who originated from the same Zhongchuan Village in today's Xiayang Town, Yongding District. Starting from his grandfather's generation, the family had been engaged in pepper cultivation in Penang. At a young age, Hu Zichun followed fellow villagers to Malaysia, where he began as an apprentice, and eventually amassed wealth through tin mining operations.

In the massive wave of Hakka emigration from the Maritime Silk Road hinterland to Southeast Asia, the vital link between the homelands and the overseas communities was maintained by "water brokers"—traveling middlemen who served as the key conduit between home villages and diaspora populations. Local specialties such as tea, shredded tobacco, and preserved vegetables from the hometowns flowed steadily abroad, while Southeast Asian goods such as medicinal herbs and timepieces were shipped back, forming a dense and dynamic trade network. Moreover, these "water brokers" served as couriers, acting as emotional bridges between overseas Chinese and their families back home. The *qiaopi*—remittance letters sent by overseas Chinese containing both financial support and personal messages—became a crucial source of income for families in the homelands.

The ancient town of Songkou in Meizhou, located at the border of Fujian and Guangdong provinces, bore witness to the bustling activities of the Hakka people along the Maritime Silk Road. At its peak, Songkou's wharf was home to over a thousand shops, with hundreds of boats docking and departing daily. In 2012, UNESCO established an "Migration Monument" in Songkou, commemorating the close historical ties between the Hakka communities of the hinterland and the Maritime Silk Road.

III. Livelihoods of Overseas Chinese

The majority of emigrants from western Fujian in Southeast Asia were engaged in commerce and industrial sectors, particularly in fields of medicine and mining, while others pursued careers in cultural education and various small to medium-sized social service-oriented enterprises. Typically, they honed their skills within industries dominated by fellow townspeople or clan members, starting from entry-level positions and advancing through perseverance and hard work.

1.Pharmaceutical Industry

A significant number of Chinese immigrants in the Malay Peninsula were involved in the pharmaceutical field. In the 22nd year of the Qianlong reign (1757), Chen Chenliu from Yongchun, Fujian, made a living in Malacca, where he successfully treated a difficult illness suffered by the local Sultan's wife and was rewarded with the right of land reclamation. Zeng Guohua, (courtesy name Wenguang), a native of Yongding, practiced medicine and traveled to Penang, where he partnered with relatives to establish the Wan'anxiang Herbal Shop. He later independently founded Wan'anhe, engaging in large-scale herbal trade. His inventions, such as the "Longbiao Headache Powder" and "Ping'an Oil," were very popular in the region. Others from the inland mountainous areas, such as Yu Zhitang from Jianyang, also ventured into the pharmaceutical industry in Penang.

With the practice of Chinese medicine practitioners in the Malay Peninsula, the diagnostic techniques and methods of traditional Chinese medicine spread there as well. Methods such as the "Four Diagnostic Methods" (inspection, listening and smelling, inquiry, and palpation), along with classic medical texts like the *Shennong's Classic of Materia Medica*, became increasingly familiar to the local population.

The most renowned enterprise in this industry was the *Eng Aun Tong* Pharmaceutical Company, founded by Hu Wenhu. Initially established in Rangoon, Burma, in 1921 the company set up its headquarters in Singapore and later expanded to cities such as Bangkok, Hong Kong, Batavia (Jakarta), Penang, Medan, Surabaya, Shanghai, and Tianjin. Another prominent figure, You Linsun from Daxi, Yongding, became one of the leading pharmaceutical entrepreneurs in the Dutch East Indies, overseeing over 130 branches under names such as Ji'an Tang, Da'an Tang, Taihe Tang, Da'an He, and Taihe Chun. Additionally, Lu Bochuan operated in Burma, eventually founding firms like Yifa Firm and Rongfa Company. From Shanghang County, You Xingnan and You Zihan also practiced Chinese medicine in Singapore and helped establish the "Association of Chinese Medicine."

2.Mining Industry

Most Yongding immigrants in Perak and Penang, Malaysia, were involved in tin mining. Hu Zichun, the "Tin King", operated more than 30 mining enterprises in Malaysia. Other prominent mining ventures included Yingfeng Mine owned by Hu Renfang, Shunyi Mine by Hu Zhongyi, and the Tin Mine by Hu Yuechu—all of which were significant in Malaysia's mining sector. In Dawei, Burma, Yongding immigrants also participated in tin mining, while Li Qinze from Wuping County engaged in salt mining in Burma.

3.Newspaper Industry

Hu Wenhu was a pioneer in the newspaper industry among Chinese merchants from the hinterland of the Maritime Silk Road. He founded *Sin Chew Jit Poh* and a series of newspapers known as the "Sing Series." In 1928, he launched *Sin Chew Jit Poh*, the first of the series, with the inaugural issue released on January 25, 1929. As the business of *Eng Aun Tong* flourished, Hu's newspaper empire also expanded to include sixteen newspapers in mainland China, Hong Kong, and throughout Southeast Asia, such as *Sing Guang Daily* in Xiamen, *Sing Yue Daily* in Guangzhou, *Sing Hua Daily* in Shantou, *Sing Zhong Daily* in Singapore, *Sing Bin Daily* in Penang, *Sing Daily* in Bangkok, and *Sing Tao Daily* in Hong Kong, forming a vast newspaper conglomerate. Among these, *Sin Chew Jit Poh* in Singapore ranked second in scale and circulation only to Tan Kah Kee's *Nanyang Siang Pau*. The newspaper was suspended during the Japanese occupation of Singapore but resumed publication after Japan's defeat.

Yongding expatriates actively participated in the newspaper industry. Hu Changyao, Hu Wenhu's nephew, founded *Gazette* (*Gongbao*), while You Ziyun established the *National Daily* (*Guomin Ribao*) in Batavia, and Su Xiaomi co-founded the *Surabaya Commercial Daily* (*Sishui Shangbao*) in Surabaya and other locations. In addition to founding their own newspapers, overseas Chinese also participated in journalism as staff members. Hu Wenhu's newspaper offices recruited many fellow townsmen as reporters and editors—over 40 overseas Chinese from Yongding, including Chen Lansheng and Zeng Daoxiu, once worked for Hu Wenhu's newspaper enterprises.

Chinese-language newspapers represented by *Sin Chew Jit Poh* held profound significance for the overseas Chinese community. From its inception, the newspaper consistently focused on reporting developments in the homelands and information about overseas Chinese communities, aligning with the general needs of the Chinese diaspora. It also strengthened the connection between overseas Chinese and their homelands, reinforced their sense of cultural identity with Chinese civilization, and inspired them to actively participate in national salvation movements during the first half of the 20th century.

4.Other Industries

After settling in their new countries, overseas Chinese utilized their skills and talents, engaging in a wide range of occupations, including the daily goods and general merchandise trade, commerce, cultural enterprises, and education.

Many Longyan emigrants became small-scale merchants and typically belonged to the lower-middle class, with few becoming major magnates. They began their careers as apprentices, menial workers, shop assistants, and bookkeepers, gradually building wealth through diligence. Some became street vendors or co-founded general stores. During the 1920s to 1940s, a significant number of Longyan expatriates in Southeast Asia worked in accounting, giving rise to the local saying, "Hainan coffee, Longyan bookkeepers." Chinese merchants, especially those of Minnan origin, competed to hire Longyan bookkeepers with high salaries. Well-known accountants of Longyan origin included Zhang Haiqing, Huang Guoren, and Wang Yuanxing, who worked for prominent firms such as Tan Kah Kee's companies in Singapore. In the late 1930s, Longyan expatriates expanded their business activities to include specialized trade in local products, agency sales of foreign goods, and distribution of Chinese-made merchandise, with some even establishing workshops locally.

Additionally, a number of Longyan expatriates actively contributed to educational development. During the Republican era, over 250 teachers from Longyan were employed in schools throughout Southeast Asia, with some serving as principals. Their presence extended to Indonesia, Singapore, Malaysia, Burma, Thailand, and the Philippines. Notable educators included Zhang Peiying, Lin Boyan, Guo Rongqi, and Zheng Rihui, along with many distinguished female teachers such as Huang Weikun, Su Xiulian, and Zheng Huiying.[1]

Other individuals from Changting, such as Xu Weitang, Xu Geting, Wu Jianji, Li Binri, Hu Pingshan, and Chen Hanchuan, operated businesses in sporting goods in countries such as Thailand, Indonesia, and Singapore. Overseas Chinese from Liancheng sold specialty products from western Fujian, such as *Yukou* paper and *Shanbei* paper. Though small in number, their ventures reflect the diversity of goods traded by Chinese expatriates.

---

1 Longyan Municipal Local Gazetteer Compilation Committee, ed. *Gazetteer of Longyan City*, vol. 29, *Overseas Chinese.* China Science and Technology Press, 1993. Longyan Regional Local Gazetteer Compilation Committee, ed. *Gazetteer of Longyan Region, Fujian Province*, vol. 28, *Overseas Chinese*. Shanghai People's Press, 1992.

Section 3 The Role of Overseas Chinese Merchants in Giving Back to Their Homelands and Serving as Cultural Bridges

Overseas Chinese who journeyed from the hinterland of the Maritime Silk Road to distant foreign lands braved hardships in pursuit of entrepreneurial opportunities and personal development. Their endeavors significantly contributed to the economic, cultural, and social advancement of host countries. Regardless of their individual success or failure, these emigrants maintained a deep emotional connection with their homelands, cared for the well-being of their families and communities, and showed concern for the peace and strength of the Chinese nation. From anti-imperialist and anti-feudal movements during the late Qing and early Republican periods, to the Xinhai Revolution, the War of Resistance against Japanese Aggression, the Chinese Civil War, and the construction of the People's Republic of China, overseas Chinese have made irreplaceable contributions with their own efforts to rescue the nation from peril and to achieve independence and rejuvenation of the Chinese People.

I. Giving Back to Their Homelands

Economic contribution was the most significant form of support provided by overseas Chinese merchants to their places of origin. In the early waves of emigration to Southeast Asia, most emigrants left home due to poverty. Like kites tethered to their native soil, they remitted the majority of their earnings back home to support their families. Wealthier individuals built houses and mansions, stimulating local economic development and transforming social landscapes, with architecture bearing Southeast Asian characteristics becoming new aesthetic benchmarks. Their hard-earned success inspired more people from their hometowns to follow in their footsteps.

After the founding of the Republic of China, the economic power of overseas Chinese strengthened, giving rise to a cohort of influential expatriate tycoons. Their ties with their ancestral homelands became increasingly close. Many not only aided newly arrived compatriots and the impoverished in host countries, but also devoted themselves to the development of their families and hometowns. Remittances from overseas Chinese typically served three functions: support for family, investment, and donation.[1] These three functions were often simultaneously present in overseas remittances, as Chinese migrants supported their families, built or renovated houses, purchased land and mountains, constructed ancestral halls and temples, assisted relatives and friends. In addition, they donated funds to establish schools, develop industries, and support charitable and public welfare causes, significantly contributing to the transformation of their hometowns. Although accurate statistics on remittances from overseas Chinese to the hinterland of the Maritime Silk Road during the Republican period are lacking, scholarly estimates based on 1938 data from counties in western Fujian suggest that total remittances from overseas Chinese in that year exceeded 1.5 million yuan.[2]

Overseas Chinese, deeply influenced by traditional Chinese culture and the belief that "studying is the highest pursuit," came to appreciate the importance of education even more through their own entrepreneurial experiences. Donating to support education in their hometowns became a key way for them to give back to their native land. During the Republican

1 Yuan Ding, Chen Liyuan, and Zhong Yunrong. *The Government's Control over Overseas Remittances in the Republic of China*. Guangdong People's Publishing House, 2014, p. 1.

2Zhang Youzhou, editor-in-chief. *The History of Overseas Chinese from Longyan*. South China University of Technology Press, 2020, p.149.

period, overseas-funded schools in Fujian accounted for a large proportion of the national education system. Among western Fujian expatriates, Hu Zichun was the first to make such contributions. In 1905, he solely funded the establishment of the Yongding Normal School—the first secondary school in Yongding—and later founded Youxing School in Xiayang, Hushan Elementary School, and Jinfeng Middle School. He also supported the construction of seven other schools in Longyan, Shanghang, and Liancheng. Following Hu's example, many others—Weng Jinchun, Zhang Caidong, Zhang Gang, Lin Yingqing, Dai Ziting, Lu Guozhen, Que Delong, You Fanwu, Li Yunxiao, Li Shizhang, and Zhou Yangyun—donated funds to establish schools either in their hometowns or elsewhere in western Fujian. Among all expatriates from the region, the most generous donor to national education was the patriotic overseas leader Hu Wenhu, a native of Xiayang, Yongding. Unlike Tan Kah Kee, who invested heavily in founding schools in Xiamen, Hu Wenhu was committed to building schools that promoted universal education across the country. In 1935, he donated 2.5 million silver dollars with the goal of constructing 1,000 elementary schools nationwide. By 1938, 300 schools had been completed. Between 1929 and 1937, Hu Wenhu made substantial donations to support education or fund the construction of school buildings and facilities for secondary schools and universities across China, including Daxia University in Shanghai, Xiamen University, Sun Yat-sen University in Guangzhou, Lingnan University in Guangzhou, Fujian College in Fuzhou, Zhongkai Agricultural and Industrial School in Guangzhou, Liangjiang Women's Education College in Shanghai, Shantou Municipal Girls' Middle School, Shantou's Huilan Private Middle School, Shantou No.1 Middle School, Haiqiong Middle School in Haikou, Xiamen Middle School, Shuangshi Middle School, Datong Middle School, Zhonghua Middle School, and Huiqun Middle School in Xiamen.

Establishing industries was also one of the ways overseas Chinese gave back to their hometowns and the motherland. During the late Qing and early Republican periods, in addition to donating to education in his hometown, Hu Zichun also invested in industry, including the Beijing–Hankou Railway, the Guangzhou–Hankou Railway, and the Zhangzhou–Xiamen Railway. Beginning in the 1930s, Hu Wenhu made substantial investments in China's economic development. He established pharmaceutical factories in Guangzhou and Shantou and opened branches of Eng Aun Tong Pharmaceutical Company and his "Sing Series" newspapers in cities such as Shanghai, Chongqing, Guangzhou, Fuzhou, Xiamen, Tianjin, Kunming, Guiyang, and Guilin. In 1933, he returned to China and founded the Fujian Provincial Construction Committee, where he proposed the establishment of the Fujian Bank and the promotion of rural economic development. These industrial endeavors were intended to revitalize the domestic economy and transform the economic landscape of both hometowns and the nation. However, due to the international and domestic conditions of the time, their efforts to industrialize China encountered significant obstacles and challenges.

II. Overseas Chinese and the Domestic Revolution

Sun Yat-sen once said, "Overseas Chinese are the mother of the revolution." In modern times, as China faced existential national crises, its people launched arduous struggles against imperialism and feudalism. It was also a period marked by a significant wave of Chinese labor migration abroad and a growing national consciousness among overseas Chinese. Each revolutionary wave at home stirred the patriotic fervor of Chinese communities abroad.

Overseas Chinese societies were supported by three institutional pillars: associations, schools, and newspapers. In the late Qing period, both the Qing government and revolutionary factions vigorously engaged in overseas Chinese affairs for their respective purposes. Overseas Chinese associations, Chinese-language schools, and newspapers flourished, raising the cultural level of these communities and spreading nationalist sentiment. Chinese migrants from the hinterland of the Maritime Silk Road became key targets of revolutionary recruitment. Figures such as Wang Shaojing, Chen Xingchu, Hu Diren, and Hu Jianyang actively participated in the Xinhai Revolution. The May Fourth Movement of 1919 marked the beginning of China's new democratic revolution. A number of overseas Chinese propagated revolutionary ideals both in China and abroad, including Zeng Daoxiu, Chen Zibin, Hu Zizhou, Li Lianxing, Zhang Zhuangfei, Hu Dingjun, Zeng Zhaosheng, Zhang Shuangming, Wei Jinshui, and Cao Juru, all of whom contributed to China's revolutionary cause. Li Lianxing, an overseas Chinese from Singapore, returned to China to study at the Guangzhou Peasant Movement Training Institute. He later served as a special commissioner for peasant movements in Zhangzhou, a member of the CPC Southern Fujian Special Committee, and a member of Fujian Provisional Provincial Committee of the CPC. Deng Chaohai once served as chairman of a county-level Soviet government. Wei Jinshui, a returnee from Malaysia, joined the revolution and led guerrilla warfare in the Fujian-Guangdong-Jiangxi border region. After the founding of the People's Republic of China, he served as deputy secretary of the Fujian Provincial Committee of the CPC, governor of Fujian Province, and a member of the CPC Central Advisory Commission. Cao Juru, who had previously worked in the region of Southeast Asia, including Indonesia and Malaysia, returned to western Fujian and joined the Industrial and Agricutrural Bank. He later participated in the Long March and served as governor of the People's Bank of China after the founding of the People's Republic of China. Zeng Zhaosheng joined the Chinese Communist Youth League at the age of 15, participated in the Jinfeng Uprising in Yongding, and later joined the Red Army. After losing contact with the Party organization while imprisoned by the Kuomintang, he went to Singapore to make a living and reestablished connections with the Party's overseas branch. He later served as secretary of the Perak Committee of the Malayan Communist Party and returned to China under difficult conditions in 1938 to continue revolutionary work. Other overseas Chinese who returned from Southeast Asia to join the revolution and sacrificed their lives for the nation and the people include Chen Junchang, Chen Nangui (from Houtian, Dongxiao, Longyan), Lian Shaochang (from Chishui Village, Longmen, Longyan), Guo Qianzhao, and Guo Youzeng (both from Longmen Town, Longyan).

Overseas Chinese actively promoted revolutionary causes in their host countries. In 1923, more than 20 overseas Chinese from Longyan in Sumatra, including Qiu Jinghua, organized the *Green Grass Society*. They launched a literary weekly titled *Green Grass Weekly*, using the supplement pages of the *New China Daily* in Medan. This publication played an important role in promoting the New Literature Movement in Sumatra. In 1926, one issue featured imagery of an axe and a sickle, which led to the publication being banned by the Dutch colonial authorities, forcing it to cease operations. In that same year, news of the victory of the Northern Expedition brought celebratory marches among Longyan overseas Chinese and other members of the diaspora. In Bagansiapiapi in eastern Sumatra, Longyan immigrants composed a widely circulated victory song, with lyrics proclaiming,

"Revolutionary troops, the Northern Expedition completed.
Warlord tyranny, from now on overthrown.
Good governance thrives, the nation grows strong each day.
We, overseas kin, exiled far abroad,
Rejoice at this news, leaping with joy.
Bless our homeland—may it prosper and flourish!"

After 1930, Su Yiyun, Ma Ning, Qiu Shizhen, and Qiu Xuxu wrote novels and poetry. Figures such as Wang Yuanxing, Huang Fukang, Zhang Aiting, Lian Xiao'ou, and Wu Dizhou supported cultural initiatives, helped launch newspapers and journals, and contributed articles, all significantly impacting the local new cultural movement in their host countries.

During the War of Resistance against Japanese Aggression, Longyan-born overseas Chinese actively joined the anti-Japanese cause. In April 1939, the Longyan Association in Singapore published the *Inaugural Commemorative Issue*, whose foreword outlined the association's sole mission: to unite the community, unify its will, concentrate its strength, and consolidate the anti-enemy front. It stated,

> Because we are far from our homeland, living abroad, we are unable to serve on the battlefield and make the heroic sacrifice of dying wrapped in horsehide. Nor have we experienced the terrifying bombardments of enemy planes and artillery. Compared with our compatriots who are separated from their families or have lost limbs, how comfortable our lives are!

"We will publicize various developments through written means, enabling the overseas Chinese to better understand the situation and truly shoulder their responsibilities, fighting for the nation and the people." These words expressed the deep patriotic sentiments of the Longyan overseas Chinese in their resistance against Japanese aggression and efforts to save the nation. In the same year, the Longyan Association in Penang organized a committee to raise funds for wounded soldiers and refugees of the motherland's resistance against Japan's aggression, raising 8,000 Straits dollars—more than any other group in Penang. Subsequently, it also established the *Yanqing* harmonica troupe, *Yansheng* Chinese Music Group, and *Yanguang* Drama Troupe to hold charity performances in support of the anti-Japanese cause. In the Philippines, Zhang Xugao and his wife Zheng Huiying, who were engaged in education, actively participated in anti-Japanese propaganda among the overseas Chinese community. They were arrested by the Japanese military police, and Zhang Xugao was later executed. A memorial was erected in his honor by the local Filipino community. In 1941, Longyan expatriate Huang Wei founded *The Overseas Chinese Herald* in the Philippines to report on global anti-fascist developments and promote the Chinese war effort. Even after the newspaper was shut down by the Japanese military and some staff members were arrested, the publication persisted in its struggle, continuing to publish through alternative means. In the summer of 1943, Longyan native Guo Sanmin risked his life to shelter patriot Wang Renshu (who later became the first PRC ambassador to Indonesia) and his wife in his own home, secured residence permits for them and skillfully evaded repeated searches by Japanese forces. He later arranged for their safe transfer. In the same year in North Borneo, Malaysia, thirteen Longyan expatriates—Chen Jinxing, Yang Jinxing, Liao Yuqing, Wu Mujin, Guo Debao, Lin Lianghai, Huang Boxing, Zhang Shaohui, Wei Bofa, Wei Muhai, Lin Biran, Lin Tianfang, and Lin Boxing—died heroically in anti-Japanese guerrilla warfare. The Longyan Association in Kota Kinabalu later erected a monument in their honor, and in 1968 their remains were interred at the Chinese Cemetery.

Section 4 The Eminent Navigator Wang Jinghong

Wang Jinghong, a native of Xujiashan Natural Village, Xiangliao Village, Jixian Tow, Longyan County, Zhangzhou Prefecture of the Ming Dynasty (present-day Xiangliao Village, Chishui Town, Zhangping City), was known among the people as "Wang Sanbao (王三保)," "Wang Sanbao (王三宝)," "General Wang," and "Wang Sanpin." He was an outstanding navigator and diplomat of the Ming Dynasty.

Wang entered the imperial court during the Hongwu reign of the Ming Dynasty and served the Prince of Yan, Zhu Di. He distinguished himself in the Jingnan Campaign during the Jianwen reign. Beginning in the third year of the Yongle reign (1405), he was commissioned alongside Zheng He and Hou Xian to lead the maritime expeditions to the Western Seas. Until 1436, when Emperor Yingzong ordered the cessation of such missions, Wang participated in seven voyages over a span of more than 30 years—five jointly with Zheng He, two as a logistical coordinator, and one (the eighth voyage[1]) as the sole commander. His journeys extended across the South

1The *Veritable Records of Ming Emperor Yingzong* states, "A request was made to designate four hundred swift ships from various garrisons as warships, and to appoint Commander Chen Zheng to take charge of naval operations on the River. The emperor ordered the eunuch Wang Jinghong to plan and execute this." This means Wang Jinghong was still responsible for naval training and, in the ninth year of Xuande reign (1434), was commissioned for the eighth overseas expedition. The *Ming History: Account of Sumatra* records, "In the fifth year of Xuande reign, the emperor, noticing that foreign tribute missions frequently failed to arrive, dispatched He [Zheng] and Wang Jinghong to visit various countries, more than twenty in total, including Sumatra. The following year, emissaries were again sent to pay tribute. In the eighth year, a tribute of a *Qilin* was received. In the ninth year, the king's younger brother, Halizihan, came to pay homage and died in the capital. The emperor pitied him, posthumously conferring upon him the title of Vice Director of the Court of State Ceremonials and granting him a posthumous name. Officials were assigned to manage his funeral and tomb upkeep. At that time, Jinghong made another mission to his country and the king sent his younger brother, Hani Zhehan, to accompany him to pay homage."

China Sea and the Indian Ocean. Wang made an indelible contribution to peaceful diplomatic relations between China in the Ming Dynasty and various Western nations, the dissemination of Chinese culture, the promotion of maritime trade, and the prosperity of the Maritime Silk Road.

Statue of Wang Jinghong

I. Wang Jinghong's Status and Role in the Maritime Expeditions

For a long time, Wang Jinghong was regarded merely as Zheng He's deputy. However, increasingly more contemporary scholarly sources have revealed that Wang Jinghong, like Zheng He, held the position of Grand Eunuch Envoy, the highest command rank of the expeditions. In historical records, their names are frequently mentioned in parallel. As a principal figure of the maritime missions, Wang made immense contributions to the Western Seas, and in terms of navigation, his achievements in some respects even surpassed those of Zheng He.

First, Wang Jinghong and Zheng He were both de facto leaders of the maritime expeditions. Their careers during the Ming Dynasty closely paralleled each other—they shared similar status and were both distinguished diplomats and navigators. Over their thirty years of collaboration, they worked in harmony, jointly accomplishing a naval enterprise unprecedented in history. According to official records, Wang participated in five voyages with Zheng He and independently commanded one.

> In the sixth month of the third year of the Yongle reign, "He and his associates, including Wang Jinghong, were ordered to serve as envoys to the Western Oceans."[1]
>
> In the *dingshi* year of Yongle (the fifth year), "Eunuchs Zheng He, Wang Jinghong, and Hou Xian were ordered to visit the southeastern countries with imperial gifts and proclamations."[2]
>
> In the seventh year of Yongle, *jichou* year, "The Emperor commissioned Grand Eunuchs Zheng He and Wang Jinghong to lead over 27,000 officers and troops to visit various foreign countries and bestow gifts and edicts. They traveled through the southeastern maritime realms to establish communication with the Western Seas."[3]
>
> In the sixth month of the fifth year of the Xuande reign, "As the Emperor had been on the throne for years but some distant countries had yet to send tribute, He and

---

1(Qing) Zhang Tingyu, et al. *History of the Ming Dynasty*, vol. 340, *Biography of Zheng He*. Zhonghua Book Company, 1984, p. 776.

2(Ming) Lang Ying. *Classified Drafts on the Seven Cultivations*, vol. 12, *Eunuch Sanbao*. Series of Notes from Past Dynasties. Shanghai Bookstore Press, 2009, p. 121.

3(Ming) Lu Rong. *Miscellaneous Notes of Shuyuan*, vol. 3, *Collected Historical Notes of the Yuan and Ming Dynasties*. Zhonghua Book Company, 1985.

> Jinghong were again dispatched to seventeen countries, including Hormuz, and returned thereafter." Other records show that in the spring of the nineteenth year of the Yongle reign, Zheng He, Wang Jinghong, and Ma Huan embarked again for the Western Seas.[1]
>
> In the spring of the nineteenth year of the Yongle reign, Zheng He, Wang Jinghong and Ma Huan again voyaged to the Western Seas. According to the *Record of the Manifest Efficacy of the Celestial Princess: Zhang Yuan, Guardian of the East Sea,* "In that year (the nineteenth), Grand Eunuch Wang Gui (note: referring to Wang Jinghong) and others were again commissioned to voyage to the Western Oceans."

From these records, it is evident that at least by the third voyage, Wang Jinghong had already attained the status of Chief Envoy Grand Eunuch, co-equal with Zheng He.

Second, Wang Jinghong primarily oversaw navigational affairs within the fleet. Historical accounts describe Zheng He as "physically robust and commanding, articulate and quick-witted," with military expertise and strategic acumen, making him a military leader. In contrast, Wang Jinghong was described as poised and intelligent, erudite and refined, fluent in Sanskrit and local dialects, trained in Shaolin martial arts, and deeply knowledgeable in maritime affairs—making him the technical head of operations. When Zheng He and Wang Jinghong embarked on their seventh voyage in the fifth year of the Xuande reign (1430), Emperor Xuanzong Zhu Zhanji personally composed two seven-character poems. One praised

---

1(Qing) Zhang Tingyu, et al. *History of the Ming Dynasty*, vol. 340, *Biography of Zheng He*. Zhonghua Book Company, 1984, p. 776.

Wang Jinghong,

> In former times you bore the imperial mandate most loyally, Great ships swept past the Dragon King's halls. With the might of the flying wind god you pierced the mists, Traversing islands and soaring over vast valleys.

The poem clearly reflects that Zheng He and Wang Jinghong were held in equal regard by the emperor, albeit with different responsibilities. Being a native of Fujian, Wang was familiar with maritime conditions and local languages. Moreover, most of the sailors and shipbuilders in the fleet were recruited from Fujian. During the voyages with Zheng He, Wang demonstrated remarkable leadership in managing the fleet. According to the preface of *Records of the Barbarian Nations in the Western Oceans*, the mariners

> journeyed back and forth over a span of three years, navigating the vast and misty oceans, where sky and water met, and nothing could be seen on all sides. One could only judge direction by the rising and setting of the sun and moon; distances were measured by the height of the stars. Mariners carved wooden disks, inscribed heavenly stems and earthly branches, floated magnetic needles on water for navigation, and sailed day and night for months on end. The shapes of islands and reefs at sea varied—some appeared ahead, others to the sides—and these served as guides for adjusting course. Precision in calculating shifts and stops was essential to reach the intended destinations.

These accounts highlight the harsh maritime conditions and underscore the exceptional skills of the crew and the organizational and command capabilities of their leaders. In *Records of the South Seas* by Chen Lunjiong, folklore tells of Wang Jinghong guiding the fleet by calling birds and planting arrows in the Seven Islands Sea, "It is said that when Wang Sanbao sailed to the Western Seas, he summoned birds and planted arrows to mark the route in the ocean."

Third, Wang Jinghong was responsible for military logistics and support during the maritime expeditions. Throughout the voyages, he was in charge of recruiting soldiers from the coastal provinces of Fujian, Zhejiang, and Guangdong, training sailors, and selecting personnel. At the time, many of the shipboard specialists responsible for navigation, steering, anchor operation, sail management, rowing, ship carpentry and metalwork, and astronomical observation were recruited from Fujian and Guangdong. These roles were assigned to experienced maritime personnel known as "boatmen skilled in the navigating the open seas." The ships required for the expeditions were primarily constructed in Fujian. According to the *Veritable Records of Ming Emperor Taizong*, on the day Xinsi of the fifth month of the first year of the Yongle reign (1403), the emperor ordered the Fujian Regional Military Commission to construct 137 oceangoing vessels. On the day Guihai of the first month of the second year of Yongle, "as envoys were to be dispatched to countries of the Western Seas, the emperor ordered the construction of five sea vessels in Fujian." The *Miscellaneous Records of the Capital of Fujian* notes,

> Upon issuance of the imperial edict, local officials first organized the construction of ships in the Shiyang of Changle, employing thousands of craftsmen. The region quickly developed into a commercial hub, bustling with people and trade. Upon completion of the vessels, the Grand Eunuch Sanbao and his companions arrived in Changle, and boarded the sea vessels. Over 500 ships

> loaded with bestowal, provisions, troops, armors and weapons, and various craftsmen assembled at Taiping Harbor, where they embarked at Wuhangtou.

In the Jiaqing reign of the Qing Dynasty, Cai Yongjian transcribed *Miscellaneous Records of Mount Xishan,* in which *Sanbao's Voyages to the Western Seas* records,

> In the third year of Yongle, Emperor Chengzu, suspecting that the deposed Emperor Huizong had fled south, ordered eunuchs Zheng He, Wang Jinghong, and Zhang Wen to construct 100 large ships and lead a force of over 27,000 men. Wang Jinghong, a native of southern Fujian, chartered Quanzhou vessels and coordinated local coastal boats from Dongshi to guide the fleet. They set sail from Liujiagang in Suzhou, made a stopover in Quanzhou, and prayed for favorable winds at Jiuri Rock and the Mosque. The fleet was heavily laden with porcelain, silk, and fine textiles, and proceeded through Zhangzhou, Chaozhou, and Qiongya to Champa.

Although Wang did not directly participate in the fourth and fifth voyages led by Zheng He, he made thorough preparations for both expeditions. Historical records document Wang Jinghong's involvement during these missions: In the tenth year of the Yongle reign (1412), he was ordered to recruit a large number of sailors and shipbuilders along the coasts of Fujian and Zhejiang, to train naval forces and supervise ship construction in Taicang, Changle, Fuzhou, and Quanzhou, as well as to renovate the Temple of the Celestial Goddess; in the eleventh year of Yongle (1413), he concurrently took on responsibilities in Nanjing for recruiting naval personnel and overseeing shipbuilding.

Fourth, after the end of the maritime expeditions, Wang Jinghong oversaw post-expedition affairs. In the first year of the Zhengtong reign (1436), acting on behalf of Emperor Yingzong, the regency ministers ordered Eunuch Wang Jinghong, the Guard Commander in Nanjing, to cease all purchases and shipbuilding activities, thereby officially ending the largest maritime expedition in history. Though he had laid down his military command, Wang Jinghong continued to handle the disposal of expedition supplies and the resettlement of personnel. Historical records note,

> On the first day of the third month of the first year of Zhengtong, an imperial edict was issued to Wang Jinghong, the supervising eunuch of Nanjing and its surrounding areas, and to other officials, to manage the large volume of goods stored annually in the eight imperial warehouses at Yongchengyun in Nanjing, to prevent deterioration over time and to relieve the burden on the custodians.
>
> On the twenty-first day of the same month, an imperial order instructed Wang Jinghong and others to distribute 3 million *jin* of pepper and sappanwood from government storehouses and dispatch officials to transport the goods to Beijing for submission to the court. They were explicitly ordered not to cause disturbances or inconvenience to the populace along the way.[1]

"On the sixth day of the sixth month, one hundred fast transport ships loaded with pepper and sappanwood departed from Nanjing en route to the capital."[2] After this, Wang Jinghong gradually withdrew from court affairs.

1 *Veritable Records of Ming Emperor Yingzong*, vol 15. Shanghai Bookstore Press, 2015.

2 *Veritable Records of Ming Emperor Yingzong*, vol 18. Shanghai Bookstore Press, 2015.

In Nanjing, he compiled the navigational records and experiences of the voyages into a manual titled *Voyage Routes to the Western Seas*, which was regarded as a treasured rare navigation text by maritime personnel throughout the Ming and Qing dynasties.[1]

Fifth, Wang Jinghong independently commanded the return of the seventh expedition and led the eighth voyage himself. During the return leg of the seventh voyage, Zheng He passed away in Calicut (Kozhikode), India, in the sixth month of the eighth year of the Xuande reign (1433). It was Wang Jinghong who assumed command and successfully led the fleet back to China. In the subsequent eighth voyage, Wang Jinghong served as the sole commander of the expedition, fully assuming the leadership of the naval fleet.

II. Wang Jinghong's Legacy Along the Maritime Silk Road

Wang Jinghong remained largely obscure in official historiography for several reasons. First, historical records often mention him alongside Zheng He, but always in subordinate position; thus, the expeditions became popularly known as Zheng He's voyages to the Western Seas. Second, Zheng He, responsible for military operations and diplomatic engagement with foreign nations, enjoyed higher visibility, while Wang Jinghong, in charge of technical and navigational matters, received less public

---

1In the *Records of Official Missions Across the Taiwan Strait*, Huang Shujing of the Qing Dynasty remarked, "Sailors in every ocean each possess a secret manual, said to have been left by the Ming envoy Sanbao. I borrowed and copied one, naming it *Yang Geng*." This *Yang Geng*, also known as *Zhen Bu*, *Zhen Pu* or *Zhen Jing,* was highly practical in nature. It covered an extensive range of matters to be observed during navigation, including the seasonal patterns of monsoons, the direction and strength of currents, the rise and fall of tides, the distance to mountains and islets, the locations of sandbanks and reefs, the time of day, the depth and color of the water, compass bearings and course changes, methods for sounding water depth, safe anchorage points, precautions against hazards, the ship's altitude, and the observation of constellations for navigation. In short, it encompassed virtually everything that a sailor needed to take note of during a voyage. (Cited from Guangdong Maritime Silk Road Museum, *"The Sailors' Secret Manual" and Zhen Bu.*)

recognition. Third, Confucian scholar-officials generally harbored deep-seated distrust and disdain for eunuchs, and were reluctant to record or praise them in official history. For example, the Qing-era historical novelist and scholar Cai Dongfan once remarked,

> Though Zheng He extended imperial prestige abroad and reached across the South Seas—an unprecedented feat in Chinese history—it is a grave affront to national dignity that such high-level diplomatic missions were entrusted to eunuchs. Moreover, to lavishly bestow gold and silk in order to attract foreign tribute stands in stark contrast to the colonial policies of Western nations. While others praise Zheng He's contributions, I remain unconvinced.[1]

Fourth, after the eight voyages had ended, the Ming court—having effectively eliminated maritime threats—shifted its strategic focus northward. Moreover, the expeditions and the tributary system of "ten thousand states paying homage" imposed a tremendous financial burden on the government. After the cessation of the voyages, to prevent any future revival of such costly ventures, the scholar-official class destroyed or suppressed nearly all the original records of the expeditions, including the *Nautical Charts of Zheng He's Voyages*.[2]

Since the launch of China's Reform and Opening-Up policy, as the country's international exchanges have grown, there has been broader recognition in the historical significance of the voyages. Scholars have deliberately sought out materials from archival records and overseas

1Cai Dongfan. *Romance of the History of Ming Dynasty*, chapter 27. Huaxia Publishing House, 2018, pp.170–176.

2According to legend, it was burned by Liu Daxia, but the records are contradictory and controversial, and detailed historical materials on the voyages to the Western Oceans have not reappeared.

sources, gradually enriching the image of Wang Jinghong. His contributions to the Maritime Silk Road have since become widely recognized.

In Taiwan, numerous local gazetteers from the Qing Dynasty, such as the *Gazetteer of Taiwan Prefecture* compiled under the supervision of Gao Gongqian during the Kangxi reign, and the *Gazetteer of Fengshan County* edited by Chen Wenda and later revised by Wang Yingzeng and others during the Qianlong reign, contain multiple references to Wang Jinghong. According to the *Gazetteer of Taiwan Prefecture*, volume 1, *Territorial Administration: Historical Evolution*, "During the Xuande reign, Eunuch Wang Sanbao passed by this place en route to the Western Seas due to adverse winds." In volume 9, *Supplementary Records – Ancient Sites – Medicinal Waters*, it is noted that in Danshui Community of Fengshan County, "Legend has it that the Ming eunuch Wang Sanbao once cast medicine into this water; today, if indigenous people bathe in it when ill, they are cured." The same volume, *Supplementary Records – Ancient Sites – Great Well,* further states,

> The date of its excavation is unknown. Legend says that during the Xuande reign of the Ming Dynasty, Eunuch Wang Sanbao came to Taiwan and drew water from this well. It is now known as the Great Meritorious Well in the western part of the prefectural seat.

Throughout Southeast Asia, there are dozens of sites, temples, and monuments commemorating Wang Jinghong and Zheng He. In Thailand, 10 kilometers south of Ayutthaya (Ayudhya) stands the Sanbao Temple, which houses the country's largest bronze Buddha statue, known to the Chinese community as the "Sanbao Buddha." A couplet in the temple reads, "Sanbao's divine power brings favorable winds and timely rain. The Buddha's blessings ensure national peace and prosperity." Near Bangkok is another Sanbao Temple, and the estuary of the Chao Phraya River features a port called Sanbao Port. In Melaka, Malaysia, on Sanbao Hill stands a mountain-stele said to bear an inscription in the hand of the Yongle Emperor. Nearby are several revered historical landmarks, including Sanbao City,

Sanbao Well, Sanbao Temple, and Sanbao Palace—places highly venerated by both the local government and the populace. About two kilometers southeast of Kampong Cham in Cambodia, within the remains of an ancient city, there is also a Sanbao Temple with a couplet that proclaims, "Three expeditions to foreign lands, pacifying the barbarians and securing the realm—his image endures for all to revere. Protecting the people with loyal service, assisting governance and nation-building—his heroic spirit lives on through the ages." A Sanbao Monastery stands in Ha Tien in the southern region in Vietnam, and in Brunei's capital, Bandar Seri Begawan, there is a street named "General Wang Road" in honor of Wang Jinghong.[1]

Wang Jinghong's most prominent legacy is found in the city of Semarang, Indonesia. According to Zheng Jianlu's *Records of Three Months in the South Seas: A Visit to the Historical Site of Sanbao Cave*,

> A nearby burial mound next to Sanbao Cave is said to be Wang Jinghong's tomb. When he accompanied the envoys to the South Seas and died there, he was buried on site. This later gave rise to the mistaken belief that it was Sanbao's final resting place. The tomb is surrounded by dozens of wooden tablets —wide at the base and narrow at the top, pointed like a pagoda—inscribed with the names of disciples or female devotees offering thanks, and some tablets also engraved with Javanese script. Years later, a stone tablet was erected by Huang Zhixin. In the fifth year of the Guangxu reign (1879), Huang Zhixin, a Chinese emigrant in Semarang, erected a stone stele to commemorate the event. The inscription reads, "It is now believed that this is the final resting place of Lord Wang Sanbao. The mountains are scenic, the waters graceful, and the trees lush. At the foot of the hill is a stone gate naturally forming a cave. The divine spirit of Sanbao

1The relevant account in this passage is quoted from: Wen He. "Magnificent, Seven Voyages of Zheng He and Wang Jinghong to the Western Oceans." *At Home & Overseas*, no. 8, 2005, pp.31–35.

> reveals its presence here, hence the place is called Sanbao Cave and is named after the deity."

Whether Wang Jinghong actually reached Semarang and died there remains unresolved due to conflicting historical accounts and ongoing academic debate.

In 1945, the Nationalist Government of the Republic of China renamed Sin Cowe Island in the Nansha Islands "Jinghong Island" in his honor.

Section 5 The Formation and Development of the Hu Clan's Commercial Culture in Zhongchuan

I. The Origins of the World's First Hometown of Overseas Chinese

According to the *Gazetteer of Yongding County* compiled during the Daoguang reign of the Qing Dynasty, "Merchants conducted long-distance trade with Wu, Chu, Dian, and Shu, and travelers were never lacking; the people of Jinfeng, Fengtian, and Taiping crossed the seas to various foreign lands as if visiting their own courtyards."[1] Among the many emigrants from western and northern Fujian who journeyed to Southeast Asia, the Hu clan of Zhongchuan in Jinfengli, Yongding, stood out prominently as a representative entrepreneurial lineage along the Maritime Silk Road. Zhongchuan Village in Xiayang, Yongding, is a renowned hometown of overseas Chinese, often described as "a village of 3,000 residents and 20,000 overseas Chinese." The number of overseas Chinese originating from this village was five times greater than that of its local population. The majority settled in Malaysia (approximately 8,000), followed by Indonesia (around 3,000), and Singapore (over 2,000), with others dispersed globally. Thus, Zhongchuan has earned the sobriquet "Number One Hometown of Overseas Chinese." It is also the birthplace of renowned overseas Chinese magnates such as Hu Zichun, known as the "Tin King," and the patriotic overseas Chinese leader Hu Wenhu, dubbed the "Tiger Balm King."

The Hu clan's migration into Fujian began in the late Southern Song Dynasty, with the clan's founding ancestor Hu Jiulang arriving from Jiangxi.

---

1 Fang Lyujian, comp., and Wu Yifu, eds. *Gazetteer of Yongding County*, Daoguang edition, vol. 16, *Customs*. Xiamen University Press, 2012, p. 279.

His third son, Hu Qilang, settled in Xiayang, and the ninth-generation descendant Hu Tieyuan moved to Zhongchuan, establishing the ancestral home of the Zhongchuan branch. During the Ming and Qing dynasties, the Hu family produced numerous talented individuals, with consistent success in the imperial civil service examinations. The clan's emigration to Southeast Asia began in the 1720s and peaked in the mid-nineteenth century. Among the earliest migrants were Hu Zhaoxue, Hu Yingxue, and several dozen others, who ventured to various locations such as Sarawak, Dungun, Kapar, and Perak (present-day Perak State) in Malaysia, as well as Cirebon in Indonesia. In the 19th century, brothers Hu Yongchun and Hu Yonghe went to Indonesia's Kapitan; Hu Menlin and others to Cirebon; Hu Yiyu, Hu Zengrui, and Hu Wuzhuan to Penang , Malaysia; and Hu Yilin to Perak , Malaysia. In the 1920s, following the footsteps of Hu Zichun, other major tin mine magnates such as Hu Chongyi, Hu Yuechu, and Hu Yuejie emerged from the family.

II. Origins and Characteristics of Commercial Culture

The formation of the commercial culture of the Hu clan in Zhongchuan is deeply rooted in their unique cultural values of "striving, kinship, filial piety, education, talent, and wealth." Located in a region characterized by barren land and a high population density, Zhongchuan residents developed the saying, "Men tied up their trousers to go overseas, while women carried shoulder poles in straw sandals to do labor," vividly reflecting the gendered division of labor during the wave of migration to Southeast Asia. "Going abroad" (*guo fan*) became a vital means for the villagers to alleviate the tension between population and land. The trajectory of Zhongchuan's transformation into an overseas Chinese village can be summarized in twenty characters: "from poverty to emigration, from emigration to wealth, from wealth to education, from education to talent, from talent to prosperity."

The village's overseas Chinese culture possesses a distinct "cultural code"[1] and a deeply rooted spiritual core. The ancestral hall of the Hu clan serves as a spiritual symbol of the clan's cultural heritage. Originally built in the 12th year of the Wanli reign of the Ming Dynasty (1584), it underwent six major renovations in the 29th year of the Kangxi reign (1690), the 56th year of the Qianlong reign (1791), the 14th year of the Daoguang reign (1834), as well as in 1926, 1934, and 1984.[2] In front of the ancestral hall, 36 merit flagpoles (21 wooden and 15 stone) stand on the courtyard, erected by the Hu clan to commemorate members who achieved academic distinction through the imperial examination system. According to the *Hu Genealogy of Tongyong*, during the Ming and Qing dynasties, Zhongchuan produced five *jinshi* (advanced scholars), thirty *juren* (recommended scholars), 123 *gongsheng* (tribute students), and 108 civil and military officials. One of the existing flagpoles was erected in honor of Hu Zichun, who, in recognition of his achievements, was successively granted the titles of Minister of Posts and Communications and Grand Master for Glorious Happiness by the Qing court. The Hu ancestral hall, as the most prominent landmark in the village, continues to inspire future generations of the Hu clan.

1Zhang Yaoqing, editor-in-chief. *Historical Memory: The Cultural Heritage of Western Fujian*. Haichao Photography and Art Press, 2007, pp.214–217.

2 The Cultural, Historical and Educational Committee of the Longyan Municipal Committee of the Chinese People's Political Consultative Conference, eds. *Historical Materials* of *Western Fujian, vol. 12: Famous Ancestral Halls and Ancient Tombs of Western Fujian*. The Cultural, Historical and Educational Committee of the Longyan Municipal Committee of the CPPCC, 2010, p. 35.

The Ancestral Hall of the Hu Clan in Zhongchuan, Yongding (Photographed by Guo Shusheng)

The Hu clan of Zhongchuan "embraces wealth without taboo". For instance, Hu Zhanxiang, who served as an educational official in Zhanghua County, Taiwan, built his *tulou* (earthen building) in the shape of the Chinese character for "wealth", making it the only character-shaped *tulou* among all those in Yongding. Wealth in the Hu clan is linked to benevolence and philanthropy. Many of Zhongchuan's commercial giants were also noted for their charitable acts, including Hu Taixing, the overseas Chinese leader and "Pepper King" of Penang; Hu Zichun, the "Tin King" of Malaysia; Hu Wenhu, a famous overseas Chinese leader in Southeast Asia; his daughter Hu Xian, "Queen of the Press" of Hong Kong; and Hu Xiubo, Indonesia's "Chemical Industry King." Their pioneering entrepreneurial endeavors in Southeast Asia and their generous contributions to hometown development reflect the cultural values embedded in their very nature. Even among second- and third-generation overseas Hu descendants, a strong awareness of their ancestral origins has remained intact. Though geographically distant from home, emotionally and spiritually they maintain a strong bond with their place of origin and motherland. The commercial success achieved by the overseas Hu clan from Zhongchuan demonstrates that although the hinterland of the Maritime Silk Road lies far from the sea, merchants who emerge from it are neither conservative in business thinking nor inferior in entrepreneurial ability compared to "maritime peoples." The Hu clan's commercial culture, deeply influenced by the Hakka values of "loyalty" and "filial piety," embodies a spirit of diligence, enterprise, and deep love for the nation and their native land.

Section 6 Representative Merchants from the Maritime Silk Road Hinterland

I. Hu Taixing

Hu Taixing, courtesy name Yuedong, was a native of Zhongchuan Village, Xiayang, Yongding County. His father, Hu Zengyu, migrated to Southeast Asia during the late Qianlong reign of the Qing Dynasty and began as a hired laborer from scratch in Balik Pulau, Penang. After accumulating some capital, Hu Zengyu leased land to cultivate crops such as pepper and cloves. Before long, he had built up a modest fortune, married and started a family in Penang. During his childhood, Hu Taixing was once sent back to Zhongchuan, where he received elementary education in the clan school and was introduced to Chinese culture, before returning to Penang. Hu Zengyu's pepper plantation business continued to flourish, and by the time it was handed down to Hu Taixing, the Hu family already owned a sizable pepper estate. He leased large tracts of uncultivated land from the Tua Pek Kong society in Penang to grow pepper, cloves, and sugarcane, and soon reaped significant profits. At its peak, the Hu family's plantation enterprises rivaled and even surpassed those of the British colonial farm owners. Hu Taixing also opened a trading house in the city, earning him the title "Pepper King of Penang."

Hu Taixing served as a contractor in the British colonial government's farm system. In Penang's early colonial days, the British administration faced two pressing challenges: first, due to the implementation of a free trade policy, the government was unable to collect customs duties; second, as more and more Chinese immigrants arrived to settle and develop the land, the colonial authorities needed to find a way to tax the Chinese population. They observed that the Chinese had strong consumption habits for items such as tobacco, alcohol, and opium, and decided to impose taxes on these commodities as a way to extract revenue. Thus, the farm system was established. Under this system, the government auctioned off the right to collect specific taxes to the highest bidder. The winning contractor would pay the government an agreed-upon rental fee and retain any surplus revenues; if the actual tax revenue fell short, the contractor would bear the loss. In early Penang, Chinese were one of the major ethnic groups. Known for their hard work and business acumen, they were particularly better positioned than other groups to participate in the farm system. Hu Taixing was among those who took part in. By contracting the taxes on tobacco and gambling, he was able to rapidly accelerate his capital accumulation.

Hu Taixing actively participated in community affairs. He once served as the president of the Canton and Tingzhou Association of Penang and also contributed generously to the construction of Kek Lok Si Temple in Penang. His economic success earned him considerable social prestige, and he later served as a municipal councilor in Penang. During the major riot that broke out in Penang in August 1867, the British colonial government established an investigative committee to help restore order. Hu Taixing was one of the eight members appointed to this committee. In recognition of his outstanding contributions to the development of Penang Island, a street in Penang—"Hu Taixing Road"—was named in his honor.

II. Wu Dezhi

Wu Dezhi, a native of Sixian Village, Xiayang Town, Yongding County, was born in 1861 in Balik Pulau, Penang. His father, Wu Xiang, had migrated from his hometown to Malaysia in his early years to seek a livelihood, cultivating crops such as nutmeg and pepper in Balik Pulau. Wu Xiang married a woman surnamed Zhang, and the couple had four sons, of whom Wu Dezhi was the youngest. In his childhood, Wu Dezhi attended the Anglo-Chinese School on Light Street in Penang. After graduation, driven by financial necessity, he entered the business world as an apprentice.

Diligent and capable, and possessing a certain level of English proficiency, he quickly earned the trust of his employer. Over the course of more than a decade, he rose to become the manager of the Ruixing Company. After the company ceased operations due to a fire, Wu Dezhi, with the help of British friends, founded a department store specializing in the sale of British goods. Because he sourced his merchandise directly from the United Kingdom or production centers in Europe, he became the first major Chinese merchant in the area to trade in foreign goods. His store, named after himself, was known locally as "Wu Dezhi Tukhu" (with *tukhu* meaning "warehouse" in Hakka). His advantageous position as a first-hand importer and strong business acumen led to rapid success, and he soon became one of the wealthiest men in the area. After achieving success, Wu Dezhi enthusiastically engaged in philanthropic endeavors and gradually rose to prominence as a well-known Chinese figure in Malaysia. He served as Vice President of the Penang Chinese Chamber of Commerce and Honorary Director of the Yongding Association in Singapore. In recognition of his contributions, the British colonial government conferred upon him the title of Justice of the Peace.

Although Wu Dezhi was born and raised overseas and never returned to his hometown in his lifetime, he was deeply influenced by his family upbringing and, having lived for a long time within the Chinese community, still retained a strong sense of patriotism and attachment to his ancestral land. After the First Sino-Japanese War, Wu made several donations to the Qing government for national defense. When a famine struck his hometown of Dengshan in Xiayang, he also contributed funds for disaster relief on multiple occasions. In 1906, following the Qing court's prohibition of opium, Wu convened leaders of various Chinese associations in the region to issue a joint statement urging the Malayan authorities to ban opium and calling upon overseas Chinese to abstain from its use. Together with fellow community leader Hu Zichun, he founded the "Zhenwu Charitable Society" to promote opium cessation. This initiative sparked widespread support and emulation among Chinese communities across the northern states of Malaya, giving rise to a large-scale anti-opium campaign. In 1907, when a smallpox epidemic broke out in Penang, Wu learned that traditional Chinese medicine offered effective treatments and preventive measures. He then single-handedly funded the establishment of the Jisheng Hospital, and hired well-known Chinese physicians from across Malaya. The hospital not only treated infected patients but also conducted public outreach on disease prevention. As a result, hundreds of lives were saved. In 1915, during World War I, Malaysia experienced severe shortages and soaring prices of rice and sugar. Rumors and panic ensued, leading to incidents of rice looting. The local government deployed troops to maintain order, casting a pall of fear over the city. As the colonial authorities were unable to resolve the food crisis at its root, public anxiety intensified. At this critical moment, Wu Dezhi stepped forward and brought together twelve leading figures from various commercial sectors, including Ke Mengqi, Zhu Hele, and Liang Yuancao. Together, they raised substantial funds to purchase and store grain through the government's granaries and distribute it regularly as relief rice. Wu also urged the government to assure rice merchants of a stable grain supply in the market. Through these concerted efforts, the rice crisis was effectively resolved.

Shortly after the rice riot, Penang's financial market was shaken by new turmoil. With the deepening impact of World War I, copper—a key raw material—became scarce, making it difficult to mint and supply copper subsidiary coins (copper cents) that circulated in the Malaysian market. The local government failed to coordinate coin supply with neighboring areas such as Singapore and Malacca, resulting in a severe "copper coin shortage" in Penang. Taking advantage of the situation, some merchants imported lower-quality copper cents from Sarawak in North Borneo to circulate locally, which caused financial losses for some residents and posed a threat to the government's fiscal stability. In response, the British colonial government ordered a strict investigation and harsh punishments, sparking widespread concern in the business community and public discontent. Wu Dezhi stepped forward to negotiate with the government. As a result, authorities cracked down on illegal copper coin traders, transferred copper coins from Singapore and Malacca, and established a Copper Coin Bureau. The Bureau urged merchants and citizens to exchange Sarawak copper coins at regulated rates. This measure benefited all parties and successfully resolved the copper coin shortage. As a result of his efforts, Wu Dezhi's reputation rose significantly among the local business community and overseas Chinese residents.

In 1916, Wu Dezhi was elected by the overseas Chinese community to serve as Chairman of Penang's Tongshan Hall. Tongshan Hall was a charitable organization in Penang, established through donations from merchants and local residents, and dedicated to providing social relief. It had long offered assistance to refugees, the elderly, the disabled, and the poor, and was also responsible for the burial of unclaimed corpses—expenditures that incurred enormous costs. After the outbreak of World War I, due to currency depreciation and poor management by previous leaders, the Tongshan Hall's funds were rapidly depleted, threatening its continued operation. Upon taking office, Wu Dezhi took the lead in contributing his own funds and mobilized other overseas Chinese merchants to donate, thereby replenishing the foundation's resources. At the same time, he reorganized the institution internally and implemented strict financial regulations. Before long, Tongshan Hall resumed its operations and continued to benefit many impoverished Chinese immigrants in the area. Subsequently, Wu also spearheaded the establishment of the "Tongshan

School" to provide education for children from poor Chinese families. In 1915, he had also founded the "Wunei Girls' School," adopting a tuition-free model, thereby contributing significantly to the advancement of women's education in Penang.[1]

III. Hu Zichun

Hu Zichun (1860–1921), also known as Guolian, was a native of Zhongchuan Village, Xiayang, Yongding County. His father, Hu Yuqi, was born in British-controlled Penang and returned to his hometown as an adult to marry. Orphaned at a young age, Hu Zichun was raised by his grandmother, Li Meiniang. At the age of 13, he followed fellow villagers to Penang , where he sought refuge with his aunt. At 16, he apprenticed under his maternal uncle to learn tin ore prospecting techniques. At 20, he moved to Kinta, Perak where he worked in the tin mines owned by the prominent mine owner Zheng Jingsheng. Impressed by Hu's abilities, Zheng Jingsheng arranged for him to marry his daughter. Over time, Hu Zichun expanded his presence in Perak's tin mining industry and rose to become one of the most prominent tin mine entrepreneurs in Southeast Asia. At the height of his success, Hu diversified into various industries. In addition to tin mining, he managed rubber plantations as well as clove and cardamom estates, with his rubber holdings alone spanning several thousand acres. His business empire extended throughout the Malay Peninsula and even reached southern Siam, establishing him as a leading commercial figure of his time.

Hu Zichun was one of the overseas Chinese industrialists of the late Qing period who invested most heavily in China and was the first overseas Chinese from Western Fujian to return home and make large-scale

1Luo Yi. "Wu Dezhi, An Overseas Chinese Leader from Malaysia." In *Yongding Hakka Figures*, edited by the Editorial Committee of *Yongding Hakka Figures*, 2008, pp.394–398.

investments. He actively invested in domestic mining, railways, salt production, and plantation agriculture, becoming a model for Chinese merchants in Southeast Asia investing in their homeland. In 1906, when Chen Baochen, then General Manager of the Fujian Railway Company, traveled to Southeast Asia to raise capital, Hu Zichun enthusiastically invested and became a major shareholder. As a result, he was jointly recommended by officials across the province to serve as associate director of the company and was later granted the honorary title of a third-rank minister by the Qing court. In 1907, Hu partnered with Wu Zicai to invest in the Anxi coal mine and other mineral ventures in Fujian. When the mining rights of Jianning, Shaowu, and Tingzhou were reclaimed in 1907, Fujian gentry and merchants advocated for the cancellation of contracts with foreign merchants and for the self-management of mining enterprises. Recognizing Hu Zichun's financial resources and influence, they remarked, "Minister Hu is a prominent and reputable Southeast Asian businessman. If he raises shares, it will certainly be easier. Moreover, having risen from the mining industry, he will certainly not fall behind others in future developments."[1] In 1908, Chen Bi, Minister of Posts and Communications, and Vice Minister Guo Zengxin, jointly submitted a letter to the Ministry of Foreign Affairs requesting that Hu Zichun be appointed to oversee mining affairs. Later that year, the Ministry of Agriculture, Industry, and Commerce, under the imperial decree, appointed Hu as General Manager of Fujian's merchant-operated mining enterprise and later extended his oversight to Guangdong as well.

Hu Zichun was also among the earliest overseas Chinese leaders to propose and implement development plans for Hainan Island. In the spring

1Ma Hongmo, ed. "Yan Jinting: The History of Mining Affairs." In *Selections from Minhu, Minxu, and Minli Newspapers (May 1909–December 1910)*, Henan People's Publishing House, 1982, p.132.

of 1907, he personally traveled to Hainan to conduct investigations and draft a development plan. Emperor Guangxu approved the proposal and appointed him to "oversee mining affairs in Qiongya." To implement the plan, Hu co-founded the Qiaoxing Company in 1908 with Qu Tangliang and others, undertaking development projects in land reclamation, mining, animal husbandry, and remittance services across the Qiongya region of Guangdong. In Guangzhou, they established the Overseas-Chinese-Initiated Reclamation and Mining Company to manage the tin mine in the Niaoqiang Ridge and the gold-tin mine in the Najin Ridge on Hainan Island.

From a young age, Hu Zichun had lived abroad, and it was not until 1906 that he returned to China to attend his grandmother's funeral. He remained in the country for nine months to conduct an inspection tour before returning to Penang in July of the following year. In fact, even before this trip, Hu had already considered investing in the mining industry in China. During his return, aside from visiting relatives, he traveled extensively throughout Fujian and Guangdong to explore potential investment opportunities. In 1907, just days after returning to Penang, Hu delivered a speech in which he recounted his observations from the tour. He noted the rich mineral resources in Fujian and Guangdong, the convenient transportation along the southeastern coast, and the Qing court's open and supportive attitude toward overseas Chinese investing and starting businesses back home. He believed there were promising prospects for developing industry and commerce in these two provinces. Soon afterward, Hu Zichun joined with Zheng Luosheng, Li Xiaozhang and others to establish the Perak Chinese Chamber of Commerce. In December of the same year, at the invitation of the Qing Ministry of Agriculture, Industry, and Commerce, Hu personally traveled to Hainan to survey mineral resources. In 1908, based on his findings, he proposed a development plan titled "One Guiding Principle and Ten Objectives", which was submitted by Vice Minister of Commerce Yang Shiqi and received official approval from the Ministry. In November that year, he co-founded the Qiaoxing Company with Qu Zhaoren to engage in land reclamation, mining, animal husbandry, and remittance services. They began mining cassiterite (tin ore) in Nada and Xibin in Danxian County. He also established the Qiaofeng Company, which specialized in salt production and built saltworks near Sanya Port. Later, he founded the Qiaolun Company, which focused on transporting salt between Haikou and Guangzhou.

Between 1907 and 1908, Hu Zichun and his partners invested a total of 9.43 million yuan in mining and agricultural reclamation projects across Fujian and Guangdong.[1] However, the Qing Dynasty was nearing collapse, and its failed reforms, coupled with deep-rooted corruption and operational mismanagement, hindered the success of the enterprises he had invested in. As a result, most of the projects were ultimately abandoned.

Hu Zichun came to realize that in order to save the nation from peril and achieve national prosperity, it was not enough to strengthen the country and enrich the people through industrial enterprises alone—it was also essential to promote education, advance science and technology, and reform social customs. Thus, he devoted himself to educational initiatives. He had long established schools for overseas Chinese in Malaysia, providing educational opportunities to Chinese children living abroad. In 1905, after the Qing government abolished the imperial examination system and promoted modern schooling, Hu founded an academy and a school in his hometown of Zhongchuan Village in Xiayang, Yongding, and later established a normal school in the county seat of Yongding. He was also a strong advocate for women's education. His establishment of the Chinese

---

1Yan Qinghuang. *Research on the History of Overseas Chinese.* Association of Asian Studies in Singapore, 1992, p.56.

Girls' School in Southeast Asia was a landmark event in the history of overseas Chinese women's education. In addition to education, Hu Zichun was also dedicated to public welfare. He founded the Zhenwu Charitable Society, actively promoted the anti-opium campaign among the overseas Chinese community in Southeast Asia, and provided free herbal remedies to help addicts quit smoking, thereby benefiting the community. He generously supported charitable causes and assisted fellow overseas Chinese in need. Hu served multiple terms as a member of the local Civil Affairs Council and acted as a consultant for the Advisory Bureau. He was also a prominent figure behind the establishment of numerous overseas Chinese associations and was widely respected as a community leader. His contributions earned him the title "Lord Mengchang of Southeast Asia" for his benevolence and philanthropic efforts among the overseas Chinese.

IV. Zhou Yangyun

Zhou Yangyun (1885–1964), originally named Shu Ying, was a native of Wenheng Town in Liancheng County. He was born during the late Qing Dynasty, a time when the nation was in decline, and his family had also fallen on hard times. As a young boy, Zhou had to give up his studies and shoulder the burden of supporting his family, becoming an apprentice at a paper shop in the Gutian area. Intelligent, diligent, and literate, he gradually displayed exceptional business talent. Before long, he earned the trust of the shop owner, who sent him to Chaozhou, Guangdong, to promote handmade paper. Starting in the 1920s, he partnered with friends in Chaozhou to run a business selling dyes produced by the German company Bayer. However, during World War I, maritime transportation was severely disrupted, and prices fluctuated unpredictably, causing the dye business to collapse. Zhou Yangyun returned to his former trade and resumed operation of the Lianxingchang Paper Company in Chaozhou. In 1930, he co-founded the Guangfu Tobacco Company in Shantou, selling high-quality tobacco from the Yongding area in Fujian. As business rapidly expanded, he established branch offices in Shanghai and Bangkok, Thailand. Later, Zhou moved to Thailand to manage Guangfu Company, achieving great success. Zhou also founded the Jianfeng Rice Import and Export Company in Saigon, Vietnam. While residing in Hong Kong, he and his friends successively opened several paper businesses, including Guangchengchang Paper Company and Guanghuachang Paper Company. His business empire reached its peak in the 1930s. Zhou's success in Thailand aroused the jealousy of British firms engaged in the local tobacco trade. After failing to lure Zhou into selling his brand and patents with a large sum of money, the British merchants pressured the Thai government to intervene and demand Zhou transfer his patents. Zhou firmly refused. His experience reflects not only the hardships faced by Chinese entrepreneurs operating abroad but also their perseverance and indomitable spirit.

After the outbreak of the War of Resistance against Japanese Aggression, Zhou took the lead in fundraising to support the nation in its time of crisis. He also mobilized his employees to contribute donations totaling 10,000 silver dollars every month, which were regularly remitted through the Bank of Fujian to aid the war effort. Deeply aware of the critical role of cultivating talents for national revitalization, he heavily invested in his hometown's educational development. He solely funded the founding of Mingchi Middle School (the predecessor of Liancheng No. 1 Middle School). The school's name, derived from the *Zuo Zhuan* phrase "*ming chi jiao zhan*" (to be enlightened by humiliation and instructed to fight), reflected his earnest hope that the youth of his hometown would study diligently and safeguard the nation. In addition, Zhou contributed to the development of many local schools, including Jinshan Primary School, Zhouwu Primary School, Gechuan Primary School, Jinhua Primary School, and Beituan Xiewei Central Primary School, ultimately benefiting more than 20,000 students. He was also active in local public welfare, financing the 1938 edition of the *Gazetteer of Liancheng County,* to which his contribution accounted for 40% of the total funding. He also donated to the construction of key infrastructure projects such as Pengfang Bridge and Ding'an Bridge, and engaged in other charitable acts such as funding hospitals and aiding disaster victims.

V. Wang Yuanxing

Wang Yuanxing (1910–1974), also known as Jianxin (or Jianchu), was a native of Dayang Village, Xipi Town, Longyan. Born into a poor family, he only received basic education at a primary school, where he learned basic arithmetic. In 1924, while working as an apprentice in Zhangzhou, he became acquainted with fellow Longyan youths Cao Juru, Zheng Rihui, and Lin Caizhi, who were contributors to *Yansheng Bao* (*The Voice of Yan*), a progressive publication edited by revolutionary youth such as Deng Zihui and Zhang Duqi. This exposure instilled in Wang the patriotic spirit of the May Fourth Movement.

In 1926, Wang Yuanxing traveled to Singapore in search of a livelihood. Over the years, he worked successively as a laborer, street vendor, rickshaw puller, and shop assistant. In 1931, he went to Palembang, Indonesia, where he co-founded the Hengfeng Company with partners and served as its manager. After the outbreak of the nationwide War of Resistance against Japanese Aggression, Wang took on leadership roles in the overseas Chinese community, serving as director of the Palembang Chinese Chamber of Commerce and vice-chairman of the Palembang Chinese Relief Association. Between 1938 and 1940, he served as the Palembang delegate to the Federation of Chinese Relief Funds in Southeast Asia (the Federation of Southeast Asia), an organization initiated by the patriotic overseas Chinese leader Tan Kah Kee to raise relief funds for wounded soldiers and refugees in China. In 1941, when Japanese forces bombed Singapore and invaded the Malay Peninsula and the Indonesian Archipelago, Tan Kah Kee mobilized the Chinese community in Singapore for anti-Japanese resistance. Wang Yuanxing, in turn, led the Palembang branch of the Federation of Southeast Asia. He actively raised funds to aid Chinese refugees, rallied overseas Chinese to support the anti-Japanese cause, and worked with local Indonesians to resist Japanese invasion, becoming a prominent leader among the younger generation of overseas Chinese. Wang's resistance activities soon attracted the attention of the Japanese authorities, who sought to arrest him. He narrowly escaped and went into hiding in Julok, a town in western Sumatra, where he survived by farming. Even after the fall of Singapore, and despite having fled with his family, Wang continued to provide substantial financial assistance to the wartime Cultural Work Corps of the Chinese community in Singapore, led by literary figures Yu Dafu and Hu Yuzhi. Together with local organizations, he helped raise 400 guilders to support Yu Dafu's establishment of the Zhaoyuji Distillery, which provided an economic lifeline for a large number of exiled intellectuals.

After Japan's surrender, Wang Yuanxing returned to Palembang, where he was elected Chairman of the Palembang Overseas Chinese General Association. Under his leadership, the Hengfeng Company flourished. Beyond developing his industrial ventures, Wang was a generous patron of cultural and journalistic causes, becoming a well-known supporter and leader of the cultural and media enterprises in the overseas Chinese community in Southeast Asia. At the time, a number of progressive publications—including *Democracy News* (founded by Ba Ren and Wang Jiyuan), *Musi River Semi-Monthly* in Palembang, and several newspapers in Jakarta such as *Life*, *Under the Wind* and *Women's Life*, as well as Hong Kong's *Chinese Business Daily*—all benefited from his financial assistance. After the Hengfeng Company relocated its headquarters to Singapore, Wang served as a board member of the *Nan Chiau Jit Pao* founded by Tan Kah Kee, appointing Hu Yuzhi as the editor-in-chief and giving his full support to the newspaper's growth. The *Nan Chiau Jit Pao* became an influential voice in the postwar struggle against imperialism and colonialism, and in the movement for national independence and liberation.

Wang Yuanxing was among the first overseas Chinese leaders to return to invest in the newly founded People's Republic of China, making him a pioneer in "three-capital" enterprises (ventures involving state, private, and overseas Chinese investment) and a leader of the All-China Federation of Returned Overseas Chinese. In 1951, he organized an Overseas Chinese Industrial and Commercial Delegation to inspect investment opportunities across China, visiting Guangzhou, Wuhan, Beijing, Tianjin, Qingdao, and other cities. Upon returning to Guangzhou, he founded the Public–Private Joint Overseas Chinese Industrial Development Company in August of that year, serving as vice-chairman. The company was later reorganized into the Guangdong Overseas Chinese Investment Company. Subsequently, he established a series of modern industrial enterprises, including the sack factory, the sugar refinery, the paper mill, and the cement plant. He also served as Director of the Guangzhou Overseas Chinese Affairs Bureau, initiated the founding of an Overseas Chinese Primary School, and donated funds to help establish Huaqiao University and the Overseas Chinese Museum. Wang's efforts made significant contributions to industrial development in Guangzhou during the city's early post-liberation years.

VI. Hu Wenhu

Hu Wenhu (1882–1954), a native of Zhongchuan Village in Jinfengli, Yongding County, was born in Yangon, Burma. At the age of ten, he returned to his ancestral hometown, but four years later, he returned to Yangon to assist his father in managing the Chinese medicine business of Yong An Tang, and also studied medical techniques. In 1908, when Hu was

27, his father passed away, and he, along with his younger brother Hu Wenbao (his elder brother Wenlong had died young), inherited the family enterprise. In the first year of the Xuantong reign (1909), Hu returned to China and traveled to Siam and Japan to inspect both Chinese and Western pharmaceutical industries. Upon returning to Yangon, he employed several Chinese and Western physicians and chemists to research traditional Chinese medicinal pastes, pills, powders, and plasters. Eventually, they successfully developed five patent medicines under the Yong An Tang brand—Tiger Balm, Headache Powder, Pain Relief Powder, Refreshing Water, and Bagua Pill—which rapidly gained popularity across Burma and Malaysia, bringing considerable wealth to the Hu brothers.

In the period of early Republic of China, Hu Wenhu co-invested with overseas Chinese to establish the *Yangon Daily*, and soon afterward launched *The Morning Post*. Later, he left Burma for Singapore, where he founded the Yong An Tang Pharmaceutical Factory. He gradually expanded operations throughout Singapore and Malaysia and opened additional branches and manufacturing plants in Hong Kong. He later established pharmaceutical plants in Shantou and Guangzhou, and branches in Xiamen, Fuzhou, Shanghai, Tianjin, Chongqing, Guiyang, Kunming, Macau, Zhanjiang, Wuzhou, and Guilin, as well as in Taiwan, Vietnam, Siam, the Philippines, and the Dutch East Indies. In 1923, he established the Yong An Tang headquarters in Singapore, where Tiger Balm products flourished across Southeast Asia and were even exported to Europe and America.

Hu Wenhu and the Hu family were also deeply engaged in the newspaper industry. In 1929, Hu and Deng Lisheng co-founded *Sin Chew Jit Poh* in Singapore, which later came under Hu's sole ownership, with him serving as chairman of the board. In July 1931, he launched *Sing Hua Daily* in Shantou. In September 1935, he founded *Sing Guang Daily* in Xiamen and, in the same month, *Sing Chung Daily* in Singapore. In June 1938, Hu was appointed as a member of the first National Political Council. In August of that year, he established the *Sing Tao Daily* in Hong Kong, with his third son, Hu Hao, serving as publisher. That same year, he attempted to found *Sing Yue Daily* in Guangzhou, but due to the city's fall to enemy forces, the publication was suspended; later, *Gong Zheng Daily* was published in Guangdong instead. In 1939, he founded *Sing Pin Jih Pao* in Penang. In 1940, Hu Wenhu acquired the *Zong Hui Bao (General News)* in Singapore with his own capital. In 1941, when Hong Kong fell to the Japanese, Hu happened to be in the city and was detained by Japanese authorities for three days before being released, after which he remained in Hong Kong. That same year, the *Sing Tao Daily* ceased publication and resumed under the name *Heung Tao Daily*. He also established the General Management Office of the Sing Series Newspaper in Singapore. In 1942, after the death of Hu Wenbao in Burma, Hu Wenhu established Zhongqiao Company in Hong Kong and launched *Sing Tao Morning Post*, with plans for another publication, *Sing Hu Daily* (Hu means Tiger). After the victory in the War of Resistance against Japanese Aggression in 1945, Hu returned to Hong Kong and prepared for the launch of *Sing Hu Daily* (Hu means Shanghai) in Shanghai and *Sing Tao Evening Post* in Hong Kong. In 1947, he published *Sing Min Daily* in Fuzhou. In March 1949, he founded the English-language newpaper *Hong Kong Standard* in Hong Kong. After October of the same year, the Yong An Tang businesses in various locations gradually ceased operations, and the Sing Series newspapers in Guangdong and Fujian were taken over. The Sing Series continued publishing overseas, making it the largest Chinese-owned private media group abroad. In July 1950, Hu launched the *Singapore Standard*, an English-language newspaper with Hu Hao as general manager, while the Hong Kong papers were managed by his daughter, Hu Xian. In January 1951, he began publishing *Sing Siam Daily* in Bangkok, and later added an evening edition titled *Sing Thai Evening Post*.

The Building of *Sin Chew Jit Poh* in Singapore

Throughout his life, Hu Wenhu was dedicated to building Fujian and his hometown. In his article entitled *Striving to Build the Hometown*, he wrote,

> This is our Fujian, where the ancestral homes and graves of our forefathers lie. My descendants and I will also live and thrive here. If, in our own lifetime, we still wish to evade difficulties and make no effort to build, then when will the construction of Fujian ever be realized?[1]

In pursuit of unity and support among Malaysian Chinese from Fujian, Hu published several special editorials in newspapers. In August 1945, he called on overseas Chinese from Fujian to pool capital and support industrial production in the province. He subsequently authored articles

1Hu Wenyu. "Striving to Build the Hometown." *Sing Guang Daily*, 21 Jan. 1947.

such as "*On the Economic Development of Yongding*," "*Preliminary Thoughts on Developing Fujian*," "*Strive to Build the Hometown*," "*Heaven Helps Those Who Help Themselves*," and "*The Future Fate of Overseas Chinese*," advocating for the development of Fujian and his hometown, Yongding. To gain government approval, from 1946 to 1947, Hu traveled between Hong Kong, Singapore, Xiamen, Fuzhou, Shanghai, and Nanjing to promote the establishment of the Fujian Economic Construction Co., Ltd. In 1946, he wrote to the then Kuomintang Provincial Governor of Fujian, and to Directors of its Finance and Construction Departments, proposing to develop the coal mines in Longyan and to construct railways from Longyan to Zhangzhou and from Longyan to Dapu in Guangdong, thereby linking raw materials with markets and supplying fuel to the areas in southern Fujian such as Xiamen, Zhangzhou, and Quanzhou.

Hu Wenhu was also a prominent leader among the Hakka overseas Chinese in Southeast Asia. He actively promoted the construction of Hakka community organizations. In 1923, Yinghe Guild in Singapore and Fung Yun Thai Association initiated a proposal to convene an All-Eight-County Hakka Assembly, with the aim of forming a large-scale transregional Hakka organization—the General Association of Hakkas. The Hakka overseas Chinese across Southeast Asia enthusiastically responded with financial and organizational support, and Hu Wenhu contributed the most. His motivation for promoting regional unity among Hakka associations was based on the belief that "all Hakkas across the world are one family; we share the same language, customs, and traditions, and should not be estranged by geographic divisions." He aimed to break down geographical boundaries among Hakka groups to unite and strengthen the Hakka people. [1]

1Zhang Kan. "A Preliminary Study of Hu Wenyu's Relationship with Malaysian Hakka Associations." In *The Chinese Heart, Hakka Sentiment: Proceedings of the First Hakka Studies Symposium*, edited by Lin Jinshu. Hakka Studies Association of Malaysia, 2005, pp. 43–76.

Construction on the headquarters of the General Association of Hakkas in Southeast Asia began in 1926, and was completed two years later. On August 23, 1929, the association was officially established, with Hu Wenhu being elected as its first president. The founding of the General Association fostered bonds of kinship and mutual development among Hakka compatriots in Southeast Asia and greatly enhanced the ethnic cohesion and solidarity of the Chinese nation, especially the Hakka, overseas.

Tiger Balm Garden in Hong Kong with a Blend of Chinese and Western Styles

Tiger Balm Garden in Yongding with a Blend of Chinese and Western Styles

The Paifang Outside Tiger Balm Garden in Singapore

VII. Chen Xingchu

Chen Xingchu (1871–1939), also known as Qingshan, courtesy name Jiaxiang, was a native of Fuman Village, Jingcheng Town, Zhangping County. Born into a relatively well-off family, he studied at a private school in his early years. As a youth, he participated in the local imperial examinations in Zhangping County and Longyan Prefecture, ranking at the top and earning the nickname "Little Three-First Scholar" (referring to the first place in the county, prefectural, and provincial examinations). In the 21st year of the Guangxu reign (1895), Chen passed the provincial-level exam, became a *xiucai* (licentiate) and gained the favor of Wang Xifan, the then Governor and Education Commissioner of Fujian. However, the late Qing period was marked by internal turmoil and foreign aggression. The signing of *the Treaty of Shimonoseki* in 1895 further ignited nationwide indignation. Consequently, Chen gradually lost interest in the imperial examination system and became actively involved in social movements. In the 28th year of Guangxu (1902), Chen abandoned the imperial exams and, following his fellow townsmen, journeyed to Southeast Asia, arriving in Batavia in the Dutch East Indies (present-day Jakarta, Indonesia) to learn the business trade. With the support of fellow countrymen, he quickly integrated into the local overseas Chinese community. During this time, he was exposed to Sun Yat-sen's revolutionary ideals and began participating in the democratic revolutionary activities of the revolutionaries. In 1911, together with Wang Jingshu, he co-founded the Overseas Chinese Intellectual Association in Batavia, actively promoting Sun Yat-sen's democratic revolutionary thoughts. After the founding of the Republic of China in 1912, Chen worked actively in Batavia to raise funds, which he sent back to support national development. To better serve the local Chinese community, Chen, along with Chen Songhe and Chen Jinshan, co-founded the Fujian Association in 1912, where he was elected as an advisor. In 1921, he collaborated with Lin Jianliu, Huang Tianxi, and others to establish the newspaper *Industrial and Commercial Times*, serving as a board member. This newspaper played an active role in providing valuable information and protecting the rights and interests of the Chinese diaspora. In 1932, Chen joined forces with prominent Fujianese merchants such as Zhuang Xiyan and Chen Bingding to establish the Fujian Overseas Chinese Hometown Relief Association, where he served as an executive member and secretary.

The association aimed to mobilize the resources of overseas Chinese to support the economic development of China and their hometowns. Chen also rallied the Chinese community in Batavia to express solidarity with China's resistance efforts against Japanese aggression. After 1933, Chen served in successive positions, including committee member and secretary of the Chinese Medical and Pharmaceutical Relief Association in Batavia, member of the Batavia Anti-Vegetarian Preparatory Committee, and secretary-director of the Dutch East Indies branch of the Central National Medical Institute. He was devoted to developing medical, charitable, and relief services, offering assistance to impoverished members of the Chinese community. At the same time, he volunteered as a correspondent for two Chinese-language newspapers in Batavia, *Sin Po* and *Tian Sheng Daily*, conducting in-depth investigations among the overseas Chinese community and giving them a voice. After the Marco Polo Bridge Incident (also known as the July 7th Incident), Chen was appointed as an executive committee member of the Kuomintang's directly affiliated branch in Batavia and became actively involved in organizing anti-Japanese resistance efforts within the Chinese community there. He used his pen to publish articles, supporting resistance against Japan and inspiring patriotic fervor among his fellow compatriots. In 1939, Chen was summoned back to Chongqing to attend the third session of the Party and Government Training Program at the Central Training Institute of the Kuomintang. After completing the program, he joined a morale-support delegation to visit and encourage Chinese soldiers on the anti-Japanese frontlines, where he witnessed firsthand the hardships of the war effort. Later that year, on his way back to Batavia via Kunming, he passed away in Kunming.[1]

1 Zhang Youzhou, editor-in-chief. *The History of Overseas Chinese from Longyan*. South China University of Technology Press, 2020, pp.386–387.

Chapter 7 Cultural Exchanges Between the Hinterland and the Coast

Section 1 The Overseas Dissemination of Zhu Xi's Philosophy

Zhu Xi (1130–1200) brought together the achievements of Neo-Confucianism since the Northern Song and established a complete and rigorous philosophical system. His school of thought, known as Zhuxi's Philosophy, is also called Min Philosophy, as it originated with Southern Song Neo-Confucian scholars from Fujian—such as Yang Shi, Luo Congyan, You Zuo, and Li Tong—and was further developed by Zhu's disciples and later followers. Zhu Xi presided over the Bai Ludong Academy and the Yuelu Academy, where he lectured for more than fifty years and mentored numerous students. His school of thought came to be known as Min Philosophy or the Cheng-Zhu school. He authored influential works including *Collected Commentaries on the Four Books*, *Records of the Origins of the Yi and Luo Rivers*, *Record of Words and Deeds of Famous Officials*, and *Outline of the Comprehensive Mirror for Aid in Government.* Later generations also compiled works such as *Quotations of Master Zhu* and *Collected Works of Zhu Wengong* (Zhu Xi's posthumous name). As the officially endorsed orthodox philosophy from the late Southern Song through the Qing Dynasty, Zhu Xi's thought long held a dominant position in Chinese intellectual history. Its ideological content and philosophical doctrines transcended ethnic and regional boundaries, spreading eastward to Japan and Korea where it became a shared spiritual asset of East Asian civilizations. Through the influence of Western missionaries, it also entered the consciousness of Western intellectuals, becoming part of the world's philosophical heritage.

I. Zhu Xi's Philosophy in Asia

In East Asia, Zhu Xi's philosophy reached Korea and Japan around the beginning of the 13th century. Frequent diplomatic, commercial, and scholarly exchanges between China and Korea and Japan throughout history greatly facilitated the dissemination and integration of Chinese culture. After its formation, Zhu Xi's philosophy swiftly spread to both nations. Vietnam was also a significant region for the dissemination of Zhu Xi's philosophy in Asia, where it exerted a profound and lasting influence.

Portrait of Zhu Xi (from *Sancai Tuhui*, compiled by Ming scholar Wang Qi, Wanli edition)

In Japan, the transmission of Zhu Xi's philosophy largely depended on the interaction and exchanges between monks and scholars from both China and Japan. In the fourth year of the Jiading reign during the Southern Song (1211), the Japanese monk Shunjo returned to Japan carrying 2,103 volumes of Chinese books, many of which contained works of Zhu Xi's philosophy. At the time, Zen Buddhism and Shintoism dominated Japanese thought, and Zhu Xi's teachings were initially integrated into the existing intellectual framework, producing a phenomenon referred to as "the unity of Confucianism and Buddhism," with many monks incorporating Zhu Xi's philosophy into their Zen practice. Because Japan had not implemented a universal imperial examination system, the development of Zhu Xi's philosophy was relatively gradual. By the 14th century, however, the emphasis in Zhu Xi's philosophy on ethical principles, benevolence, righteousness, and morality resonated with Japan's traditional social system, leading his philosophy to become part of Japan's national ideology. During the Edo period (1603–1868), the Tokugawa Shogunate designated Zhu Xi's philosophy as official orthodoxy. This marked the flourishing of Japanese Zhu Xi studies, inaugurated by Fujiwara Seika and represented by figures such as Hayashi Razan, Yamazaki Ansai, and Kaibara Ekken. At this stage, Zhu Xi's philosophy gradually moved away from its integration with Buddhism and harmonized with Japanese Shinto thought, resulting in a uniquely Japanese variant of Neo-Confucianism. Thinkers such as Hayashi Razan, Yamazaki Ansai, Kaibara Ekken, and Arai Hakuseki further advanced Zhu Xi's ideas by distinguishing them more clearly from Buddhism, emphasizing Zhu Xi's method of "to investigate things in order to fully understand their principles", and highlighting the school's advocacy of practical ethics and statecraft in response to the needs of society and the times. Kaibara Ekken advocated combining Zhu Xi's principle of "investigating things to attain knowledge" with empirical scientific methods. Arai Hakuseki likewise argued that Zhu Xi's philosophy of "exhausting principles" was intellectually compatible with Western scientific thinking. He advanced the idea of "Eastern morality and Western arts, with neither the fine nor the coarse omitted, embracing both inner essence and outer form," which in practice meant advocating Western arts (science and technology) as practical application, and Eastern morality (a fusion of Zhu Xi's thought and Shinto philosophy) as the guiding essence. In addition, the Osaka school of Zhu Xi studies, represented by Goi Jiken and Nakai Riken, disseminated and applied Zhu Xi's doctrines from the perspective of commercial development, showing that during the Edo period, Japanese Zhu Xi studies reflected the pressing concerns of the era. Objectively, these intellectual trends supported the reforms of the Tokugawa

Shogunate and laid the ideological groundwork for Japan's transition to capitalism, while also fostering a modern national spirit that valued practical utility and promoted scientific thinking. However, it should also be noted that during the dynastic transition between the Ming and Qing dynasties, Hayashi Harukatsu, son of the renowned Zhu Xi scholar Hayashi Razan, compiled the work *The Reversal of Chinese and Barbarians*, proposing the concept of "Chinese-barbarian reversal," whereby Japan saw itself as the rightful "center of civilization" and began to perceive China as a land of "barbarians." This ideological shift had close ties to the development of Zhu Xi studies in Japan.

The development of Zhu Xi's philosophy in Korea began with its introduction among the common people, and was later officially adopted by the government. According to some scholars, based on genealogical records and local histories, in the late Southern Song period, Zhu Qian, a great-grandson of Zhu Xi, traveled across the sea to the Korean Peninsula with his children and seven disciples. He became the first transmitter of Zhu Xi's philosophy to Korea, and the progenitor of the Korean branch of the Zhu family. During the Goryeo period, the Korean court promoted Confucianism, with Zhu Xi's Neo-Confucianism serving as a key component of education. In the subsequent Joseon period, Korea emulated the Chinese imperial examination system and adopted Zhu Xi's canonical texts as official educational materials. As a result, Zhu Xi's philosophy developed rapidly in Korea. By the mid-16th century, Zhu Xi studies in Korea were represented by two major figures—Yi Hwang (pen name Toegye) and Yi I (pen name Yulgok). The renowned Confucian scholar Yi Hwang, often referred to as the "Korean Zhu Xi," was considered a philosopher of the Joseon era who inherited Zhu Xi's philosophy, holding an extremely important position in the interpretation and development of Zhu Xi studies in Korea. He established a comprehensive theoretical system known as the T'oegye Theory, which also influenced prominent Japanese Neo-Confucians such as Fujiwara Seika. Yi I, on the other hand, was a major promoter of institutionalization of the Korean *seowon* (Confucian academy) education in Korea. He advocated, based on Zhu Xi's principles, the development of *seowon* education centered on Confucianism and Zhu Xi's philosophy. In the history of Korean *seowon* education, Zhu Xi's philosophy occupied a central position. In the Joseon era, *seowon* not only commonly held memorial rites for Zhu Xi, ancient sages, worthies, and eminent Confucian scholars of past dynasties—thereby strengthening the scholars' identification with and adherence to Confucian thought—but also trained a number of outstanding Confucian scholars, thus establishing Korea's Confucian system. Throughout the Goryeo and Joseon dynasties, Korean scholars engaged in nearly 500 years of intense philosophical debate centered on Zhu Xi's "Four Beginnings and Seven Emotions" theory in the context of his philosophy of principle (*li*) and vital force (*qi*). Nearly all Korean Neo-Confucians, directly or indirectly, participated in this discussion. This sustained engagement significantly advanced and enriched Korean Zhu Xi studies. As a result, the Korean interpretation of Zhu Xi's philosophy came to emphasize practical governance and ethical morality, fostering development and innovation that ultimately contributed to the emergence of "Enlightenment Thought" in modern Korea.

Zhu Xi's philosophy was introduced to Vietnam in the 13th century. During the Trần Dynasty (1225–1400), Vietnam adopted a Confucian-based education system modeled on China's imperial examination system. Zhu Xi's teachings spread rapidly, and major works such as *The Complete Collection of the Four Books* and *Essentials of the Complete Treatise on Principle and Vital Force* were widely printed in Vietnam. During the Lê Dynasty, Confucianism was institutionalized as the state philosophy, and the eminent scholar Lê Quý Đôn further promoted Zhu Xi studies, elevating it to new heights in the late Lê period. In the Nguyễn Dynasty, however, Zhu Xi studies gradually declined. Nevertheless, for over 600 years, Zhu Xi's philosophy remained a significant part of Vietnamese cultural history.

The dissemination of Zhu Xi's philosophy in Southeast Asia differed markedly from its spread in Korea and Japan. In Southeast Asia, Chinese immigrants served as the principal transmitters of Zhu Xi's philosophy. From the 19th century onward, large numbers of Chinese migrated to Singapore, Malaysia, Thailand, and Indonesia, bringing with them the values, ethics, moral codes, mindsets, and even lifestyle patterns rooted in Confucianism and Zhu Xi's teachings. These values not only offered Chinese immigrants a culturally distinct framework to pursue economic development but also helped reinforce their ethnic and cultural identity, distinguishing them from other ethnic groups in their host societies.

II. The Global Dissemination of Zhu Xi's Philosophy

Due to geographical distance and cultural divergence, the transmission of Zhu Xi's philosophy to Europe occurred much later than its spread in Asia. In the late Ming and early Qing dynasties, European Jesuit missionaries such as Matteo Ricci, driven by the need to facilitate their missionary work among the Chinese scholar-official class, conducted in-depth studies of Confucianism and introduced Confucian classics to Europe, sparking tremendous interest among European intellectuals in Chinese thought. Subsequently, figures such as Longobardi, Giulio Aleni, Johann Adam Schall von Bell, and François Noël also discussed the Confucianism in the Song Dynasty and introduced several Zhu Xi doctrines through their translations. However, significant doctrinal differences between Catholicism and Zhu Xi's philosophy posed obstacles to deeper integration. Catholicism advocated monotheism and regards God as the ultimate truth, whereas Zhu Xi's thought, with its ambiguous treatment of concepts such as "God", "Heaven", or "the Way", adopted a more reserved and equivocal stance toward spiritual beings and religion. Furthermore, Zhu Xi's philosophy formed the cornerstone of China's official ideology, shaping the lifestyle and values of the time. In particular, Confucianism's emphasis on venerating the "Most Sage Teacher" Confucius and on ancestor worship clashed sharply with Catholic doctrine. These differences contributed to the famous "Rites Controversy" in the history of Sino–Western cultural exchange.

During the European Enlightenment, numerous works on China emerged. Major thinkers of the 17th and 18th centuries such as Descartes, Leibniz, Voltaire, and Montesquieu showed keen interest in and discussed Confucian thought. Malebranche's *Dialogue Between a Christian Philosopher and a Chinese Philosopher on the Existence and Nature of God* compared two philosophical traditions with far-reaching influence in the East and West, becoming a classic in the history of comparative philosophy between China and the West. In 1711, François Noël, in translating the *Four Books*, adopted the commentaries of Zhu Xi and Zhang Juzheng, producing what was at the time the clearest and most complete Western-language edition of the Confucian classics. Zhu Xi's philosophy thus became a component of European Sinology, serving as both a reference system and a comparative framework for European philosophers and intellectuals. The influence of Zhu Xi studies on European philosophy stands as an example of the mutual interaction and integration of Chinese and Western cultures. In 1736, the French Sinologist and Jesuit Missionary Jean Baptiste du Halde, in the second volume of *Description géographique, historique, chronologique, politique, et physique de l'empire de la Chine et de la Tartarie chinoise*, introduced China's canonical texts and educational system, and included selected translations from Zhu Xi's works. This book, described as an encyclopedia on China, influenced figures such as Voltaire and Baron d'Holbach in their studies of China.

Zhu Xi's philosophy reached North America even later. After the 18th century, works on Zhu Xi's philosophy translated and introduced by European missionaries in the late Ming and early Qing periods began to attract the attention of North American scholars. The United States established the American Oriental Society, with the aim of studying Oriental cultures, particularly that of China. In 1849, the American Sinologist Elijah Coleman Bridgman selected and translated portions of *The Complete Works of Zhu Xi* and published them in the *Chinese Repository*. This publication is generally regarded as the starting point for Zhu Xi studies in the English-speaking world.

In conclusion, as a key component of traditional Chinese culture and East Asian civilization, Zhu Xi's philosophy deeply permeated the daily life practices of East Asian societies and participated in shaping the civilizations of East Asian countries. Moreover, it transcended geographical, ethnic, cultural, and temporal boundaries to become one of Chinese philosophy's most profound contributions to global intellectual heritage.

Section 2 The Overseas Dissemination of Hakka Culture

The Hakka people have been an important force in the transmission of Chinese civilization. Hakka culture, as an integral part of China's rich traditional heritage, is a regional culture with distinctive ethnic characteristics, cultivated in the cultural soil of China. While it took shape in southern China, Hakka culture has been disseminated globally through the overseas migration of Hakka communities.

First, the primary means by which the Hakka people spread Chinese culture is through the establishment of schools and the promotion of education.

The countries of Southeast Asia, where Hakka people have primarily settled, are also the main arenas for the dissemination of Chinese culture by the Hakka diaspora. The southward migration to Southeast Asia constitutes a collective historical memory for the Hakka people. During the arduous years of migration and the pioneering struggles in foreign lands, the Hakka dispersed the seeds of Chinese culture across Southeast Asia, where they took root, blossomed, and bore fruit.

Valuing literature and education, and upholding the tradition of "farming and studying to pass on the family legacy," are central Hakka values. The Hakka place great importance on education, and even in hardship they have been willing to devote tremendous effort to the schooling of their children. Most early Hakka immigrants were farmers with relatively little formal education. Having built their livelihoods from scratch in their host countries and experienced hardship firsthand, they came to appreciate the importance of education even more. Once they achieved success in their host countries, many prominent Hakka merchants and community leaders actively established schools both in their ancestral homelands and in the places where they lived abroad. For example, in Indonesia in 1901, the Batavia Chinese Association—led by Hakka community leaders—founded the first modern Chinese school in Indonesia, the Zhonghua School. By 1949, there were already 724 Chinese schools in Indonesia, with more than 170,000 students.[1] Likewise, the Hakka leader Hu Wenhun founded several schools in his ancestral county of Yongding, and over his lifetime established and sponsored more than 400 schools of various types across Southeast Asia. Education greatly improved the knowledge and abilities of overseas Chinese youth, giving the new generation stronger competitiveness, enabling them to obtain better jobs in local society or assist more effectively in their family businesses. At the same time, the schools established by the Hakka in their host countries emphasized traditional Chinese culture, instilling in overseas Chinese youth the values and moral principles of Chinese civilization, and strengthening their cultural identity and sense of self in relation to their ancestral homeland. Growing up in such an educational environment, the new generation of overseas Chinese "played an even more important and positive role in the spread of Chinese culture."[2]

Second, another important channel through which the Hakka have spread Chinese culture has been Chinese-language newspapers and magazines.

In the modern era, many Hakka migrants in Southeast Asia made notable contributions to journalism. By founding and editing Chinese

---

1 Luo Yingxiang. "A Brief Discussion on the Status and Role of the Hakka People in Southeast Asia." *Journal of Jiaying University*, no. 5, 1996, pp. 90–95.

2Chen Yande. "The Role of Chinese Filipinos in the Dissemination of Chinese Culture: Based Mainly on Interview Records of Chinese Filipinos and Returned Overseas Chinese and Their Families." *Journal of Maritime History Studies*, no. 2, 2012, pp.48–64.

newspapers and magazines, Hakka intellectuals and entrepreneurs helped disseminate information about both their ancestral homes and host societies, fostering unity and development within the overseas Chinese community. For example, Hakka figures in Thailand such as Zhang Zongling and Wu Jiyue operated the *Xin Zhongyuan Bao* (New Central Plains Daily), edited several important publications, and promoted Chinese culture in the region. Another notable figure was Hu Wenhu, a Hakka businessman from western Fujian who became a "press magnate." His "Sing Series Newspaper" exerted far-reaching influence across Southeast Asia. Hu Wenhu believed that newspaper served three key purposes: to remedy deficiencies in spiritual civilization and enhance the educational function of society; to realize spiritual unity and consensus among overseas Chinese; and to form a force of public opinion to urge governments to implement industrial plans and development. Among these, he placed cultural development as the highest priority. He argued that while Singapore at the time had developed materially, it still had many deficiencies in spiritual civilization that did not match the progress of material civilization. Therefore, "the educational function of society should be strengthened to remedy this imbalance. For example, the bad customs of the patriarchal society and the outdated ideas of the feudal era should be thoroughly reformed, while modern culture, politics, economy, education, and the arts should be more widely disseminated."[1] From this, it is clear that he believed culture should undergo a comprehensive renewal, and that building a modern society required the full development of culture. The press could serve as a base for such cultural dissemination. For this reason, Hu Wenhu's "Sing Series Newspaper" consistently maintained the correct orientation in its cultural communication, becoming an important stronghold for overseas Chinese in

1Luo Yingxiang. "A Brief Discussion on the Status and Role of the Hakka People in Southeast Asia." *Journal of Jiaying University*, no. 5, 1996, pp. 90–95.

Southeast Asia to promote China's outstanding traditional culture. It also effectively enhanced the national identity and patriotic enthusiasm of overseas Chinese, especially during the War of Resistance against Japanese Aggression, when it contributed to unprecedented unity across all sectors of the Chinese community in Southeast Asia.

Third, the Hakka have spread Chinese culture through their lifestyle and aesthetic arts.

When the Hakka settled and formed communities in their host countries, the first things they brought were their language and script. In parts of Indonesia, Malaysia, and the Philippines, local languages were influenced early on by the Minnan dialect, while Vietnamese also contains elements from Cantonese and Fujian dialects. Similarly, the Hakka brought the Hakka language to Southeast Asia, and Hakka vocabulary has been widely integrated into the linguistic and cultural fabric of various countries. Overseas Hakka communities have long maintained their dialect. In Southeast Asia especially, the Hakka were in fact not merely a geographic community, and certainly not purely a kinship-based one, but rather a dialect-based community. They established numerous Hakka associations and clan organizations to unite Hakka people and strengthen internal bonds. Within families and Hakka organizations, the older generation of overseas Chinese insisted on speaking Hakka and actively taught it to their descendants. In recent years, however, younger generations of overseas Hakkas have shown a weaker sense of identification with the Hakka language, and the dialect now faces the danger of decline, with its transmission encountering difficulties. Fortunately, overseas Hakkas have become aware of this issue and are taking active measures to address it—such as organizing interregional Hakka assemblies (e.g., the World Hakka Conference), returning to their ancestral homes to search for relatives and perform ancestral rites, and rebuilding ancestral halls—in order to help younger overseas Hakka restore cultural links with their homeland.

After venturing overseas, the Hakka also brought along their culinary traditions. Shaped by a unique historical, cultural, and geographical environment, Hakka cuisine is both part of the broader Chinese culinary tradition and distinctive in its own right. In Southeast Asian countries, it enjoys a certain reputation. Signature Hakka dishes such as salt-baked chicken, stuffed tofu, and braised pork with preserved mustard greens are commonly found in restaurants across local streets and alleys, enriching the food culture of their host countries. Through Hakka cuisine, local communities have also gained a deeper understanding of Hakka history, culture, and the Hakka spirit.

The Hakka have also spread Chinese traditional literature and theatrical arts. As early as their first settlements in Southeast Asia, Hakka people brought novels, poetry, and other works of traditional Chinese literature to the region. Some of these were introduced directly by Hakka migrants, while many others became known through translations by their descendants. Art forms such as string puppetry and Han opera from western Fujian likewise took root locally through Hakka cultural transmission.

Hakka migrants have steadfastly preserved their traditional customs and folk culture. In their host countries, Hakka overseas Chinese continue to uphold traditional practices—whether in worship and ancestor veneration, life rituals, or festival gatherings. Even in everyday hospitality or family celebrations, they consciously maintain elements of Chinese cultural tradition.

It is worth noting that with the steady growth of the overseas Chinese population and shifts in naturalization policies across Southeast Asia, since the late 20th century many Chinese migrants in the region have come to regard their host country as their homeland. In Indonesia, for example, government decrees simplified the naturalization process for overseas Chinese, shortening the timeline for citizenship and accelerating their integration. In Thailand, relatively lenient naturalization policies have led to a large number of Chinese gaining citizenship. Once naturalized, many overseas Chinese identify politically and economically with their host country and actively participate in its national economy, while culturally growing more distant from their ancestral homeland. How to inherit and promote the cultural traditions of overseas Chinese and maintain their cultural ties with their ancestral country has thus become an urgent challenge today.

Section 3 The Spread of Mazu Belief in the Hinterland

I. The Introduction of Mazu Belief into the Hinterland of the Maritime Silk Road

According to legend, Mazu was born by the sea and manifested her divine presence on the ocean, thus becoming widely regarded as a maritime protector deity. Remarkably, Mazu temples are found even in inland mountainous regions far removed—by thousands of miles—from the coast, and the veneration of Mazu in these hinterland areas remains closely tied to maritime culture.

During the Song Dynasty, Mazu was officially canonized as a deity, yet scholars held sharply different views toward the belief. For instance, Chen Chun expressed a negative attitude, while Chen Mi, Zhen Dexiu, Wei Liaoweng, and Liu Kezhuang all praised and honored her. Among them, Zhen Dexiu played a role in promoting the spread of Mazu belief. Zhen Dexiu, courtesy name Jingyuan (later changed to Xiyuan), styled Xishan, was a native of Pucheng. In the fifth year of the Qingyuan reign (1199), he passed the imperial examinations with the degree of *jinshi*, and shortly afterward succeeded in the special examination for broad learning and talent. He served twice as prefect of Quanzhou, and during his tenure composed multiple dedicatory prayers addressed to Mazu.[1] Zhen Dexiu possessed substantial influence within scholarly circles. Historical records note,

> (Zhen) Dexiu was tall, with a broad forehead, and a jade-like countenance, and those who beheld him

1(Song) Zhen Dexiu. *Collected Works of Xishan*, vol.1174 of Photographic print of the Complete Library of the Four Treasuries (Wenyuan Pavilion Edition). Taiwan Commercial Press, 1986, pp. 858, 863–864, 859, 850–860.

> invariably saw him as destined for high office. Within less than a decade at court, he submitted memorials numbering in the tens of thousands of characters, all of which addressed urgent matters of state, his upright voice echoing through the court. Scholars across the land recited his writings, imagining his noble bearing. Wherever he served in office, his benevolent governance was deeply felt, living up to his words; thus he was praised both at home and abroad. In his later years, Zhen Dexiu alone took it upon himself to uphold scholarly orthodoxy, both teaching and practicing it. After the factional prohibitions were lifted, the Confucian orthodoxy was thus clarified throughout the realm, thanks largely to his efforts.[1]

Through his authority among scholars and his administrative experience, Zhen Dexiu contributed significantly to legitimizing and disseminating Mazu worship.[2]

At the grassroots level, Mazu belief gradually became integrated into the everyday life of the Maritime Silk Road hinterland. In the Song Dynasty, Mazu belief in Changting was closely connected with Chaozhou and the salt trade. Since Tingzhou did not produce salt, it had to be transported from elsewhere for sale. The people of Tingzhou originally consumed “Fu salt,” which came from the Fuzhou region. After the salt was produced, it was first shipped upriver along the Minjiang River, then transported overland through Nanjian Prefecture to Tingzhou —a long and difficult journey that made salt prices very high. As a result, in Tingzhou Prefecture and

---

1(Yuan) Tuo Tuo. *History of the Song Dynasty*, vol. 37. Zhonghua Book Company, 1985, p. 12964.

2Lin Dongjie. “The Dissemination of Mazu Belief by Zhu Xi’s Later Disciples in the Southern Song Dynasty.” *Religious Studies*, no.4, 2018, pp.262–267.

neighboring areas such as Qianzhou in Jiangxi (today's Ganzhou), smuggling of private salt was rampant. During the Shaoding reign of Emperor Lizong of the Southern Song (1228–1233), Song Ci served as magistrate of Changting County. Seeing the hardship the people faced in buying salt, he proposed rerouting salt purchases from Chaozhou instead. The new route sent salt upriver along the Hanjiang River, then via the Tingjiang River into western Fujian for sale. This greatly shortened the transportation distance, facilitated salt trade management, and reduced salt prices. After the salt route was redirected to Chaozhou, the county officials and boatmen responsible for salt transport frequently traveled between Tingzhou and Chaozhou. It is very likely that in this process they learned of the legend of Mazu as a sea-protecting deity and naturally adopted the belief. In this way, Mazu belief was introduced into western Fujian. The San Sheng Fei Temple in Changting was probably the earliest Mazu temple in Tingzhou and was likely established by "dividing incense" from a San Fei Temple in Chaozhou.[1]

Mazu belief in the upper reaches of the Minjiang River spread upstream along the river, reaching the important town of Yanping in the upper Minjiang River region. From there, it continued to expand northward and westward along the river's various tributaries, moving upstream via the Jianxi Creek, Futun Creek, Shaxi Creek, and Youxi Creek. This allowed Mazu worship to take root in the societies of the three prefectures of Yanping, Jianning, and Shaowu. Parts of Tingzhou Prefecture were also incorporated into the network of Mazu worship transmission due to their economic and trade ties with the Minjiang River Basin. The connection between Mazu worship and the Maritime Silk Road can be evidenced by the story of "*Shaowu Garrison Troops Being Rescued During a Campaign*

1Xie Chongguang. "Mazu Belief in the Hakka Region of Western Fujian." *Studies in World Religions*, no. 3, 1994, pp. 74–84+155.

to the Western Seas." According to the important record *Register of Military Appointments*, which documents Zheng He's voyages to the Western Seas, most of those who followed Zheng He came from coastal military garrisons, including 18 soldiers from the Shaowu garrison. During the Yongle reign of the Ming Dynasty (1403–1424), soldiers from the Shaowu garrison built a Temple of the Celestial Goddess (formerly called the Lingci Palace). In the 16th year of the Qianlong reign (1751), this Temple was rebuilt in the southern part of the city near Changfeng Granary in Zhongzhen Lane. The original Temple of the Celestial Goddess was later converted into the Temple of King Yu during the Jiaqing and Daoguang reigns.

The zenith of Mazu belief's expansion into the hinterland occurred during the Ming and Qing dynasties, particularly from the mid-Ming period onward. The Ming government's delineation of administrative regions, establishment of garrison towns, implementation of the *lijia* (household registration) system, and the agricultural population tax regime enabled greater institutionalized management over borderlands and coastal areas. These systems directly or indirectly affected the economic links between the mountainous hinterland and the Maritime Silk Road. In particular, during the Ming and Qing periods, China's coastal regions entered a vibrant stage of civilian overseas interaction. Civilian-led commercial activities (including maritime smuggling) flourished, and the hinterland of the Maritime Silk Road benefited directly or indirectly from maritime trade. This change in fact challenged the hinterland's traditional livelihood pattern centered on agriculture. Continuous natural disasters and social upheavals also prompted people in the hinterland to choose migration overseas as a means of survival. Under the combined influence of internal and external forces, Mazu worship continued to extend into the hinterland, even reaching regions inaccessible by ship.

In the late Ming and early Qing, the renowned scholar Li Shixiong from Ninghua County in Tingzhou Prefecture recorded the county's major temples and religious practices in his compiled *Gazetteer of Ninghua County*. Regarding Mazu, he observed, "Ninghua has no knowledge of sea vessels; for no reason it worships the Celestial Goddess —could this not be flattery?"[1] Li Shixiong had traveled through Fujian, Guangdong, and the regions south of the Yangtze River. He believed that Mazu was a sea deity, and since Ninghua County, located in the mountainous area along the Fujian–Jiangxi border, was too far removed from the maritime world, the people there worshipped Mazu out of "flattery"—that is, for utilitarian purposes, believing that the more deities they honored, the more blessings they would receive. Li Shixiong's opinion represented the general attitude of the intellectuals in the mountain regions toward Mazu worship at the time. However, it also indirectly proves that, by the late Ming at the latest, Mazu worship had already spread widely within the folk society of hinterland counties along the Maritime Silk Road.

After the Mazu belief spread into the hinterland of the Maritime Silk Road, it exhibited several fundamental characteristics.

First, the number of temples was large, and the followers were numerous. Although Mazu worship was introduced to Tingzhou in the late Song Dynasty, it was not until the mid-Ming period that it began to develop in western Fujian, and it only flourished after the Qianlong and Jiaqing reigns of the Qing Dynasty. By the mid-Qing, temples dedicated to Mazu as the principal deity could be found in counties and villages throughout the hinterland of the Maritime Silk Road, many of which were of considerable scale. Particularly in counties engaged in frequent foreign exchanges, Mazu had increasingly become the most important deity in the religious life of

---

1(Qing) Zhu Wenyu, comp., and Li Shixiong, ed. *Gazetteer of Ninghua County*, vol. 7, *Records of Altars, Temples, and Ancestral Halls*. Fujian People's Publishing House, 1989, p. 417.

local people—for instance, every town and village in Yongding County had a Tianhou Palace or Mazu Temple.

Second, the channels through which Mazu belief was transmitted were diverse. In addition to officials, Mazu devotees included those who traveled to or resided in the mountainous areas of western and northern Fujian. Merchants formed the main body of Mazu followers, and some Mazu temples were funded and constructed by them. For example, the Tianhou Temple at Mount Taiping in the east part of Wuping County, was reportedly built in the late Ming by Lin Qiqing, a Wuping native engaged in trade in Putian; the Tianhou Palace in Fengshi, Yongding, was established by timber traders known as *Mugang*. Certain Mazu temples were built by immigrants newly settled in Hakka areas, such as the Tianhou Palace in Xipi, Yongding, whose founding ancestor migrated from Fuqing and once served as magistrate of Yongding during the Jiajing reign of the Ming Dynasty. Boatmen engaged in inland river shipping were also active promoters of Mazu worship. The numerous Mazu temples scattered along riverbanks served a practical function for boatmen, as they often doubled as inns for long-distance freight crews.[1] These boatmen, frequently in and out of Mazu temples, naturally deepened their devotion to the deity and carried her worship to the places they visited.

The spread and development of Mazu worship in mountainous areas also exhibit distinct mountain-region characteristics.

First, it inherits the core elements of coastal Mazu belief. From the geographical distribution of Mazu temples, the characteristics of Mazu worship in the mountainous hinterland of the Maritime Silk Road can be observed. Based on their locations, Mazu temples in these inland areas can

1 Shi Yilong. "On the Relationship Between the Mazu Belief, the Shipping Industry, and the Surname Lin in the Inland Areas of Fujian and Guangdong." *Journal of Putian University*, no. 1, 2008, pp. 75-76.

be categorized into two types: those along waterways and those in the mountains. The former includes temples located along main waterways such as the Huangtan River and Yongding Creek, tributaries of the Tinjiang River. Most Mazu temples in the mountainous areas remain associated with water, usually built near river mouths, creek banks, or bridges—for example, the Tianhou Temple in Hongkeng Village, Yongding County. Additionally, Mazu temples in the Maritime Silk Road hinterland often coexist with guild halls, that is, the temple may serve as a guild hall or such halls would enshrine Mazu statues. Some boat crews engaged in waterborne activities set up shrines on their rafts to worship Mazu, forming a mobile mode of belief. Thus, Mazu worship in the Maritime Silk Road hinterland inherits the fundamental core of coastal Mazu faith: praying for the safety and smooth navigation of rivers and waterways, as well as the success of commercial activities.

Second, the transformation of Mazu worship in the mountainous areas. Besides temples along waterways and streams, many Mazu temples are located within villages or even atop high mountains in these regions. This reflects how Mazu worship was adapted and adjusted within the local cultural context. Unlike coastal Mazu beliefs, the mountain-area Mazu worship developed its own unique legends and stories, exhibiting distinct mountainous characteristics. Some scholars suggest that besides merchants, boatmen involved in shipping and Lin-family immigrants were important agents in spreading Mazu worship in the mountainous hinterland of the Maritime Silk Road.[1] While many Mazu temples are situated along navigable rivers, most inland temples were likely built by Lin clans. In many mountain villages with Lin-family populations, many venerate Mazu as their "ancestral deity" or "ancestral Buddha." For example, the Tianhou

1Chen Jiansheng. "Mazu Belief in the Upper Reaches of the Minjiang River." *Journal of Fujian Institute of Socialism*, no. 2, 2012, pp. 59-63.

Temple at Mount Taiping in the east part of Wuping County, was founded by a patron with the surname Lin; similarly, the Mazu temples in Hongkeng Village, Hukeng Town, Yongding, and Xipi Village, Gaobei Town, Yongding County, were established by local Lin clans.[1] This reflects a common folk religious practice in South China known as "ancestral deity" worship, where some clans regard deities sharing their surname as part of their own family and honor them accordingly in some villages in the provinces of Guangdong and Fujian. This kinship-like "both deity and ancestor" belief strengthens the bond between the deity and local people, helping the worship tradition to sustain and flourish locally.

Overall, Mazu worship in the hinterland of the Maritime Silk Road shares similarities with that of the coastal regions, but also shows clear differences. In the coastal areas, where Mazu worship is rooted in the cult of Meizhou Mazu, veneration of the deity is closely tied to the maritime-based modes of production. It forms what has been described as "a core maritime cultural belief jointly shaped by coastal folk rituals, imperial endorsement from the political center, and the commercial interests of overseas Chinese migrant communities."[2] In other words, protecting fishing activities, uniting clans and overseas migrants, and safeguarding maritime trade become the main functions of coastal Mazu worship. In the mountainous hinterland of the Maritime Silk Road, however, Mazu worship is an extension and transformation of the coastal tradition, in most cases introduced by local merchants. In particular, in emigrant-sending areas, Mazu worship was closely connected to the growth of the overseas Chinese merchant economy. But because mountain areas were far from the sea,

---

1Shi Yilong. "On the Relationship Between the Mazu Belief, the Shipping Industry, and the Surname Lin in the Inland Areas of Fujian and Guangdong." *Journal of Putian University*, no. 1, 2008, pp. 75-76.

2Peng Zhaorong. "The Encounter Between Mountains, Seas, and the Tianhou Palace." *Reading*, no.7, 1999, pp.144-148.

Mazu worship there lacked its original maritime foundation and thus underwent adaptation after the mid-Ming period. In this process, the cult was adjusted to fit the local religious landscape: it absorbed elements from Guanyin (Deity of Mercy) worship, Daoist legends, and local Dragon King folklore, and, through reinterpretation by the gentry, took on Confucian overtones of loyalty and filial piety. As a result, inland Mazu worship not only retained the coastal function of ensuring smooth commerce for merchants, but also came to reflect the practical hopes and needs of the mountain people.

II. Representative Mazu Temples in the Hinterland of the Maritime Silk Road

1. Tianshang Palace in Mount Wuyi, Northern Fujian

The largest Mazu temple in northern Fujian is the Tianshang Palace in Xingcun Village, Mount Wuyi. It is located on the Huanghua Ridge in Xingcun Village, by the banks of the Jiuqu Creek in Mount Wuyi. The temple was first built in the 38th year of the Kangxi reign (1699), rebuilt during the Jiaqing reign, and underwent multiple renovations in the 1990s. The name Tianshang Palace (Palace in the Heaven) differs from those of Mazu temples in other regions. One explanation is that Mount Wuyi, being the highest mountain in the Fujian–Guangdong–Taiwan area, stands at a higher elevation than both coastal and other inland Mazu temples. Furthermore, one of the sources of Jiuqu Creek in Mount Wuyi, the Tongmu Creek, is also known as the "River to Heaven" and local legend holds that Xingcun Village was formed from celestial stars. For these reasons, the Mazu temple in Xingcun Village was named Tianshang Palace.

The layout of Tianshang Palace is boat-shaped, with a frontage of 33 meters, a depth of 30 meters, and a total area of 864 square meters. The complex consists of three main halls in sequence, arranged along a central axis with a balanced and symmetrical design. It includes the gatehouse, the worship pavilion, the main hall, the rear hall, courtyards, and surrounding corridors. The main hall enshrines a standing golden statue of Mazu, while the rear corridor houses a seated statue of the Bodhisattva Guanyin. Flanking the main hall are side halls; the right side contains both the Wenchang Hall (for the Deity of Culture and Literature) and the Caishen Hall (for the Deity of Wealth).

The emergence of Tianshang Palace in Mount Wuyi is closely tied to the region's tea trade. Since the Ming and Qing dynasties, Mount Wuyi relied on the Chongyang Creek to develop water transport. Large quantities of tea, timber, dried bamboo shoots, rice, and other goods were shipped on bamboo rafts and other vessels down the Jiuqu Creek, Dongxi Creek, Xixi Creek, Meixi Creek, Huangbo Creek, and Langu Creek, converging into the Chongyang Creek, which connected to the Minjiang River and eventually reached the sea via Fuzhou. Villages along these major waterways thrived on the movement of goods and external trade, and Xingcun Village was one such settlement.

The inscription of the plaque above the entrance of Tianshang Palace reads "*Yinjiang Juxiu*" (Gather Splendor of the Yinjiang River). The Yinjiang River is another name for the Tingjiang River, suggesting that the Tianshang Palace was likely built as a guild hall by tea merchants from Tingzhou. According to the *Gazetteer of Chong'an County,*

> The tea market in Xingcun Village draws people from all directions. Prices are high and the local customs are extravagant. Even servants are adorned in fine clothes. Most are from Jiangxi and Tingzhou, with some from Zhangzhou and Quanzhou. In early spring, baskets fill the mountains, carriers crowd the roads, warehouses and

temples are nearly overflowing.[1]

This shows that during the tea trade's peak, Tingzhou merchants frequently visited Xingcun Village. Since Mazu worship had spread to Tingzhou from Chaozhou during the Song Dynasty and flourished there, it is highly probable that Tingzhou merchants, when building their guild hall in Xingcun Village, enshrined the familiar Mazu to bless and safeguard their commercial ventures. Over time, what began as a guild hall with a Mazu shrine eventually became a dedicated Mazu temple.

2. Tianhou Temple in Tingzhou

According to statistics from Board of Directors of the Tingzhou Tianhou Palace in 2006, there were still 86 temples in Changting County—the seat of the former Tingzhou Prefecture—that enshrined Mazu (44 as the principal deity and 42 as an accompanying deity).2 The Tingzhou Tianhou Palace in the urban center of Changting is one of the earliest Mazu temples in the region and is also the largest Tianhou Palace in inland Fujian.

The Tingzhou Tianhou Palace is located on a sandbar by the banks of the Tingjiang River outside the Chaotian Gate on East Street in Changting. It is a single-structure palace-style building, complete in layout and grand in scale, covering an area of about 10,000 square meters and surrounded on all sides by water. The Mazu statue enshrined in the main hall is said to have been crafted by artisans from Chaozhou during the Yongzheng reign of the Qing Dynasty. Despite nearly 300 years of historical changes, it has been preserved to this day.

1(Qing) Wei Daming, comp. *Gazetteer of Chong'an County*, Jiaqing reign, vol. 1, *Customs*. In Wu Juenong, ed., *Selected Historical Materials on Tea from Chinese Local Gazetteers*. Agricultural Publishing House, 1990, p. 322.

2The Fourth Board of Directors of the Tingzhou Tianhou Palace, ed. *Tingzhou Mazu*. The Fourth Board of Directors of the Tingzhou Tianhou Palace, 2006.

The Tianhou Temple was originally established during the Shaoding reign of the Southern Song Dynasty under the name "Three Holy Consorts Palace." Its construction took place after the development of the Tingjiang River in the Song period and was closely linked to Tingjiang River shipping. According to the *Gazetteer of Linting*, "The Three Holy Consorts Palace is located at Fuwen Lane in the southern part of Changting County, aligned with the ancestral temple in Chaozhou... It was founded during the Jiaxi reign. Nowadays, when the prefectural and county officials transport salt shipments, they must pray here before setting off."[1] This suggests that during the Song Dynasty, the temple served as a key location where officials offered sacrifices to pray for the smooth and safe transportation of salt. After this salt-transport route was opened, the Tingjiang River became the most important waterway between Fujian and Guangdong provinces, and also the busiest goods transportation route linking Hakka areas across Fujian, Guangdong, and Jiangxi. The prosperity of the Tingzhou Tianhou Palace was thus not limited to official patronage. It flourished thanks to Tingjiang River shipping, and merchants, boatmen, travelers, and local residents of Tingzhou were all deeply influenced by Mazu worship. An inscription carved on a donation stele from the fifth year of the Daoguang reign (1825), commemorating the reconstruction of the Tianhou Palace, lists the names and contributions of the sponsoring businesses and merchants.

1(Song) Hu Taichu, comp., and Zhao Yumu, ed. *Gazetteer of Linting*. Fujian People's Publishing House, 1990, p. 65.

The Tianhou Palace in Tingzhou

In the 18th year of Zhiyuan reign of the Yuan Dynasty (1281), the "Three Holy Consorts Palace" was renamed "Tianfei Palace" (Celestial Goddess Palace) and relocated to Pangui Lane in eastern Changting. In the 23rd year of Kangxi reign of the Qing Danasty (1684), when Mazu was posthumously elevated to "Tianhou" (Heavenly Empress) by imperial decree, the "Tianfei Palace" of Tingzhou was accordingly renamed "Tianhou Temple." Both Ming- and Qing-era local gazetteers of Tingzhou record this change. The Ming-dynasty *Gazetteer of Tingzhou Prefecture* even included an illustration of the Tianhou Palace, and the *Gazetteer of Changting County* in the 5th year of Guangxu reign of the Qing Danasty (1879) marked its location. These records affirm that since its introduction via water routes during the Song Dynasty, Mazu belief has maintained a prominent place in Tingzhou's religious life. In the 1950s, the temple was requisitioned for use by the county's electric power plant. After the Reform and Opening-Up period, the plant was relocated, and beginning in 1994, a systematic restoration effort was launched. In 1997, devotees from Longtian Temple in Taichung, Taiwan, visited Changting to ceremonially receive the spirit of the Mazu and enshrine it in Taiwan, revering the Tingzhou Tianhou Temple as the ancestral temple.

The ritual activities at Tingzhou Tianhou Palace fall into two categories: daily rites and festival rites.

On the 1st, 15th, and 23rd days of each lunar month—designated as days for offering prayers and reciting scriptures for the blessing of all people—Mazu devotees gather for collective worship, and the Tianhou Palace holds small-scale ceremonies such as scripture recitation and memorial petitions. On the 9th day of each lunar month, the Fuhui Lotus Society, a scripture-reciting group voluntarily formed by believers from Changting's urban area, makes a pilgrimage to the Holy Mother and conducts scripture-recitation and memorial-petition rituals in the Tianhou Palace.

During the first lunar month, numerous celebratory events take place. The New Year's greeting ceremony on the first day begins on Lunar New Year's Eve, when the temple invites a drum and music troupe to perform incense-drum rituals. After the temple doors are opened on New Year's Day, sacrificial rites are held, and the chanting group recites scriptures throughout the day to offer petitions, praying for favorable weather and the peace and prosperity of the nation. On the 8th day, residents of Changting's eastern district observe Mazu's festival, locally called "Watching the Bodhisattva." On that day, villagers visit the temple to pay their respects to Mazu and also prepare lavish feasts to entertain visiting relatives and friends. On the 15th day, the Lantern Festival features a ceremonial lighting event at the Tianhou Temple.

The 23rd day of the third lunar month, Mazu's birthday, and the 9th day of the ninth lunar month, the day of Mazu's ascension, are the two most important annual Mazu festivals, with Mazu's birthday being the grandest. Celebrations for Mazu's birthday begin on the 21st day of the third lunar month and last three days, including sacrificial rites, birthday warm-up ceremonies, communal banquets, opera performances, and the Three Offerings ritual. Celebrations for Mazu's ascension last from the 7th to the 9th day of the ninth lunar month, with activities similar to those for her birthday.

The Mazu temple fair at Changting Tianhou Palace is a local folk religious event involving the whole community, though merchants are the main participants. One key activity during Mazu's processions is the "River-Cleansing Rite," organized by merchants from the paper and bamboo-timber trades, to pray for Mazu's blessing for safe and smooth shipping on the Tingjiang River and for prosperous business.

Section 4 Chinese Deities (from the Hinterland of the Maritime Silk Road) Worshipped Overseas

Tua Pek Kong (Thai Pak Koong) is revered as the guardian deity of Hakka Chinese communities in Malaysia and Singapore. Temples dedicated to this deity are commonly referred to as Tua Pek Kong Temples, such as the Tua Pek Kong Temple at the Hengshan Ting, the Tua Pek Gong Temple in Gohchor, and the Tua Pek Gong Temple on the Peak Island; or as "Fude Shrines," such as the Fude Shrine in Tanjong Pagar and the Hai Choo Fude Shrine in Telok Ayer of Singapore.

In the 10th year of the Qianlong reign of the Qing Dynasty (1745), Zhang Li and Qiu Zhaojin—both Hakkas from Dapu, Guangdong—and Ma Fuchun from Yongding, Fujian, traveled to Penang and became sworn brothers. They are regarded as the pioneering founders of the Chinese settlement in Penang. It is said that Zhang Li, the eldest, was literate and possibly a private tutor; he was elected as the provisional "island chief." The second brother, Qiu Zhaojin, was a blacksmith, while the third, Ma Fuchun, was a charcoal burner. The three quickly established dwellings, cleared land, and cultivated grain and other crops. They soon diversified their operations by opening a blacksmith shop for making farm tools, building charcoal kilns, and cutting timber for charcoal production. Under their leadership, Hai Choo Island was developed. Zhang Li was also reputedly knowledgeable in medicine and would often gather herbs in the mountains to treat both Chinese settlers and indigenous inhabitants. After the three brothers passed away, local Chinese descendants honored them as "Pek Kong" (Elder Uncle)—Zhang Li as *Tua Pek Kong* (the First Elder), Qiu as the Second Elder, and Ma as the Third Elder. Their remains were interred together, and a temple was built on Hai Choo Island for public veneration.

Paifang of Tua Pek Kong Temple on Hai Choo Island

Initially, the tomb of Tua Pek Kong was relatively modest. In the fourth year of the Jiaqing reign of the Qing Dynasty (1799), Penang had grown into a market town. In 1801, the Hakka leader Chen Chunsheng received official approval to build a temple on what is now known as Tua Pek Kong Street. He raised funds to construct the *Fude Shrine Tua Pek Kong Temple*, which occupied over 2,000 square meters and served as the main sanctuary on Hai Choo Island. A secondary temple was later established in the city center of Penang to serve as an auxiliary shrine. Notably, Clementi, who served as Governor of both Hong Kong and Singapore, is said to have made a special pilgrimage to the temple in Penang.

As the Chinese migrants, especially the Hakka, gained a foothold in local society, belief in Tua Pek Kong became increasingly influential. One inscription within the temple states, "In Southeast Asia, when one speaks of deities, it is customary to refer to the 'Great Deity of the Three Treasures,' and some say it refers to the Ming eunuch Zheng He. In Southeast Asia, when one speaks of Buddhas, all revere Tua Pek Kong. The tomb bears the names Zhang, Qiu, and Ma—surnames without given names—unified under the veneration of Tua Pek Kong."[1] This shows the wide influence of Tua Pek Kong worship across the regions in Southeast Asia. Another stele bears the inscription, "Among the overseas Chinese from five counties of Meizhou, whenever they reap a harvest, they do not credit themselves but instead attribute their success to Tua Pek Kong." This demonstrates that Chinese immigrants attributed their pioneering and entrepreneurial achievements in their host countries to the inspiration and protection of Tua Pek Kong. According to Chen Da's research on Penang, the Hakka from Jiaying exhibited particular reverence for Tua Pek Kong. Among overseas Chinese in Southeast Asia, regardless of their occupations—agriculture, industry, or commerce—it was customary to offer sacrifices to Tua Pek Kong before beginning construction on homes or factories to ensure safety. The Tua Pek Kong belief was widespread among various Chinese subgroups, including those from South Fujian, Hainan, Guangzhou, Chaozhou, and Meixian. Many places held ceremonial processions in which Tua Pek Kong "went on tour," though the specific dates varied among regions and dialect groups. The name for the deity also differed; for instance, Chinese migrants in Siam (Thailand) referred to him as Bentou Gong.

In the 28th year of the Guangxu reign (1902), Zhang Bishi—a patriotic industrialist from Dapu County, Guangdong—was serving as the Chinese Consul in Singapore. During this time, he donated 10,000 taels of silver, under the name of "Tua Pek Kong" Zhang Li, to aid victims of the Yellow River flood in China. Zhang Bishi regarded Zhang Li as being from the same clan, referring to him in official memorials as his "ancestral uncle," and petitioned for imperial recognition. In response, the Qing court conferred upon Tua Pek Kong the honorary rank of First-Class Official with

1 Chen Da. *Overseas Chinese in Southeast Asia and the Societies of Fujian and Guangdong*. The Commercial Press, 2011, p. 272.

Feather Insignia.

Although academic opinions vary on the precise origins and nature of Tua Pek Kong, it is widely agreed that the deity was introduced to Southeast Asia by Hakka migrants. As Basu notes, "Tua Pek Kong is a symbol of the Chinese pioneer spirit." This sentiment is echoed in the inscription left by Zhang Yunan, the Consul of Penang during the Guangxu reign, in Tua Pek Kong temple, which reads, "You come from the homeland, with the heroic resolve, pioneering among wild lands and foreign tribes; with the mountains fading into the plains, the sea gates not far ahead, soon you shall see the dragons rise amidst the wind and rain." The rise and flourishing of Tua Pek Kong worship in Southeast Asia is emblematic of the Chinese diaspora's integration into their new environments, while Ma Fuchun—one of the three deified brothers—epitomizes the Hakka spirit of venturing from inland China to Southeast Asia. What the Hakka people venerate overseas is precisely this pioneering spirit. The transformation of Pek Kong from mortal to deity encapsulates the Hakka's spirit of survival against all odds and their perseverance in arduous endeavors abroad.

Section 5 Missionaries and the Introduction of Foreign Religions

Human mobility within the maritime and inland exchange along the Maritime Silk Road not only involved the outward movement of commercial and migrant populations but also reciprocal flows—particularly the arrival of foreigners into the hinterland of the Maritime Silk Road, who observed the region through the lens of the "Other."

One of the earliest Western accounts of Fujian comes from the 13th-century Italian merchant and scholar Jacob d' Ancona, who described Quanzhou in his work *The City of Light*.[1] Later, figures such as Marco Polo, the traveler Odoric of Pordenone, and the missionary Matteo Ricci further introduced Fujian to the world. However, existing foreign documents mainly record Fujian's coastal cities—particularly Fuzhou and Quanzhou—and prior to the 17th century, few foreign travelers had entered the inland regions of the Maritime Silk Road.

In the 14th year of the Kangxi reign of the Qing Dynasty (1675), Nicolae Milescu Spătaru, as a Russian envoy to China, wrote *Travel Notes to China* and *Travels in China* upon returning to Russia. Though he did not visit Fujian, he devoted two chapters to describing the province, with Chapter 48 offering an overview of Jian'ning (present-day Jian'ou), Yanping, Tingzhou, and Shaowu—key inland prefectures along the Maritime Silk Road. He also brought tea back to the Russian Tsar, marking one of the earliest references to tea in Russian literature. His writings portrayed the prosperity of Fujian, especially in the coastal regions, and

1 (Italy) d'Ancona Jacob. *The City of Light*. Edited and translated by David Selbourne(Britain), translated into Chinese by Yang Min et al. Shanghai People's Publishing House, 2000. Note: Authenticity of this work remains in doubt.

through his observations of its long-standing maritime trade tradition, he insightfully identified the maritime disposition of the Fujian people.

In the mid-to-late 19th century, the renowned British travel photographer John Thomson made several journeys throughout China. In 1898, he published in Britain *China, Through the Lens of John Thomson.*[1] During his travels from late 1870 to early 1871, he entered Xiamen from Shantou, journeyed east to Taiwan, then crossed the sea northward to Fuzhou. From there, he traveled upriver along the Minjiang River to Nanping, recording in detail the entire voyage from Fuzhou to Nanping by boat. His observations provided a close-up look at Fujian in a period of transition at the end of traditional society, and he left behind valuable photographic records of the upper Minjiang River.

Overall, however, among Westerners who set foot in the hinterland of the Maritime Silk Road, travelers like Thomson were in the minority; the majority were Western missionaries.

I. Missionaries in the Late Ming Period and the Hinterland of the Maritime Silk Road

Fujian, historically known as "Eight Min," is a province of rugged hills, intersecting rivers, diverse dialects, pluralistic religious beliefs, and rich folk traditions. It is also the birthplace of Zhu Xi's Neo-Confucian philosophy, boasting strong cultural confidence and distinctive local cultural features. When missionaries and overseas religions entered Fujian, they faced differences in language, faith, and customs.

Catholicism entered China during the late Ming Dynasty, often interwoven with commercial activities and intellectual exchanges with

---

1(Britain) Thomson John. *China, Through the Lens of John Thomson*. Translated by Yang Boren and Chen Xianping. China Photography Publishing House, 2001.

Confucian scholarship. The 16th and 17th centuries saw the development of maritime trade routes between the East and West, which facilitated missionary access to China. Merchant ships traveling between Europe and Asia carried not only goods but also many Christian missionaries. Once in China, missionaries often wore Confucian robes and disguised their Catholic teachings under the guise of Confucian culture.

The earliest verifiable missionary to reach the hinterland of the Maritime Silk Road was Giulio Aleni (1582–1649), known in Chinese as Ai Rulue and styled Siji. He was regarded as the most successful Jesuit missionary to China after Matteo Ricci and was honored with the title "Confucius of the West."[1] Aleni entered inland China in 1613 and preached for several decades, forming close friendships with notable figures such as Xu Guangqi, Ye Xianggao, Han Lin, and Yang Tingjun. In 1625, Aleni followed Ye Xianggao back to Fujian, where, through Ye's introduction, he gained acquaintance with officials and scholars in Fuzhou and developed close relations with Zhang Ruitu, He Qiaoyuan, Lin Tong, and others.[2] During the turbulent transition from the Ming to Qing dynasties, Aleni served as the Jesuit Superior of the South China District and made Fujian one of the two major Jesuit dioceses in China. In 1644, the Ming Dynasty collapsed, and surviving members of the imperial family established a series of short-lived Southern Ming courts. In 1645, Zhu Yujian, the ninth-generation descendant of Zhu Yuanzhang and a Southern Ming monarch hopeful for restoration, was enthroned in Fuzhou as the Longwu Emperor. He held a favorable attitude toward Catholicism and once visited the

1 (Ming) Han Lin, and Zhang Geng. *Testimonies of the Saints*. In vol. 1 *Third Compilation of Catholic Missionary Literature in the East*, Student Bookstore, 1972, p.274.

2Lin Jinshui. "Aleni and Fuzhou Society in the Late Ming Period." *Maritime History Studies*, no. 2, 1992, pp. 56–66.

Catholic Church —known as Futang—founded by Ye Yifan, grandson of Ye Xianggao. He even bestowed the plaque "Imperially Established Catholic Church of Central Fujian." *Futang* also printed Aleni's works. During his time in Fujian, Aleni associated with over 205 literati, the majority of whom were "young Confucian scholars and local gentry, such as Confucian instructors, students, and tribute students."[1] In 1646, the Qing army captured Fuzhou. Aleni fled to Puyang (present-day Putian), and the following year sought refuge in the mountains near Yanping (modern-day Nanping), where he died in 1649. He was buried at Mount Shizi near the north gate of Fuzhou.

Aleni was the first Jesuit missionary in China to pioneer grassroots evangelism. Over the 25 years he spent in Fujian, he traveled extensively through Fuzhou, Fuqing, Putian, Xianyou, Yongchun, Anxi, Dehua, Quanzhou, and Zhangzhou, as well as inland regions such as Nanping, Jian'ou, Chong'an, Jianning, Taining, Shaowu, and Mingxi. Wherever Aleni went, he made many friends and spread Christian teachings. He built 22 large churches and countless smaller chapels, which were distributed across more than 20 prefectures and counties in Fujian Province. The number of local people baptized under his influence was the highest among all provinces.[2] Fujian's literati, through their interactions with Aleni, gained a deeper understanding of Western religion and civilization. In the 10th year of the Chongzhen reign (1637), the Nestorian Church in Jinjiang published Aleni's work *Responses to Questions about the West* (edited by Jiang Dejing). This book introduced Western social customs and medical knowledge to local Fujian scholars and officials.

1Lin Jinshui. "The Social Network Between Aleni and Fujian Scholars and Officials." *Studies on the History of Sino-Foreign Relations*, no.5, World Affairs Press, 1992, p.182.

2Zhang Xianqing. *Aleni and Fujian Society in the Late Ming Period.* MA thesis, Fujian Normal University, 1995, pp. 25–26.

II. Missionaries in the Hinterland of the Maritime Silk Road Since the Modern Era

After the Ming-Qing transition, due to the Qing government's comprehensive ban on Christianity, Western missionaries faced strong resistance, and their activities in China entered a low ebb. After China's defeat in the First Opium War in 1840, Britain intensified its cultural penetration. After the signing of the Sino-French *Treaty of Whampoa* in 1844, the Qing government was forced to open treaty ports and grant missionaries the right to preach freely. Subsequently, various Protestant missionary societies began to evangelize in China's coastal cities, gradually expanding their presence into the inland hinterlands. Among the five treaty ports open to foreign trade, Fujian had two: Fuzhou and Xiamen. Through the Minjiang River and Jiulong River, Christianity spread to various regions. Xiamen served as a base for missionary societies such as the American Reformed Church, the British London Missionary Society, the British Presbyterian Church, the American Presbyterian Church, and the Seventh-day Adventist Church. Fuzhou was the base for societies including American Board of Commissioners for Foreign Missions, the Methodist Episcopal Mission, and the Anglican Church. Additionally, there were other societies like the Baptist Mission, Irish Presbyterian Mission, Scottish Presbyterian Mission, Canadian Presbyterian Mission, and Christian Assembly.

Fujian's mountainous terrain and dense forests posed significant hardships for missionary work. The American missionary Joseph Edkins, who worked for an extended period in northern Fujian, described the region as a "kingdom composed of continuously extending mountain ranges,"[1]

1 Lin Jinshui, Wu Weiwei, Cui Junfeng, et al. *Studies on Fujian and the History of Cultural Exchanges Between the East and West*. Ocean Press, 2015, p.337.

with only narrow mountain paths for travel. Aside from walking, the only other transport option was sedan chairs. Another missionary from American Board of Commissioners for Foreign Missions, Samuel Wells Williams, recorded,

> Upstream from Fuzhou, parts of the river are obstructed by reefs and shallows, making navigation difficult. Boats could only reach about 30 miles to Minqing County; beyond that, the water currents become swift and reaching Yanping is extremely difficult—even during high water levels, towing the boats by manpower remains ineffective.[1]

Other missionaries from the same American Board made similar observations, noting that as they went further upstream along the Minjiang River, conditions became increasingly difficult, "The Minjiang River is full of rocks, with rapid currents, making navigation slow and dependent on manual labor."[2] After switching from water to land routes, they had to traverse rugged mountain trails, where it was difficult to find enough porters to carry their luggage, and horses were a rare sight.

Despite these obstacles, missionary activities in Fujian's mountainous regions continued to advance during the late Qing period. Some missionaries began to establish medical, educational, social welfare, and publishing institutions to support their evangelical missions, which objectively contributed to local social progress.

In western Fujian, the principal Christian missionary societies included

1(America) Williams Samuel Wells. *A General History of China*, vol. 1. Translated by Chen Ju. Shanghai Ancient Books Publishing House, 2005, p. 89.

2Lin Jinshui, Wu Weiwei, Cui Junfeng, et al. *Studies on Fujian and the History of Cultural Exchanges Between the East and West*. Ocean Press, 2015, p.338.

the London Missionary Society, the Presbyterian Church, the Baptist Mission, and the Reformed Church. Each society had its own primary mission areas, though overlap in missionary zones sometimes occurred. The London Missionary Society mainly operated in Changting, Liancheng, Shanghang, Qingliu, Ninghua, and Mingxi counties; the Presbyterians concentrated their efforts in Shanghang, Yongding, and Wuping; the Baptists worked predominantly in Changting, Shanghang, Yongding, Wuping, and Xinluo District; the Reformed Church focused on the Xinluo area of Longyan. As an important node along the Tingjiang River, Shanghang became a hub where multiple missionary societies converged. Given the region's geography, missionary routes in western Fujian were primarily overland, supplemented by river travel, with major transportation junctions serving as mission centers. During the early phase, missionary work was mainly conducted through "itinerant preaching," with subsequent construction of churches, hospitals, and schools. The different societies coordinated with one another, and missionaries actively trained local believers to share the evangelistic workload. One distinctive feature of Christian missions in western Fujian was the comparatively high number of female converts, which exceeded that of other areas in Fujian.

1. Longyan Region

In the spring of the 9th year of the Guangxu reign of the Qing Dynasty (1883), the London Missionary Society stationed in Xiamen dispatched Western pastors such as Bu Maolin and Ban Yi Lai Hua, alongside Chinese pastors Lin Zhenghui and Zhou Zhide, to preach in Longyan. Initially, they rented a private residence outside the East Gate in Pingzai Lane to serve as a church and soon gathered more than ten believers and inquirers. In the 25th year of Guangxu reign (1899), a Catholic church was established at the salt depot in Shangban, Longyan, enrolling 112 believers, of whom 56 were baptized and 24 were approved as a donor. Evangelism was initially led by

Zhong Shanbao and continued by Chen Fuliang. In the 31st year of Guangxu reign (1905), Father An Wulang rented the Jiang family shrine at the foot of Meiting Hill as a church. Catholic activities revived, but after some church members committed offenses and the priest shielded them, Longyan prefect Li Jingsong punished them severely. The priest fled, the believers dispersed, and the mission stopped. The spread of Christianity in Longyan was under the jurisdiction of the American Reformed Church. In the early Republic of China era, American pastors such as Li Zhenduo and Wei Pingsheng established a church (chapel) at Pingtou, Pingzai Hill. In 1919, a missionary society founded Ai Hua Hospital at Mont Huling, and in 1923, Mingde Primary School was established. In the spring of 1941, a church was constructed outside the West Gate of Longyan city (now Jiuyi Road), with branches later established in Xiaochi, Yanshi, and Longmen townships. Churches were also built in Longmen and Yanshi, with the total number of believers exceeding 800.[1]

During the early period of evangelization in Western Fujian, missionaries primarily employed the methods of "selling books while preaching" and "distributing leaflets"—methods that proved largely ineffective. As American Baptist missionary Frank. J. Wiens (Wei Yingshi), who worked actively in Shanghang County from 1912 to 1927, remarked, these strategies were "not an effective method for preaching"[2] to the Hakka, who seldom left their homes. After the initial setbacks, missionary societies in western Fujian adjusted their strategies, establishing hospitals, schools, and charitable organizations as extensions of their religious missions. For

1Chen Jiadong. *A Brief History of the Church in Longyan*. 1987. Quoted in Lu Ping. *Christianity and Hakka Society in Western Fujian*. MA thesis, Fujian Normal University, 2002, p. 24.

2(America)Wiens Frank. J. *Fifteen Years Among the Hakkas of South China*. Translated by Ding Lilong. Xiamen University Press, 2017.

instance, Frank. J. Wiens founded Meihua School, a girls' school, and a Western hospital in Shanghang.

Church hospitals introduced modern Western medical practices to local communities. The mountainous regions of western Fujian were prone to infectious diseases such as skin disorders and malaria. Church hospitals and doctors developed specific medications and treatments to address these local conditions. However, some residents held deep prejudices against Western medicine, referring to it as "foreign devil's sorcery," with rumors claiming that Western drugs would "render women infertile and men sterile"[1]—a particularly alarming notion among the Hakka, who place high value on fertility. Initially, only the impoverished sought treatment at church hospitals, but as more patients experienced successful outcomes, public perception gradually improved. Notable Christian hospitals in the Longyan region included Ai Hua Hospital, the Gospel Hospital in Tingzhou, and the Gospel Hospital in Shanghang. In addition to treating patients, Hakka Christian hospitals in western Fujian began training local Chinese doctors. In 1884, missionaries such as Bu Maolin, Ban Yidi, and Zhou Zhide of the London Missionary Society established a church and a medical clinic in Xinluo (present-day Xinluo District of Longyan), with plans to build Longyan hospital. However, due to public mistrust, the project was abandoned and funds were redirected to establish the Zhangzhou Hospital instead. Using the Zhangzhou Hospital as their base, missionaries from the London Missionary Society frequently traveled between Longyan and Zhangzhou. Despite the inconvenient transportation, the missionaries were known to be "constantly on the move…enduring hardship and fatigue."[2] In

1Zhou Zhide. *A History of the London Missionary Society in Southern Fujian*. Gulangyu Sacred Church Press, 1934.

2"Short Notes." *Sacred Church Bulletin of Southern Fujian*, July 1944, p. 2.

1919, missionaries Li Zhenduo, Wei Pingsheng and the doctor Xia Liwen from the Beixi District of the London Missionary Society in southern Fujian arrived in Longyan to assist with missionary work. That same year, Ai Hua Hospital was established at the foot of the Huling Ridge in Xinluo District. It became one of the most advanced hospitals in western Fujian at the time. In addition to providing routine medical services, it also incorporated evangelistic preaching into its patient care.

2. Sanming Region

In the 36th year of the Kangxi reign (1697), Spanish Catholic priest Anmin traveled from Fuzhou to teach the Gospel in Jiangle, establishing a Catholic church in the county seat that occupied 600 square meters. The congregation grew from just over 100 in its early days to over 500 by the early Guangxu era. During the Qing Dynasty, Catholicism also reached Jianning County, where a church was built. However, due to imperial edicts during the reigns of Emperors Yongzheng and Qianlong prohibiting Catholic activities, church operations in Jianning were suppressed. In the 24th year of Guangxu reign (1898), a Catholic church was built in the county seat of Taining. During the Republican era, Catholic churches were successively established in Shaxian, Zhukou of Taining, Ninghua, and Xikou of Jianning.

The first Catholic organization in Shaxian was established in 1912 by French priest Feng Mengxiong in Qingzhou. Between then and 1926, churches were successively built in West Gate of the county seat, Xiamao, Yongxi, Gaoqiao, and Shangzhuangyuan Lane within the county seat.

In the early years of the Republic of China, Spanish priest Xue Bingdu held considerable influence in Jianyang, to the extent that even the county magistrate yielded to him. He boldly promoted the idea that Catholics would be exempt from harsh taxation and would win legal disputes; anyone displaying a cross at their door would prevent *yamen* runners for entering. As a result, the Catholic population in Jianyang quickly grew to more than 3,400. Catholic lay organizations such as the Sodality of Our Lady, the Society for the Souls in Purgatory, and the Sacred Heart League were established, along with four mission stations in Gaotang, Huangtan, Shanfang, and Wan'an. An additional church was built in the county seat. In 1926, the German missionary Shen Minwang came from Shaowu to take charge of church affairs in Jianning, where he oversaw church construction. Between 1927 and 1940, other missionaries who successively served in Jianning included Sister Shi Cihang, Lan Chunru, Qi Lishi (Belgian), Nie Duowen (German), Zhao Mofan (Irish), and Zhang Weiren (from Nanfeng, Jiangxi Province). From 1929 onward, Spanish missionaries including An Meida, Luo Peide, Lu Xinghui, Ma Ruilin, and Bai Guizhang continued their mission in Jiangle. By 1942, Taining had more than 2,300 Catholics. In 1934, the Catholic Church was formally established in Shaowu. In 1944, the Catholic Diocese of Changting dispatched Czech priest Bo shitu, Sister Yuan Dezhen (a native of Shanghang), and evangelist Li Yuting to establish a chapel and carry out missionary work in the county seat of Ninghua. As Catholicism had no local social base in Ninghua, and the church was simply furnished, early missionary efforts yielded little success. The following year, a well-equipped church building was built in Ninghua, along with auxiliary facilities, to attract believers. In 1948, the Diocese of Tingzhou sent evangelists including Zhuo Zhengxian to carry out missionary work in Qingliu. By the eve of the founding of the People's Republic of China, there were already over 1,000 Catholic believers throughout both the urban and rural areas of Qingliu County.

Christianity was introduced into the Sanming region in the tenth year of the Tongzhi reign of the Qing Dynasty (1871) from Yongchun, spreading to Datian, Jianning, Taining, Qingliu, Jiangle, and Ninghua. American missionaries Xue Cheng'en and Wu Linji traveled from Yongchun to Datian to preach and established a Methodist Episcopal Gospel Hall in the county seat. Gospel halls were subsequently founded in various localities. During the Republican period, as Christianity spread, churches were successively constructed across the region. By the eve of the founding of the People's Republic of China, there were already 63 Christian churches in Sanming, with a total of 6,000 believers. Notable churches included Youxi Mission Church (1942) in the county seat, Yong'an Gospel Hall (1917), Shaxian Gospel Hall (1928), Jianning Christian Church (1927), and Guangping Church in Datian (1929).

In the eighth year of the Guangxu reign of the Qing Dynasty (1882), Pastor Huang Daozhen of the Christian General Church in Shaowu traveled to Jianning to preach, using the Liming residence in Xiafang Lane as the preaching site. Shortly afterward, American pastor Tang Le'er carried out missionary work in Jianning and purchased a house to serve as a Gospel Hall. In the nineteenth year of Guangxu reign (1893), American missionary Joseph Edkins preached in Taining. In the twenty-first year of Guangxu reign (1885), Fan Xianshi from Shaowu also engaged in missionary work in Taining. In the twenty-ninth year of Guangxu reign (1903), the Tingzhou Christian Church sent Pastor Zhou Zhide to preach in Qingliu. Zhou first developed a congregation in the county seat and in Changxiao, then established the Qingliu Branch of the Christian Church in the county seat, under the jurisdiction of the Tingzhou District Church. In the third year of the Xuantong reign (1911), Pastor Yu Mingqian from Shaowu preached in Jiangle. In 1913, Tingzhou Church pastors Wu Kuiguang, Zhan Jiade (female, British), Xiu Zhongcheng (American), Wang Yongzhang, Wei Muzhen, Wu Zijie, Wang Jie'en, and Wu Shaotang rented private homes in Qingliu for missionary work. That same year, the church in Datian County was destroyed in a bandit raid; soon afterward, a new Western-style church and pastor's residence were built at Ximendou in the county seat, covering about 2 *mu* (approximately 1,333 square meters). In the early Republican period, Guan Xifu from Changting and Kang Xinan from Gutian preached in Ninghua. In 1913, the Changting Church District sent Ma Bocheng, also from Changting, to take charge of church affairs in Ninghua, where he also served as an English teacher at the county-run Longyun Higher Primary School. He developed over 50 believers and purchased a house to serve as a church. In 1916, Fan Xianshi from Shaowu established a Gospel Hall in Zhukou, Taining. In 1917, seeing the rapid growth of the Qingliu Church, the Tingzhou Church sent Wu Cunsong and others to assist in missionary work and establish schools there. In 1919, with funding from the North Fujian Christian Conference and donations from Jiangle believers and pastors, the Yang ancestral hall in the county seat of Jiangle was converted into a church. In 1928, the Methodist Episcopal Church in Datian reached its peak, with 2,700 believers and 30 churches countywide. In 1930, Christianity in Jiangle entered a period of prosperity, with more than 200 regular participants and four branch churches in Huangtan, Wanan, Wanquan, and Zefang. That same year, when the Chinese Workers' and Peasants' Red Army entered Qingliu, foreign pastors and missionaries returned to their home countries one after another. In 1936, the Datian branch of the Methodist Episcopal Church was renamed the Datian Branch of the Church of Christ in China and placed under the jurisdiction of the Yongde District of the Southern Fujian Assembly. That same year, the Changting church sent Pastor Zhang Lun to resume ministry in Ninghua, who was later succeeded by Lan Yuhui, also a Changting native. The number of believers grew to over 90.

3. Nanping Region

Catholicism was introduced to Nanping in the early Qing Dynasty. In the 12th year of the Shunzhi reign (1655), a private residence in Yanfang

Lane within the city was repurposed as the Church of Our Lady. By the 23rd year of the Guangxu reign (1897), the Catholic Church in Nanping was under the administration of Spanish priests. From the late Qing period to the founding of the People's Republic of China, Spanish clergymen such as An Wuqing and Bai Jinlan successively carried out missionary work in the area.

In the 3rd year of the Tongzhi reign (1864), American missionary Xue Cheng'en began preaching in Nanping. He established the Gospel Church and founded Yide Theological School, an institution dedicated to training evangelists. Education and medicine were the primary means through which he conducted his missionary work. He founded Liufang Primary and Secondary School and Shuxin Girls' Primary and Secondary School. In addition, he established several medical institutions including the Methodist Hospital, the Methodist Advanced School of Nursing, a leprosy hospital, and a public health station. On the second day of the eleventh lunar month in the fifth year of Guangxu reign (1879), the "Yanping Missionary Case" occurred, during which missionaries were assaulted in the areas of Xiaoshui Gate and Lyuzhu Ridge of Yanping. The following day, the Yanping Prefect dispatched officials to escort Xue Cheng'en back to Fuzhou. The peak of Methodist missionary activity in Nanping occurred between 1920 and 1930, during which time there were three church districts and more than ten churches, staffed by over one hundred preachers and serving more than 5,000 believers. After 1927, however, the rise of anti-Christian movements among the populace weakened the momentum of church development.

III. Cultural Inclusiveness and Conflict: The Case of Hakka Communities in Western Fujian

Chinese civilization possesses a profound inclusiveness, whereas Western Christianity is characterized by exclusivity. Among the most common issues Christianity faced upon entering Hakka regions was the conflict of belief systems. Christianity had to contend directly with long-standing Hakka concepts such as the unity of heaven and humanity, ancestor worship, polytheism, and geomantic (fengshui) beliefs. The Hakka areas of western Fujian, being remote rural localities, regarded honoring one's ancestors, maintaining clan harmony, and showing reverence for the past as the highest virtues. In every household, ancestral tablets of close kin were enshrined in the central hall. During the Spring Festival, portraits of ancestors would be prominently displayed. Villages were dotted with ancestral halls of various sizes, and ancestor worship constituted the most important annual event in the village life. Hakka clan activities included renovating ancestral halls, compiling genealogies, purchasing clan land, and establishing charitable estates. Unlike the theistic worship of the Christian God, the Hakka of western Fujian revered Confucius and Zhu Xi, valued education, maintained academies of classical learning in many places, and engaged in an unceasing array of folk cultural activities. The populace did not regard the foreign religion of Christianity as possessing absolute authority. Moreover, the Hakka attached great importance to ecological and fengshui considerations: the siting of an ancestral hall required the consultation of a geomancer, and major life rituals paid particular attention to selecting auspicious dates. The spread of Christianity in Hakka regions often took education and medical care as points of entry, rarely directly confronting the ancestral veneration practices of the Hakka.

It is undeniable that the spread of Christianity in western Fujian's Hakka regions during the modern era introduced elements of Western civilization to the local society. However, the Church's refusal to localize its teachings and practices, combined with strong resistance from Chinese cultural traditions, posed significant challenges to missionary work. This tension illustrates the deep cultural confidence of Hakka society, which is rooted in Confucian civilization.

Section 6 Cultural Identity in Overseas Chinese Communities

With the increasing outflow and settlement of immigrants from the hinterland of the Maritime Silk Road, many localities saw the emergence of small migrant communities organized according to places of origin and geographic ties. Among these, kinship- and hometown-based associations became the most significant form of social organization in the formation and development of overseas Chinese settlements. These migrant communities were bound together by traditional cultural ties and emotional connections to their homelands. As a result, they exhibited a distinctive cultural identity that combined the characteristics of their ancestral cultures with those of their host societies.

1. Hometown-Based Associations and Ethnic Identity

During the Ming and Qing dynasties, the Maritime Silk Road had a profound impact on the global trade system. From the 16th to the early 19th centuries, although China remained in a state of relative seclusion for a considerable period, the outside world's understanding of China continued to deepen. Beneath the surface of Sino-foreign relations, the influence of the external world on China intensified, and the unequal status between the two began to shift. From the late eighteenth century onward, the scale of trade between China and the Western world, led by Britain, expanded rapidly. In particular, the abnormal opium trade—driven by the political and military power—became an accelerator of China's economic decline. China's connections with the outside world shifted from gradual and latent to radical and disruptive, entering a revolutionary stage.

Into the 20th century, Chinese—especially from the southern regions—continued migrating overseas. As Philip A. Kuhn has noted, the phenomenon of modern Chinese migration was a reflection of world economic development as manifested in China. In modern history, the economic links between Europe, China, and Southeast Asia provided a stage for Chinese engagement overseas.[1] Among these participants, the people from the hinterland of the Maritime Silk Road—most notably the Hakka—formed a significant group who migrated from Southern China to settle and take root overseas. They were active participants in China's integration into the world and made distinctive contributions to the formation of the global maritime trade system. From the 16th century onward, the Hakka engaged in continuous overseas migration, evolving from sporadic voyages abroad to a broader trend, transcending geographical barriers and merging into the great current of the Maritime Silk Road, thereby linking its hinterland with the wider world.

One of the migration routes of the Hakka people from the Maritime Silk Road hinterland was to cross the "Black Ditch" (the Taiwan Strait) to Taiwan, where they gradually engaged in reclamation and settlement. Within the migrant groups heading to Taiwan, it is generally believed that the Hoklo preceded the Hakka. However, some scholars have pointed out that the Hakka in fact arrived in Taiwan at roughly the same time as the Hoklo (referring mainly to the Minnan–speaking residents from Zhangzhou and Quanzhou in Fujian). After entering Taiwan, the two ethnic groups engaged in land reclamation in different regions. The Hakka tended to settle in mountainous areas with geographic conditions similar to those of their ancestral homeland. They underwent a long and arduous process of development and eventually became one of the four major ethnic groups in contemporary Taiwan, numbering several million people across the island.

---

1 (America) Kuhn Philip A. *Chinese Among Others: Emigration in Modern Times*. Translated by Li Minghuan. Jiangsu People's Publishing House, 2015, p. 6.

A second migration route of the Hakka from the Maritime Silk Road hinterland was toward the southeastern coastal areas, and subsequently to countries along the southern rim of China and the Indian Ocean in search of livelihoods, giving rise to the well-known "Southeast Asia migration" in China's history of overseas migration. Hakka communities left their footprints across the entire region of Southeast Asia, becoming an important component of the local Chinese diaspora.

Having "gone down to Southeast Asia," the Hakka people moved away from agricultural labor in their native regions, leaving behind traditional rural communities to participate in processes of industrialization and urbanization. By the mid-Qing Dynasty, the number of Hakka emigrants abroad gradually increased, leading to the emergence of the so-called "Hakka gang." According to Luo Xianglin's research,

> By the mid-Qianlong and Jiaqing periods, Jiaying natives such as Luo Fangbo had established the Lan Fang Grand Administration (of a republican nature) around Pontianak in Borneo. At that time, there were already several tens of thousands of Hakka emigrants there, many of whom had migrated prior to Luo Fangbo's arrival.

In Southeast Asia, Hakka immigrants established themselves in places such as Penang, Malacca, and Singapore, forming two primary occupational groups: miners and craftsmen, with the former being larger in number. A nascent Hakka society began to take shape in the region, forming a relatively independent community. The so-called "Hakka gang" also began to form only after the mid-Qing period. In terms of residential patterns, they tended to live relatively concentrated in Hakka villages and used the Hakka dialect internally. As a result, different ancestral and dialect groups established ethnic boundaries and often experienced significant estrangement or even conflict with surrounding communities. In the 11th year of the Yongzheng reign (1733), after the establishment of Jiaying Directly Administered Prefecture in Guangdong, the "Five Jiaying Districts" became the core strength of Hakka communities overseas. Through hometown associations (guild halls), they maintained social and cultural ties with their native region, displaying a stronger sense of ethnic identity, which further promoted the self-recognition and cohesion of the Hakka people.

Guild halls, associations, and similar organizations played an even more significant role in shaping the ethnic identity of the Hakka people. After the 19th century, hometown-based groups developed within the overseas Chinese communities in Southeast Asia. "In terms of origin and function, Chinese guild halls both preserved the fundamental core of their counterparts in mainland China and adapted innovatively to the needs of life abroad."[1] Guild halls served as key points of contact and networks of communication, functioning as centers for market information as well as social hubs for cultivating friendship and interpersonal relationships. Hakka guilds also established schools, promoted Chinese-language education, and carried forward the virtues of Confucian tradition. Consequently, guild halls became carriers of the transformation from Hakka society to modern social forms. By the 19th century, Hakka people throughout Southeast Asia had generally joined such organizations. Although the majority of guild halls were established by Hakkas from Guangdong, some were founded by Hakkas from Western Fujian.

1The Compilation Committee of Chinese Guild Halls, ed. *Records of Chinese Guild Halls*. Fangzhi Publishing House, 2002, pp. 218–219.

Table 7-1 Major Western Fujian-Based Associations in Southeast Asia Before the 1950s

Name	Year Established	Location	Place of Origin
The Kwangtung and Tengchow Association, Penang	1795	Penang, Malaysia	Guangdong and Tingzhou natives
Yong-Da Association	1840	Penang, Malaysia	Yongding and Dapu natives
Anding Hall of the Hu Clan of Yongding, Penang	1863	Penang, Malaysia	Hu clan from Xiayang, Yongding
Yongding Association, Penang	1863		
Lord Guan Hu Company, Penang	1864	Penang, Malaysia	Hu clans from Xiayang, Yongding and Tong'an, Fujian
Wushu Association of Penang	1899	Penang, Malaysia	Natives of Huizhou, Jiaying, Dapu, and Zengcheng in Guangdong, and Yongding natives
Yinjiang Association of Renggam	1908	Renggam, Johor, Malaysia	Hakka natives from Tingzhou
Yongding Association, Singapore	1918	Singapore	Yongding natives, Fujian
Yongding Association, Yangon	1918	Yangon, Myanmar	Yongding natives, Fujian
Hu Clan Anding Hall, Yangon	1919	Yangon, Myanmar	Natives primarily from Yongding (Fujian) and Meizhou (Guangdong), also from provinces such as Yunnan, Hainan, and Hubei
Yong'an Society, Penang	1919	Penang, Malaysia	Yongding natives, Fujian
Longyan Association, Yangon	1923	Yangon, Myanmar	Longyan natives, Fujian
Longyan Association, Medan	1923	Sumatra, Indonesia	Longyan natives, Fujian
Longyan	1924	Sabah, Malaysia	Longyan natives, Fujian

Name	Year Established	Location	Place of Origin
Association, Kota Kinabalu			
Longyan Association, Bangkok	1925	Bangkok, Thailand	Longyan natives, Fujian
Longyan Association (Pematangsiantar, Tebing Tinggi, Asahan, Kota Langsa, Palembang)	After 1926	Sumatra, Indonesia	Longyan natives, Fujian
Longyan Association, Penang	1929	Penang, Malaysia	Longyan natives, Fujian
Longyan Association, Dindings (Manjung)	1936	Dindings, Malaysia	Longyan natives, Fujian
Longyan Association, Singapore	1938	Singapore	Longyan natives, Fujian
Longyan Association, Jakarta	1938	Jakarta, Indonesia	Yongding natives, Fujian
Yongding Association, Bandung	1938	Bandung, Indonesia	Yongding natives, Fujian
General Association of Longyan Natives in Sumatra	c. 1940	Medan, Indonesia	Longyan natives, Fujian
Nanyang Shanghang Association, Singapore	1941	Singapore	Shanghang natives, Fujian
Kedah–Perlis Longyan Association	1945	Kedah, Malaysia	Longyan natives, Fujian
Yongding Association, Perak	1946	Ipoh, Malaysia	Yongding natives, Fujian
Yongjing Association, Samarinda	1946	East Kalimantan, Indonesia	Yongding and Nanjing (Zhangzhou) natives
Nanyang Hu Clan Federation, Singapore	1946	Singapore	Natives of Yongding (Fujian), Zhaoqing and Meizhou (Guangdong)
Yongding	1947	Penang,	Yongding natives, Fujian

Name	Year Established	Location	Place of Origin
Association of Northern Malaysia		Malaysia	

Source: Zhang Youzhou. *The History of Overseas Chinese from Longyan*. South China University of Technology Press, 2020.

1. The Kwangtung & Tengchew Association, Penang (The Guang-Ting Association)

The Kwangtung & Tengchew Association, Penang, founded during the Xianfeng reign of the Qing Dynasty, was jointly established by Hakka people from Tingzhou, Fujian, and from Guangdong. It is the oldest association in Penang and, indeed, on the entire Malay Peninsula. Penang was an important port city along the Maritime Silk Road. During the Ming and Qing periods, merchants from Tingzhou joined with Hakka merchants from Guangdong to engage in maritime trade, and the establishment of this association stands as a prime example of such collaboration.

Founded in 1795, the association initially served mainly to manage public cemetery lands and did not have a dedicated premises. In 1919, overseas Chinese merchants from Guangdong donated four shop units and a temple dedicated to the deity Guan Sheng Di Jun (Lord Guan), thereby endowing the association with immovable property. In 1923, one of these units was renovated into the association's premises. In 1925, the Kwangtung & Tengchew Association was formally registered as a social organization. In 1941, its main building was completed, and the statue of Lord Guan, originally enshrined in the Liesheng Palace was relocated to the new hall. Organizationally, the association adopted a board-of-directors system, with its 19 affiliated counties of origins in Guangdong and Tingzhou each electing one to six representatives to form the Board of Directors and the Executive Council.

In addition to continuing its role in managing the public cemetery lands, the association expanded its functions as the overseas Chinese from Guangdong and Tingzhou grew in number and influence. It became a key facilitator of connections among fellow townsmen and an advocate for various welfare and relief efforts for overseas Chinese. From the early 20th century until 1920, the association successively established multiple educational institutions, including Shizhong School for Hakka students, Commerce School for Cantonese, Yihua School for Qiongzhou natives, Taishan School for Cantonese, and Hanjiang School for Chaoshanese—spanning various regions and dialect groups.

The Kwangtung & Tengchew Association, Penang, Malaysia

2.Yong-Da Association of Penang

Originally known as “Yong-Da Company,” the Yong-Da Association was founded by emigrants from Yongding (Fujian) and Dapu (Meizhou, Guangdong). Although Yongding and Dapu belong to two different provinces, the two areas share adjacent geographies, economic interactions, and linguistic commonalities. After improvements in the Tingjiang River navigation in the Song Dynasty, trade between the two regions flourished, and the Chayang Wharf in Dapu became one of the main departure points for people from Yongding and western Fujian to sail for Southeast Asia. The earliest group of migrants to arrive in Penang in 1745—including Zhang Li, Qiu Zhaoxiang, and Ma Fuchun—originated from Dapu and Yongding, respectively.

These two migrant communities cooperated in pioneering and developing Penang, forging deep connections in geography, kinship, and finance. Although the pioneer overseas Chinese from both places participated in activities at the Tua Pek Kong Temple and the Guang-Ting Association, the former's activities were mainly religious rituals, while the latter had a broad organizational scope and could not provide the most practical care specifically for the emigrants from Yongding and Dabu. In light of the practical need to strengthen hometown ties and promote common development, Chen Hongkui, a blacksmith originally from Xiayang, Yongding, took the initiative to establish the Yong-Da Association and donated a shophouse for its use. After the Yong-Da Association was founded, emigrants from Yongding and Dabu joined enthusiastically, and the association organized spring and autumn ancestral worship ceremonies every year to foster fellowship among its members.

3. Lord Guan Hu Company of Penang

The Lord Guan Hu Company of Penang (Bingcheng Dijunhu Gongsi) was a joint initiative established on the foundations of two earlier Hu clan halls in Penang: Dunmu Hall of Dingmei and Anding Hall of Xiayang. Dunmu Hall was founded in 1872 by Hu clan members originating from Dingmei Village in Tong'an County, Fujian, and functioned as a clan ancestral shrine. Anding Hall, established in 1883 by Hu clan members from Xiayang Town in Yongding County, Fujian, was composed of descendants of the clan's founding ancestor in Fujian, Nian Balang, and, in practice, functioned as an ancestral hall. The Anding Hall operated under a patriarchal system, with different family branches and factions, and was managed by twelve family heads. After Malaysia's independence, Anding Hall was restructured in 1957 to comply with governmental regulations on social organizations, replacing the patriarchal model with a committee system. Every year in the third lunar month, all clan members would gather at the Hu ancestral tombs for the spring worship, and in the seventh lunar month for the autumn worship. Despite being called a "company," the Lord Guan Hu Company was founded with the purpose of venerating the Hu clan's ancestor Nian Balang and his wife, as well as the deity Lord Guan. Through this, it aimed to strengthen ties among Hu clansmen. Membership was restricted to descendants of Nian Balang from Zhongchuan, Xiayang. Each year, the company convened clan members to conduct worship and ancestral rites on the 13th day of the first lunar month, the 13th day of the fifth lunar month (Lord Guan's birthday), the 15th day of the seventh lunar month (Ghost Festival), and the Winter Solstice.

4. Longyan Association of Penang

Migration from Longyan to Penang began in the 1890s, and by 1929, the Longyan Association was formally established. The typical migration route involved traveling from Longyan to Zhangzhou, then to Xiamen, and finally sailing to Southeast Asia. During the early Republican period, the number of Longyan migrants surged, with Penang serving as their primary port of entry into Malaya. In 1908, Longyan immigrants formed the Cangyan Qingming Fu Company in Penang. According to records, As the number of Yan (Longyan) people in Penang increased, that year, Weng Zhipeng, Chen Shuiwang and his brother Shuifa, together with Wang Zhanfu and others, initiated the organization of the Cangyan Qingming Fu Company. Each year, donations were collected from fellow townsmen overseas to be used for the spring and autumn ancestral worship ceremonies.

Any surplus from the worship funds was deposited in shops owned by fellow townsmen to generate interest."[1] "Qingming Fu" literally means "praying for blessings during Qingming," indicating that the Cangyan Qingming Fu Company was a mutual-aid society for ancestral worship, funerals, and tomb-sweeping activities among Longyan migrants. By the 1920s, Longyan-owned businesses in the area had become well established, and they donated funds for the company to purchase property, as well as to provide assistance to newly arrived Longyan migrants in Penang. Gradually, "Qingming Fu" evolved from a mutual-aid society for ancestral worship activities into a new stage in which it "handled all affairs concerning Longyan migrants."

In the 1920s, following the trend among overseas Chinese in Southeast Asia to refer to large-scale native-place organizations as "associations", the Longyan community promoted the expansion of Qingming Fu's scope and management capacity. This effort culminated in the official establishment of the Longyan Association of Penang in November 1929, which became the earliest and most influential native-place organization of the Longyan diaspora in Malaysia.

5. Yongding Association of Singapore

The Yongding Association of Singapore was established in 1918, making it the earliest and largest Yongding native-place organization in Southeast Asia. It was founded by Yongding natives residing in the Malay Peninsula and Singapore, including Hu Biyu, Hu Huashan, Hu Xiurong, Zhang Zilou, and Hu Xingjie.

At its inception, the Yongding Association of Singapore functioned

---

1 Jiang Renqi. "A Brief History of the Longyan Association in Penang." *The 22nd Anniversary and New Building Completion Commemorative Publication of the Longyan Association in Penang*, p. 29.

effectively as the overarching organization for Yongding natives across Southeast Asia, with appointed liaison officers in various countries and territories such as the Malay Peninsula, the Dutch East Indies, Burma, and Thailand. These officers were responsible for maintaining communication with local Yongding communities and mobilizing new members. Notably, Hu Wenhu served as the association's liaison for Rangoon, Burma, during its early days.

The association's mission was to foster solidarity among townsmen and promote mutual welfare. It established a headquarters, a charitable cemetery, and the Chongde Ancestral Hall, providing support and relief to compatriots traveling between Southeast Asia and their home region, as well as to local migrants—especially those in poverty. During the Japanese occupation of Singapore in 1942, the Yongding Association temporarily functioned as a refugee shelter for displaced Chinese. After Japan's defeat in 1945, the guild hall of the Yongding Association was rebuilt, and Hu Wenhu's eldest son, Hu Jiao, was elected president. Under his leadership, the association drafted new work plans, revitalized its operations, and launched *Yongding Monthly*, one of the earliest publications issued by a Chinese association in Southeast Asia, focusing on educational affairs in the homeland Yongding. In addition, the Yongding Association of Singapore also participated actively in the activities of the Chongde Ancestral Hall affiliated with Fung Yun Thai Association.

6. The General Association of Hakkas in Southeast Asia and the Chongzheng General Association

The General Association of Hakkas in Southeast Asia held significant influence across Southeast Asia. Initiated by Hakka organizations such as the Yinghe Guild and Fung Yun Thai Association in Singapore, the idea of founding the association was proposed in 1923. In 1929, after approval by the Registrar of Societies under the British colonial government, it was officially established in Singapore. The General Association of Hakkas in Southeast Asia served as a united body for many Hakka associations across Southeast Asia, with Hu Wenhu being its largest donor. Upon its founding, it garnered widespread enthusiasm and support from Hakka communities across the region, and Hu Wenhu was unanimously elected as its first president. Following its establishment, numerous regional branches affiliated with the association were founded: 43 in Malaysia, 7 in Indonesia, 2 in Sarawak, and 1 in Burma. The association and its branches made great contributions to uniting Hakka people across Southeast Asia, supporting the development of Hakka-owned businesses, and promoting cultural, recreational, and welfare activities. During the War of Resistance against Japanese Aggression, the association, under Hu Wenhu's leadership, along with the Federation of Overseas Chinese in Southeast Asia led by Tan Kah Kee, mobilized overseas Chinese to support China's resistance against Japan. These efforts included organizing large-scale anti-Japanese propaganda campaigns, fundraising, purchasing national defense bonds, and even returning to China to join the resistance.

The fact that the association bore the name "Hakka" shows that a broad-based Hakka self-identity had already emerged within the Hakka community in Southeast Asia. Over the course of several decades, the General Association of Hakkas in Southeast Asia played an important role in uniting overseas Hakkas and deepening their collective sense of ethnic identity.

II. Cultural Identity of Overseas Chinese

According to Scholar Zhang Youzhou and others, the cultural identity of overseas Chinese communities is primarily reflected in three aspects: dialect, customs, and folk beliefs.[1]

---

1 Zhang Youzhou, editor-in-chief. *The History of Overseas Chinese from Longyan.*

1.Dialect

Dialect serves as the main basis for distinguishing different sub-ethnic groups and possesses a strong cohesive force among people. In overseas Chinese communities, dialect becomes a salient marker of regional origin. According to the research of Zhang Youzhou and others, in areas such as the mining districts of Batu Gajah and Chenderiang in Perak, Malaysia, the Bagan Ajam area of Penang, the commercial district of Ipoh, as well as Sabak Bernam and Sekinchan in Selangor, and in Yangon, Myanmar—places where people from Xiayang, Yongding have settled—Xiayang dialect functions as the common language of communication. These overseas Chinese also pass their dialect down to their descendants as a mark of identity. Even if later generations have no direct connection to their ancestral homeland, they can still speak the hometown dialect. While Chinese immigrants from Longyan are also present throughout Southeast Asia, they have not formed as concentrated "dialect enclaves" as those from Yongding. Nevertheless, in Longyan-populated areas such as Penang, Kuala Lumpur, and Kota Kinabalu in Malaysia, Singapore, Jakarta in Indonesia, and Yangon in Myanmar, migrants are still able to communicate with each other in the Longyan dialect.

Dialect serves as a natural bond among overseas Chinese, partly due to the economic structure of migrant communities. Chinese immigrants often migrated together with family members or fellow villagers and engaged in the same or related occupations abroad. For instance, Hu Wenhu's Eng Aun Tong Pharmaceutical Company employed many members of the Hu clan, while the *Renhe Tang* Pharmacy operated by Luo Hongguang and Zhang Jixian also involved clan members from both families. After migrating overseas, these Chinese often joined guilds or

---

South China University of Technology Press, 2020, pp.104–108.

hometown associations based on regional ties. As discussed in the previous section, such organizations either served as hubs for sharing information, organized ritual activities, or provided mutual aid. As a result, hometown-based organizations reinforced the internal use of a common dialect. On a cultural level, many migrants—especially Hakkas—were influenced by the traditional concept of "Better to sell the land of one's ancestors than to forget the language of one's ancestors." This notion enabled local dialects to transcend spatial barriers and be preserved across generations.

2.Seasonal Festivals and Folk Customs

Overseas Chinese also brought with them seasonal festivals and folk customs rooted in Han Chinese traditional culture. For instance, in areas such as Ipoh in Perak, Malaysia, where many Yongding Hakkas reside, members of the Hu clan continue to celebrate the Lunar New Year following the customs of their ancestral hometown, Xiayang. Hu Wandu, son of the "Tin King" Hu Rijie, once recalled,

> On New Year's Eve, our family would carefully take out and hang portraits of our ancestors on the family altar. All family members would solemnly offer a three-sacrifice ritual to the deities and ancestors, burn incense, light candles, and worship with utmost sincerity.[1]

This custom is consistent with current Spring Festival practices in some Hakka villages in Western Fujian. Additionally, traditional folk activities such as dragon and lion dances and lantern parades are still practiced in places like Ipoh (Perak), Sabak Bernam (Selangor), and Penang.

Overseas migrants hold strong beliefs in honoring ancestors and

---

1Hu Wandu. "True Words of Hu". *Oriental Daily*, 13 Feb. 2010. Quoted in Zhang Youzhou, editor-in-chief. *The History of Overseas Chinese from Longyan*. South China University of Technology Press, 2020, p.105.

remembering the past. Among Hakka and Hoklo communities in Southeast Asia, it is customary to worship ancestors during traditional holidays, particularly on Lunar New Year's Eve, Qingming Festival, and the Mid-Autumn Festival—all days that are especially significant for ancestor veneration among overseas Chinese from western Fujian. Several ritual organizations emerged in response to these needs. For example, in 1798, the Kwangtung & Tengchew Association was established by Chinese migrants from Tingzhou (mainly Yongding) and Guangdong for the purpose of ancestor worship. Around 1840, the Yong-Da Association of Penang and the Fung Yun Thai Association of Singapore were founded, both responsible for managing communal graves and conducting sacrificial rites. The Cangyan Qingming Fu Company of Penang, established in 1908, was one of the earliest social organizations among Western Fujian migrants explicitly focusing on Qingming rituals. In the same year, the Yinjiang Association of Renggam was formed in Renggam, Johor, Malaysia, with autumn ancestor worship as its main activity.

3.Folk Beliefs

Folk beliefs refer to a set of deity worship concepts and ritual practices widely found among the people, usually accompanied by fixed ceremonies. When emigrants from the hinterland of the Maritime Silk Road sailed to Southeast Asia, they also brought with them the folk beliefs and corresponding customs of their homeland.

The Yongding Hakkas, as a primary force in the southward migration from the Maritime Silk Road hinterland, carried with them the Hakka traditions of worshipping *Gong Wang* (Lord Gong) and Pek Kong. In the Hakka villages of Yongding, every natural village has its own *Gong Wang* and Pek Kong. *Gong Wang* shrines are usually located at the village's water entrance, while *Bo Gong* shrines could be found under a cliff, beneath a tree, at a bridgehead, beside a well, or even in the fields—serving as local guardian deities. Upon arriving in Southeast Asia, the Hakka people had to adapt to unfamiliar geographic and climatic conditions while enduring emotional hardship from separation from their homeland. They projected their hopes and longing onto these guardian deities and began establishing Pek Kong and *Gong Wang* altars in their plantations or settlement areas. The worship of Tua Pek Kong in Penang, Malaysia, is essentially a projection of this homeland-based guardian deity belief system.

Beyond *Gong Wang* and Pek Kong, as the number of Chinese migrants in Southeast Asia increased, traditional Chinese religious and folk beliefs became widespread across the region. Deities such as Mazu,the Deity of Wealth, and Guan Di (Lord Guan) are commonly worshipped in Southeast Asian Chinese communities. The rituals and customs surrounding these deities have not only strengthened communal cohesion and reinforced cultural centripetal force toward Chinese traditions but have also provided spiritual comfort and motivation for personal and communal advancement. At the same time, these migrants have actively integrated into their host societies, engaging in charitable acts and public service, and have continuously contributed to local economic and social development.

Major References

I. Classical Works and Local Gazetteers

(Tang) Huang Tao. *Collected Works of Censor Huang of the Tang Dynasty*. Photolithographic Print of the Complete Library of the Four Treasuries (Wenyuan Pavilion Edition).Taiwan Commercial Press, 1986.

(Song) Hu Taichu, comp., and Zhao Yumu, eds. *Gazetteer of Linting*. Fujian People's Publishing House, 1990.

(Yuan) Tuo Tuo. *History of the Song Dynasty*, vol. 37.

(Yuan) Xiong He. *Collected Works of Wuxuan*, vol. 4. Complete Library of the Four Treasuries (Wenyuan Pavilion Edition), vol. 1188.

(Ming) Xu Hongzu. *Xu Xiake's Travel Diaries*. Chongwen Publishing House, 2014.

(Ming) Li Mo. *Collected Writings from the Jade Tower.* Cumulative Bibliography Series of the Four Treasuries, vol. 77. Qilu Publishing House, 1997.

(Ming) Han Lin, and Zhang Geng. *Testimony of the Saints' Faith,* vol. 1 of *Third Edition of Collected Documents on the Eastward Transmission of Catholicism*, edited by Wu Xiangxiang. Taipei Student Bookstore, 1972.

(Qing) Zeng Yueying, et al., eds., and Li Fu, et al., comps. *Gazetteer of Tingzhou Prefecture*, Qianlong edition. Shanghai Bookstore Publishing House, 2000.

(Qing) Li Hong, and Wang Bai, eds., and Chang Tianjin, et al., comps. *Gazetteer of Pinghe County,* Kangxi edition, *Series of Chinese Local Gazetteers*, no. 91. Chengwen Publishing House, 1967.

(Qing) Zhu Wenyu, ed., Li Shixiong, comp., and Gazetteer Compilation Committee of Ninghua County ed. *Gazetteer of Ninghua County*. Fujian People's Publishing House, 1989.

(Qing) Yang Lan. *Collected Studies of Linting*, woodblock printed edition, the 4th year of Guangxu reign.

(Qing) Ji Liuqi. *Northern Records of the Late Ming.* Taiwan Historical Sources Series, Taiwan Datong Bookstore, 1987.

(Qing) Du Shijun, comp. and ed., and the Local Gazetteer Compilation Committee of Liancheng County, comp. *Gazetteer of Liancheng County,* Kangxi edition. Fangzhi Publishing House, 1997.

(Qing) Yang Shoujing. *Rhymed Verses on Book Collecting*. Classical Literature Publishing House, 1957.

(Qing) Fang Lyujian, ed., and Wu Yifu, comp. *Gazetteer of Yongding County,* Daoguang edition, vol. 16. Edited by the Fujian Provincial Local Gazetteer Compilation Committee. Xiamen University Press, 2012.

Fujian Provincial Local Gazetteer Compilation Committee, ed. *Fujian Provincial Gazetteer: Overseas Chinese Volume*. Fujian People's Publishing House, 1992.

Local Gazetteer Compilation Committee of Longyan City, ed. *Gazetteer of Longyan City*. China Science and Technology Publishing House, 1993.

Local Gazetteer Compilation Committee of Longyan Prefecture, ed. *Gazetteer of Longyan Prefecture, Fujian Province*. Shanghai People's Publishing House, 1992.

Local Gazetteer Compilation Committee of Changting County, Fujian Province, ed. *Gazetteer of Changting County*. Sanlian Bookstore, 1993.

Editorial Committee for the Series on the Compilation and Research of Mazu Documents, ed. *Series on the Compilation and Research of Mazu Documents*, vol. 2. Strait Literature and Art Publishing House, 2017.

II. Monographs

Xie Chongguang. *A General Discussion of Hakka Culture*. China Social Sciences Press, 2008.

Xie Chongguang. *Studies on the Hakka Ethnic Group and Hakka Culture*. Guangdong People's Publishing House, 2018.

Zhou Xuexiang. *Socioeconomic Changes in the Hakka Regions Along the Fujian–Guangdong Border During the Ming and Qing Dynasties*. Fujian People's Publishing House, 2007.

Zeng Ling. *A History of Handicraft Industry Development in Fujian*. Xiamen University Press, 1995.

Zhou Zhenhe, and You Rujie. *Dialects and Chinese Culture*. Shanghai People's Publishing House, 1986.

Jin Yangchun. *Regional Development in Tingzhou and the Formation of the Hakka Ethnic Group During the Song and Yuan Dynasties*. China Social Sciences Press, 2015.

Yang Baojun, editor-in-chief. *Encyclopedia of Overseas Chinese: Volume on Personalities*. China Overseas Chinese Publishing House, 2001.

Wang Xiangrong. *Japanese Instructors*. SDX Joint Publishing Company, 1988.

Fujian Provincial Archives, ed. *Archival Historical Materials on Overseas Chinese in Fujian Province*. Archives Publishing House, 1990.

Wu Bangcai, editor-in-chief. *A History of the Development of Fujian Merchants: Nanping Volume*. Xiamen University Press, 2016.

Li Yingchun, editor-in-chief. *A History of the Development of Fujian Merchants: Sanming Volume*. Xiamen University Press, 2016.

Cai Lixiong, editor-in-chief. *A History of the Development of Fujian*

Merchants: Longyan Volume. Xiamen University Press, 2016.

Cai Lixiong. *A History of Commerce in Western Fujian*. Xiamen University Press, 2014.

(America) Brooks Joanna. *Cultural Trade: Book Commerce in Sibao from the Qing to the Republican Era*. Translated by Liu Yonghua et al., Peking University Press, 2015.

He Bingdi. *A Study on the History of Chinese Guild Halls*. Zhonghua Book Company, 2017.

Yang Yanjie. *Into the Historical Fields of the Hakka: Local Society and Cultural Traditions*. Guangdong People's Publishing House, 2018.

Chen Da. *Overseas Chinese in Southeast Asia and the Societies of Fujian and Guangdong*. Commercial Press, 2011.

Liu Xunxue. *A Travel Account in Southeast Asia*. Kaiming Bookstore, 1930.

The Compilation Committee of Chinese Guild Halls, ed. *Records of Chinese Guild Halls*. Fangzhi Publishing House, 2002.

Hu Jiaxin. *Zhongchuan*. Haichao Photography and Art Press, 2009.

Zhang Yaoqing, editor-in-chief. *Historical Memory: The Cultural Heritage of Western Fujian*. Haichao Photography and Art Press, 2007.

Lin Jinshui, Wu Weiwei, and Cui Junfeng, et al. *Studies on Fujian and the History of Cultural Exchanges Between the East and West*. Ocean Press, 2015.

Zhang Youzhou, editor-in-chief. *The History of Overseas Chinese from Longyan*. South China University of Technology Press, 2020.

(America) Williams Samuel Wells. *A General History of China*, vol.1. Translated by Chen Ju. Shanghai Ancient Books Publishing House, 2005

(America) Wiens Frank. J. *Fifteen Years Among the Hakkas of South China*. Translated by Ding Lilong. Xiamen University Press, 2017.

(America) Kuhn Philip A. *Chinese Among Others: Emigration in Modern Times*. Translated by Li Minghuan. Jiangsu People's Publishing House, 2015,

(America) Ross Sarah. *For All the Tea in China: How England Stole the World's Favorite Drink and Changed History*. Translated by Meng Chi. Social Sciences Academic Press, 2015.

(Britain) Fortune Robert. *Two Visits to the Tea Regions of China*. Translated by Ao Xuegang. Jiangsu People's Publishing House, 2020.

(America) Skinner G. William. *Marketing and Social Structure in Rural China*. Translated by Shi Jianyun and Xu Xiuli. China Social Sciences Press, 1998.

(America) Skinner G. William, editor-in-chief. *The Cities in Late Imperial China*. Translated by Ye Guangting et al. Zhonghua Book Company, 2000.

(America) Schafer Edward Hetzel. *The Empire of Min: A South China Kingdom of the Tenth Century*. Translated by Cheng Zhangcan, Hou Chengxiang, et al. Shanghai Cultural Publishing House, 2019.

(America) Chia Lucille. *Printing for Profit: The Commercial Publishers of Jianyang, Fujian (11th -17th Centuries)*. Translated by Qiu Kui, Zou Xiuying, Liu Ying, and Liu Qian. Fujian People's Publishing House, 2019.

III. Journal Articles, Conference Papers, and Theses

Lin Tingshui. "Some Observations on the Evolution of Ancient Transportation Routes in Fujian." *Studies in Chinese Social and Economic History*, no. 1, 1994.

Ge Wenqing. "A Preliminary Study on the Evolution of the Export-Oriented Economy in the Tingjiang River Basin." *Selected Essays on Hakka Studies: Commemorating the 30th Anniversary of the Journal of Longyan University*, edited by the Editorial Office of Journal of Longyan University. Hebei University Press, 2013.

Pei Yaosong. "The Jiulong Creek and Its Linkage with the Hakka Economy." *Studies on Hakka Culture*, edited by Fujian Yanhuang Culture Research Association and the CPPCC of Longyan City. Strait Literature and Art Publishing House, 2007.

Yu Dazhong. "From the Periphery to the Center: The Construction of Hakka Identity and the Expansion of Hakka Development Space Since Modern Times." *Journal of South China University of Technology*, no.3, 2016.

Tan Qixiang. "Principles and Examples of Historical Human Geography Research." *Historical Geography*, vol. 10. Shanghai People's Publishing House, 1992.

Wu Fengbin. "A Study on the Issues of Overseas Migration from Western Fujian During the Republican Era". *Southeast Asian Affairs*, no. 1, 1994,

Zhong Yifeng. *The Circulation of Tobacco: The History and Culture of Tobacco in Yongding*. PhD Dissertation, Xiamen University, 2008.

Hu Wenhu. "Striving to Build the Hometown." *Sing Guang Daily*, 21 Jan. 1947.

Zhang Kan. "A Preliminary Study of Hu Wenhu's Relationship with Malaysian Hakka Associations." In *The Chinese Heart, Hakka Sentiment: Proceedings of the First Hakka Studies Symposium*, edited by Lin Jinshu. Hakka Studies Association of Malaysia, 2005.

Li Fusheng. "A Brief Discussion on the Status and Role of the Minjiang River Basin in the 'Maritime Silk Road.'" *Fujian History and Records*, no. 5, 2015.

Lin Feng, and Song Danling. "Interactions Between Inland and Coastal Regions: The Business Orientation of Fujian Merchants During the Ming and Qing Dynasties." *Marine Culture and the Development of Fujian: Proceedings of the Second Cross-Strait Symposium on Marine Culture*, edited by Fujian Provincial Department of Ocean and Fisheries, Fujian Yanhuang Culture Research Association, Fujian Federation of Social Sciences Circles, and Fujian Academy of Social Sciences, Fujian Yanhuang Culture Research Association, 2011.

Mao Xing. "Fragments of Commercial Trade in Changting before the Founding of the PRC." *Historical Materials of Changting*, vol. 12, edited by the Literature and History Editorial Office of the CPPCC Changting County Committee, 1987.

Fang Yanshou. "Development and Influence of Jianyang's Role as a Book-Engraving Center in External Dissemination." *Research on the History of Chinese Publishing*, no. 3, 2019.

Zou Risheng. "Sibao: One of China's Four Major Woodblock Printing Centers." *Historical Materials of Liancheng*, vol. 4, 1985.

Chen Zhiping, and Zheng Zhenman. "A Study of Clan Merchants in Sibao, Western Fujian, During the Qing Dynasty." *Researches in Chinese Economic History*, no. 2, 1988.

Zhou Xuexiang. “Western Fujian Hakkas and the Maritime Silk Road: A Case Study of the Zou Clan in Wuge, Sibao.” *Fujian Tribune (Humanities and Social Sciences Edition)*, no. 5, 2016.

Xie Chongguang. “Mazu Belief in the Hakka Region of Western Fujian.” *Studies in World Religions*, no. 3, 1994.

Shi Yilong. “On the Relationship Between the Mazu Belief, the Shipping Industry, and the Surname Lin in the Inland Areas of Fujian and Guangdong.” *Journal of Putian University*, no. 1, 2008.

Chen Jiansheng. “Mazu Belief in the Upper Reaches of the Minjiang River.” *Journal of Fujian Institute of Socialism*, no. 2, 2012.

Lin Jinshui. “Aleni and Fuzhou Society in the Late Ming Period.” *Maritime History Studies*, no. 2, 1992.

Zhu Caixi. “Fragments on Water Transport Along Jiulong Creek.” In *Historical Materials of Yong’an*, vol. 19, edited by the Literature and History Committee of the Yong’an Municipal Committee of the CPPCC Fujian Province, 2001.

Lu Ping. *Christianity and Hakka Society in Western Fujian*. MA thesis, Fujian Normal University, 2002.

IV. Folk Sources

Genealogy of the Zou Family of Fanyang, fifth Revision. Compiled by the Longzu Branch of the Zou Clan in Sibao, Changting, 1947.

Tingzhou Mazu. Compiled by the Fourth Board of Directors of the Tingzhou Tianhou Palace, 2006.

Fan Yang Zou Family Genealogy (Dunben version), sixth Revision. Compiled by the Zou Clan Genealogy Committee of Wuge, Sibao, Liancheng County, Tingzhou, Fujian Province, 1996.

Postscript

Commissioned by the Cultural, Historical and Educational Committee of the Fujian Provincial Committee of the Chinese People's Political Consultative Conference and Fujian Yanhuang Culture Research Association, our team undertook the compilation of *The Fujian Maritime Silk Road: The Hinterland Volume.* The research and writing process spanned approximately four years, culminating in the submission of a first draft to the Yanhuang Culture Research Association in June 2022. The final version was completed after revisions based on feedbacks from experts of the Association and editors from Fujian People's Publishing House.

With the in-depth implementation of the 21st-century "Belt and Road" Initiative, research on the Maritime Silk Road has flourished. However, there remains a paucity of literature focusing on the hinterland of the Maritime Silk Road, and even fewer studies examine the interactive relationship—particularly the historical interactions—between the Maritime Silk Road and its hinterland. Compounded by the traditional Chinese historiographical tendency to devalue commerce and by the relatively underdeveloped commercial history of mountainous regions, our writing process encountered unforeseen challenges in data collection. To overcome these challenges, the research team conducted extensive fieldwork in Longyan, Sanming, Nanping, Fuzhou, Xiamen, Quanzhou, and other regions. We carried out in-depth investigations at museums, in rural villages, at ferry crossings, and in seaports to gather material artifacts and traces of historical memory. These were cross-referenced with local gazetteers and archival documents to establish the structural framework of the volume.

The research goals, content outline, and structural framework of this volume were proposed, revised, and finalized by Cai Lixiong. Chapters 1, 2, 4, and 5 were primarily written by Dr. Yang Linyan, while Chapters 3, 6, and 7 were drafted by Dr. Zhang Fengying, with the remaining content completed and the entire manuscript revised and finalized by Cai Lixiong.

On the occasion of the publication of this book, I, on behalf of all authors, would like to express our heartfelt thanks to all organizations and individuals who provided support and assistance throughout the writing and publication process. Special thanks go to Ms. Huang Lihua of Fujian Yanhuang Culture Research Association for her extensive coordination efforts in both the writing and publication phases. We are also deeply grateful to the editors at Fujian People's Publishing House, whose care, patience, and support made the publication of this book possible, thus creating a valuable opportunity for dialogue on the hinterland of the Maritime Silk Road in Fujian among fellow scholars and readers.

Although we have made considerable efforts to enhance the scholarly value and readability of this volume, limitations in available materials and in our own capacities may have led to shortcomings or errors. As a pioneering attempt to explore the historical role of Fujian's inland regions in the Maritime Silk Road, we sincerely welcome critical comments and corrections from experts and readers alike.

Cai Lixiong

December 2022, Longyan

www.ingramcontent.com/pod-product-compliance
Lightning Source LLC
LaVergne TN
LVHW010554100826
845148LV00014B/2714
9798901860168